then Catharine
of Woodstock
. 1397
nne m.
kingham
Humphrey
d. 1460
Anne Neville
Henry
d. 1483
e of Buckingham
Iargaret Beaufort
Henry
Beaufort
d. 1447
Bishop and Cardinal
Richard
Neville
d. 1460
Count of
Salisbury
m. Alice
Montague
William
Neville
Lord Fauconberg
Cecilia m. Ric
orge
cellor
Edward IV
d. 1483
m. Elizabeth Grey
Anne
Beauchamp
the heiress
Richard Neville
who became
unt of Warwick
Edward V
d. 1483
Richar
Duke of Y

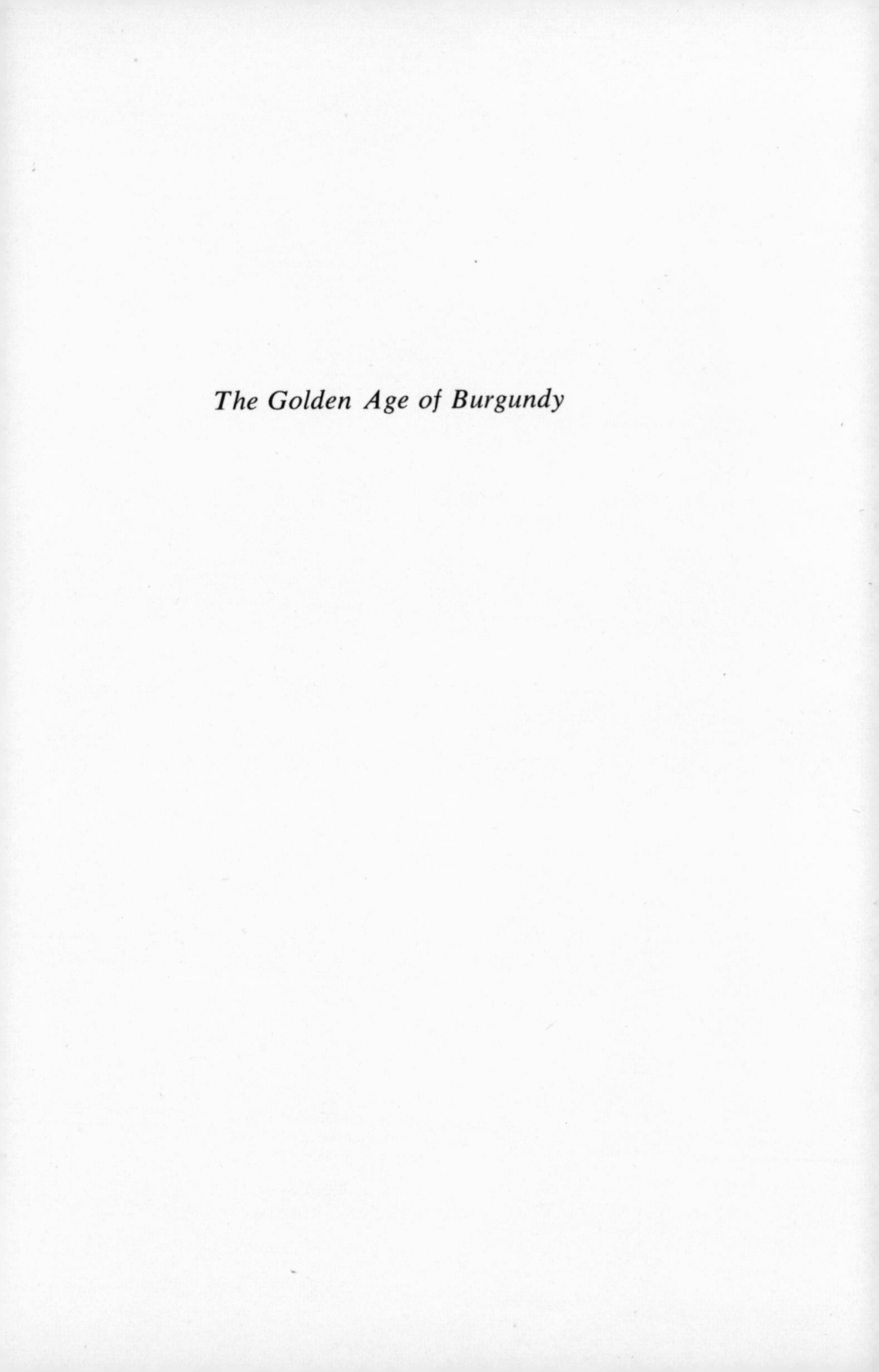

The Golden Age of Burgundy

The Golden Age of Burgundy

The Magnificent Dukes and their Courts

Joseph Calmette

Translated from the French
by Doreen Weightman

W · W · NORTON & COMPANY · INC ·
NEW YORK

FIRST AMERICAN EDITION 1963

Library of Congress Catalog Card No. 63-9876

PRINTED IN THE UNITED STATES OF AMERICA

CONTENTS

ILLUSTRATIONS

Between pages 182 and 183

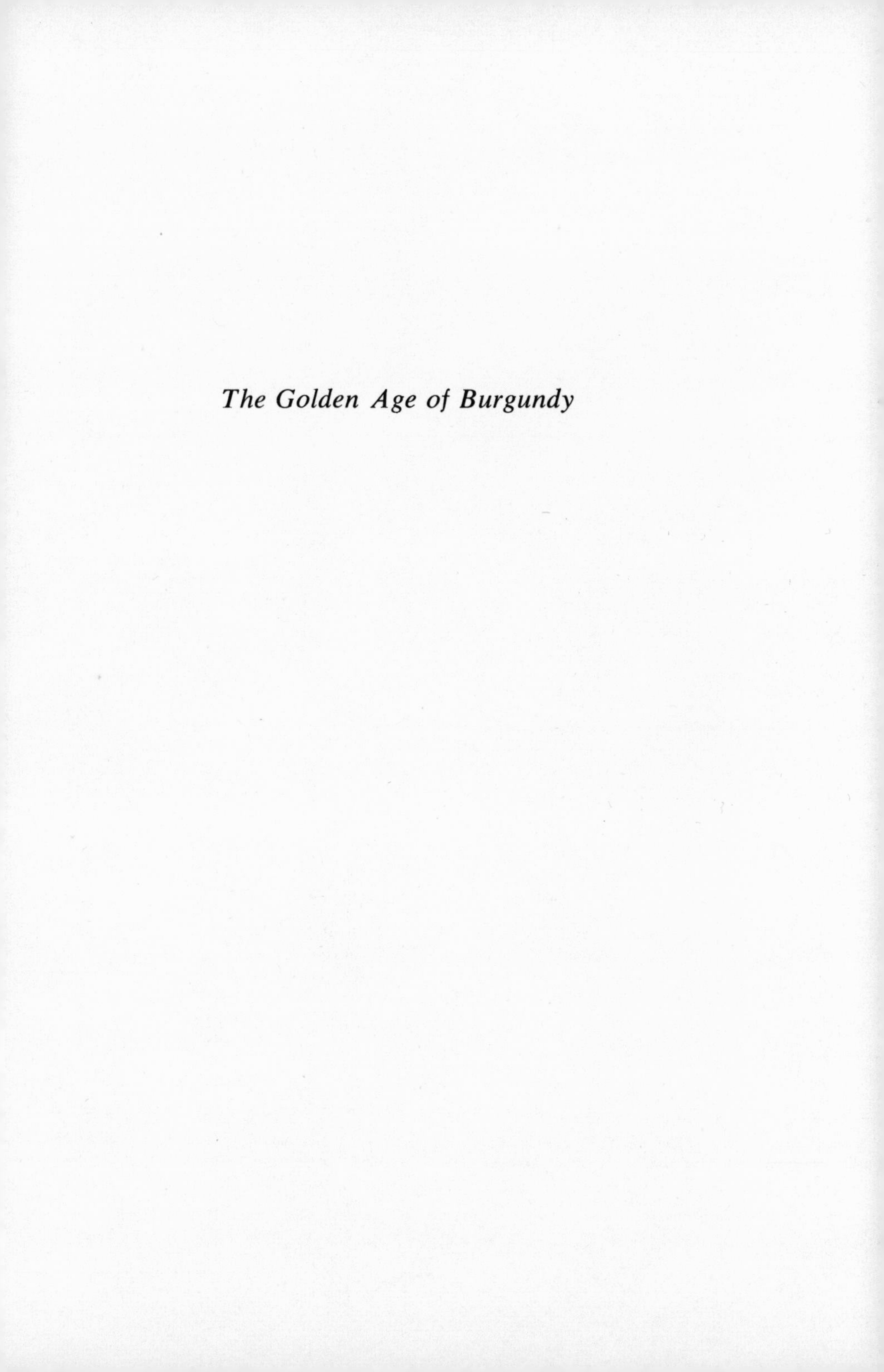

The Golden Age of Burgundy

CHAPTER I
FROM KINGDOM TO DUCHY

UNLIKE THE NAMES of most provinces, the name 'Burgundy' does not instantly call forth a mental picture of a recognizably-shaped area, whose confines are clearly outlined on the map of France. Almost all our provinces have a distinct shape with which we are familiar—one is a peninsula, a fragment of an ancient world linked to a relatively recent continent; another is a plateau; yet another is a valley, either narrow and spindle-shaped, or wide and sweeping; another again is a wedge of alluvial silt, mounted, as it were, in the setting of the surrounding hills. Burgundy, however, consists of both plain and mountain, valley and plateau, ancient soil and recent deposit. On all sides it looks towards the four slopes of France.

Burgundy in fact was not designed by nature; nature merely provided an axis along which several highways converged. Burgundy is a man-made creation. Around a star-shaped cluster of high valleys, whose streams run in all directions, a human settlement was formed, varying in size from time to time. Something different has been made of it at different periods; history has made choices among the various possibilities offered by geography.

The territory, Gallic at first then subject to strong Roman influences, of the *Edueni*, *Lingoni* and *Sequani*—to quote only the main Celtic tribes—was occupied at the time of the major invasions of the fourth and fifth centuries by a race whose name was given to, and has been retained by, the province—the *Burgundi* or *Burgundiones*. Scandinavian in origin, they settled first of all on the island of Bornholm, before moving on to the mainland where they stayed in what is today known as Eastern Pomerania. During the course of the centuries, as they moved slowly and uncertainly towards the Upper Rhine, experiencing various misadventures, the most famous of which was the bloody defeat inflicted on them by the Huns in 437 (splendidly immortalized in the *Niebelungenlied*), they finally settled round the Lake of Geneva, and from there fanned out over a vast area—along the Rhone, on either side of the Saône, over the mountain slopes of the Jura and the Alps, as far as the Morvan region and the upper reaches of the Seine, and up the valleys of its first tributaries. A *Burgundia*—let us say a *Burgundy*—then appeared in writing and began to take its place in the language of historical geography. By the time of the great king Gundobad, son of Gondioc, the name '*Burgundia*' had definitely emerged.

This Burgundy, the kingdom of the *Burgundians*, *regnum Burgondionum*, was a new and very concrete reality which flourished precisely at the period when, with Clovis—a contemporary of Gundobad, who was, incidentally, one of St Clotilda's uncles—France, *regnum Francorum*, was coming into being.

But just as France was not chiefly inhabited by Franks, Burgundy was not chiefly peopled by Burgundians. Comparatively few barbarians finally settled in imperial territory. The Burgundians, like the Franks, merged for the most part with the millions of Gallo-Romans who had accepted them in their midst. They contributed a racial factor which, although it had its importance, did not substantially alter the general ethnographic picture of the future French nation.

Nevertheless, closely allied as it was to the Merovingian monarchy through the victories of the sons and grandsons of Clovis, Burgundy stood out as one of the liveliest regions of Gaul during the sixth, seventh and eighth centuries.

First and foremost the fusion of the Burgundian settlers with the native population gave a special flavour to the area, where they were for a time the leading political force, more especially to the part which stretched towards Dijon, Chalon-sur-Saône, Mâcon, Autun, and even Châtillon-sur-Seine. So strong was their influence that a Gallo-Burgundian nation was established there, just as Gallo-Frankish and Gallo-Gothic nations were established in other parts of France. The enlightened legislation of Gundobad, a 'modern Solon',[1] had reinforced the undeniable and ineradicable racial factor by the retention of a peculiar code of law—the *loi gombette*, so called after the man who had created it, the most humane and progressive of the barbarian legal systems, and traces of which can be found in the *Coutume de Bourgogne*. Finally, credit should be given to a number of prominent personalities of the Merovingian era whose influence was most effective—King Gontran, Queen Burnehaut, King Dagobert, and the martyred Bishop of Autun, St Léger. The combination of these various factors explains a vital point, which should constantly be borne in mind throughout this study, namely the development of a well-defined Burgundian *entity*. By this we mean that from then onwards, even in the early centuries of the Middle Ages, there existed, within the confines of France, and in both a political and moral sense, a Burgundian form of regionalism.

Burgundy started then as a kingdom ruled by its own kings who extended its frontiers in all directions; Marseilles was for a time a port of Burgundy.[2] Next, the kingdom was incorporated politically with the Frankish monarchy. The Gallo-Burgundians pursued their many activities—mostly agricultural and military—under the protection of their overlords. They cultivated their vineyards and fields. They cut down their forests and reclaimed areas of waste land. They warded off attacks by the Lombardians who had settled in the Po basin and who were strongly tempted to enlarge their territory: under Gontran, the patricians Amat and Mummol defeated the Lombard barbarians who were noted for their ferocity and flung them back after two glorious campaigns. Then the wind changed and danger threatened in the south. The Saracens pillaged Mâcon, Chalon, and Autun, and swept on furiously to Sens and Langres. Charles Martel, the Merovingian king's 'Mayor of the Palace', who had conquered the Moslems at Poitiers in 732, established his authority over the whole of Burgundy, in the widest sense. He divided the old *regnum* and its dependencies into four commands: the Arles-Burgundy area, the Vienne-Burgundy area, Alamanic Burgundy and Frankish Burgundy. He appointed as governor of the latter his half-brother Childebrand, whose name, celebrated in verse, has an epic flavour.

Charles Martel's quadripartite Burgundy can be called the nebula from which the various mediaeval Burgundies emerged: these were the Kingdom of Burgundy or Arles, comprising Provence, Dauphiné and Savoy; ducal Burgundy; and the Burgundy ruled by the counts, otherwise known as Franche-Comté.

Martel belonged to the Austrasian family of the Pippinides who, as is well-known, supplanted the royal family descended from Merovacus, and assumed the crown in their place. Martel was, in fact, the first of the Carolingians. Next came his son Pepin the Short, who began the so-called 'second line' of kings. Thus Burgundy, after another vigorous reshaping, came to play a part in the empire, which Charlemagne, the mighty son of Pepin, founded about 800.

An outline of Carolingian rule in Burgundy will show how it paved the way for the transition from kingdom to duchy.

It did not take the new dynasty long to enforce a respect for order, and Charlemagne's reign was pre-eminently an era of internal peace. The period of prosperity referred to in contemporary documents was a just reward for all the hard work expended on a land which soon abounded in good tillage. Order and discipline encouraged rich harvests. It was a triumph for the Carolingian spirit, fundamentally so different from that of the Merovingians. A determined effort to achieve centralization was the most distinctive feature of the empire.[3] The conception of the State, which at one time or another had been favoured by some of the most far-seeing personalities of the Merovingian dynasty, became more clearly defined with Martel; with Charles the Great it attained its zenith. But now there was a complete change. Although the terms *Burgundia* or *regnum Burgundiae* still appeared in certain documents, there is no mistaking the fact that they had a purely geographical significance. Strictly speaking, Burgundy as such did not exist in the new Western Empire: what did exist was something quite different—a group of Burgundian 'counties'. The old *civitates* of the Gallo-Roman epoch merged into *pagi*. These were simply administrative divisions. All the counts in charge of these were on an equal footing—they were directly responsible to the Palace—that is to say to the central authority. These *comtés* or counties, considerably smaller than present-day departments, fitted together on the map like the pieces of a jig-saw puzzle. Gundobad's State had been divided up into *comitatus*.[4]

This intervening period is of paramount importance for, as can clearly be seen, the future duchy of Burgundy originated neither from the Kingdom of Burgundy nor from the Merovingian kingdom, although it remained faithful to the fundamental spirit of both: the future duchy sprang from the *pagi* of the eighth century. In other words the mosaic of 'counties' created by the Carolingians formed a necessary link between the former kingdom and the future duchy.

Just how some of these counties, which had been incorporated in the greater Burgundy of former times, happened to unite and assemble around one family, thus creating the duchy, is one of the mysteries of the ninth and tenth centuries, a prolific period but one which is exceptionally difficult to understand. The collapse of the Carolingian Empire was partly responsible; another factor was the decline of the royal house, but a more important cause was the rise of feudalism, which resulted from a mass of converging circumstances and pressures. A still further major reason was, no doubt, the economic self-sufficiency of the period.[5]

In such troubled times strong personalities come to the fore. Some of the counts and their families thrust themselves eagerly into the front rank. One of them was Guérin, Count of Mâcon under Louis the Pious, whose shrewdness did much to shape the future. He emerged during the series of civil wars which characterized the disjointed reign of the second Carolingian emperor. When the latter died, Guérin took sides in the war between the dead man's sons. He attached himself to Charles the Bald, and he it was who turned the scales in favour of Charles and his brother Louis the German at the battle of Fontenoy-en-Puisaye. The Treaty of Verdun, which pushed back the frontiers of a shattered France to the Meuse and the Sâone, also entrusted the rising local potentate with a supervisory and defensive mission ideally suited to furthering his aims and enhancing his reputation.

Burgundy, which had no clearly defined boundaries when it belonged to the unitary Empire, was reduced in size, then split into two parts by the Partition of Verdun of 843. A French Burgundy was established along the French border of Charles's Empire. An imperial Burgundy merged with Lothair's Kingdom: the dual pattern of duchy and Franche-Comté or *comté* of Burgundy was thus, to all intents and purposes, laid down for the future.

In French Burgundy which had now been reduced in size, Guérin, Count of Mâcon, was the leading figure by virtue of services rendered. By that time, it was admitted that several counties could be administered by one man provided the holder of such a privileged position arranged for viscounts to deputise for him. This practice, although a menace to kings, was a great incentive and source of profit to vassals. Guérin was one of the people who knew exactly how to acquire positions of power. He managed to accumulate quite a collection. Not only did he rule Mâcon, he also had Chalon and Nevers. In addition to being a count, he was lay abbot[6] of a considerable number of monasteries—including the one at Flavigny. Several documents bestow on him, as the administrator of numerous *pagi*, the more high-sounding title of *duke*.

It must be realized of course that the title of duke at this period only meant that he was a military leader in command of several counties. The creation of a frontier along the Saône in 843 justified the military functions which the title implied.

And yet it is impossible not to see in Guérin, who was both *comes* and *dux*, a prefiguration of the future dukes of Burgundy. His exalted yet ill-defined position corresponded exactly to the indefinite state of the Burgundian marches, which were as yet but a tentative outline of the future duchy.

With Richard the Justiciary we find a closer resemblance to the dukes of Burgundy. A step forward had been taken and the existence of a king's representative who ranked higher than a count had finally received official sanction. One duke controlled several counties—he was count of each one, unless he had delegated his duties to a viscount, and the counties, whether administered directly or indirectly, were dominated to an increasingly greater extent by ducal authority. As for the word *ducatus*—duchy—it had two meanings which were originally indistinguishable: the status of duke, and the territorial province administered by the duke.

Feudalism, which was rapidly gaining ground everywhere just at this time, instituted a scale of homage, bound men together by the close ties of vassalage, and assessed authority on land tenure. Authority and land were meted out in the form of benefices.[7] Hence the term *beneficiary dukes*, subsequently adopted by historians to indicate the first dukes—namely those who, although in theory servants of the king, in actual fact received their high office from a waning central authority. But the granting of ducal benefices became less and less dependent on the king's will. More often than not the duke took the law into his own hands and his rapidly rising prestige consolidated the position of the duchy.

Such was the process which was in train throughout the ninth and tenth centuries. A certain number of *pagi* formed themselves into organizations, for example the regions of Autunais, Beaunois, Avalois (Avallon), Lassois (Bar-sur-Seine and Châtillon-sur-Seine), Dijonnais, Mémontois (Mâlain), Attuyer (watered by the Vingeanne), Oscheret (watered by the Ouche), Auxois (Alise), Duesmois (Duesme), Auxerrois, Nivernais (Nevers), Chaunois (Chalon-sur-Saône), finally Mâconnais or Massois.

While Boso, the brother-in-law of Charles the Bald, since the latter had taken Boso's sister Richilde as his second wife, ruled the southern Burgundians, the counties listed above were more or less ruled by Richard, Boso's brother. Richard defended his territories against possible encroachments from Boso and remained faithful to King Charles and subsequently collaborated with his successors, Louis the Stammerer, Louis III, Odo and Charles the Simple. This collaboration did not go unrewarded, since he was granted several territorial benefices.

Richard the Justiciary then widened his scope. He had seized everything he could in Autunois, Avalois and Duesmois. Manassès, his devoted vassal and his 'best friend' according to a certain chronicle was not Count of Dijon as the old historian André

Duchesne claimed, arguing that Manassès founded the House of Vergy. But it is certain that he had brought Chaunois, Oscheret and Attuyer under his control. Thanks to close collaboration between suzerain and vassal, Richard and Manassès held in their possession the major part of the future duchy of Burgundy. They had even overstepped the boundary at certain points, for Richard had brought the Count of Troyes into subjection: he even ruled Tonnerrois for a time, and he was for a period in possession of the *cité* of Langres, the diocesan centre of which Dijon was, and continued to be for many long years, the ecclesiastical dependency. The 'duke' even seized Sens in 894—yet another cathedral town. He placed the bishop, who was at that time Primate of the Gauls, under house arrest and established a trusted viscount in the town as his representative.

There was, however, more to Richard's powerful personality than the bold ambition and energy coupled with tactical skill which made him one of the leading feudal lords of his day. He was after all Richard the *Justiciary.* Within the limitations of the period, he established law and order. He won the respect of kings, both lawful and otherwise. He held back the Norman invaders. He turned his 'duchy' into an asylum for hunted monks: he protected the monastic centres founded in the counties within his power. Under his rule, Burgundy stood out in contrast to the more turbulent surrounding regions; it was a comparatively privileged land and already offered a foretaste of the prosperity which successive ages were to revive.

Richard died about the 1st September 921: there could be no clearer proof of the rise of his family than his son Raoul's accession to the throne of France on the 13th July 923. Raoul's was incidentally a stormy reign and one which emphasized, as it happened, the importance of the Burgundian duchy at a time when it was consolidating its position: for the sorely tried king, whose claim to the throne was challenged from the very beginning, drew from his ducal patrimony the resources which enabled him to confront his numerous and powerful enemies.

Under Hugo the Black's administration, the clash between the *beneficiary* principle and the *hereditary* principle came to a head. The family of the Robertonians or dukes of France, which was contending with the last of the Carolingians for the control of the kingdom, was anxious to establish itself in Burgundy: it sought to subject Burgundy to the suzerainty of the *ducatus Franciae.* It did not succeed, and just when it thought it was about to achieve its aim, it was suddenly obliged to abandon the whole scheme, and to set up a separate duchy. Otto, then Henry the Venerable, both of them brothers of Capet, ruled Burgundy in turn: the duchy of Burgundy resisted all attempts to incorporate it either with the *ducatus Franciae* or the royal domain. We can only conclude that the Burgundian *entity*, whose emergence we have traced so far, was already endowed with, and was to retain, exceptional vigour and tenacity. The individuality which had managed to find expression in the cross-currents of dynastic history kept alive (and was to continue to do so) the conscious inspiration which had created what was originally Gundobad's kingdom, and what would subsequently be the duchy of the great dukes.

CHAPTER II

THE ACHIEVEMENTS OF THE CAPETIANS IN BURGUNDY

HENRY THE VENERABLE died at Pouilly-sur-Saône on the 15th October 1002, leaving no male descendants. His nephew and his son-in-law, who, it would seem, had become his adopted son and devisee, quarrelled over his fief. The nephew happened to be Robert the Pious, King of France. The adopted son was Otto-William, Count of Burgundy, vassal of the Germanic Roman Empire.

The armed struggle which broke out immediately afterwards between the two rivals took on very great significance. Otto was irresistibly attracted to the Rhone Valley and to the southern Burgundians. A victory for his forces would have reversed the effect of the Partition of Verdun and caused an historical deviation. The union, under his protectorship, of ducal and comital Burgundy at the outset of the eleventh century would most surely have resulted in the regions of Dijon, Autun, Chalon and Auxerre being wrested from the hands of the eminently French dynasty of the Capetians. It might even have brought the still somewhat ill-defined duchy administered in turn by Guérin, Richard the Justiciary and the de Capet brothers, within the German Reich's sphere of influence; this did actually happen in the case of Franche-Comté, which remained in German hands for a very long time. It is then true to say that, even if the participants in this important drama were oblivious of, and indifferent to, the issue at stake—history need not be understood by those who make it—the (future) destiny of French Burgundy lay in the hands of these two rivals: King Robert and Count Otto-William.

It was a hard, bitter and prolonged duel. Whatever happened, Robert never lost hope. He had to sustain thirteen years of arduous campaigning against his stubborn foe. But he got the better of him in the end. He succeeded in taking possession of the various counties along the right bank of the Saône and even of Dijon, which the bishop of Langres, Brunon, an ally of the opposite camp, was trying to hold for the rival claimant. With King Robert's final triumph, the vision of a new *Burgundia* vanished—although this same vision, many years later, was to inspire another duke and count of Burgundy, the last of the great dukes, Charles the Bold.

Thus, the 843 frontier, which had for a time been in jeopardy, was more firmly established than ever by about the year 1000. The duchy of Burgundy had as its ruler the king of the *regnum Francorum*. This appeared to be deferred realization of an earlier ambition of the French dukes. But the royal power was not capable, at this point, of sustaining such a tremendous advance.

It has often been said that Robert the Pious had *given* French Burgundy to his second son Robert. It is not certain that the king bestowed the title of duke on his younger son. All that can be said is that it fell to him on the death of his father. Henry I, who had come to the throne in difficult conditions, allowed his brother to be master of the duchy in 1031 with the possibility of bequeathing it to his heirs.[1] This time there could be no misunderstanding. The era of *beneficiary dukes* had given way to the era of *hereditary dukes*. A branch of the Capetian family was to rule in Burgundy, and what is more, being younger and more vigorous, it was to survive the royal dynasty, for the Burgundian stock persisted until 1361, whereas the direct Capetian line on the throne of France, as is well known, died out in 1328.

In actual fact, in spite of the all-embracing terms of the grant made by Henry I to his brother[2] the power assigned to Robert was more theoretical than real. The period of confusion between Richard the Justiciary's rule and that of Henry the Venerable, and above all the bitter war of succession which followed the latter's death, had reduced the title of duke to a purely formal appellation. The increasing number of subinfeudations which the dukes were forced to grant to pay for the co-operation they needed had deprived them, in successive cases, of the greater part of their estates. To be short of land in a century when the feudal system was in full swing and when, in consequence, political power depended on land tenure, was indeed a serious disadvantage. The Capetian House of Burgundy, like the Capetian House of France, was in difficulties from the outset, lacking as it did the security and support of a recognized territorial demesne and the backing of a powerful seigniorial hierarchy. Both dukes and kings were faced by the same task—they had at all costs to reconstitute a united demesne, they had to restore and strengthen their authority which had dwindled, or survived only in a diluted form.

It was precisely the historical mission of the Capetians of Burgundy to devote their lives to this urgent and two-fold task of rehabilitation. The French Capetians created the kingdom, while, alongside, the Capetians of Burgundy created the duchy.

It cannot be said that this tremendous task was carried out by very strong personalities. Neither the elder nor the younger branch of the Capetian dynasty numbered among its members a truly outstanding man, one of those obvious geniuses who, overcoming all opposition, leave the stamp of their personalities indelibly imprinted on events.[3] Both kings and dukes were conscientious workers, dedicated to a common task: they were persevering, realistic and methodical—quick to seize every favourable opportunity. These were, it could be argued, essentially negative attributes. If they rarely achieved anything sensational, at least they almost always avoided the obvious mistakes they might easily have made. They did not jeopardize their chances by pursuing splendid visions or glorious adventures; they were content to remain watchful, husbanding their resources, fully aware of the implications of every event and every situation, like sly, hard-working peasants who, diligent and cautious, consolidate their wealth with each new generation and climb higher and higher up the social scale. The heirs of the first Capetian duke were successful, imperceptibly at first, then later much more ostentatiously. By what miracle did the Capetians manage to carry through their Burgundy venture?

It should first of all be realized that as the king's representative in the duchy, the duke could profit by the law of escheat. Should a fief happen to have no heir capable of administering it, it automatically reverted to the duke. As a matter of fact, several inheritances fell to the Capetian duke in this way, and also to each succeeding Capetian king. For instance, it was by intestate inheritance that Auxois and Duesmois, according to their historians, passed into the duke's hands in the middle of the eleventh century.[4]

Purchase, either of land proper, or of vassalage, was another means open to the dukes. The purchase of land needs no explanation. The purchase of vassalage was rather more complicated: it involved transactions known in feudal law as renewal and increase of the fief. They consisted either in adding more land to the existing vassalage of a vassal or in acquiring a new vassal by demanding homage from an estate previously exempt from homage. It is quite obvious that

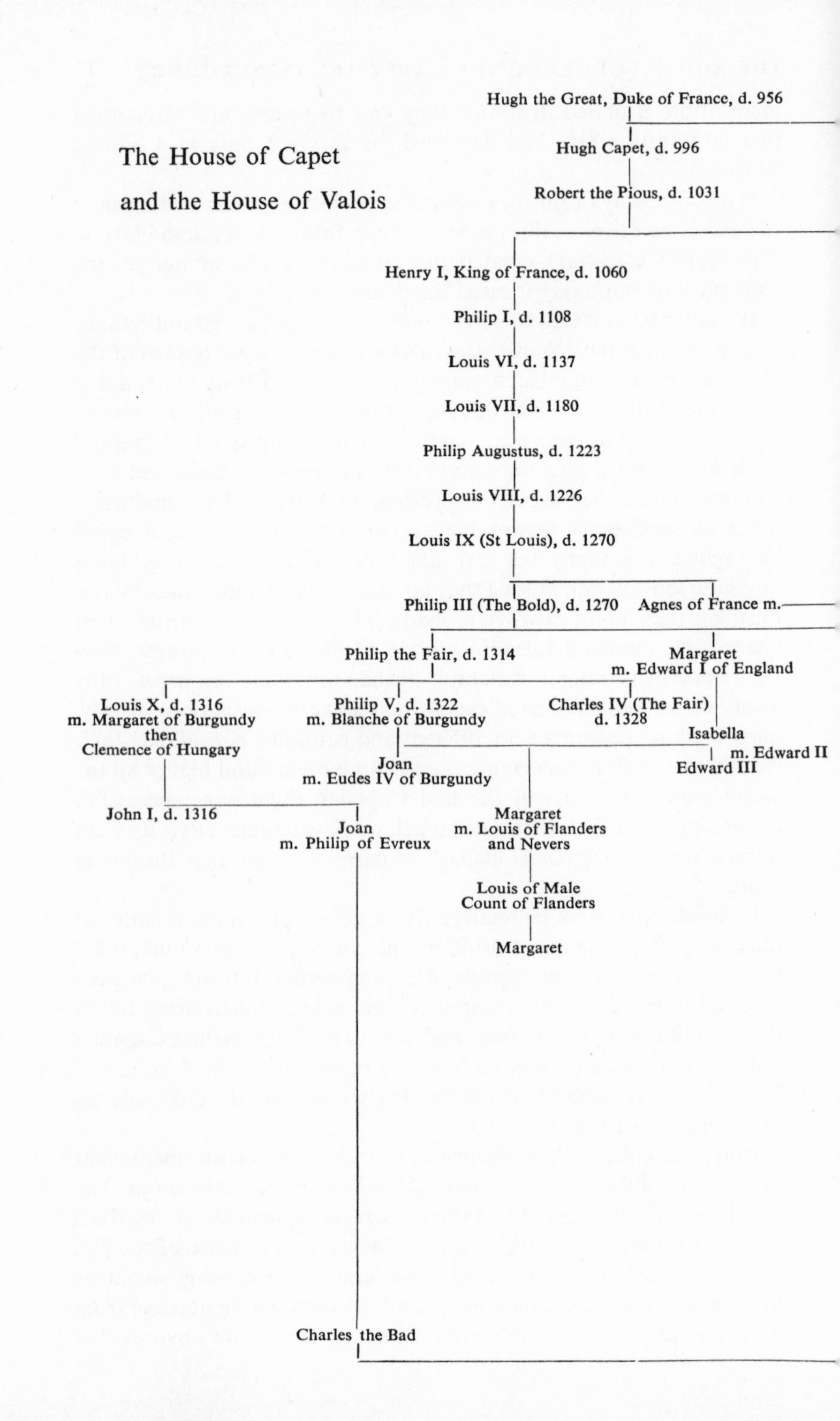

The House of Capet
and the House of Valois
Hugh the Great, Duke of France, d. 956
Hugh Capet, d. 996
Robert the Pious, d. 1031
Henry I, King of France, d. 1060
Philip I, d. 1108
Louis VI, d. 1137
Louis VII, d. 1180
Philip Augustus, d. 1223
Louis VIII, d. 1226
Louis IX (St Louis), d. 1270
Philip III (The Bold), d. 1270
Agnes of France m.
Philip the Fair, d. 1314
Margaret
m. Edward I of England
Louis X, d. 1316
m. Margaret of Burgundy
then
Clemence of Hungary
Philip V, d. 1322
m. Blanche of Burgundy
Charles IV (The Fair)
d. 1328
Isabella
m. Edward II
Edward III
Joan
m. Eudes IV of Burgundy
John I, d. 1316
Joan
m. Philip of Evreux
Margaret
m. Louis of Flanders
and Nevers
Louis of Male
Count of Flanders
Margaret
Charles the Bad

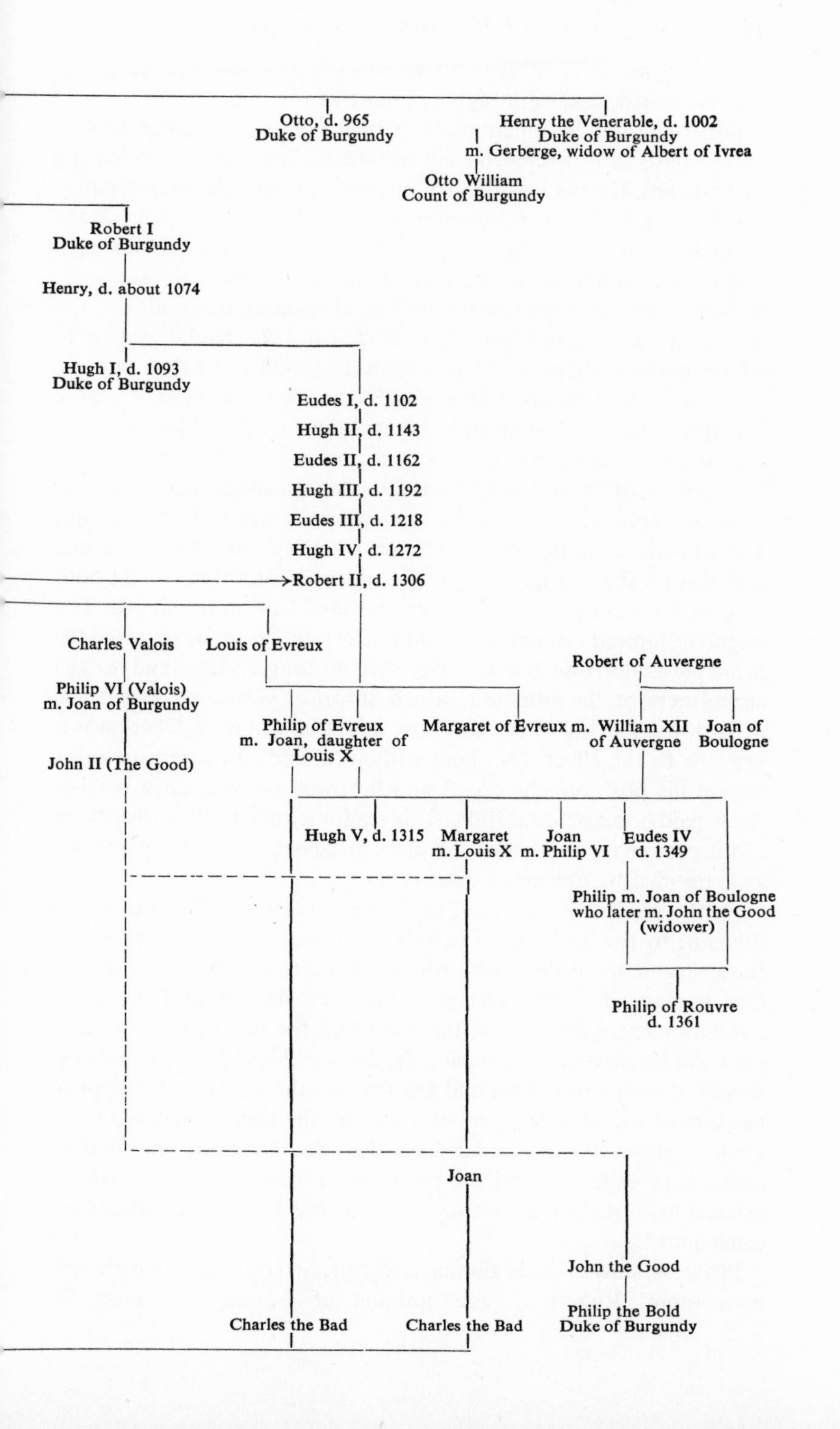
Otto, d. 965
Duke of Burgundy
Henry the Venerable, d. 1002
Duke of Burgundy
m. Gerberge, widow of Albert of Ivrea
Otto William
Count of Burgundy
Robert I
Duke of Burgundy
Henry, d. about 1074
Hugh I, d. 1093
Duke of Burgundy
Eudes I, d. 1102
Hugh II, d. 1143
Eudes II, d. 1162
Hugh III, d. 1192
Eudes III, d. 1218
Hugh IV, d. 1272
Robert II, d. 1306
Charles Valois
Louis of Evreux
Robert of Auvergne
Philip VI (Valois)
m. Joan of Burgundy
Philip of Evreux
m. Joan, daughter of
Louis X
Margaret of Evreux m. William XII
of Auvergne
Joan of
Boulogne
John II (The Good)
Hugh V, d. 1315
Margaret
m. Louis X
Joan
m. Philip VI
Eudes IV
d. 1349
Philip m. Joan of Boulogne
who later m. John the Good
(widower)
Philip of Rouvre
d. 1361
Joan
John the Good
Charles the Bad
Charles the Bad
Philip the Bold
Duke of Burgundy

these two methods of renewal and increase of the fief were very closely related, and both highly remunerative.

Otherwise, feudal inheritances in Burgundy were usually allotted on the basis not of seniority but of lineage. If a vassal died leaving several sons, the fief was divided up among them. The eldest, called 'the head of the family' (*chef-parageur*), represented his brothers at the suzerain's court, and his brothers became his vassals. With each generation, therefore, new grades in the feudal hierarchy were created; a more and more elaborate pyramid of allegiances was built up. On the other hand, non-hierarchical feudalism—the feudal system to which belonged those lords who were not bound by vassalage because their estates had always been exempt[5]–remained at a stand-still since exemption was a phenomenon dating from the past. This being so, the number of lords without a suzerain remained unchanged, while the number of those bound by the ties of vassalage increased with extreme rapidity. The case of the seignieur whose land was not subject to the condition of homage became exceptional and abnormal, and was all the stranger in that the same person often owned both land held on condition of homage and land held in fee-simple. The seignieur himself did not understand why this should be so, since the principle underlying the anomaly was no longer clear, and so the strangeness of the situation caused surprise. Where no title-deeds existed, the legality of the situation might be disputed. There was a proverb to the effect: 'No land without a lord'. In order to legitimatize his position, the seignieur who owed no allegiance instinctively paid homage to the duke. This readmission into the jurisdiction of the customary law often took place in exchange for cash payment, as is testified by numerous documents.[6]

By the genuine purchase of land, the duke gradually built up his domain; by the purchase of vassalages he acquired the allegiance of those seignieurs in the duchy who were under no obligation to pay him homage. But whatever the nature of the transactions, such purchases presupposed that the duke had the necessary resources. How did he succeed in acquiring the money? He did so, not only by means of loans from Jews and Lombards—the universally accepted bankers of the Middle Ages—but also by the skilful exercise of his feudal rights—such as feudal dues, the sale of various immunities, chancellery expenses, and the profits of justice—briefly by various expedients, not the least remunerative of which was the granting of *communes*.[7]

Progress, slow at the beginning under the first dukes, soon gathered momentum. Robert II, the husband of Agnes of France, St

Louis's daughter, had already speeded up the process by vigorous action. The development of the ducal house had often been impeded by the transfer of ownership of land to younger sons and daughters. Robert II put an end to this disastrous practice. In his will he left Hugh, his eldest son, and after him his heir, 'all the fiefs, former fiefs, seignieuries and revenue . . . belonging to the duchy'. The younger brothers and daughters were to receive only allowances: and since the income of the second son, Odo, depended on property, it was clearly stipulated that he owed liege homage to his elder brother. As a matter of fact, it so happened that this elder brother died, and the title came to Odo.

From then onwards the dynasty was established on a solid basis. It revived the idea of the 'State' for its own benefit. It was about to embark on a most dazzling future.

Hugh V was King of Thessalonica. Odo IV was for a time Prince of Morea. These titles, however, sound more impressive than they really were. The successful expeditions to the east were merely passing diversions: they never jeopardized the conduct of internal affairs any more than the crusades in which the Capetian kings took part distracted their attention from the national mission they had undertaken. Exploits in the Levant, or in Spain, in no way prevented the growing province from pursuing a steady course towards that unity which ensured and indeed accelerated the rise of the dynasty. Odo IV was first and foremost Duke of Burgundy and a French prince. He married a Capetian princess, Joan, daughter of Philip V (the Tall) and granddaughter of Philip the Fair. He was at once the son-in-law of a king of France, and the brother-in-law of two kings of France, by the marriage of his sisters, Margaret and Joan of Burgundy, to Louis X and Philip VI (of Valois). At the same time, Philip, Odo's son, married Joan of Boulogne, who after her husband's death, became the wife of King John the Good. It is apparent that these carefully planned matches were inspired by a definite marriage policy, which had already been indicated by three previous characteristic attempts at expansion—by Hugo III towards Dauphiné, Odo III towards Nivernais, and Hugh IV towards Bourbonnais, Nivernais, Torrerre, and Auxerre: this tradition, which was to persist, and was accompanied by a determined policy of buying up whatever he could, made the Duke of Burgundy one of the greatest, and one of the most richly endowed, representatives of feudal France.

Even at this early stage, Odo could almost be said to embody to a large extent all the features of a great duke. He had the duchy firmly in hand. The lesser nobility—the vassals who had divided up between them the land belonging to the old counties on the near side of the Saône—were completely under his control. And now, among the various fiefs which he had acquired by his marriage, figured Franche-Comté, that same *comté* of Burgundy into which Otto-William had once dreamed of incorporating the duchy, and which now, on the contrary, became a possession of the duchy, although it still remained subinfeudated to the Empire. A greater Burgundy was being reconstituted under the rigorous control of the powerful Capetian duke, who, it must be remembered, ruled at a time when a change of dynasty was taking place in France, and the first skirmishes of the Hundred Years' War were beginning to be fought.

A study of the dukes alone is not enough: attention must be paid to the duchy itself. Not only did the Capetians accumulate estates and vassalages, and enter into advantageous marriages, they built up a feudal State, which gained in stability with every succeeding generation and owed its organization to their careful efforts. There grew up around the dukes a court, at which all the traditional offices were represented and which was a replica, on a smaller scale, of the royal court. The *Jours Généraux* which sat at Beaune were modelled on the *Parlement*. Furthermore the dukes imitated the kings in matters of local administration by superimposing over the original provosts or lords of the manor bailiffs, such as had been newly instituted in the neighbouring monarchies,[8] and five *bailliages*—Dijon, Autun and Montcenis, Auxois, Chalon, Montagne (Châtillon-sur-Seine) maintained a closely co-ordinated system of control throughout the duchy.

The parallelism between the administrative policy of both dukes and kings is particularly noticeable here. The ducal bailiffs were quite as zealous and effective as the royal bailiffs. Like them, they were professional administrators, holding all the reins of authority very efficiently in their hands. Supported by a growing tradition, and acting on juridical principles which experience could adapt very flexibly to changing conditions, they transformed the ducal fief into a homogeneous body. They saw to it that ducal 'rights' yielded the maximum amount of revenue. It was in fact the compact, organic unity achieved by the five *bailliages* which brought into being the Capetian duchy, now superimposed upon the Carolingian counties, at the very heart of the *regnum Burgundiae*.

In short, a centralizing and unifying force was in full operation. In this respect the dukes were undoubtedly the imitators of the senior royal branch.

This centripetal drive fulfilled, as it happened, a vital need because it counteracted opposing forces, both feudal and ecclesiastical.

From the feudal point of view, several districts, which had appeared originally to have allied themselves to the duchy, had slipped out of its control: they were the greater part at least of Nivernais and Auxerrois, as well as Mâconnais, a district which had formerly belonged to Otto-William, and which was attached to the duchy by a very slender bond of suzerainty—a suzerainty much disputed at that and one which, on more than one occasion, had been subject to the direct intervention of the crown.

At the same time, religious life in Burgundy had acquired an extraordinary intensity and ecclesiastical authority had become powerful enough to counterbalance and even threaten the duke's own authority.

This was not due to the sudden emergence in Burgundy of exceptionally extensive or wealthy bishoprics, but to the fact that the regular clergy there was extremely numerous. Mediaeval Burgundy was especially renowned for its great monasteries. Two of the most illustrious and distinguished religious orders of the Middle Ages were, undoubtedly, the Burgundian orders of Cluny and Cîteaux.

Cluny, founded in 909 in the Autun diocese by William the Pious, Count of Mâcon, with Berno as abbot, established its prestige throughout the Christian world, and set up thousands of Cluniac monasteries, which gave incomparable brilliance to western Europe. When Cluny began to decline, it was replaced by the austere order of Cîteaux, founded by St Robert of Molesmes and given new life and an unrivalled position in the life of the times by the greatest pulpit orator between Jean Chrysostome and Bossuet—the eloquent ascetic, St Bernard, known as 'the man of God', an outstanding spiritual leader. A native of Fontaines-lès-Dijon he was, without any shadow of doubt, the greatest ecclesiastical figure of the twelfth century. Under the influence of Cluny and Cîteaux, old abbeys experienced brilliant revivals: Luxeuil, Moutiers-St-Jean, Bèze, St Seine, St Bénigne de Dijon, La Madeleine de Vézelay, and a host of others, not forgetting the ancient abbey at Tournus, where the relics of St Philibert had finally come to rest, after endless peregrinations from one place of refuge to another, from the island of Noirmoutier to the Saône. Cluny and Cîteaux were at once centres of dogmatic theology, artistic centres and centres of reform, and hives of social and economic activity of remarkable efficiency and inestimable value. Burgundy, as the original home of these orders, whose missionaries travelled widely the world over, became an important centre, the heart, as it were, whose pulsations were transmitted to the whole of the *Christiana Respublica.* This rare honour placed the Capetian duchy, independently of its domanial and political evolution, in the forefront of civilization, and indeed of history.

It is certain that the prestige of the clergy and of the Burgundian abbeys tended to limit the duke's authority; however, the entire duchy basked in their reflected glory and, generally speaking, Capetian Burgundy owed the harmonious equilibrium which was its essential characteristic to the action of these opposing forces of compression and expansion at the time when it was finally achieving awareness of its own identity.

A Burgundian consciousness had undoubtedly emerged, but it was a French consciousness too. And it is this last point which should now be stressed.

Ever since the Partition of Verdun had placed Burgundy next to France, along the frontier of the kingdom, it had been the mission of the dukes to defend both the kingdom and France, which meant that Burgundy had been inspired by national feeling.

Robert, in acting against Otto-William had behaved like a true patriot, whether he was conscious of the fact or not. There is no need to avoid the apparent anachronism of the word when it corresponded to the realities of the situation. The hereditary dukes, for their part, in so far as they were of Capetian stock, not only moulded the body of the duchy, they infused into it a soul, which was inevitably French.

The Hundred Years' War, which might have been expected to sever France and Burgundy, did in fact unite them in closer bonds than before. A new dynasty, the Valois, had taken over the crown; but, as has already been seen, Eudes IV became the brother-in-law of the first Valois king, the king who was elected in opposition to Edward III of England. Under the second Valois king, John the Good, himself married to a Burgundian by adoption, Burgundy suffered in the cause of France. It is always the case that great destinies are tempered in the fire of suffering.

Burgundy, then, suffered for France—suffered for her elder sister. All this comes out quite clearly in the last English campaign of John the Good's reign, the one immediately preceding the Treaty of Brétigny in 1360: a bitter campaign during which Edward III's men, after landing at Calais, advanced on Rheims which they dared not attack, and set up their winter camp around Flavigny and Saulieu, relentlessly laying waste the countryside, sacking towns and villages as if their sole aim were to transform the duchy into a hotbed of anglophobia.

The Burgundian entity, although essentially French, had its own individual tradition. Moulded by the past, it was now ready to embark on the most illustrious epoch of its history. The age of the great dukes was drawing near. The dynasty of Robert I was about to die out. It would seem that some mysterious and ineluctable law decreed that he should not outlive the royal line of the Capets. Be that as it may, the death in 1361 of the grandson of Eudes IV opened the way for Philip the Bold.

CHAPTER III

PHILIP OF ROUVRE AND THE PROBLEM OF SUCCESSION

AMONG THE CIRCUMSTANCES which had favoured the Capetian cause in Burgundy, we must count as very important the happy chance which provided duchy and kingdom alike, and for almost the same period of time,[1] with an unbroken succession of male heirs throughout several generations. From 1031 until 1361 in Burgundy, and from 987 until 1328 in France, there was always, when the time came, a lawful heir ready to take over the succession. From father to son, from grandfather to grandson, or from brother to brother, the ducal crown was handed down without a hitch. A kindly providence had spared the House any of those premature and disastrous deaths which so often ruin the most promising political undertakings. The thread which appeared to be so strong snapped on the 21st November 1361 when Philip of Rouvre, grandson and successor of Eudes IV, died. The extinction of a princely line which has ruled over a State for several centuries is inevitably a cause of extreme anxiety among the inhabitants of that country.

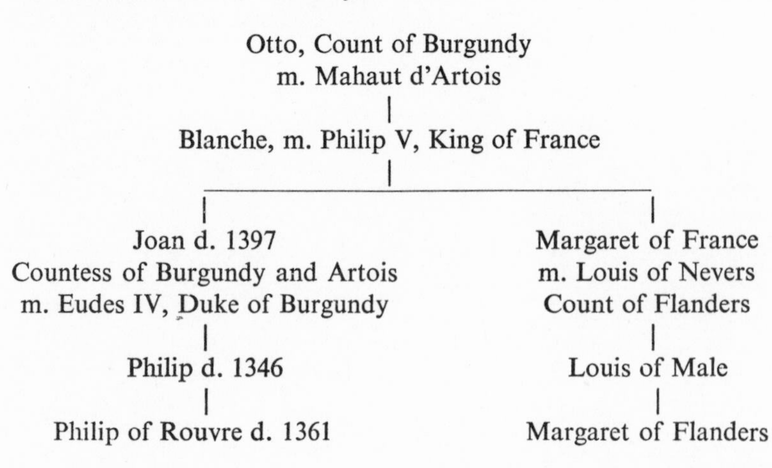

Philip of Rouvre was a young man of seventeen. Born in the castle of Rouvre, his favourite castle where he was to breathe his last and to which he owed his name, he was engaged to Margaret of Flanders, the daughter of the Count of Flanders, Louis of Male: plans for their approaching marriage had been skilfully negotiated, and it seemed to promise the ducal house a wealth of future advantages.

But it so happened that the last descendant of Robert I, who had so much to live for and so much to look forward to, died without leaving an heir. He fell victim to the plague which was raging throughout France and Burgundy, and which killed him after only a short illness.

Apparently the patient's condition did not cause any anxiety until the 11th November, the day on which the young duke made his will. Ten days later he died. This sequence of events suggests two observations. First of all, Philip of Rouvre succumbed to an acute illness of short duration. He was engaged to be married, and to all appearances, was about to embark on a normal career, which would have ensured the continuance of his race. The termination of the ducal dynasty was, then, an unexpected and disconcerting occurrence and one which had had no place in the duchy's political reckonings. Secondly, the illness may have been of short duration, but the death can hardly be called sudden. It was not like death caused by a tragic accident, the sort of accident which had killed the young duke's father, Philip, the son of Eudes IV (he had died suddenly after a fall from his horse). Furthermore, young Philip had been attacked by the plague, the dreaded scourge of his time, and it is quite certain that as soon as the illness was diagnosed—and diagnosis was easier than cure, given the limited medical knowledge of the fourteenth century—those who were closest to him must have looked upon his death as a possibility, or even as a probability. In any case, by the 11th November, when the will was made, the early likelihood of the ducal throne falling vacant could have been, and must have been, envisaged.

So, this unexpected, yet foreseeable catastrophe, did not burst dramatically, like a peal of thunder out of a clear sky. There was very little time, but there were at least a few days, in which to get used to the idea that Burgundy must look for a new heir.

These reflections are of interest to anyone who seeks to understand the sequence of events that now occurred. Although the circumstances in which Philip of Rouvre's death took place appear to the historian as having given the politicians of the period very little time to consider the problem of succession,[2] it is also true that the problems arising from his death could have been discussed coolly and calmly before the actual time of his decease. Moreover, it is an established fact that the King of France, John the Good, was kept informed of the development of the young duke's illness. Lengthy and involved deliberations were quite out of the question, given the speed with which events occurred, but the next of kin were not taken completely by surprise.

Since the deceased had made a will, we should obviously quote from it. The chief clause read as follows: 'Item, we direct and appoint as heirs to our country and to our possessions whatever they may be, those, male and female, who by law or by local custom ought or may inherit'. Nothing in the provisions of the will was intended to impede the legal transmission of the title. On looking closely at the terms, we could infer that the young duke might as well not have made a will at all and that he had really died intestate.

However, the fact that he made a will did serve some purpose. It meant that feudal principles had to be invoked. It ruled out in advance any attempt at interpretation. It became impossible to deny that Philip's possessions should go to their lawful claimants. In other words, no one had the right to say he was, or to claim that he was, on any grounds whatsoever—whether on legal grounds or by reason of State—Philip of Rouvre's executor.

Thus was established the legal procedure for determining the allocation of the various possessions left by the deceased. As far as feudal domains and rights were concerned, the only factor to be taken into account was original ownership. In each instance this had to be traced back to the last owner with lawful heirs, while observing the rules applicable in each individual case, and keeping strictly to the tenets of either civil law or customary law; this was in fact the only possible interpretation of the terms used in the will 'by law and local custom'.

Have we to suppose that the use of such explicit legal terms was prompted by fear of intrigue or greed?—or the fear of annexation, or the application of a uniform law to the estate as a whole—or even fear of disruptive rivalries and arbitrarily conducted dealings? The supposition cannot be ruled out altogether; on the other hand, we have no confirmation of it.

Actually, Philip of Rouvre's estate presented quite enough complications to warrant the cautious terms of the will. It consisted, in fact, of a conglomeration of heterogeneous elements set together like the pieces of a mosaic and each one originating from a separate source.

First of all there was the major item, the Capetian duchy of Burgundy. We have seen how this was created by the dead man's ancestors. We have seen how it was built up, and welded together; we have seen how it became an organic entity.

Then there were a number of additions to the duchy, all fairly recent. For example, the duke owned the two counties of Boulogne and Auvergne. These two counties had come to him from his mother, Joan of Boulogne, daughter of William XII of Auvergne. Now Joan, who had died leaving King John the Good a widower, had as her nearest relative her uncle John of Boulogne, her father's brother as can be seen in the genealogical table;[3] consequently, in the case of both counties, the young duke's heir was his great uncle.

Apart from the Burgundian duchy, Philip of Rouvre had received from his paternal grandfather, Eudes IV: (1) the county of Burgundy—in mediaeval parlance '*la comté*', (2) the county of Artois, (3) the Champagne lands. Tracing back the line of inheritance of each of these three fiefs separately, we arrive at a princess of royal blood, Margaret of France, the daughter of Philip V: she had inherited these domains from her mother, Joan, and was the widow of the late Louis, Count of Flanders and Nevers, and her son, Louis of Male, ruled over Flanders.

As far as the duchy itself was concerned, King John the Good, grandson of Charles V of Valois, and son of Joan of Burgundy, and a representative of both the senior and junior branches of the Capetian dynasty, possessed titles with which only Charles the Bad, King of Navarre, could vie. Charles, grandson of Margaret of Burgundy, and great-grandson of Duke Robert II, appealed to the customary law of Burgundy. He had perhaps some right on his side. He said he belonged to the direct line of Margaret, who had prior claim over Joan, her younger sister with whom the King of France claimed kinship: the latter insisted that he was one degree closer in line of descent. The King of Navarre not only challenged the right of the representative of the House of Valois, he disputed Margaret of France's right to the Champagne lands.

Now it happened that the heirs, without consulting Charles, came to an agreement amongst themselves whereby they opposed his claims. The most striking fact was that, whether or no the King of Navarre had the best legal claim, nobody gave him any serious support, for he had never been more unpopular than he was at that time. He was the sly, clandestine supporter of the English. His dubious conduct during the critical days following the King's imprisonment, after the Poitiers disaster, had been finally revealed and had been greeted with violent indignation by all Frenchmen of feeling.[4] Now we know that just at this moment when the choice of a new leader was imminent, Burgundy felt itself to be profoundly French. Widespread opposition to Charles the Bad, which had grown particularly noticeable in Burgundy, had found expression during the meetings of the estates held during the Dauphin's regency: this opposition hindered the King of Navarre's cause and favoured the cause of John the Good. At this point we can appreciate the part played by those 'imponderables' which Bismarck referred to in three of his speeches, saying that they should not be underestimated, as they so often are by politicians, who forget that what they dismiss as negligible may weigh more heavily in the balance of fate than the most involved schemes, the most skilful stratagems, and the most daring crimes.

With the English acts of pillage at Flavigny and Saulieu still fresh in men's minds, how could a friend of Edward III, the sworn enemy of the King of France, be accepted as Duke of Burgundy? In actual fact there was never any question of Charles the Bad succeeding to the title. Furthermore, the agreement reached by the other interested parties, who were joint heirs rather than rivals, settled the matter very promptly. There were three joint heirs: John the Good, Margaret of France, and John of Boulogne.

The agreement so quickly arrived at was not ratified by a written document: at least no traces of any such document have been discovered. Only one legal deed dealing with furniture and debts was subsequently drawn up at Cîteaux on the 16th January 1362.[5] This agreement was drawn up quite a long time after the three heirs had reached an understanding about the major part of the estate.

In actual fact, it was left to John the Good and John of Boulogne to concoct a plan of action, since Margaret of France was content to abide by their decision. With the elimination of Charles the Bad, the coalition formed by the three heirs had removed any possible source of dissension, and the task of sharing out the pieces of the mosaic was performed with the utmost ease, without any complications—one might almost say painlessly.

This is all the more surprising when one bears in mind the extent and complexity of the composite heritage. Yet the fact can be explained by the very nature of the claims which were put forward. All the beneficiaries, even John the Good, based their claims on their rights as individuals. The King of France did not act in his capacity as king, but as the son of Joan of Burgundy, and grandson of Duke Robert. In the fourteenth century, a line of argument such as this could only be answered by a line of argument of a similar nature. Now Charles the Bad, the only person in a position to do this, was an undesirable candidate whom nobody would consider. His reasons, which might have proved convincing if they had come from someone else, carried no weight at all coming from him.

Those who were in charge of the operations had therefore a relatively easy task. Yet it would be most unfair not to stress the remarkable skill and adroit manœuvring of John of Boulogne, who took the lead in the matter.

Just when the problem of the Burgundian succession arose, one man happened to be particularly well placed for the supervising and controlling of events: this was John of Boulogne, great-uncle of Philip of Rouvre and chairman of the ducal council. John the Good could count on this shrewd, crafty seignieur, not only because of the personal relationship between them, but because their interests coincided.

John of Boulogne was a very old friend of King John. He had been more or less involved in the execution of the Count of Eu, the worthy constable whose life the jealous king had sacrificed because he thought he was the lover of his first wife, Bonne of Luxemburg: and when the king became a widower, John of Boulogne had proposed that his own niece, Joan of Boulogne, should replace the king's late wife. Thus Joan, who was the widow of Philip, father of Philip of Rouvre, had become Queen of France. It is obvious from this that the two Johns had been hand in glove for a very long time.

And now this same John of Boulogne, as brother of the late William XII of Auvergne, turned out to be co-heir to his great-nephew's estate. Everything seemed to strengthen the bond between them. It was a foregone conclusion that they should work well together, and in fact they did.

It was entirely thanks to John of Boulogne that John the Good was kept so well informed of the illness of his son-in-law Philip of Rouvre, whose guardian he was. Once the young man had died, it was John of Boulogne who advised the king on the course of action to be taken, and who, personally, gave all necessary instructions in Burgundy, in a manner which anticipated the terms of eventual settlement of the estate. It was at Rouvre, where the chairman of the council was in residence, that every move was devised. News of the death of the last Capetian was deliberately withheld from the people.[6] Proof that John the Good, on the other hand, was informed immediately is given by the date of the letters patent whereby the duchy was restored to the kingdom.[7]

It is quite obvious what John of Boulogne's manœuvre was. He had planned everything and in secret. Furthermore, judging by the strict orders which he issued to constables and townships, he was obviously working for the king. After the many documents which disclosed exactly what his tactics were, we need only quote the memorandum issued on the 24th November, which forbade anyone, except the king's officials, from entering Burgundian territory.

By these and similar measures, John of Boulogne appears to have nipped in the bud any opposition to the King of France. It should be added that the generosity, the chivalrous bearing, the very misfortunes of John the Good, who had more or less been a father to the young orphaned duke, appealed strongly to the Burgundian nobility. The hatred inspired by his only possible rival, the King of Navarre, merely served to intensify these feelings of sympathy. Patriotism and sentiment now pleaded in favour of the man who had been defeated at Poitiers.

King John did not, however, have any faith in imponderables, to which he never gave much thought; he had mobilized his forces in Nivernais, as a measure of precaution. This may have been an unpremeditated move on his part, or he may have acted on the advice of his confederate, the other John. The fact remains that troops, borrowed from forces led by the famous Arnaud de Cervole (known as the Archpriest), were concentrated in the Corbigny area. These precautions turned out to be unnecessary because everything went off as smoothly as possible, and without a hitch.

Thanks to John of Boulogne's activities, event followed event in rapid succession. With unfaltering zeal, he urged the king on literally in every fresh despatch. His plan was obviously to present both the people and the other claimants with a *fait accompli*. It was quite clear that his intention was to keep the King of Navarre guessing and to give him as little time as possible to act.

That his primary concern was to expedite all decisive measures was revealed most clearly when he hastily summoned all the vassals in the duchy to meet on Christmas Day, the date chosen for rendering homage to the duchy's new master.

In this instance, the chairman of the ducal council overstepped the mark, for the King of France acted less promptly than he had expected. The meeting had to be postponed, and took place only on the 28th December. The Burgundian estates held an official session in honour of the occasion. Then John the Good went to Cîteaux, where a meeting of the co-heirs took place, during which they signed the document drawn up on the 16th December 1362, the purpose of which has already been explained. Later, after a visit to Beaune, the King of France went back to his kingdom, leaving one of his men, the Count of Tancarville, in charge of his new domain.

In this way the duchy was handed over without a hitch. Not a single voice was raised in protest. And yet, during his brief stay, the Head of the House of Valois may have noticed more than one unmistakable danger signal. During the December session of 1361, the estates, eagerly voicing the mood of the Burgundian entity, made several respectful but firm pronouncements. These can be briefly resumed as follows: the duchy intends to remain a duchy; it has no wish to become a province of the royal domain; there should be no administrative changes; joined to the kingdom by virtue of one man's rights, Burgundy could never agree to being absorbed into it; there had not been, and never would be, annexation, but juxtaposition; since the heir was also king, there was a personal link between the two territories, but that was all.

These were no hastily improvised ideas, for the Burgundian Charter issued in 1315 under Louis X had expressed opinions which contained the 1361 declarations in embryonic form. The delegates who had welcomed John the Good identified themselves with the aspirations of their forefathers. By embodying the historical traditions of Burgundy, whose existence they loudly proclaimed, they themselves acquired new importance. They voiced the indomitable spirit of the Capetian duchy, whose deep-rooted individuality insisted on being treated with respect. The circumstances could hardly be called propitious, since by almost universal consent, the duchy had been handed over to the Valois king, and recent events in Burgundy had quickened patriotic feelings towards France; yet their attitude only goes to show that a Burgundian entity did exist. There was here an historical potentiality whose roots were far too deeply set not to thrust forth new shoots and eventually to flower.

Regional aspirations were clearly revealed in this open affirmation that annexation would never be accepted, only juxtaposition and union under a common king. Their full force can only be grasped if they are considered alongside the wording of the letters patent of November 1361, in which King John had given quite a different twist to the problem. Having established the fact that he was taking possession of Burgundy, not by virtue of his rights as king, but as a private individual, he had immediately added that he was giving Burgundy to the crown, with which it was to be inseparably united.[8] A whole policy was contained in these few lines; the crown was secretly attempting the bold manœuvre of moving from hereditary right to annexation.

Later, the king who had tried to bring off this bold stroke was to endow his youngest son, Philip the Bold, with the appanage of this same duchy.

There is a world of difference between the letters patent of 1361, and the creation of the appanage. This change of policy, which amounted to a *volte-face*, needs to be explained.

The main reason is to be found in the reactions of the Burgundian people. The suggestion that annexation was implicit in the November document immediately came up against the proud, uncompromising statement made by the estates in December. The estates had the last word, which shows that the letters patent proved of no avail against Burgundian regional consciousness. Two factors came into play: John the Good's clumsiness, and the shrewdness of his son, Philip the Bold.

Attempts to rehabilitate the second Valois king have proved fruitless.[9] All through his unfortunate reign, his lack of responsibility and of political acumen were only too well known. Under the circumstances, to appropriate one of the great fiefs—the duchy of Burgundy which had been granted its charter in 1315—in a few lines written on a sheet of parchment, was an unforgivable piece of utopianism. To ensure the success of such an enterprise, to incorporate Burgundy, without the latter suspecting anything, within the framework of French unity, was a task requiring both tact and time. King John was not capable of such a *tour de force*. He embarked on too difficult an operation, and failed. His objective, which even subtle and flexible tactics could hardly have achieved, was now even further out of reach. By his very first gesture—so remarkably rough and tactless—he had jeopardized the best solution of the difficult problem which faced the royal house now that the ducal throne of the Capets had fallen vacant.

When exactly the idea of recreating a Duke of Burgundy as distinct from a King of France became clear in John the Good's muddled mind, it is difficult to say. But it can be confidently supposed that by the time the Valois king had secured from his brother-in-law, the Emperor Charles IV of Luxemburg, the secret letters of the 15th January 1363, in which Philip the Bold was promised

Franche-Comté, a fief subinfeudated to the German Empire, the installation of the young prince in the duchy had been definitely decided upon.[10]

Philip the Bold was just the man to make the most of such a generous gift. Since the battle of Poitiers in 1356, he had acquired tremendous prestige. The 19th September, a tragic day for so many others, had been for him a day of triumph. Everyone knew of the gallantry shown by this lad, only fourteen years eight months old, who had gone on to the battlefield to assist his father in the memorable feats of valour which took place just before the surrender. The words uttered by the youth to direct the last thrusts of the very parfait knight, words which have been handed down to us in the vivid account by the Italian chronicler, Villani: 'Defend yourself, father . . . to the right . . . now to the left . . .' were still ringing in everyone's ears. Such a splendid performance at the outset of his career made Philip, King John's youngest son, his favourite. He was soon to reap his reward.

Philip combined valour, good nature and irresistible charm with sound commonsense. Under cover of the confidential relationship with which his father honoured him, he succeeded in making brilliant use of any opportunities which came his way.

His ingenuity was shown with striking clarity during the events leading up to his accession to the ducal throne. Everything was carried out in secret, and, if the expression may be permitted, with a good deal of string-pulling. Philip had no intention of making any definite move to take Burgundy by force—he wanted the duchy to fall into his lap, as it were. He seemed apprehensive in case he should be thought to be on the watch and he was most careful to conceal his purpose. Such unerring tactical skill could never have been achieved by crude manœuvring in the manner of John the Good. Nothing could have been further removed from the rough, clumsy subterfuge of the letters patent. There was no mistaking the stamp of an intelligent and crafty mind, such as Philip the Bold was always to be noted for. To tell the truth, Philip the Bold—bold on the battlefield yet in diplomacy the most prudent of men—displayed such cunning before his accession to the throne, that at times, even the historian loses the thread of his intricate plots.

The man who had taken charge of Burgundy's policy possessed all the adroitness to deal with the infinitely difficult situation, whose various elements have already been examined. The state of the duchy explains and justifies the moves which Philip engineered with such skill. Feelings were running high, and many vital individual interests were at stake; the English plunderers or the mercenaries had left in their wake a trail of misery and poverty; the country was torn and confused by the passions and greed unleashed by the Hundred Years' War; the accumulation of all these difficulties would have discouraged a less self-controlled statesman, and one with less implicit confidence in his star. But this circumspect representative of the Valois line could call on inexhaustible reserves of perspicacity and ingenuity. Patiently he directed events so as to further the ends he had in view, and waited until the time was ripe to show his hand.

After the imperial writ of January 1363, which indirectly revealed the ambitions of the young prince, and the proposals he had suggested to his father, Philip made no move at all for six months. During these six months he remained in close attendance on the king. It is impossible not to believe that all this while he was furthering his policy.

On the 27th June he did in fact abandon his cautious tactics and make a positive move. He became governor of Burgundy in place of Tancarville. The count had met with reversals and had fallen into disgrace. Philip, who had acquired the title of lieutenant-general, arrived in the duchy as his father's representative.[11] On the 3rd July the estates met at Dijon. This first decisive meeting of the future duke with his future subjects was a solemn moment. It so happened that the estates of 1363 granted Philip subsidies which they had refused Tancarville. There was no mistaking the fact that the estates' real intentions were being accomplished; the lieutenancy granted to Philip was but a transparent, provisional veil through which the dukedom of the future could clearly be discerned.

The most curious feature of the whole affair, and one which could be interpreted in various ways, was that the *secret* was kept, and the pretence maintained throughout the latter part of John the Good's reign. On the 6th September, the king created Philip Duke of Burgundy, but this fact was not made public. It was left to the letters patent of the 2nd June 1364 issued by Charles V on the death of his father, to make the setting up of the Valois duchy of Burgundy an established fact.[12]

It may be asked: why the mystery, why the precautions?

Perhaps we should look upon this perpetuation of a fiction that no one believed in any longer as a way of not too openly disavowing the official writ of 1361. There may have been a desire to avoid any suggestion of a change of heart. Or it may have been necessary to facilitate good relations between the Dauphin and his young brother. This very probably accounts for the hesitations which lasted for such a surprisingly long time. But it must be confessed that we know nothing whatsoever of inter-family transactions to which the Burgundy question gave rise, from the time when it became apparent that union with the crown was an idle dream right up to the moment when an official announcement placed a new duke at the head of the duchy. This represented a return to the Capetian settlement, since it created, alongside the elder branch of the Valois who reigned in France, a junior branch in possession of the duchy and its dependencies. At all events, Philip the Bold, on whom this splendid gift was bestowed, was now ready to undertake his task; he was to be the first of the four great dukes.

CHAPTER IV

PHILIP THE BOLD: THE STATESMAN

PHILIP THE BOLD, the youngest of John the Good's sons, was born on the 17th January 1342: he came into the world on St Anthony's day. This explains why, when he grew up, the duke liked to observe this particular day, professing as he did a quite remarkable devotion to St Anthony; it was his favourite practice to sacrifice to the saint as many well-fattened pigs as there were living members of his family.[1]

Philip, after being for a time without any land of his own, had at first received the appanage of Touraine. It was the habit of the kings of France to grant their sons, when they reached a certain age, and in order that they might live in a fashion befitting their rank,[2] an important fief, transmissible to their descendants, but only on condition that it must return to the crown, should the male line of the initial beneficiary become extinct. The same rule held good when Philip exchanged Touraine for Burgundy. He made his solemn entry into Dijon on the 26th November 1364, and there in the church of St Bénigne confirmed the privileges to be enjoyed by the town and the duchy.

Tall, strong, well-built and amply proportioned, the new duke of Burgundy was, we are told, '*noir homme et laid*'. From this we can assume that he was dark-skinned and heavy-featured; his lower jaw must have been marked by the prognathism which he apparently passed on to the House of Austria as the characteristic stamp of his race. His countenance, which was normally friendly, was lit by the fire which flashed from his eyes: their lively glance was wonderfully expressive of a keen, subtle intelligence. The duke was affable, frank and charming. Shrewdness was his main quality, and was accompanied by a sense of timing and quickness of decision. He was 'far-seeing', according to Froissart. Christine de Pisan states that he was 'supremely wise and sensible'. The monk of St Denis assures us that he was 'the most prudent of the fleur-de-lys princes'. The portraits which we possess of him bear out these brief but eloquent eulogies; still more so, more indeed than any other work of art, does the kneeling statue of the duke which the famous sculptor, Claus Sluter, placed at the door of the Chartreuse of Champmol and which will be described in due course.[3]

Although untiring in political matters and acutely conscious of his duties as head of the state, Philip nevertheless found time for the lighter side of life.

He liked to watch play-acting and miming. He was fond of '*le jeu de paume*', and he played dominoes. Family affections were close to his heart. To his wife, who was far from beautiful, he was bound, if not by a great love, at least by a sincere and loyal affection. He was always very attached to his children. Even his nephews came in for a good deal of benevolent attention. On one occasion he gave his nephew, Charles VI, aged ten, an ornate, painted flageolet.[4] At the same time, he was fond of ceremony, enamoured of the ostentatious mode of contemporary court life, and very careful to create for himself a style of life worthy of his position. Generous, excessively so at times, like his brothers Louis and John, he had like them a supreme contempt for thriftiness; the consequences of this were only too apparent on more than one occasion during his career, and finally at the time of his death.

A keen collector and an enlightened lover of the arts, his rôle as patron was of such paramount importance that we shall be obliged to devote a separate chapter to this one aspect of his activities.

Once established in the duchy, Philip's first ambition was to unite Franche-Comté with Burgundy. After all, it had in the past belonged to his two predecessors: it was a necessary complement to the duchy and had been taken away from Burgundy by the unnatural Partition of Verdun in 843, and now belonged to Margaret of France. Charles V's representatives set to work to recover it and it soon became apparent that the best way would be by means of a marriage. This was one of the arguments in favour of Philip's union with the granddaughter of Margaret of France, the daughter of Louis of Male, Count of Flanders, the same Margaret, heiress to the Belgian lands and to many other desirable seigneuries, who had been affianced to Philip of Rouvre.

The Count of Flanders, disappointed by the unexpected death of his daughter's first fiancé, had in the meantime encouraged the advances of another prince, Edmund of Langley, son of Edward III.

It had been for a long time a traditional policy of the English to aim at an alliance with the country which was later to be known as Belgium. The area, the most industrialized in Europe, was subinfeudated to France, but it was dependent, economically, on Great Britain. Flanders, a purely textile-producing area, needed wool, the raw material provided by English sheep. The English kings, by prohibiting the export of this vital raw material, had it in their power to bring Flemish trade to a standstill. Edward III had already resorted to this means of intimidation. There is some degree of truth in the assertion that he followed a 'wool policy'.

The marriage of Margaret with Edmund of Langley, Earl of Cambridge and the future Duke of York, would have given England indirect control of Flanders, and would have represented a serious threat to France.

As the young Flemish princess was to inherit territory not only from her father, but also from her grandmother, the marriage would have put a great many fiefs into the hands of the Plantagenets—Artois, Nivernais, Rethel, Franche-Comté, and a number of less important seigneuries. It was difficult to accept the idea that such a combination of territories should be allotted to a son of Edward III.

Charles V accordingly set to work and appealed to the Pope of Avignon, Urban V. The ecclesiastical authorities had already granted the dispensation which would allow the Anglo-Flemish marriage to take place, and Margaret and Edmund were already engaged.

The Pope now attempted to thwart the scheme. The two young people were cousins, only remote cousins, it is true, but all the same closely enough related to fall under the ecclesiastical ban. The Holy See decided that the objection could not be overruled, and Urban revoked the dispensation already granted. He forbade both French and English priests to carry out the marriage ceremony.

Faced with such resolute opposition, Louis of Male and Edward III were forced to give way. Another betrothal scheme for Margaret had come to nothing.

However, Charles V was not satisfied with this negative solution, which was not enough to satisfy the requirements of his policy as a whole. He had set himself as the main task of his reign to get even with the English king, to make good the reversals suffered by Philip VI and John the Good, and to revise the Treaty of Brétigny. What better counter-move could the French make than to ensure that Philip the Bold became the heir of Margaret of France and Louis of Male? It was quite obvious that Margaret of Flanders, her parents' only child, and the former fiancée of Philip of Rouvre, should become the wife of her first betrothed's successor. The two brothers directed their diplomatic activities to this end.

Yet for a long time, Louis of Male showed great reluctance to accept the idea. There is no doubt that London was deliberately bringing pressure to bear on him, and attempting to thwart the new plan, which was an obvious and direct blow at England.

It seems clear that the intervention of Margaret of France, the young princess's grandmother, forced the issue. Margaret, a Capetian and French to the core, acted in the interests of the crown and finally convinced her son.

Some historians have thought fit to dramatize the episode or even give it a fictional gloss. Here, for instance, is the account which de Barante composed for the entertainment of his readers and which has become a classic version:

> Negotiations for the marriage had been going on for seven years without arriving at any conclusion; in the hope of furthering the business the King of France had travelled as far as Tournai, but the Count of Flanders, feigning illness, had refused to go to Tournai. Finally, Madame Margaret, angered by the lack of control she had over her son, went to see him; as he still showed no sign of yielding, she suddenly pulled her dress to one side and, revealing her breast, said with passion: 'Since you refuse to obey the wishes of your King and your mother, I intend, in order to shame you, to cut off this breast which fed you—you and no one else—and to throw it to the dogs. I would have you know that I hereby disinherit you and that you will never have my county of Artois.' The count, deeply moved and alarmed, threw himself at his mother's feet and promised to give the heiress of Flanders to the Duke of Burgundy.[5]

The truth was that the Franco-Flemish negotiations had not been concluded without some hard bargaining, and Charles had to pay for what he got by agreeing to a most painful sacrifice, the return to Flanders of the territories formerly annexed with such difficulty by Philip the Fair. The third Valois king had to resign himself to restoring to the count the Walloon part of Flanders, that is the castellanies of Lille, Douai and Orchies which had been brought within the royal domain through the efforts of the last of the great Capetian kings.

So, in order to deny the English access to the Belgian coast, the 'wise king' had to make his young brother's fortune in a way that could hardly have been foreseen. The entire inheritance of Margaret of France along with the estate which Louis of Male had inherited from his paternal ancestors, was to fall into Philip's hands. The counties of Burgundy, Rethel, Nevers, Artois and Flanders, with the addition of the three castellanies retrieved from the royal domain, not to mention several less important seigneuries—such was the dazzling prospect which opened up before the penetrating gaze of the Duke of Burgundy. He glimpsed, in a brilliant vision, the vast, rich state whose existence had already been foreshadowed under his Capetian predecessors. Charles V had, from the outset, launched the newly-founded house on a policy of vast territorial aggrandizement. It was scarcely possible for him to foresee that, as a result of this policy, which in later years was to be most zealously pursued, there would spring up on the eastern flank of the Valois domain a state powerful enough to threaten the authority of his successors.

The marriage of Philip and Margaret was a typical, great dynastic union. It was celebrated with impressive pomp.[6] The union was solemnized in the church of St Bavon at Ghent on the 19th June 1369. Philip did everything on such a lavish scale that, in order to give a farewell banquet to the notabilities of Ghent and pay for the return journey, he had to leave very valuable precious stones in pawn with three burghers of Bruges.

This was a fateful hour for France under Charles V. The Treaty of Brétigny had been denounced.[7] Duguesclin was recalled from Spain after placing an ally of France, Henry of Trastamare, on the throne of Castille, and took charge of the main war in his capacity as constable. Charles V's brothers, Louis, Duke of Anjou, John, Duke of Berry, and Philip, Duke of Burgundy, did their duty as princes of the blood and joined forces with the famous soldier who was waging war for the greater glory of the fleur-de-lys.

Philip entrusted the administration of Burgundy to the faithful Eudes of Grancey, who was paid at the rate of three florins a day, and spent most of his time fighting the English, apart from the short spells he spent now and again in the duchy.[8]

Let us, then, follow the fortunes of Charles V's youngest brother while he was in the service of France from 1369 until 1390.

The duke took part in each of the campaigns of the period,[9] but he distinguished himself chiefly in the 1373 campaign. The Duke of Lancaster, John of Gaunt, had been placed by his father, Edward III, at the head of a huge body of cavalry. On the 25th and 26th July, powerful forces were landed at Calais. A most impressive general staff accompanied the English prince, who, on the strength of claims which he felt entitled to make through his wife, Philippine, daughter of Peter the Cruel, styled himself 'King of Castille'. Into the bargain, Edward had conferred on him the title of 'special lieutenant and general commander both of the Kingdom of France and the duchy of

Aquitaine'. Thomas, Earl of Warwick, William, Earl of Suffolk, and John IV, Duke of Brittany, who had rallied to the English cause, were fighting alongside the brilliant Lancaster. Starting from Calais, the invaders marched on Doullens by way of Hesden: on the 19th August they crossed the Somme between Corbie and Bray.

The Duke of Burgundy was stationed at Amiens. Starting from there, he manœuvred along the enemy's right flank and so prevented him from marching on Paris. Lancaster was forced to move away in the direction of Laon and to skirt the hill on which the town is built. John of Vienne and John of Bueil, acting in conjunction with Philip the Bold, inflicted several defeats on the English, notably the bloody battle of Oulchy-le-Château.

Lancaster then tried to make off towards the Loire; Philip managed to take up his position on the enemy's left flank so as to cover the Loire valley. He thus forced Lancaster to divert his troops towards Limousin and Périgord. After an exhausting march, the English arrived in the Gironde in a pretty sorry state. As both sides were exhausted after so much strenuous fighting, the Pope was able to intervene and arrange for the Bruges conferences to take place in 1375. Philip the Bold was placed at the head of the French delegation. On the 25th March, on Lady Day, he held a huge banquet and helped to achieve a settlement. The Bruges truce gave France a breathing space, but in 1377 the struggle was resumed.

The Duke of Burgundy had lent such effective help to Duguesclin that he was given the honour of carrying on his task. When Charles V's great captain succumbed to a mysterious illness during his siege of Châteauneuf-de-Randon, in Lozère, the king offered the command to his youngest brother, who thus had to fight the cavalry led by Edward III's youngest son, Buckingham.

In 1380 the British cavalry started from Calais just as the previous force had done in 1373. They moved off on the 22nd July, St Madeleine's Day, with the intention of cutting across France, pillaging as they went, and eventually occupying Brittany. Duke Philip, faced with a fresh British offensive, adapted to the situation the tactics which had been so successfully put into operation by Duguesclin: no pitched battles, but a constant harassing of the enemy, who was thus worn down and prevented from obtaining any important objectives.

Closely watched by Philip the Bold, Buckingham moved past Laon: he crossed the Marne at Condé and reached Troyes, where Philip had entrenched himself. The Plantagenet offered battle, but the challenge was naturally refused.

Disappointed, Buckingham made his way westwards. He crossed

Flanders and Burgundy

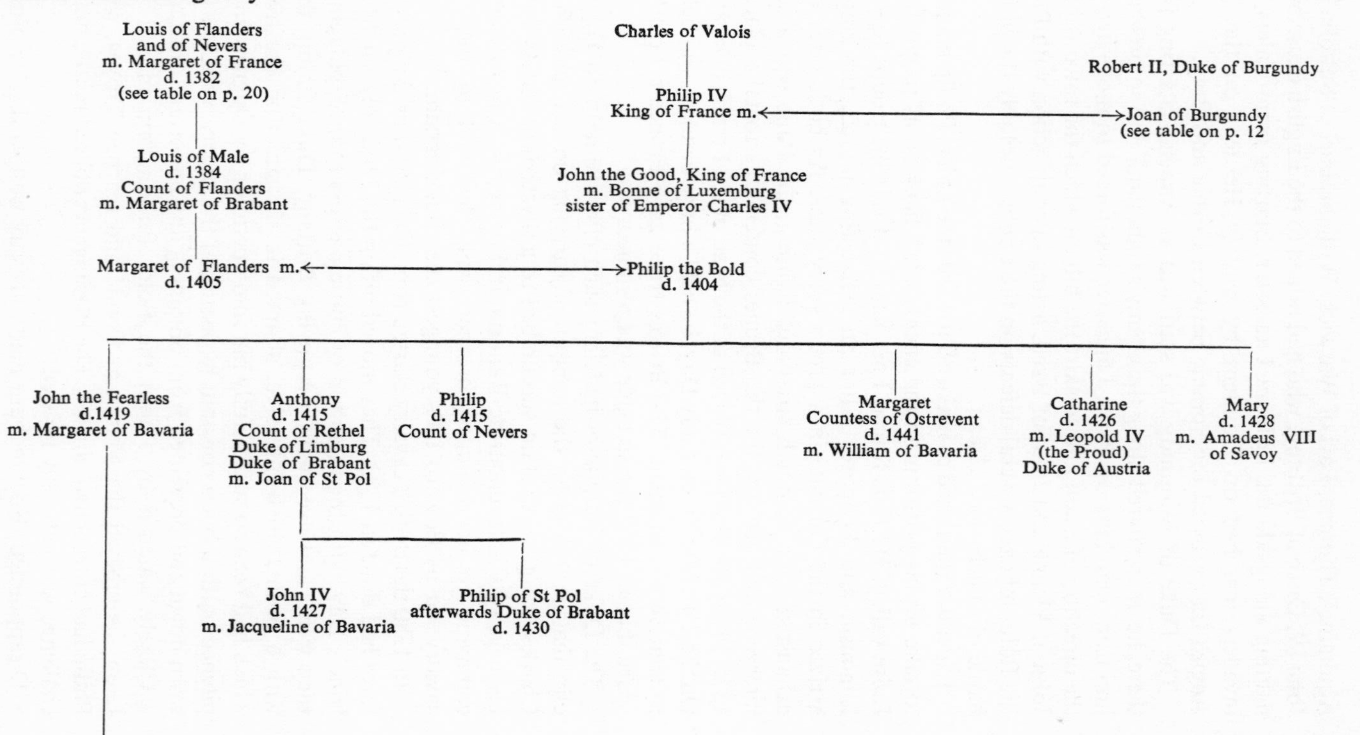

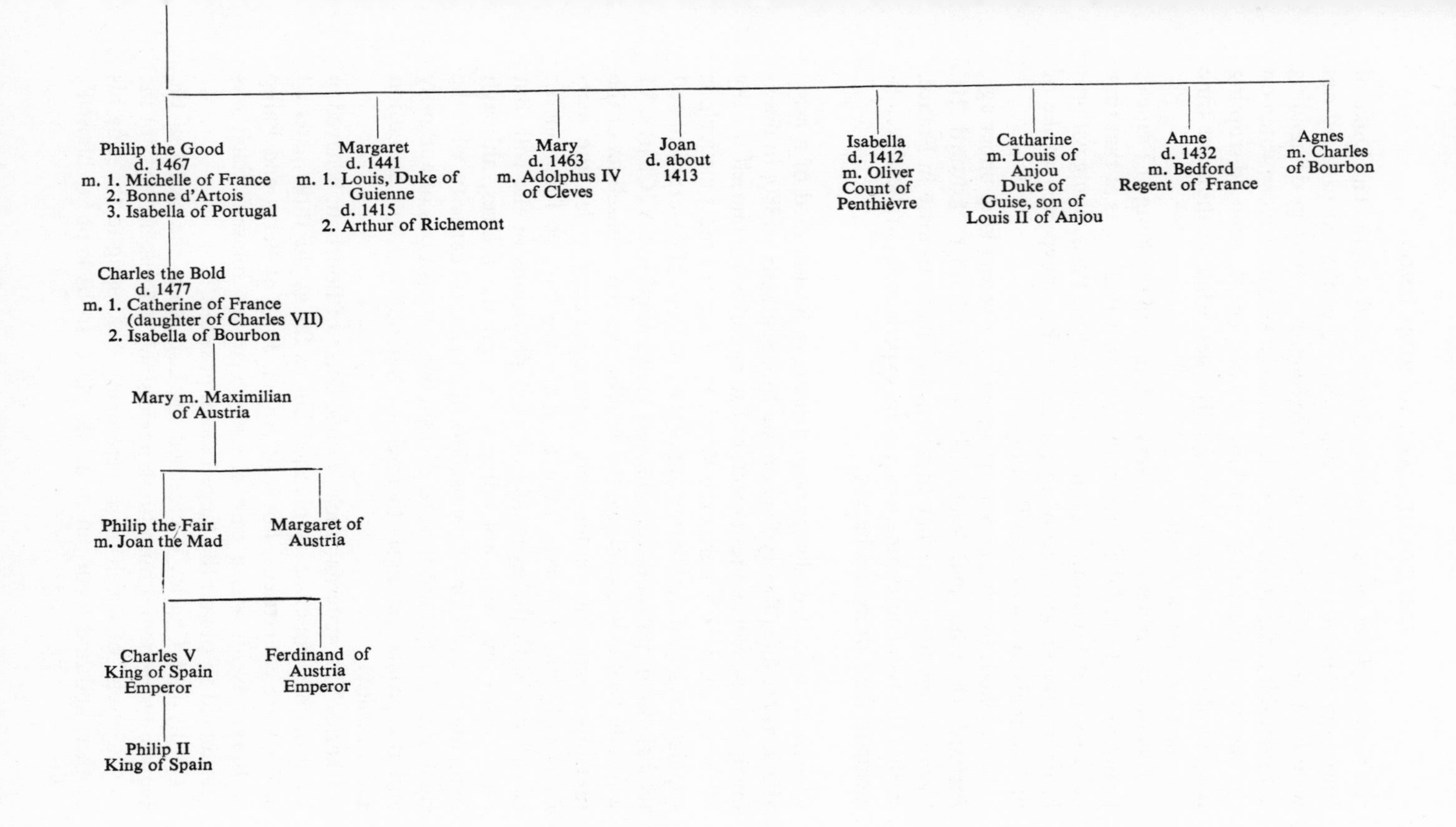
Philip the Good
d. 1467
m. 1. Michelle of France
2. Bonne d'Artois
3. Isabella of Portugal
Margaret
d. 1441
m. 1. Louis, Duke of Guienne
d. 1415
2. Arthur of Richemont
Mary
d. 1463
m. Adolphus IV of Cleves
Joan
d. about 1413
Isabella
d. 1412
m. Oliver Count of Penthièvre
Catharine
m. Louis of Anjou Duke of Guise, son of Louis II of Anjou
Anne
d. 1432
m. Bedford Regent of France
Agnes
m. Charles of Bourbon
Charles the Bold
d. 1477
m. 1. Catherine of France (daughter of Charles VII)
2. Isabella of Bourbon
Mary m. Maximilian of Austria
Philip the Fair
m. Joan the Mad
Margaret of Austria
Charles V
King of Spain
Emperor
Ferdinand of Austria
Emperor
Philip II
King of Spain

the regions of Sénonais, Gâtinais, Beauce, and Anjou. The Duke of Burgundy followed at a short distance. He continued to carry out what Froissart calls 'the pursuit of the English', a strategy demanding considerable sang-froid, and which involved keeping a close watch on the enemy's movements, attacking isolated enemy units, disrupting communications and harassing supply lines, while at the same time avoiding any serious clash.

This was the situation when very bad news of the King of France's health reached the duke's camp. It seems that Philip was at that time at Saurs, near Chartres. He immediately left for Paris, along with his brothers. Buckingham took advantage of this unexpected stroke of luck to make his way into Brittany.

In England, the throne was occupied by a young king under age, Richard II, who had succeeded his grandfather, Edward III. Curiously enough, a similar situation was about to arise in France, so that the two contending monarchies experienced parallel developments in their domestic history.

Charles V, who had always been delicate in health, died of a heart attack at the age of forty-five, on the 16th September 1380. In drawing up his last will and testament, he had again shown himself worthy of the appellation, 'Charles the Wise'. He made the most meticulous stipulations about the sharing out of the functions of government and the balance of power during the new king's minority. As Charles VI was only twelve years of age, the princes and the counsellors of the previous reign (the latter were contemptuously styled the *marmousets* by the former) were to share the various functions in accordance with the extremely detailed provisions of the will. But these provisions were not adhered to, and the princes, although retaining the dead king's counsellors in a technical capacity, with the right to advise but not to vote, divided out the positions of authority and the profits amongst themselves, but not without dissension and difficulty.

Charles VI's maternal uncle, Louis, Duke of Bourbon, behaved in a reasonable, conciliatory manner, but as far as the three paternal uncles were concerned—Louis of Anjou, John of Berry and Philip of Burgundy—it was a case of every man for himself. Each was determined to obtain the biggest share possible.[10]

Hardly had Charles V breathed his last, when the eldest of the fleur-de-lys princes, Louis, 'took possession', so Froissart says, 'of the crown jewels, of which there were many, belonging to the king his brother, and had them put in a safe place, to be kept for himself'.

This was not all. He arranged for 32,000 golden francs, saved by the late king and placed for safe keeping in the Château of Melun, to be handed over to him. At the same time, he took the title of regent and used it in the signing of documents.

But the Duke of Burgundy, who had arrived with all possible speed, protested. He demanded that the provisions of the will should be carried out, not because he felt that Charles V's last wishes should be respected, but because this was a sound tactical move. Louis of Anjou was the eldest of the dukes, but Philip was the most powerful. Men at arms began to mass in the Paris area and it seemed as if a clash might occur at any moment. However, a compromise was effected. It was agreed that Louis should be regent, but only until the boy king's coronation, which was to take place without delay. After the anointing, Charles VI, in spite of his tender years, would take over the reins of government. In this way, a troubled regency would be avoided. Nevertheless, the princes were to be in control of affairs pending the day when the young lad would become king in more than name.

The government of the uncles—under cover of an entirely theoretical kingship since in actual fact the king played no part whatever—now began to take shape. John of Berry accepted a sort of proconsulship and went off to control Languedoc and Guienne. Louis of Anjou was to be Chairman of the Council, although he would be unable to take important decisions except with the agreement of the twelve members of the Council, which was to constitute a virtual polyarchy. There can be no doubt about it; Philip had managed to curb his elder brother's authority. Furthermore, he kept a close watch on his administration of royal affairs. And while Louis of Anjou was scheming to collect money for his Italian venture—he wanted the Kingdom of Naples—Philip was quick to see, in the military strength of royal France, a factor that would help him in his Flemish policy.

Louis of Male [11] found himself in a very difficult situation, in which he was struggling as best he could, but with little success.

In the Belgian lands, where manufacturing was carried out on a large scale, the burgesses were wealthy and the *communes* very touchy about their privileges. Unrest was widespread among the weavers and all sections of society showed increasing resentment at the old type of feudal authority as personified by the arrogant count. Ghent, Bruges, and Ypres were the most prosperous towns, and the most 'progressive'.

Even in the reign of Philip VI, there had very nearly been a revolution among the *communes*, which would have turned Flanders into a trading republic modelled on the important maritime republics of Italy. Jacob van Artevelde had led the uprising and it was only his death which brought about a lull. But since then a fresh outburst of unrest had occurred. A league, called the *Chaperons Blancs* (White Hoods), spread subversive ideas and increased the frequency of clashes with the feudal overlord.

It so happened that by now, Flemish unrest was indisputably linked with a broader movement which was astir in all the countries of Europe. Of course, it would be quite wrong—and at the time some people made the mistake—to imagine that the movement was part of a vast conspiracy involving the whole of Christendom. The uprisings were quite spontaneous but certain rather disturbing coincidences can be noted. They are explained by the widespread uneasiness which prevailed at the period. In most French towns disturbances occurred, beginning by a refusal to pay taxes, and in Paris too, there was '*la commotion des Maillets*'.[12] In Florence, the *Ciompi*, workers with no political status, seized power and set up a veritable dictatorship of the proletariat. In England workers proclaimed a form of communism and seized the Tower of London. Similar upheavals were reported from Bohemia and Germany. Even the south of France did not go unscathed: it was ravaged by the bloody exploits of the *Tuchins*, literally *maquisards*.[13]

But Flanders was the scene of the main disturbances. One incident, which occurred in 1375, brought matters to a head. The count gave permission to the people of Bruges to construct a canal which would connect the Lys to the port of Bruges, thus diverting the river traffic away from Ghent. The inhabitants of Ghent resorted to armed rebellion, put the county bailiff to death and set fire to Wondelghem castle.

Ypres gave whole-hearted support to Ghent. Even Bruges, where the weavers suddenly seized power by stripping the '*lignage*' (a group of influential burgesses representing the better-class trading families), of its authority, sided with Ghent. The 'three limbs of Flanders' joined forces against Louis of Male. An army of artisans was raised and took to the field, and the 'low country' perforce followed suit. The whole of Flanders was in a turmoil.

Louis of Male, outflanked and taken by surprise, gave way. On the 1st December he announced his agreement to the franchises of the towns and to the setting up of a commission of twenty-six members, nine from Ghent, eight from Bruges and nine from Ypres, to carry out an enquiry into the abuses which had given rise to complaint. In this way the count hoped to gain time. He was calculating that the conflicts of interests which often occurred between the towns would break up the popular front which they had just formed against him and that their rivalries would play into his hands. As it happened, the *lignage* re-established its hold over Bruges, and the weavers' party, which in the other two towns had lost a good deal of its assurance, adopted a more conciliatory tone.

However, discontent persisted in Ghent and the workers remained in control. Abandoning his conciliatory policy, the count advanced on Ypres, seized the town, hanged some leaders and sent others into exile, and disarmed all those who surrendered. After which, he laid siege to Ghent.

Now Ghent was the only town strong enough to hold the count at bay. Although the Ghent militia suffered a defeat at Nivelles in 1381, it did more than merely resist the count, it deliberately went over to the offensive. And such was the force of the attack that it was difficult to say whether the count still retained the initiative or whether he had not lost it to the townspeople. Feelings ran high. An obsessional fury took possession of the wildly excited crowd; on both sides the fighting became pitiless and prisoners were massacred. After being raised twice, the blockade was re-established for yet a third time in 1382.

The people of Ghent then chose as their leader the brewer, Philip van Artevelde, who endeavoured to repeat the exploits of his father, Jacob van Artevelde, the great popular leader of Philip VI's time.[14]

Philip van Artevelde proved himself to be at once an orator and a tactician. He wasted no time. With amazing audacity he advanced on the count's army, which was reinforced by soldiers from Bruges, and, thanks to a surprise attack, he won a brilliant and resounding victory not far from the town of Bruges.

The Bruges militia had apparently soon given way, and their collapse turned into a rout. 'The knights could not even try to hold them together or to resist the enemy; they were swept along in the disorderly retreat. The Count of Flanders himself was knocked off his horse and was rescued from the mêlée only with the greatest difficulty. Everyone was seized with panic. People escaped as best they could; fathers ran off without waiting for their sons, and sons without waiting for their fathers.'[15]

The count made a dash for Bruges. He tried to shut the city gates but he was not quick enough. The men of Ghent arrived at the same time as the panic-stricken fugitives. When the count tried to hold a meeting in the market square by lantern light, because night was falling, he was warned that his opponents were out to capture him.

After hastily ordering the lights to be put out, he rushed into a back street, quickly exchanged clothes with a valet and fled through the town, only managing with difficulty to conceal his identity. Shortly after midnight, he succeeded in finding shelter with an old woman to whom he revealed his name and who was prepared to hide him. He finally managed to get out of the town without being recognized and took refuge in Lille.[16] Meanwhile, the *Chaperons Blancs* had gained control of Bruges, and the population were left in no doubt of the fact.

The triumphant workers immediately took revenge by massacring the rich merchants who had been against them, and sacking their houses. The castle of Male, the count's birthplace, which lay about a mile out of Bruges, was ransacked: the cradle in which he had slept as a child was seized and melted down. Throughout Flanders, the populace had won the day.

Never, indeed, had democracy in Flanders been in such a flourishing state. The established authorities found themselves in a most grave situation, since it was clear that the whole structure of society was being threatened. If a republic were to be set up in Belgium under the leadership of the *mécaniques*[17] the whole political system, based on feudal hierarchy and a privileged nobility, would surely collapse. This was the sort of argument heard in castles amongst the *gentillesse* (gentility), as Froissart called them.

Louis of Male appealed to his son-in-law as the only person capable of helping him out of his predicament, and the latter passed on the request for help to his nephew Charles VI. This was the beginning of Franco-Burgundian intervention. At this crucial moment the 'uncles' régime' took fright and called upon the full resources of the fleur-de-lys to help the feudal cause.

Not only royalty, but the papacy, too, was summoned to the rescue. The Great Schism had existed since 1378. The elected popes, Urban VI in Rome, and Clement VII at Avignon, were in open conflict. The Flemish, like the English, supported Urban; the King of France supported Clement. The latter excommunicated the rebels and the expedition sent against them took on, to some extent, the appearances of a crusade.

Philip van Artevelde was not a man to be intimidated even by such ominous signs. He is credited (quite wrongly, perhaps, because French chroniclers, writing for the lords and ladies of their time, tended to embroider) with the insolent comment: 'What does this kinglet imagine he is up to? He still has a year to go before he can frighten us with his massed armies. By what route does he think he can get into Flanders?'

By blocking the isthmus between the Lys and the coast and by destroying the bridges, the leader of the *Chaperons Blancs* hoped to deny the king and his lords access to the territory over which he had brazenly assumed control; he proudly styled himself 'regent of Flanders'; wherever he went, he was heralded by endless fanfares; he used the count's superb table-silver which he had appropriated.

Artevelde set great hopes on help from England. He had sent ambassadors to London to request the co-operation of the British army and, pending this, the payment of a debt, 40,000 *livres*, which was outstanding against Edward III in Ghent.

However, the opposition was not inactive; both the French and the Burgundians had taken the field. The Marshal Louis de Sancerre and the Constable Olivier de Clisson accompanied the king. Several noblemen took part in the expedition—mainly Bretons, since the Duke of Brittany was Louis of Male's brother-in-law.

The advance met with considerable opposition. The people of Rheims tried to prevent Guy de Pontailler, the Burgundian Marshal, from reaching Arras. Laon refused to contribute thirty cross-bowmen. Rouen lent 5,500 *livres*, but only with great reluctance. The towns felt that a feudal victory would be followed by stern repressive measures, and would threaten municipal independence.

But in spite of this overt or clandestine opposition, the Franco-Burgundian army pursued its forward march. By now, it was the month of October. A company of soldiers in the count's service, led by one of his illegitimate sons, was the first to open the attack. It was surrounded and massacred. At the news of this victory, Artevelde's self-assurance, and the enthusiasm of the *Chaperons Blancs*, knew no bounds.

Constable Olivier de Clisson, and Marshal Louis de Sancerre realized the seriousness of the impending struggle and knew that victory would not be easy. They were in some doubt as to the best place at which to force a break-through. Clisson was all for following the course of the Lys upstream. He was dissuaded from doing this because of the marshy nature of the region. Finally, Sancerre, on the advice of the Lord of Saimpy, a nobleman from the Hainault region, crossed the river near Comines with some Breton troops among whom were the Lord of Rohan, the Lord of Laval and the Lord of Malestroit. The Lord of Rieux, also a Breton and a nephew of the Constable, joined the company. A bridge was constructed, and under cover of night reinforcements crossed over. The Flemish troops who were guarding the sector were under the command of Dubois, the man who had brought Artevelde into the limelight, but he was wounded at the very outset of the attack, and his men were routed. The little town of Comines was pillaged. The King of France journeyed there in person, overjoyed at the success of this first feat of arms.

It was now November. Artevelde was besieging Audenarde, a town which had remained loyal to the count. The Franco-Burgundian forces were aiming for Ypres. At this juncture, the Flemish democratic leader had the choice of either withdrawing and waiting for the assault in a strong, tactically chosen position, or of taking the initiative and risking battle in open country. Elated by the victories he had already won, he chose the latter course. He argued—perhaps rightly so—that if he followed up his victory over the father-in-law by defeating the son-in-law and then by beating their common overlord into the bargain, the artisan Republic of Flanders would be established on unshakeable foundations.

Fate solved the problem in a way quite contrary to his hopes. Whether internal dissensions, the full significance of which he underestimated, had already reduced his strength,[18] or whether he committed purely strategic errors, Philip van Artevelde ended his brief career with a deplorable defeat.

The onslaught took place on the 29th November, at Roosebeke, between Ypres and Courtrai. A thick mist blanketed the two armies. Artevelde, who commanded the entire force of the *Chaperons Blancs*, had deliberately put himself at the head of the Ghent divisions. Every town had its own banner; the men wore their distinctive local dress, and advanced *en masse*. On the French side, the knights carried the sacred banner of St Denis which had been solemnly handed over to Charles VI at the Abbey of St Denis by the abbot on the 18th April. Legend has it that a white dove hovered round the king's head, thus forecasting victory. This tendency of chroniclers to embroider freely on the history of the war shows how intense feeling was, and it was no less so on the other side. Two worlds confronted each other. The fate of fifteenth century society was at stake.

Seeing the massed force of his opponents advancing heavily, like a charging boar, Marshal Sancerre gave orders to his men to execute a two-fold encircling movement. Sancerre, like Clisson, was a faithful disciple of Duguesclin, as was shown, beyond all possible doubt, on this particular day.

While the centre, shaken by the first onslaught, retreated slightly, carrying out a tactical withdrawal, and taking the young king with it, the two wings launched a shattering attack. Artevelde had completely failed to protect his flanks. All at once, the soldiers, finding themselves unexpectedly surrounded, lost their heads and took to flight.

Even the bravest had no other choice but to allow themselves to be butchered on the spot, Artevelde amongst them. Louis de Sancerre, who had engineered the victory, was later deemed worthy of burial in the royal Abbey of St Denis alongside his master, Duguesclin.

The chroniclers relate that Charles VI, elated by the victory, insisted on burning Courtrai. They say that the Count of Flanders flung himself on his knees before his young suzerain but was unable to obtain the town's reprieve.

It was, in fact, reduced to ashes. Among the trophies which Philip of Burgundy brought back from the campaign was the *Jacque-mart*, the famous Courtrai clock which shows Jacques Marc and the members of his family, dressed in fourteenth century costume, striking the hours by hitting the bells with hammers. This clock can still be seen today, in the middle of the twentieth century, at Dijon, on the church tower of Notre Dame where it still commemorates the victory of Courtrai.

The battle of Roosebeke proved decisive. The whole of Flanders was now at the mercy of the conquerors. The 1382 revolution had failed.

It had failed not only in Belgium, but everywhere else, too, and particularly in France. In Paris, the letters announcing the débâcle of the men of Ghent were read on the 12th December by the provost, standing on a marble table. A missive from Clisson conveyed the great news to the Pope at Avignon, and Clement VII conferred the title of gentleman usher on the messenger. Philip the Bold ordered 'the history of the battle of Roosebeke' from an Arras weaver; this was a huge tapestry, fifty-six ells long and five ells wide which he was fond of using as a carpet, because he liked to walk over Philip van Artevelde, whose death had been such a relief to him.

The tide of reaction was now at its height throughout Belgium. Only the town of Ghent still held out with grim determination. It was commanded by none other than the intractable Pierre Dubois, who would only agree to opening peace negotiations if the town were placed under the immediate suzerainty of the king; and neither the count nor the duke would accept this condition. It was just conceivable that help from England, which had not come in time to save Artevelde but which the people of Ghent were still counting on, might cause a change in the fortunes of war in the spring of 1383.

In the meantime Paris had to face the after-effects of the defeat of the *Chaperons Blancs*.

The wealthy burgesses, dissociating themselves from the *maillotins*, had made fruitless attempts to come to terms with the king's representatives. All the agreements which had been entered into were now repudiated. The most moderate element was involved in the wave of ruthless repression. Although Parisians and Flemings were bound by common interests, no alliance or understanding had existed between them. In spite of this, Parisians were held partly responsible for the *Chaperons Blancs* affair. Evidence of collusion, it was said, had been discovered in Flanders. On their way back from Roosebeke and Courtrai, and after solemnly handing back to St Denis the sacred banner which had led them to victory, the king's men, eighteen thousand strong, drew near Paris on the 11th January 1383. A mile from the city wall they met with a procession of supplicants: the provost of the merchants, John of Fleury, the city magistrates and five hundred citizens—all in full ceremonial dress, and anxious to pay their respects to the king. The latter curtly referred them to his judges. To emphasize the brute strength of the monarchy, the soldiers wrenched the doors of the St Denis gate off their hinges and marched over them, like conquerors.

Charles VI entered the city on horseback, followed by his three uncles, Bourbon, Berry and Burgundy, who were followed in turn by several noblemen. At least Paris did not share the fate of Courtrai. After the singing of a Te Deum in Notre Dame, the city was placed under military occupation. The uncles were quite ruthless, and a number of people were put to death. Furthermore the office of provost of the merchants was abolished and all power was placed in the hands of the Provost of Paris, who was the king's head of police.

When he agreed to these measures, Philip the Bold, we may be sure, was less concerned with the royal capital than with his Flemish subjects, whose indomitable and disquieting spirit of defiance he was determined to crush.

Perhaps, however, intervention from across the Channel, although it had not yet materialized, would jeopardize the achievements so dearly won by the royal armies.

Charles VI had transformed the 1382 campaign into a Clementine crusade. England retorted with an expedition which had every appearance of an Urbanist crusade. It was organized by the Cardinal of Ravenna, Pileo de Prata.[19] The leading figure of the expedition was the fiery Bishop of Norwich, Henry Despenser. In his youth this pugnacious prelate had fought in Italy against Bernabo Visconti and had been given the bishopric of Norwich by Urban V in 1370. More recently he had played an active and effective part in the repressive measures taken against the 'English workers', and he considered himself as something of a strategist. Urban VI appointed him Papal Nuncio of the expedition and in the bull *Dignum censemus* of the 17th September 1382 invested him with full powers. Fundamentally, the English government was less concerned with serving the Roman pope than with seizing the Kingdom of Belgium, rendering void the effects of the Flemish-Burgundian marriage, adding Bruges, as well as Calais, to their possessions, and acquiring, by fair means or foul, the monopoly of the woollen industry. The religious pretext was merely a screen concealing what was at once a political and a commercial undertaking.

A motley army was formed, comprising fanatical mercenaries, greedy profiteers, and young adventurers. It landed at Calais on the 17th April 1383, joined up with the citizens' army, took Gravelines, then Dunkirk, overcame several of Louis of Male's divisions on the 25th May not far from Dunkirk, seized Cassel, Nieuport, Bourbourg and Furnes, and finally laid siege to Ypres on the 9th June. Many inhabitants of Ghent took part in this siege.

Philip the Bold, realizing the danger, had once more called on Charles VI for help. At a meeting of princes and wealthy barons held at Compiègne, it was decided that further armed intervention was imperative. The army was to assemble at Arras on the 15th August. The Duke of Brittany was to send two thousand men-at-arms.

Ypres, however, held out. All the excesses committed during the various stages of the crusade—massacres of innocent people, rape, and arson—only served to strengthen the determination of the citizens of Ypres. Realizing that the Franco-Burgundian forces were drawing closer, Despenser launched a final onslaught on the 10th August but it failed. The English withdrew by way of Bergues. After their hurried evacuation of the town, the Franco-Burgundian army made its entry and set fire to the houses.

The English now retreated towards Bourbourg, but the numerical superiority of the royal army gave it the upper hand. Chaos reigned during the closing episodes of the campaign. Bourbourg was pillaged by Breton soldiers. The English set fire to Gravelines, but even so the Bishop of Norwich had to negotiate his way out of the country. He left the Continent with some loss of dignity.[20] The British crusade fizzled out.

The King of England, Richard II, was personally all in favour of peace. And although the Bishop of Norwich's escapade was not followed by a treaty settling Anglo-French differences once and for all, at least a truce was arranged, covering, amongst other things, the question of Ghent. Apparently, this conciliatory move was not at all to Louis of Male's liking, but as it happened he died on the 30th January 1384, leaving his superb inheritance to Philip the Bold—the counties of Flanders, Artois, Rethel and Nevers, the domains of Malines and Salins, and the lands of Isle in Champagne, Villemaur and Jully. In spite of acquiring these vast domains, the duke was still in serious financial straits; he made one request for money after another to the king; a hundred thousand francs to begin with, then a hundred and twenty thousand, after which he asked for his allowance to be increased; it was raised from one thousand francs a month to fifteen hundred, and eventually to three thousand.

His newly acquired estates inevitably involved him in greater expense, for he had a natural liking for pomp. When he went to take possession of his new domains in May 1384, his journey was marked by his usual extravagant liberality. Contrary to his hopes, his generous gifts did not win back the towns of Belgium. Bruges and Ypres joined indomitable Ghent, in a renewed attempt to withstand the threat to their municipal liberties.

The truces which had been signed were only valid for two years, and both sides were making preparations against the day when they would expire. A Flemish noble, the Lord of Escournay, did not even wait for the agreed period to elapse, and, without warning, seized Audenarde. Philip the Bold was informed of this incident by the people of Ghent and denounced Escournay, but the latter argued with such insistence, that he was finally allowed to keep Audenarde.

In the circumstances, it was an easy enough matter to see that a fresh crisis lay ahead. Philip, on yet a third occasion, obtained the help of Charles VI. Artevelde's successor as leader of the Ghent democrats, Frans Ackerman, was subsidized by Richard II. But the new Count of Flanders was in no hurry to destroy the splendid fief which was to become the key territory of the vast State he was building up. He came with a huge army to show how powerful he was, carried out a number of executions, and then made a great show of good-will. The duke's personal charm, helped by the weariness which was everywhere in evidence, produced its effect. Wars interfered with business and the burgesses had had enough. More important still, Philip proved himself to be a clever statesman by showing the greatest possible tolerance towards the Urbanists. His conciliatory attitude with regard to the schism pleaded eloquently in his favour throughout the whole of Flanders. At the same time he made several equally adroit attempts to soothe local susceptibilities. For example, he even saw to it that letters issued by the royal chancellery were written in Flemish.[21] Such political shrewdness is not surprising on the part of the duke who 'looked ahead'. Naturally it brought its reward. The Peace of Tournai on the 18th December 1385, set a seal on the reconciliation between Ghent and the count-duke. The old privileges of the rebellious city were ratified and a general amnesty quietened public opinion. At the same time, a gateway, very threatening to France, had been barred against the English.

Success was so complete that a daring plan for a Franco-Burgundian invasion of Great Britain was now evolved. The idea of launching such an attack revived an ambition once dear to Charles V and preliminary outlines of which had even been drawn up by the 'wise king'. In the year 1386 circumstances seemed particularly favourable. In his island kingdom, 'the beardless youth' (the Duke of Burgundy's code term for referring to the King of England) was encountering ever-increasing opposition, which was to lead finally to his downfall. Why should it be impossible to do to Richard II what William the Conqueror had done to Harold? This was just the sort of project to appeal to Philip *the Bold.* Cabaret d'Orville, the chronicler, relates how Philip advised Charles VI to abandon a policy of 'small-scale enterprises'—or shall we say a policy of little by little—and to strike a heavy and decisive blow at 'the overweening pride of the English'. In an attempt to work up popular enthusiasm, the poet Eustache Deschamps[22] wrote in one of his ballads:

Princes passez sans tant de demourée
Vostres sera le pays d'Angleterre
Autre foiz l'a un normand conquesté
Vaillant cuer peut en tout temps faire guerre.

(Princes, tarry no longer
The land of England shall be yours
Formerly a Norman conquered it
A brave heart is always ready to fight.)

The appeal did not go unheard. Men-at-arms, cross-bowmen and archers volunteered in such numbers that the treasurers in charge of war finances did not know which way to turn. How could such an army be supported and maintained? It was to embark from Sluys, the port of Bruges. When in September, Charles VI travelled from Paris to take over command of the invading army, he was astounded to see all the villages from Arras onwards packed with troops, who had come from every corner of France, from areas as far apart as Comminges and Picardy, Brittany and Hainault. To avoid overcrowding, the hordes which were pouring through Flanders 'in order to cross the sea' were not allowed to billet in the towns.

Supplies were concentrated at Sluys. All the fiefs, including Burgundy, had been asked to make a contribution: huge loans had been contracted. Nothing was lacking in the way of either food or arms: there were barrels of biscuits, hams, sides of salt pork, smoked salmon, cured herrings, beans and peas, salt and verjuice, and as many as twenty-five hand mills so that the corn could be ground on board ship. As far as arms, missile weapons and artillery went, a never-ending procession of waggons carrying suits of armour, military equipment, shields, arrows, explosives, incendiary rockets and guns, moved along the road. In a construction yard near Rouen in Normandy, a collapsible wooden enclosure seven yards high, made of stout logs from the Romare forest, had been prepared, complete with look-out turrets and reinforced every twenty yards by eighteen-foot high towers. This huge 'wooden town' which was said to measure seven English leagues in circumference and which had an area of eight hundred acres, was virtually a fortified camp composed of movable parts. No fewer than seventy-two ships were needed to transport this gigantic defensive structure from Rouen to Sluys.

The navy had made just as intensive preparations as the army. The galley yards at Rouen which dated from the days of Philip the Fair and which had been reorganized in 1373 by Charles V, had been commissioned to construct, caulk, repair and fit out the ships. There were *galéasses* and *dromons*—that is to say heavy transport vessels; there were also light sailing boats for patrolling the coast. The king had had so many ships built that, according to a letter written by an Italian living in Avignon to a friend in Florence, 'they made the finest sight that was ever seen'. Ships were requisitioned from every possible source. From Seville to Prussia, says Froissart, 'there was not a single large vessel sailing the high seas which was not seized on behalf of the king and his followers, if the French could lay their hands on it.' There were enough ships, so it is said, to stretch from Calais to Dover. And indeed, during the latter months of 1386, the port of Sluys looked like a veritable forest of masts. A visitor from Florence who was present when all these preparations were in progress, estimated the fleet at twelve hundred ships, six hundred of which were equipped with fighting-tops—that is to say wooden towers which served as shelters for the cross-bowmen. The ships were all painted in the brightest possible colours: the royal ship, for example, was painted a vivid red to show, as a somewhat malicious English chronicler, the Monk of Malmesbury, put it, that the king was prepared to shed blood: all bore coats-of-arms, and linen banners and twill war-flags, emblazoned by well-known painters with oil-paintings of the French royal arms, the armorial bearings of the princes of the blood, or Charles VI's own emblem, the golden-winged stag-beetle.

While waiting for the fleet to sail, the princes whiled away the time by boat-racing. Charles VI was very proud of not being sea-sick, and very anxious for the expedition to start. But the signal was never given. The chroniclers seem to think that the Duke of Berry is to be held responsible for the miscarriage of his brother of Burgundy's scheme. They accuse Duke John not only of having slowed down the preparations but also of having deliberately postponed his own arrival on the scene, and of putting forward the argument that winter was now approaching, in the hope that the whole project would be abandoned. It was decided to postpone the expedition, which was now to take place in the summer of 1387, starting from Honfleur instead of Sluys. In actual fact the expedition never took place at all. From now on Philip the Bold's policy underwent a change; the duke counted on frightening the English into concluding, if not a real peace—which was hardly conceivable given the great differences of opinion between the rival camps—at least a relaxation of hostilities and periods of extended truce which would have all the effects of a permanent peace.

As the conquest of England had been abandoned, plans for territorial expansion on land now began to take shape.

Even before the 'wooden city' episode, the growing state of Burgundy had felt that its future lay in the east. By becoming ruler of Malines and Antwerp, the duke had acquired as neighbours two powerful Houses, which occupied positions of supreme importance in the Holy Roman Empire, and in fact, contended for control over it—the Bavarian House of Wittelsbach, and the House of Luxemburg. At this time, the House of Luxemburg had assumed the imperial crown. Anyone wishing to expand eastwards had to be prepared to negotiate a way between these two powerful dynasties, always bearing in mind that they were rivals. While still retaining his authority as overlord of the northern fiefs subinfeudated to France—and he showed how keen he was to keep them under his control by refusing to give Lille, Douai and Orchies back to the king,[23] on the ground that his marriage, conditional on the gift of these towns, had been concluded in the interests of France—Philip the Bold could not resist the temptation to extend his sphere of influence to fiefs held under German jurisdiction. He already held Franche-Comté which was a dependency of the Reich. Thus a cosmopolitan spirit came into being and was to grow steadily stronger until, in the case of the first of the great dukes, and still more so in that of his successors, it was to counterbalance the ambition of a feudal magnate who was a peer of the French realm twice over and considered because of this as 'the senior peer', destined to play a feudal rôle of supreme importance in the kingdom of the fleur-de-lys. The dual pattern now discernible was later to have highly significant consequences.

Wenceslas, Duke of Brabant, who belonged to the Luxemburg family, had died. The heir apparent of his widow, Joan, through whom he had acquired Brabant, was her niece, Margaret of Flanders, Duchess of Burgundy. An expectative granted by Wenceslas to the House of Luxemburg seemed likely to interfere at one and the same time with hereditary rights, Joan's intentions and Margaret's interests. The dowager duchess, in connivance with Philip, evolved a plan of arranged marriages to safeguard her position and ensure that her estate was passed on to the rightful heir. The idea was to join in wedlock the children of Duke Aubert of Bavaria with those of the Duke of Burgundy. John, Count of Nevers, eldest son and heir of the Duke of Burgundy was to marry Margaret of Bavaria: William of Bavaria, Margaret of Burgundy.

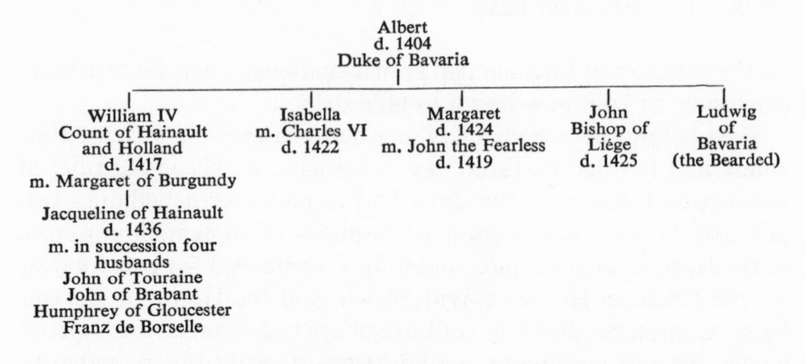

The Bavaro-Burgundian marriages took place amid impressive pomp and pageantry at Courtrai on the 12th April 1385, and the royal marriage was celebrated at Amiens on the 17th July. As Pirenne—the outstanding historian of Belgium—has so appropriately and forcibly expressed it, the main outcome of these marriages was 'to render Philip's position in the Low Countries absolutely impregnable'.

Moreover, the marriage policy became a special feature of the House of Burgundy, just as, in the past, it had been adopted by the ducal dynasty of the Capets. In 1393, Philip the Bold married his daughter Catharine to Leopold IV of Austria, and his daughter Marie to Amadeus VIII of Savoy.[24]

Needless to say, all these marriages helped the duke tremendously in the pursuit of the eastern policy on which he had embarked after 1386–1387. The first major indication of the new trend was the Gelderland expedition.

Joan of Brabant, whose heir, as has already been explained, was Margaret of Flanders, was being threatened by the Duke of Gelderland acting in the interests of the House of Luxemburg. As England supported Gelderland, Philip the Bold enlisted once more the support of Charles VI, whom, moreover, the Duke of Gelderland had stupidly and insolently challenged to combat: the result was the 'German expedition'.

In order to spare Brabantine territory, the Franco-Burgundian army had to face the difficulties of an arduous march across the Ardennes and the Eifel district. Guy de Trémouille and the Count of St Pol accompanied Charles VI and his uncle Philip. The slow progress of the 1388 expedition, unrelieved by any dramatic feats of valour, came in for a good deal of criticism in France. But it was most profitable from the Burgundian point of view. Not only was the whole of Germany greatly impressed by this show of power; Joan of Brabant, saved by her niece's husband from an alarming predicament, was from then onwards completely won over to the cause of Philip and his wife. There could be no doubt about it: Burgundy was winning, in Brabant, against Luxemburg.

How could Joan of Brabant hesitate between the sluggish, worthless Wenceslas of Luxemburg on the one hand, and Margaret of Flanders's alert and energetic husband on the other? Ignoring the various agreements contracted in his lifetime by her irresponsible husband, and which were now being invoked by the House of Luxemburg, the dowager duchess boldly placed herself under Burgundy's protection. According to an agreement drawn up on the 28th September 1390, she ceded the ownership of her estate to Philip, while retaining the control of the domain for the rest of her life.

Philip possessed to the highest possible degree a sense of proportion and an instinct for knowing just how far he could go. He was most careful not to press his advantage to the point of annexing the estate for himself. To avoid hurting the feelings of the Brabantines he put forward in 1393 the proposal that Joan's inheritance should go, not to Margaret of Flanders, but to his second son Anthony. Joan agreed. In 1396 she made the journey to Paris, for she wanted, so she said, to see 'the princes of the fleur-de-lys' before she died. Then she asked Philip to let Anthony come to stay with her, so that she could get to know him better. In the course of her journey to Paris the old duchess had handed Limburg over to Philip. All the agreements contracted between Brabant and Burgundy were ratified by the estates of Brabant in 1403. Throughout the whole of the Brabant episode, Philip the Bold, as H. Laurent and R. Quicke have so conclusively shown, was 'in complete control of events'. On this occasion more than any other he justified in masterly fashion the eulogies of Froissart and Christine de Pisan.

In the *Somnium super materia schismatis*, Honoré Bonet, who was a very well-known writer in his day, addressed himself in the following terms to the first of the great dukes: 'I observed, when I was a young man, that you were called Philip Lackland: now God has generously bestowed on you a great name, and placed you alongside the mighty ones of the earth.'[25] This is a highly significant piece of evidence, because it shows the realization on the part of Philip's contemporaries that a vast and imposing structure was taking shape under their very eyes.

His policy of expansion in the east did not prevent Philip at the same time zealously pursuing a policy as uncle of the King of France and a prince of the Valois line.

It so happened that the situation at the French court changed with startling suddenness just after the return from the Gelderland expedition. At Rheims, on the 3rd November 1388, Charles VI had thanked his uncles and announced that in future he would rule without their guardianship. Having failed, on their return to Paris, to make their nephew change his mind, the Duke of Berry and the Duke of Bourbon had resigned themselves; in any case their elder brother, Louis of Anjou, had died in 1384 and his son Louis II was entirely absorbed by Italian affairs. The Duke of Berry had been extremely annoyed but Burgundy placated him with the words: 'Brother, we must put up with the situation. The king is young. If he follows youth's advice, he will be disappointed. The time will come when those who advise him will be sorry—and the king too.' 'The time will come' was, as it happened, the Duke of Berry's motto. On this occasion the Duke of Burgundy adapted it to his own purposes. When necessary he could forget his own motto 'I cannot wait'.

In actual fact the Rheims coup was the outcome of a conspiracy led by the young Duke of Orleans, the king's brother, and Charles VI's former advisers, called the *marmousets*. A rather surprising sharing out of functions gave an ambiguous colouring to this curious two-

Burgundy and Luxemburg

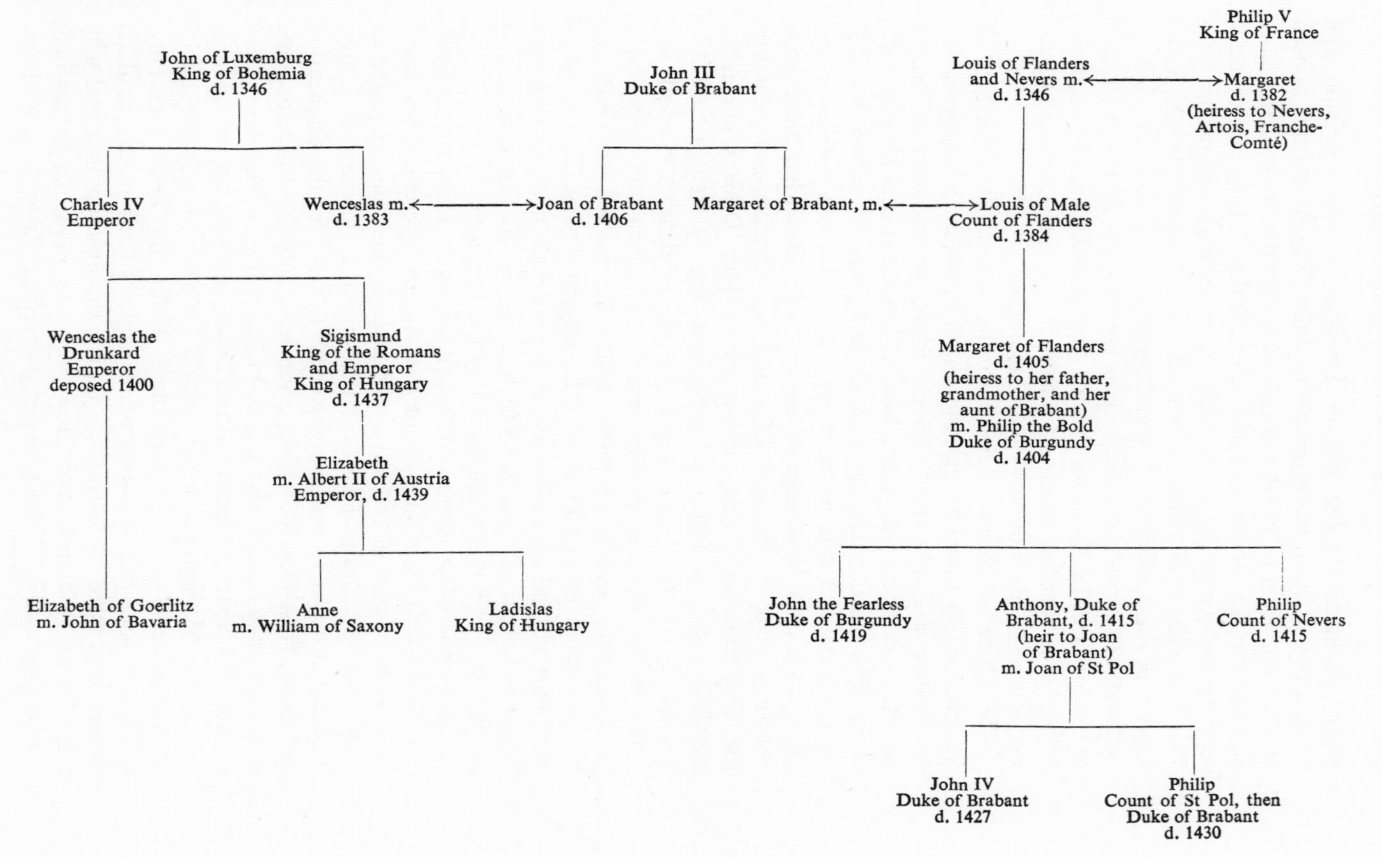

sided arrangement; the tedious business of administration and book-keeping fell to the *marmousets*, while Orleans devoted himself to the organizing of court festivities and the directing of the more adventurous side of external affairs. The Duke of Burgundy's eastern venture was partly the result of his being cold-shouldered in 1388. The four years after 1388 were turned to good account thanks to the success of the marriage policy and the Brabantine negotiations.

Charles IV's madness, which, as is well known, first showed itself in the forest of Le Mans on the 5th August 1392, put an end to the 1388 régime. The *marmousets* fell from favour and Louis of Orleans was forced to come to terms with his uncles.

The Duke of Berry returned to the profitable lieutenancy of Languedoc, so that Orleans and Burgundy were left to confront each other in the Council of State. Philip abandoned court entertainments to Louis who threw himself heart and soul into the task, along with the German queen, Isabella of Bavaria, whom scandalmongers claimed was his mistress. But Louis was ambitious and greedy. He took advantage of his brother's somewhat naïve good nature so that, in moments of sanity and feverish sentimentality, the king showered lands and money on him. Orleans pursued a two-fold policy of territorial expansion, first in Italy, where Asti had come to him as the dowry of his wife, Valentine Visconti, and where he had designs on the seignieury of Milan, and secondly, in the Ardennes and Luxemburg, which he wanted to make the nucleus of an important state, after buying Coucy. The Duke of Burgundy curbed his ambitions at every turn[26] and the first signs began to appear of a quarrel which, as it grew in intensity, was to weigh heavily on the future history of the kingdom.[27]

The Genoa affair illustrated this rivalry in its most typical light. Louis of Orleans was represented at Asti by a certain Enquerrand de Coucy, a man of initiative and tact. Enquerrand managed to secure for the Duke of Orleans the suzerainty of Savona, a preliminary move which was meant to pave the way for the subjugation of Genoa. Now Flemish trading companies had vital interests in the port of Genoa, which was a link between the manufacturing and commercial centres of Italy and the Low Countries, and the annexation of the Mediterranean port would have been highly prejudicial to the interests of the Count-Duke, Philip the Bold. Naturally, Philip had been put on his guard by Coucy's bold moves, in which he was supported by Valentine's father, the unscrupulous and wily Jean Galéas Visconti. A counter-plot was immediately hatched. Genoa appealed to Charles VI for protection. After prolonged and stormy disputes, Philip the Bold got the royal Council of State to accept the Genoese proposal, and the standard of the fleur-de-lys was hoisted over the gates of the Marble City alongside the imperial standard with the eagles. A little later, Marshal Boucicaut, who had just returned from captivity in Nicopolis, became the King of France's representative in the great Mediterranean port. Louis of Orleans gave in. He got Charles VI to agree to generous compensation for the renunciation of Genoa and Savona, and Visconti himself, with some ill-grace, had to yield to the Valois. Burgundy had won the day: indeed, whenever he cared to take the trouble, he could always get the better of Orleans.

A reference has just been made to 'Nicopolis' in connection with Marshal Boucicaut. This expedition to the east, of which the Marshal had been one of the prime movers, had brought the House of Burgundy both fame and sad bereavement. The 'Nicopolis Crusade' had been undertaken at the earnest entreaty of the King of Hungary —with the purpose of safeguarding the Danubian frontiers of Christendom which were being attacked by the Turkish Sultan, the redoubtable Bajazet the Thunderbolt. At the head of the crusade was John, the Count of Nevers, the future Duke John the Fearless. With him were the Count of Eu, commander-in-chief of the French armies, John of Vienne, Admiral of the French fleet; Marshal John le Meingre, known as Boucicaut; the Lord of Bar and the Count of la Marche, both cousins of the king; the Lord of Saimpy; and Guillaume de la Trémoille and his son Pierre. The Count of Nevers had a magnificent retinue, lavishly emblazoned with his emblem, the hop plant. Tents and flags were of green silk, his favourite colour. The glittering procession left Paris on the 6th April 1396, passed through Dijon, where magnificent celebrations were staged and then crossed the French border into German territory. Eventually it reached the Danube and laid siege to Nicopolis. Battle was joined beneath the walls of the city on the 26th September and the future duke, although victorious during the initial stages when the enemy failed to withstand the force of his attack, suffered a shocking disaster at the end of the day. Admittedly splendid feats of valour were performed on the Christian side, John of Nevers, the admiral and the marshal particularly distinguishing themselves, according to contemporary opinion. But the Christians suffered appalling losses. Philip of Bar and both members of the Trémoille family were among the dead. John of Nevers, Boucicaut, Henry of Bar and the Count of la Marche were among those taken prisoner. To the vast expense of a costly and disastrous campaign were inevitably added the heavy ransoms demanded for the prisoners. John was only released on payment of the enormous sum of two hundred thousand florins, which was advanced in instalments by a financier of Lucca. John and the marshal came back, and the fame of their exploits, which had carried far and wide, allowed the courtly society of the time to forget the bitterness of defeat and the heavy price which had been paid.[28] Far from being discouraged, Philip the Bold, following the example of all the princes of his time, chose this moment to found a new Order of Chivalry. It was a forerunner of the famous Order of the Golden Fleece which his grandson was to found and was called more simply 'The Golden Tree'. The emblem consisted of 'the golden tree with an eagle and a lion enamelled in white', and copies were distributed among relatives and friends. They involved the duke in such expense that, alarmed at the total cost, he sent his own emblem back to the goldsmith in order to cut down the bill.

During the last years of his life, the Valois duke's chief task was to achieve and maintain a *modus vivendi* with England. He worked consistently and adroitly to bring about an agreement useful to both France and the Burgundo-Flemish state, whose economic interests he shrewdly aimed at fostering.

It is not within the scope of the present work to recall the complex patterns of Franco-English negotiations under Charles VI, but the main stages of the *rapprochement* must be mentioned in passing.

As early as the 18th June 1372 truces had been signed at Levlinghen between England and France. Richard II gave back Cherbourg on the 21st January 1394: on the 19th April 1396 he married Isabella, daughter of Charles VI: the twenty-eight-year truces which were signed on the 11th March to celebrate the engagement, replaced the Levlinghen truces and ushered in one of the longest periods of peace in the Hundred Years' War, although they were destined to be broken before the end of the agreed period.

Meanwhile, Richard II's dramatic fall and the stormy accession of his cousin, Henry IV of Lancaster, did not produce any essential change in the situation, since Henry ratified the twenty-eight-year truce. He was faced by too many difficulties at home to rush into foreign ventures. From now until his death, Philip the Bold, whose Flemish domains prospered as a result of the peace, was able to feel that the war, which he had once waged alongside the famous Breton, Duguesclin, was a thing of the past.

Age was now gradually creeping on him. Like the patriarch he was, he lavished more and more of his affection on his children and grandchildren. One of his major preoccupations was finding husbands for his daughters and granddaughters.

As we have already mentioned, he had arranged a marriage between his daughter Mary and Amadeus of Savoy; but the girl was too young to embark on married life and she had remained at her father's court; she was despatched to Savoy in 1403. Margaret, the daughter of John the Fearless, had been first of all engaged to the Dauphin Charles, but had lost her fiancé while she was still a child. She was later betrothed to the Dauphin Louis, who succeeded his brother as heir presumptive to the Kingdom of the Fleur-de-Lys. It is obvious that these repeated attempts to ensure that his grandchild would one day be queen, were part of a preconceived plan.

All these family events occasioned a great show of munificence. The rich and varied costumes of the princesses, details of which will be given later in the account of court life, were specially intended to create, in France and Savoy alike, a great impression of the power of Burgundy.

The Duchess of Brabant, who was also growing old, had expressed the desire that Anthony, her great-nephew, and her heir, should take over the administration of his future estate. Anthony, who had been created Count of Rethel, while awaiting his future elevation, was sent off to his aunt. She came to Brussels to meet him, and this gave the Duke of Burgundy an excuse for lavish celebrations in the city. But at the end of his stay, the duke caught an infectious type of influenza, which was very widespread at the time. Realizing that he was seriously ill, he arranged to be transported to the neighbouring castle of Hal, where he breathed his last on the 27th April 1404, in his sixty-third year.

His life had been one long search for money. Death suddenly and unforeseeably claimed him during one of those moments, only too frequent throughout his career, when he was out of funds. He did not leave enough to pay for his funeral or to settle current expenses. Such was the situation that Margaret, afraid lest the assets of their joint estate should prove insufficient to pay off the creditors, did what 'even the most humble housewife could not do without being overcome with shame: she genuinely waived her claim to the estate and it is said that, to prove she had surrendered her possessions, she placed, as was the custom, her purse, her bunch of keys and her girdle on her husband's coffin'.[29]

The gesture was purely formal. It might have cast a slur on a lower-class woman's reputation, but in the eyes of the courtly society of the time it could not cause the slightest damage to the authority and prestige of the Duchess of Burgundy.

The day after the duke's death, his sons made the brave gesture of putting his silver in pawn with a financier, in order to pay the initial cost of his funeral. A neighbouring convent lent the Carthusian monk's habit in which Philip had expressed the wish to be attired on his death bed. A procession was formed to take the body on the various stages of its final journey, with all the pomp befitting the occasion, from the Brabantine manor, which fate had decreed should be his last earthly home, to the capital of the duchy. The official funeral was held at Champmol, where the prince, although he had died in such penury, was to lie for many hundreds of years in the most magnificent of tombs—the one which at that very moment was taking shape in Claus Sluter's workshop. This tomb, now empty and considerably restored, is today one of the most prized possessions of the splendid Dijon Museum.

CHAPTER V

PHILIP THE BOLD: PATRON OF THE ARTS

THE REFERENCE TO Philip the Bold's tomb provides a natural link between the discussion of his rôle as a statesman and his activity as a patron and protector of the arts.[1]

It should be made clear at the outset that, on this score, the Duke of Burgundy was by no means an exception among his contemporaries. On the contrary, his brother Charles V zealously fostered the arts of his day. He never tired of collecting books, rare manuscripts, illuminated manuscripts and precious *objets d'art*. He had a splendid *Librairie* at the Louvre, and the catalogues, which are still extant, list an astonishing and varied choice of works.[2] The *Bibliothèque Nationale* of our day, which emerged from the *Librairie du Louvre*, via the *Bibliothèque Royale* of the *ancien régime*, bears eloquent witness to the taste and munificence of the 'Wise King'.

Philip's brothers, Louis and John, shared their elder brother's tastes. Louis of Anjou was more especially interested in jewels and tapestries.[3] He counted among his treasures emblazoned cups adorned with lions, and tapestries showing Charlemagne alongside Godefroy de Bouillon, Lancelot and Arthur, and the Nine Doughty Knights with the Revelation of St John. John of Berry, an enthusiastic builder—he was responsible for the design and decoration of the magnificent castle of Mehun-sur-Yèvre, André Beauneveu's masterpiece, which was his home and later that of his nephew, the 'King of Bruges'—was an outstanding connoisseur of *objets d'art* and valuable curios; at the same time, he not only carried sartorial elegance to extremes, but also liked to display on his library shelves—at Mehun, as it happened—some of the most famous illustrated manuscripts of his day, such as the well-known '*Très Riches Heures du duc de Berry*', which eventually came into the possession of the Duke of Aumale, and are one of the glories of the castle of Chantilly, so fittingly bequeathed to the *Institut de France* by its last princely owner.[4]

Louis of Orleans, the nephew of these ardent collectors, emulated his uncles.[5]

They were all anxious to outdo each other in the exchange of lavish presents. The trade in *objets d'art* enjoyed an inevitable boom thanks to the stimulus given by the constant flow of orders which even the most disturbing events at home or abroad failed to interrupt, because the buyers ran up bills without giving a thought to the morrow. The most grievous mistakes made by the most adventurous and even the most frivolous of the Valois princes, were nobly redeemed by their passion for works of art.

Both Philip and Charles V are, however, unique and worthy of high praise in that they combined their passion for art with a strongly developed political sense and never allowed their rôle as lavish patrons to interfere with their obligations as statesmen.

Philip was, moreover, superior to Charles, because he not only gave the most effective encouragement to the art of his day, but also founded an incomparable school of art which owed its inception and subsequent fame entirely to him. His patronage of the arts was thus as important as the extraordinary impetus—more important perhaps for history—that his initiative had given to the Burgundian State. The ducal State, as it developed after Philip's time, certainly acquired a dazzling splendour, but it collapsed before attaining its full expression. Burgundian art, on the contrary, reached its full expression. It originated in connection with the Chartreuse of Champmol; it was founded by Philip and under his successors it produced a series of masterpieces which have remained an undying source of inspiration to succeeding generations.

Let us first of all inspect the duke's library, jealously guarded by his barber. To begin with, it contained prayer-books, missals, breviaries, psalters and books of hours, bibles, some with commentaries, some illustrated, some in Latin or French, some in Flemish, together with a few—very few to be honest—patristic works, for example, the *Dialogues* of saintly Pope Gregory the Great. But these pious volumes do not represent the most valuable part of the collection. Secular literature had a far greater appeal for the duke than theological writings. There are even a few works belonging to the pre-Christian era of antiquity—a magnificent Livy in gold lettering, an 'illuminated' copy and a gift from the Lucca financier, Dino Rapondi, to his most faithful customer. Several Aristotelian treatises occupy an important place, and although Greek manuscripts are missing, Greece is present through Romance poetry, in

Hector de Troie, which was a translation and paraphrase of works of the Homeric cycle. The Age of Chivalry is amply represented. French chronicles and chronicles of the Flemish counts furnish the well-stocked historical section. To these may be added the '*chansons de geste*', which at that time were considered as history in story form: Ogier the Dane, Baudouin of Jerusalem, Saladin, the capture of Constantinople, *and the Fleur des Ystoires d'Orient*. It seems only fitting that the Holy Land should figure in the books belonging to the man whose son and heir was the hero of Nicopolis. The *bestiaries* and *mappemondes* represented the fantastic element. *Fabliaux*, books of Proverbs and the Twelve Months, were contemporary productions. Thirteenth-century works such as the *Roman de Renart*, the *Roman de la Rose*, which were going out of fashion in the fourteenth, were side by side with the latest works to appear—*Ballades et Virelais* by Eustache Deschamps (whose real name was Eustache Morel), *Cent Ballades* and also *Mutacion de Fortune* by that much-praised writer, Christine de Pisan, who also wrote (on the duke's instructions) *Le livre des faits et bonnes moeurs du Sage Roi Charles Quint*. The same author was also commissioned to write another work—in verse this time—*Epîtres et Ditiés*. Mention should be made of a copy of a miscellany which enjoyed a great vogue at the time—*Le livre des Propriétés des Choses*—a sort of practical encyclopedia of natural phenomena—compiled by Bartholomew the Englishman in the thirteenth century, and still very popular at the end of the fourteenth. A hundred years later, there was a hand-written copy of the translation by Corbechon, in the library of Edward IV, King of England, a proof of very lasting popularity.[6]

The tapestries and the books are closely linked, since the woven pictures illustrate in their own way the works written on paper or parchment. Philip never tired of adding to his store of rich tapestries. Arras, the centre for this craft among the 'pays' belonging to the duke and the home of *arrazi*, was commissioned to make quite as many tapestries as Paris. It was the Arras weavers who started the magnificent series 'worked in cypress gold' which was to continue during the four reigns: these tapestries were so valuable that a special department was set up for their preservation, under the management of a man referred to in the account-books as '*Le Gambier*', or '*le petit Cambillon*', in all probability a cripple.

After the library, let us examine these tapestries. Interest immediately focuses on a splendid sequence of religious tableaux—scenes from the Life of Christ, and the Life of the Virgin; the *Credo* of the Apostles; the Revelation of St John—the work of Robert Poinçon of Paris. The saints are not forgotten, those honoured by the family holding a foremost place; St Louis obviously takes the lead, for the French royal family were still proud of the man to whom they owed all that was most noble in their renown; St Denis, whose oriflamme was carried in battle, comes immediately after him; then follows St John, who gave his name to both the father and elder son of Duke Philip; finally St Anthony, to whom Philip, as we know, showed special devotion, always observing his birthday. Next, the duchess's saints, Margaret and Catharine; the latter because she was worshipped traditionally by the Counts of Flanders, the former because she was patron to the heiress who had brought so many splendid seignieuries to the Valois of Burgundy.

Alongside this fine gallery of religious figures, we find an equally splendid and equally profuse array of heroic knights. First of all, scenes from the '*chansons de geste*': the Round Table cycle, Charlemagne and his Peers, Charlemagne in Jerusalem, William of Orange, Renaud de Montauban, King Arthur, Lancelot of the Lake, Perceval the Welshman, Tristan, the Nine Doughty Knights and the Nine Virtuous Ladies: next, as is only fitting, the 'tenth Doughty Knight', the famous Duguesclin—already admitted to the realm of art, just as he had been a legendary figure in his own lifetime. The series was continued to include a topical episode—the magnificent tapestry commissioned from Michel Bernard depicting the Battle of Roosebeke, to which reference has already been made.[7] As we pass from the noble exploits of legend to more recent or even very recent events, we cannot overlook the tapestry depicting Godefroy de Bouillon, the hero of the First Crusade, whose sword the duke acquired on the 13th March 1393. This superb weapon should have brought better luck than it did to the Count of Nevers at the battle of Nicopolis. One wonders if the defeat casts doubt on its genuineness.

A tapestry illustrating Jason's deeds foreshadows the future Order of the Golden Fleece, although the duke was quite unaware of this. Beside it, we find Hector of Troy, then Semiramis of Babylon, 'the destruction of Troy the Great', Alexander's conquests, the Seven Wise Men, 'Octavian of Rome', Octavius and the Sibyl, 'Pharaoh and the nation of Moses' and 'the story of Mohamet'. Finally, after this admirable display of eclecticism, indicative of a very liberal culture, comes what can be called the literary section: all the minor heroes of chivalry are shown in turn, also a choice of those abstractions of which the '*rhétoriqueurs*' were so fond, such as the '*donaiements*' and the '*souhaits d'Amours*': we find too '*l'Amant et l'Amie*', the '*Dame entre Deux Amants*', the '*Verger de Souffisance*' and the '*Verger de la Nature*'. These pastoral themes have been legitimately compared by an intelligent critic to the 'fresco by Orcagna at the Campo Santo of Pisa, in which lovers are conversing at the edge of a sacred wood'.[8] There could surely be no clearer sign that the Renaissance was on the way.

The same rustic note was echoed, with more pronouncedly pastoral overtones, in the duchess's personal collection of tapestries. Here, *marguerites* occupied a place of honour, and, looking at the sort of scene she delighted in, it is easy to visualize the lady who bore the name of these delightful flowers disporting herself in a sort of Trianon: the verdant landscape is dotted with black and white ewes, shepherds and shepherdesses: violets, roses, forget-me-nots, hawthorn and other glories of field and garden mingle with the marguerites. Such was the normal background for the princess's emotional life, suggested by the mottoes, eg: 'love's sickness holds me in its grasp'. The heiress of Flanders did not, however, live entirely in an idyllic world, and her collection reflects the traditions of chivalry of her House. Aimery de Narbonne and his six sons, the 'doughty' King Tristan, and 'Manfred routed by Charles of Anjou' were well to the fore. And although classical mythology provided only one scene, it must be agreed that it corresponded to the lady's sentimental tendency: it was The Judgment of Paris.

In these matters Philip shared his wife's tastes. At the castle of Germolles, a relief, the work of Claus Sluter, and now unfortunately lost, showed the duke and duchess under an elm surrounded by sheep. Bunches of marguerites, the intertwined initials P and M were scattered everywhere: the finest and most memorable example of the intertwined initials is to be seen at the Chartreuse of Champmol, where it commemorates the founders.

In fact, the duke and duchess surrounded themselves with works of art; their costumes, their toilet requisites, furniture, and china were all exquisite. Margaret's personal linen was embroidered with hawthorn leaves. She possessed a great variety of dresses and the account books reveal that some of them were most elaborate. The duke too appeared in completely new clothes on all the important occasions in his life. The clasps—called *fermaux*—on the ducal apparel were embellished with various plant motifs—sage, lily, violet, broom and a hundred others: some had animal motifs—eagles, lions, bears, monkeys, peacocks, falcons, etc. The falcon recalled the common pastime of hunting. Dogs, larks, pheasants, partridges and doves were also connected with the sport of hunting. Hunting scenes were frequently used as ornamentation: an eagle making off with a coney—that is, a rabbit—a falcon seizing a golden heron, 'a stag drowning in water'; and when we read of 'wild pigs, men and trees' it is easy to guess that the reference is to a boar hunt.

The stories and pastimes of feudal life inspired such scenes as 'the lady with the unicorn', or children playing the '*jeu de paume*'.

Salt-cellars were often decorated with mermaids. Jewellery flashed with every sort of precious stone—especially with the balas ruby, which was the prince's favourite gem. On one occasion, he gave the Duke of Anjou a golden goblet in the form of a sheaf of corn, set on hollow stalks with the bond twisted like rope and with each grain separately carved: at the bottom of the goblet was an enamelled picture of a swan wounded in the breast, floating on water among lilies and green foliage: the lid was encrusted with ears of corn: the terminal bud was a pomegranate flower.[9]

The richness of the gold and silver plate beggared description, and that was why, whenever security had to be found for a financial loan, it offered a source on which the duke could freely draw, because it was worth millions. The silver plate used at table was in keeping with the rest. Among the goldsmiths who were commissioned to work for the first duke, the king's own goldsmith, Hennequin du Vivier, should be given first place, although Philip the Bold had an official goldsmith of his own, John of Brabant.

Henriet Orlant and Benedict du Gal, who both lived in Paris, were also called upon to work for the duke.

Financiers of the Rapondi family acted as intermediaries for purchases made in Italy, while the Balducci were the chief agents for purchases made in Venice.

Thus, not only the art of feudal France and Burgundy, but the whole range of western art was called upon to enrich the duke's store of treasures. Even Germany contributed. Hermann and Venant of Cologne did work commissioned by the duke, as did the goldsmith Hermann Ruissel, who was better known. A compatriot of Sluter, Rollequin de Haarlem also received commissions, but he had been living in Paris since 1383.

Some of the duchess's jewels, we are told, featured two ewes holding a wolf: gentleness triumphing over savage cruelty was one of the idealistic hopes of the sentimental princess.

The ducal chambers were decorated in various ways, often with great originality, yet always with great taste. One, for example, was adorned, we are told, with boughs of red and white oak arranged around a tiger quenching his thirst at a fountain. The duke's chamber at Dijon was the colour of gold, at Montbord it was red, at Rouvre, green.

The duke was fond of adorning his clothes with ewes and swans, and sometimes, in accordance with current fashion, these creatures were 'animals which made a tinkling sound', because they had bells round their necks. Sometimes real bells formed part of the costume, when this was the current craze. Shoes, naturally, had long pointed toes and were adorned with ornate buckles. The cloak, which throughout the whole of the Middle Ages was the most lavish garment worn by courtly society, was trimmed with the most expensive varieties of fur. Cloth of gold or silk from Lucca, cloth of gold from Damascus, cloth from Arras, Douai, Lille, Malines, Termonde, etc, graced in turn the duke's wardrobe, in which every garment was exquisitely finished, tastefully arranged, and artistically cut. Hats and hoods were also works of art and adorned with expensive jewels.[10] Every day of his life the duke lived in an atmosphere of magical luxury. It is hardly surprising that, in order to keep up this mode of life—the terrifying extravagance of which will be described elsewhere, in the chapter dealing with the court—the richest of the Valois should so often have found himself, in spite of his vast fortune and fame, with an empty purse and at the mercy of money-lenders.

Art involved the duke in expenditure in another sphere, which has not yet been mentioned and which proved to be the most costly of all: architecture, including naturally both sculpture and painting. These were the three major forms of art in the fourteenth century.

The duke, of course, had several residences, but he had three main residential areas; in the Ile de France, in his capacity as a prince of the blood, he owned the castle of Conflans, and the Hôtel d'Artois in Paris: as count of Flanders and Artois he owned castles in Arras, Lille, Ghent, Bruges, or near big towns: as duke of Burgundy he had his town house in Dijon, the manors of Rouvre, Talant, Montbard and the hunting 'lodges' in Châtillonnais. He used the castle of Argilly as his own private residence, and the duchess preferred the castle of Germolles.

The greatest possible care was taken of these numerous residences; they were constantly being improved upon, enlarged and adorned with fresh embellishments. There is no need to mention the duke's bedrooms, the varied decorative schemes of which have already been noted. It is worth remembering, however, that every castle had a '*chambre du poêle*' or state chamber set aside for high-ranking guests. The *grande salle* was what in the language of today would be called 'the main drawing-room': there were also baths, a covered gallery for wet days, and the '*jeu de paume*'. Coloured panes were very fashionable, and often took the form of stained-glass windows depicting scenes from history or legend. The chapel was a church in miniature, an exquisite replica on a smaller scale of the finest examples of religious art. The Gothic style was at its height, and was ending in a burst of splendour with the wonderfully ornate lines of the *flamboyant*, sometimes quite wrongly condemned as decadent, but representing, on the contrary, the full flower of Gothic architecture.

The chief architects, sculptors, and painters of the century were commissioned to work for the duke. The man who restored the Louvre under Charles V, the king's master mason Raymond du Temple, had a meeting on the 30th April 1384, at Rouvre, with André or Drouet de Dammartin, who was in charge of all the duke's stone-work, and with Jacques de Neuilly, the mason of the Chartreuse; when three such men got together it was presumably to discuss some important undertaking. A few years later, John of Beaumetz, the painter, arrived at Rouvre castle to supervise painting operations.

Beaumetz's team also worked at Argilly from the 20th March 1389 until the 31st October 1391 and a document definitely establishes the fact that the fire-place in the main hall of the castle was the work of a mason from Rheims, Jean Herbelay, who copied the one in the royal castle at Creil. Similarly, Dammartin, when working at Germolles, along with John of Marville who had won such high praise for his work at the Chartreuse, took his inspiration from Corbeil. It would take too long to enumerate all the repairs and improvements which were carried out at the other residences, at Montbard in particular, as well as at the duke's *hôtel* in Dijon, and at those he owned in the Ile de France and other counties.[11]

We finally come to the famous Chartreuse of Champmol which owed its foundation solely to the first of the four dukes and which would be sufficient in itself to win him a place of honour in the history of art. Its aesthetic merits will be dealt with in a later chapter; what it is important to note at the moment is the way in which the lavish prodigality of the duke made possible this achievement, unequalled in France by any other feudal lord and the like of which even the Kings of France failed to achieve. Only the royal Abbey of St Denis can be compared with the Chartreuse and it took hundreds of years to complete and was not the work of one particular prince; the Kings of France were generous enough in looking after their private burial ground, but St Denis was not associated with the name of any one of them in particular.

Philip, who wanted to be buried in a Carthusian monk's habit, had considered the possibility of founding such an order at quite an early age. Even in 1375 his pious dreams were disclosed when he made a contribution towards repairing the *Grande Chartreuse* which had been damaged by fire. Pictures commissioned in 1378 from John of Beaumetz were intended for the Chartreuse of Lugny and in the same year a cloth 'painted with pictures' was presented to a monk of the same house. A plan was then formulated for the erection near Dijon of a monastery with twenty-four cells, a main cloister and a smaller cloister and which was to contain a chapel and a burial-place for the dukes. Work was begun almost immediately. The first and second stones of the building were officially laid on the 20th August 1385 on St Bernard's day. The duchess herself laid the first stone 'with her own hand' and the second was laid by the duke's heir, John, aged twelve. Raymond du Temple and Drouet de Dammartin were the architects and great artists such as John of Marville and Claus Sluter were responsible for the sculpture; more will be said in the chapter on Burgundian art about the masterpieces produced by these illustrious craftsmen. But it should be mentioned here that the erection of the Chartreuse and all the distinguished works of art which it housed, cost the House of Burgundy stupendous sums of money: in the account books mention is constantly made of payments, either for stones and the transport of stones, or for the work done by masons, painters and sculptors commissioned by the prince.[12] And since the Chartreuse was a burial-place, the duke's tomb was established there, which brings us back to the starting-point of this chapter. Work had hardly begun on the tomb when death—a rather premature death—cut short the career of the founder of the dynasty. The work was continued under the auspices of the second duke, John the Fearless, and the succession of ducal tombs was to carry on from one reign to the next, an eloquent symbol of that patronage of the arts, which, although never again as brilliant as it had been under Philip the Bold, was nevertheless, as the generations followed each other, to make as great a contribution as war or diplomacy to the fame of the great dukes.

CHAPTER VI

JOHN THE FEARLESS

THE SECOND OF THE DUKES was baptized John, after King John, his grandfather, to whom the ducal House owed its rise to power. He was, we are told, 'a small dark man, with blue eyes, a full face, an unfaltering glance, an uncompromising jaw', and 'a massive, squashed head'; he was coarse and devoid of charm, he had no fluency of speech, cared little about his appearance, neglected his clothes, except on those occasions when he went to the other extreme, and appeared ostentatiously in heavily ornamented garments. He was 'a Fleming with Hainault blood in his veins'. He took after his father, but was even more like his mother. He was brave, daring, wily and his ambition knew no bounds.[1] His slovenly appearance and his somewhat crude manners appealed especially to the common people. Yet he impressed everybody by the quickness of decision and strong determination which lay beneath the surface. Although he was ugly and ungainly, his ugliness had a masculine quality and his ungainliness denoted strength and physical robustness so that he had all the outward appearances of a great prince. His unprepossessing exterior expressed a strong personality. His aquiline features had a compelling charm; he was at once repellent and attractive, strange and disturbing. He himself never experienced fear but he took a wicked pleasure in inspiring fear in others, and he used that fear as one of the mainsprings of his policy. He was to use flattery too, at which he also excelled. His career, like his personality, was to be full of contrasts. He was to make a vigorous impact on his century, vigorous yet equivocal, as equivocal as his features, or as the quirks of his enigmatic psychology.

Since his birth on the 28th May 1371, he had lived mostly in Flanders, and he spoke Flemish, a language which his father had never known. His tutor was a Fleming, Baudouin de la Nieppe, Provost of St Donat in Bruges. At twenty the future duke was given the leadership of the Nicopolis Crusade after receiving the title of Count of Nevers. 'I am eager to distinguish myself,' he said at this time, according to Froissart. He always acted on the principle that it was best to forge ahead. The Flemish motto *Ic houd* which means 'I will never give up', 'I will hold fast', revealed his doggedness of purpose. The eastern venture ended in failure, but although it inflicted on the head of the dynasty and his subjects the terrible burden of the ransom of two hundred thousand florins, it won the heir to the duchy a lasting reputation for valour.[2] Whether, as some people think, he earned his nickname at Nicopolis on the 25th September 1396, or, as one chronicler has asserted, he won it at the Battle of Othée, it is difficult to say.[3] The fact remains that Philip the Bold's successor, by outshining his father's reputation for daring, has gone down in history as the *fearless* duke.

Feudal custom dictated the initial events of John's reign. Immediately after the funeral rites at the Chartreuse of Champmol, the official entry into Dijon took place, along with the customary ratification of privileges;[4] then the new duke paid a visit to the royal court to see the betrothal celebrations of his daughter Margaret with the Dauphin, Louis, Duke of Guienne; the marriage had been arranged by Philip the Bold but he had not lived to see it officially confirmed. This new family union inevitably brought John face to face with the only brother of the reigning monarch, Louis of Orleans.

The antagonism between Orleans and Burgundy, already evident towards the end of Philip the Bold's principate, was soon to become, under John the Fearless, the central issue round which all political action revolved.

The death of the uncle who had so often curbed his activities, gave Louis of Orleans the opportunity to do more or less as he liked with the Royal Council and to exercise the royal favour as he wished. During the latter years of his life Philip the Bold had had considerable difficulty in restraining the impetuosity of Valentine's husband, who was set on reviving the war with England, whereas it was in the interest of both the Flemings and the French to maintain the existing truce. Louis, imagining perhaps that he was following in the steps of the 'Wise King', but oblivious of the untimeliness of his plan, had even gone so far as to challenge Henry IV of Lancaster to a duel, which the English king had disdainfully declined.[5]

The Duke of Orleans' policy seemed to be to revive the war with

England and extort as much money as possible from the king. John the Fearless, on the contrary, aimed at putting a stop to tax increases, in order to gain popularity, and at preventing the break-down of the Franco-English truce, which would be prejudicial to the interests of the Burgundian state.

On this last point, John, while continuing his father's policy, dictated by the obvious demands of the Belgian provinces, was even more resolute since important Anglo-Flemish trade negotiations, started by Philip the Bold, were still in progress. John of Thoisy and another faithful servant of the House, Thierry Gherbode, were making every effort to establish a basis for agreement, under the supervision of the Chancellor, John Canart. The latter died in 1405, but his successor, John of Saulx, Lord of Courtivron, continued his work and a treaty was drawn up in December 1406 and published on the 20th April 1407.

In this way the alliance which, in accordance with the first duke's policy, had been binding England and Burgundy closer together, became firmly established during the reign of the second duke, counterbalancing and restraining the rash escapades of the Duke of Orleans and his friends who seemed bent on fanning the flame which could, at any moment, lead to a general conflagration.

As well as taking a firm stand on this major issue of foreign affairs, John set himself up as champion of the French taxpayers, who were being exploited to further Louis's bellicose and wasteful schemes. Louis found in Isabella, his sister-in-law, the ideal 'partner'[6] with whom to pursue a round of pleasures which was becoming more and more extravagant and dissolute. John, with a total lack of discretion, spoke up in the Royal Council to demand an account of how the money was being spent. The people, he said, were weighed down under their burden of taxes. A proposal had been made to levy a fresh tax before the end of the financial year, because the tax returns for the current year had all been spent. John declared himself hostile to the new measure, which he would not in any case agree to impose on his own vassals. If what was still left of the last tax returns was not enough, he was prepared to make up the deficit from his private purse, rather than allow extortionate demands to be made on the people.

Such language had never before been used by any prince—it could almost be called 'electioneering'—and it was exactly what was needed to win quick popularity for the man who had the wit to use it. The duke would have found it far from easy to make up the financial difference, but the offer was just the sort of thing to find favour with the common people: here for the first time, the prince showed signs of his vocation as a popular leader, as a master of the art of winning the approbation of the masses.

But to make a public stand in the Council on this point was inevitably to arouse the animosity of the Duke of Orleans. From this moment onwards the now open rivalry between the two cousins was to become more and more acute.

John made the additional act of homage, which he had to pay after his mother's death on the 21st March 1405, an excuse for a visit to Paris. His stay in the capital, according to the chronicler Enguerrand de Monstrelet, was to give him an opportunity of 'attending to and expediting his affairs'. This explanation was hardly necessary. The duke set off with five thousand men-at-arms. At Louvres-en-Parisis, one of the stages of his journey, he learned that the news of his arrival had made Louis and Isabella decide to flee the capital; they left the sick king behind, and went to Melun, leaving instructions to the Dauphin and his wife to join them and to travel under an escort commanded by Isabella's brother, Louis of Bavaria. On the 19th August, John swept through Paris and dashed straight off in pursuit of the fugitives. The leader of his advance-guard, William of Vienne, Lord of Saint George, caught up with the Dauphin's suite at Juvisy and brought it to a halt. The duke then arrived on the scene, severely rebuked Louis of Bavaria, dispersed his men, and replaced the Orleanist escort by an escort of Burgundian soldiers. He then brought the Dauphin and his wife back to Paris, where the people greeted the royal couple and their protector with highly significant enthusiasm.

Immediate advantage was taken of this initial success. On the 26th August, homage for Margaret of Flanders's estate was offered by John and also by Anthony, Count of Rethel, in respect of his inheritance. On the same day, protests were lodged with *Parlement*, the *Chambre des Comptes* and the university. Addressing themselves to the king, before these august representatives of the State, the Burgundian princes condemned 'all that was being done to harm you and your kingdom'. Monstrelet, a Burgundian himself, is careful to give full details of this first indictment, which was to be followed by many others. It criticized the behaviour of the Orleanists, disclosing details of the heavy burdens imposed on the common people. It declared the need for reforms. It denounced the unheard-of outrage of carrying off the Dauphin and his wife. The duke would not disband the men he had brought with him unless he saw some improvement in a state of affairs which had become intolerable. In short, the indictment was a full-scale accusation levelled against the Duke of Orleans.

When Orleans retaliated on the 2nd September, the dispute took on fresh violence and became a sparring match. The queen, in making the young couple leave Paris, had only done her duty. Surely she was responsible for 'the welfare and management of her children'! It was moreover outrageous to have arrested the heir to the throne and to keep him prisoner in the Louvre. On the 8th September, Burgundy refuted all these arguments. Troops were now being massed on either side. With every day that passed civil war seemed more likely and tension was widespread.

Doubt was no longer possible; the quarrel was serious and open. Grimly the two cousins confronted each other. Each was out to win and to eliminate his rival. Two irreconcilable policies and violent personal hatred, which every fresh incident only served to intensify, gave the quarrel its highly dramatic character.

John the Fearless had already added a second emblem, the nettle, to his first choice, the hop. It was a hint of things to come. Whoever touches me, will get stung. But Louis of Orleans had chosen a knobbly stick with the motto 'I will vex him'. John then adopted the plane as a badge and this was supposed to 'smooth down' the stick: he added the motto *Ic houd*, Flemish for 'I hold fast'. Round the plane were 'shavings'; these were silver clips, often decorated with precious stones, which people wore to show they supported the Burgundian cause and which were given away as ornaments at the Burgundian court to friends and sympathizers.

Burgundian ideas were certainly gaining ground: they were liberal ideals, plans for reform. The stand taken by the Duke of Burgundy was bound to win the support of all victims of abuses; the vigorous way in which he advocated remedial measures for the only too glaring evils of his time and the steps he suggested to remove the structural weakness of the State could not fail to win over all those, and they were legion, who longed for a new form of government.

All of them, no doubt, had read *Le Songe Véritable*, a bitter pamphlet, containing relentless attacks on contemporary vices, but one that was not written for the purpose of furthering the Burgundian cause. We propose to give a brief summary of it, because it provides an explanation of the popularity of John the Fearless.

The author deals ruthlessly with the people who are pillaging the mad king's country while the unhappy monarch leads a wretched existence, playing *chapifol*, or blind-man's-buff. He is surrounded by a whole army of swindlers, who keep him under their thumb and fleece him right and left. These are the people on whom the lash of satire falls most heavily. Not one is spared: the gentlemen who served the king at table, the carving squires, the chief pantler, the chief cup-bearer, the steward at Beauté-sur-Marne, the palace stewards in Paris, the high master of woods and forests, the clerks, notaries and inspectors of chancellery documents, the masters of the rolls and the councillors of the *Parlement*. But among this swarm of parasites of uncertain and lowly birth who had risen by favouritism to the most important offices, the financial administrators are singled out as chief offenders: the treasurers of France, the war treasurers, counsellors and custom dues collectors, district tax collectors, councillors, and special officials of the *Chambre des Comptes*, the master of the privy purse, the king and queen's master of the mint, the treasury's money-changers, the keeper of the savings-fund, the keeper of the state coffers, the keeper of the jewels and of the gold and silver plate which was housed at the Louvre, the Fortress of St Anthony, Vincennes and Saint-Germain-en-Laye.

All the members of this 'vast band' who 'are basking in the bright sunshine of Dame Fortune's favours', not only receive as presents and New Year gifts, cloth for their livery, palfreys or sumpters, lined boots, ostrich feathers with which to adorn their robes, and silver-gilt table services, they also see to it that they are provided with enormous allowances. It would not be so bad were they experienced financial experts, but most of them are incompetent and obsessed only with power and money. However, like true apothecaries, they know how to cure their own pecuniary ills, and to make good the gaps in their private fortunes. They 'snatch and grab'. They steal the silver dishes of the king's own table service; they help themselves to his tapestries and even his clothes. Everything is grist to their mill. A district tax collector, Alexandre le Boursier, called 'Close Fist', sells wine; a money-changer at the treasury is director of a business firm; a chamberlain carries on a black market trade in untaxed salt. They all 'cram their wallets full'. They all advance loans at an exorbitant interest to the king and the princes, using the money they draw from the State coffers. All have bought fine mansions, in Paris, in the fashionable districts—the rue Ste-Croix-de-la-Bretonnerie, the rue Vieille-du-Temple, the rue de la Parcheminerie, the rue de la Heaumerie, the rue Bourg-Tibourg; for instance, Milet Baillet, a blackmailer and treasurer who owns a mansion in the rue de la Verrerie where there are as many glass windows as there are days in the year. They all provide themselves with a house 'in the country', that is to say, on the outskirts of Paris, either just outside the town in the old suburbs, at Clichy, St Ouen, Bry-sur-Marnes, Romainville, or in the outer suburbs at Luzarches, Meaux, Corbeil, Palaiseau, Rambouillet and Pontoise. Raymond Raguier, controller of the public funds, has been able to save enough money to build a magnificent castle at Orsay. The famous John of Montagu, 'comptroller of all the royal finances', has had a church costing six hundred thousand francs (gold francs, of course) built on his domain of Marcoussis for Celestine monks.

In short, confusion reigned, corruption was widespread, and dishonest dealing was at a peak. By proclaiming his intention of reforming the régime, the Duke of Burgundy made a strong emotional appeal and could count on popular support. Moreover, he went beyond mere verbal promises. He restored to Parisian citizens the right to put up safety chains at night, a right which had been abolished during the repressive measures of 1382. He was deliberately seeking to earn the gratitude of the common people, who were indeed grateful for the amends thus made to them.

It almost seemed as if the son of the man who had opposed the *Chaperons Blancs*, and had been a party to the reactionary measures which followed Roosebeke, was out to become a French Artevelde, so zealously did he cultivate the friendship of the Parisian people, always ready to approve of opposition to the powers that be.

But alongside the aggressive spirits who were undaunted by the prospect of a clash of arms, or even of political upheavals, there were also moderate, peace-loving men, who were dismayed by the violent turn that the controversy was now taking. A good many of these men were to be found at the royal court. The Duke of Bourbon, and the Duke of Berry, in particular, were most disturbed when they saw their nephews hurling defiance at one another, and the thought that they might actually come to blows filled them with panic.

The court, alarmed, brought pressure to bear on the two cousins: a first reconciliation took place, on the 16th October 1405, when they were prevailed upon to eat and drink together and to promise that they would disband their forces. The first scare was over. But before long, feelings once more ran high. The uncles, increasingly dismayed by the challenges and counter-challenges that were exchanged, again tried to patch up the differences between the two opponents. They were invited to stay in the same places, were made to take Holy Communion together, and to embrace each other. These contrived scenes of reconciliation were short-lived.[7] Isabella, whom some people were trying to set up as regent, manœuvred as best she could, but she had little authority, being undecided and changeable.[8]

It was John who got rid of Louis. The famous crime which startled the whole country was committed on Wednesday, 25th November 1407. On that particular evening Louis of Orleans had gone to Barbette House, in the Marais, the residence of the queen, where she had given birth to her twelfth child, Philip, who lived just long enough to be privately baptized. The gang hired by the Duke of Burgundy had put up in a nearby inn with the sign '*l'imaige Notre Dame*'. The crime had been planned down to the last detail. Thomas Courteheuse, the king's *valet de chambre*, had been let into the secret. He went to Charles VI's brother, who was with the queen, and said: 'My lord, the king instructs you to go to him without delay because he wishes to speak with you about an urgent matter closely concerning both himself and you.' Thus was the trap laid.

Without stopping to think how unlikely it was that he should be asked to go to the king at such a time—it was about eight o'clock and dusk had fallen—the Duke of Orleans mounted his mule and set off. 'It was a fairly dark night' we are told by Monstrelet, who describes the scene. The prince was accompanied by two equerries on horseback, and by five or six footmen carrying torches.

Suddenly, eighteen or twenty men emerged from the shadows. Taken aback, Louis exclaimed: 'I am the Duke of Orleans'. The reply came: 'That's the man we want'. Whereupon they set to with might and main. After killing two valets as well as the prince's German equerry, and putting the others to flight, the hired assassins got to work on their main victim. Louis fell to the ground. His head was smashed open, his right arm broken and mutilated, his left wrist cut right through, and his brains scattered in the mud. The curt order was heard: 'Put out all lights. Let us be off. He is dead. Behave like men.' The body, which they left lying there, was taken during the night to the church of the Guillemites, later called the church of the Blancs-Manteaux, while awaiting burial, which took place in a Celestine monastery.

The leader of the assassins, who were most generously rewarded by the Duke of Burgundy for carrying out their mission successfully, was one of the Duke's regular servants, called Raoulet d'Anquetonville. Queen Isabella had in the past had him convicted for swindling, and he was head over heels in debt. A whole group of hired assassins were, like Raoulet, in the duke's pay, and ready to carry out his orders, even when it was a question of murder. John, in fact, belonged to that category of statesmen who are so dominated by ambition that they consider the means to justify the end, and who do not hesitate to commit any sort of crime, if by so doing they can relieve a tense situation.

And on the morning following the death of his cousin, the Duke of Burgundy took his place at the funeral service without any sign of embarrassment, and displayed the feelings that were expected of him as a kinsman of the dead man.

The enquiry, conducted by the shrewd and conscientious Provost of Paris, Guillaume de Tignonville, could not fail to lead directly to the household staff of the royal dukes.[9] Rumours were already beginning to circulate.[10] Two days after the event, at the close of a session of the Council, John admitted his share in the affair to the Dukes of Anjou and Berry. He told them that 'led on by the devil, he had had the murder committed'. The next morning, which was a Saturday, he left Paris for Flanders.

There should be no mistake about the significance of the confession or the reason for John's departure; he was not running away. By making his declaration to the princes, the murderer showed his unwillingness to wait for the results of the enquiry which could not fail, as he well knew, to reveal his responsibility. Being John the *Fearless*, he took the initiative. He set off for Flanders because he needed to allow time for the shock to wear off, for public opinion to crystallize, and for friends, enemies and waverers to work out *in his absence* what attitude they were going to adopt. But he was convinced that the climate of opinion would soon be such that he could return, not to apologize for his deed, but to boast of it, and to reap the benefits it would yield.

As was understandable, the crime of 1407 at first gave rise to contradictory reactions. At court people were still dazed and their grief seemed genuine enough. Louis of Orleans had great faults, but he was a generous man, a decent fellow on the whole, and a gay dog. In spite of his escapades and his squandering of public money he still retained the allegiance of the knights and feudal lords. He was loathed, on the other hand, by the common people and the burgesses. The latter looked upon him as the man who frittered away their money, and the former held him responsible for the duties, tolls and tithes to which they were subjected. People who did not know him personally imagined him to be wicked. For them the gay companion was a saturnine character, the light-hearted rake, a double-dealer, the irresponsible duke, a malevolent schemer. Valentine was widely believed to be a witch. It was said that the king was given potions which made him ill, so that advantage could be taken of him. To many people, then, Louis appeared as a hateful tyrant, whereas John was the defender of liberal ideas. Since the sword alone could end the enmity between the two cousins, the man in the street was relieved that Orleans had been the one to succumb.[11] Those who had set their hopes on reforms—and they were in the majority—were certainly relieved that the 'knobbly stick' had been 'smoothed down' by the 'plane'.

No sooner had John reached the safety of his Flemish lands, than he set to work to win the allegiance of his subjects. It was not difficult to hoodwink them. The duke called his barons and clerks together at Lille, and gave them his version of what had happened, and then did the same at a session of the Flemish estates at Ghent. With a profound understanding of the power of propaganda, John, whose craftiness was such that he could anticipate any move in the political game, spread abroad tendentious rumours presenting the crime either as a necessary step to safeguard the nation, or as a legitimate act of vengeance. The Duke of Orleans was accused of having planned the murder of the Duke of Burgundy, so that the latter had really only acted in self-defence. Another line of approach was also used. Orleans was accused of having tried to seduce the Duchess of Burgundy,[12] from which it could be inferred that the blow struck on the 23rd November was a fitting punishment for an irreparable outrage. It was, moreover, common gossip that Louis was ambitious and tyrannical; that he wanted the throne for himself; that he and his wife Valentine practised black magic on the king in order to hypnotize or poison him; that he had nothing but contempt for the common people, and squandered the money he extorted from them in the form of tolls and aids. With a dexterity which had never before been witnessed, the guilty duke made it seem as if he had rid society of an unworthy character, thereby performing an act of liberation and justice; and this interpretation of the facts was so skilfully presented that it came to be accepted in Flanders, Burgundy and Paris—so readily, indeed, that we can gauge the moral confusion of these troubled times, when it was becoming increasingly difficult to discriminate between good and evil.

The duke was undoubtedly past master of the arts of slander and political strategy. He had introduced into his entourage two different sets of henchmen who served his purpose admirably: first, hired assassins like Raoulet d'Anquetonville, who were ready to do away with anyone who stood in their master's way, and second, clerks, like John Petit, whose bold propaganda we shall shortly have an opportunity of appreciating, recruited in rather dubious university circles and able to turn out an endless succession of broadsheets and polemical statements which confused the issues and covered up the duke's tracks so successfully that the average Frenchman was totally unable to distinguish what was lawful from what was not.

Without going as far as Thomas Basin,[13] who maintained that John had long had the idea of killing his cousin, it must be admitted that he made the most of the corpse, thus revealing a sound grasp of the psychological possibilities of the situation. He slipped away from the court and the capital. He knew that the initial reaction would be one of sympathy towards the dead man, however unpopular he had been but that, in the case of the 'tyrannical' Orleans, the sympathy would only be short-lived. He had only to wait. The tide would turn and he could help to speed up the process.

Events confirmed these calculations. To begin with, Louis's widow, Valentine, who had taken refuge at Château-Thierry and then at Blois, aroused some feelings of sympathy. Along with her children, she gave vent to a rather melodramatic display of grief, which nevertheless evoked some response. Later, taking advantage of the murderer's absence, she came back to Paris. With her eldest son, Charles, Count of Angoulême, and her daughter-in-law, Isabella, she stayed at the Hôtel St-Pol; clad in severe though costly mourning which caused quite a sensation, Valentine, together with Isabella, threw herself at the king's feet in tears and demanded that justice be done. A petition was put before the Council. The circumstances of the assassination, the details of the Duke of Burgundy's crime, the appalling confession, all these were recalled. The petition also gave an account of the recent publication in Flanders of an abusive and infamous document which cast a slur on the honour of the Duke of Orleans.[14] The king raised the weeping Valentine Visconti and her daughter, Isabella, to their feet, consoled them as best he could, and assured them that the petition would receive legal attention.

But in Paris, the masses proved more and more sensitive to Burgundian propaganda. The idea of reform was increasingly linked in their minds with assumption of the power by the duke. Who but he was capable of ruling? Was he not the only remaining statesman of the House of Valois? At the Hôtel St-Pol, the Orleans family lived in terror of what the morrow would bring. It was known that the Duke of Burgundy was mobilizing his forces. Given the confused state of the public mind it was unlikely that he would meet with any opposition. The advisers of the Duchess of Orleans and her children were too weak and irresolute to take any sort of action. John was obviously the strong man of the hour, and this he realized full well. It was not surprising that he was prepared to play a bold game.

From then on the fearless duke voiced his intentions more and more openly. When his uncles advised him not to return to Paris, he ignored their warning. He knew that propaganda had achieved its object of counteracting the emotional appeal of Valentine's grief, as well as the arguments put forward by her lawyer Guillaume Cousinot. The rumour was spread abroad that the duchess, during her stay in the capital, had tried once more to cast a spell over the king. Feeling that she could not count on the king's extremely vague promises, she withdrew to Blois. A gathering of Burgundian men-at-arms was a clear signal that the duke was about to make a show of force. His army assembled at Arras, under the direction of the Marshal of Burgundy, John of Vergy. Isabella, panic-stricken, appealed to the Bretons. But her brother-in-law had every intention of 'gaining the upper hand, if there were any means of doing so'.[15] He pressed on. By the 28th February, he had reached St Denis. Three days later he entered Paris and was cheered by the crowd. He went to the Louvre to join his son-in-law, the Dauphin and his daughter, the Dauphin's wife. He dined at the Hôtel de Nesle, the elegant residence of the Duke of Berry, whose disapproval of his nephew had been short-lived. With perfect composure he took up residence in his own town house, the Hôtel d'Artois. There could be no mistaking the fact—he had, by sheer effrontery, won the first round in the game.

In the game that John the Fearless was playing, the stake was nothing less than the control of France. The fact that the man responsible for the Barbette crime should be acclaimed by the Parisian crowd clearly showed that public opinion was confused and that this was one of those moments in history when human life counts for little, when the dagger and the battle-axe—or it may be the machine-gun—are accepted as the normal means of conducting political controversies, and power goes to the man who is bold enough

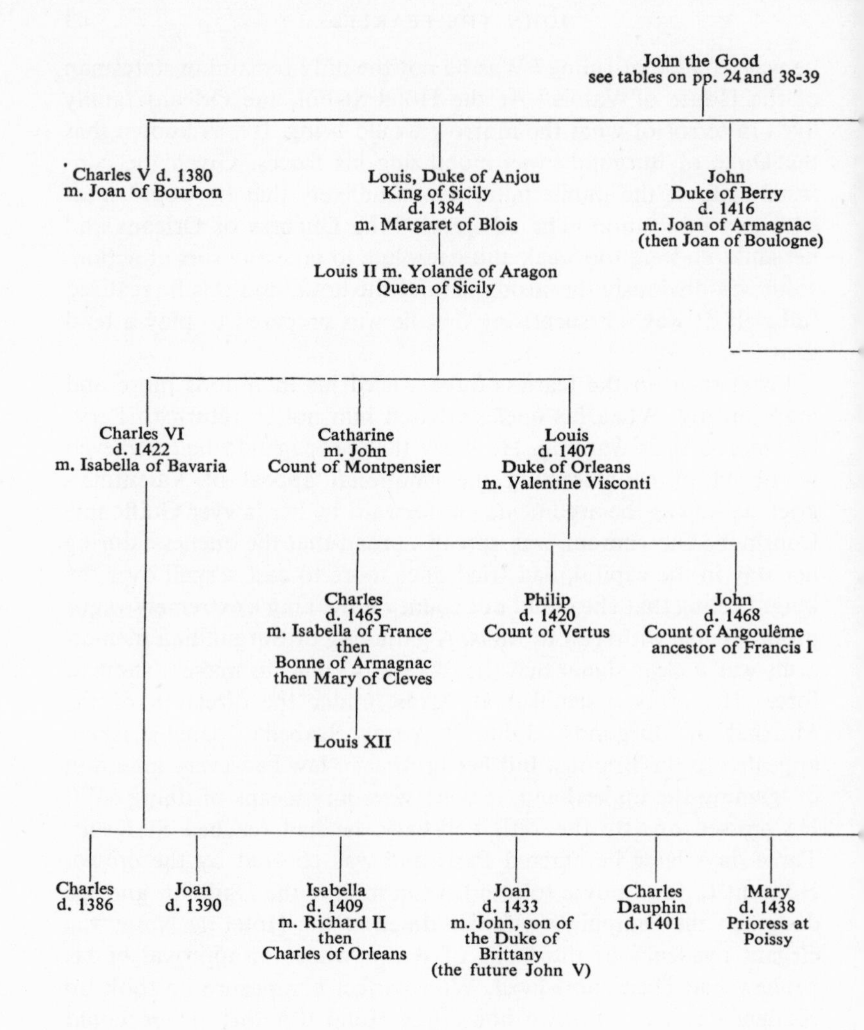

The Valois of France and Burgundy

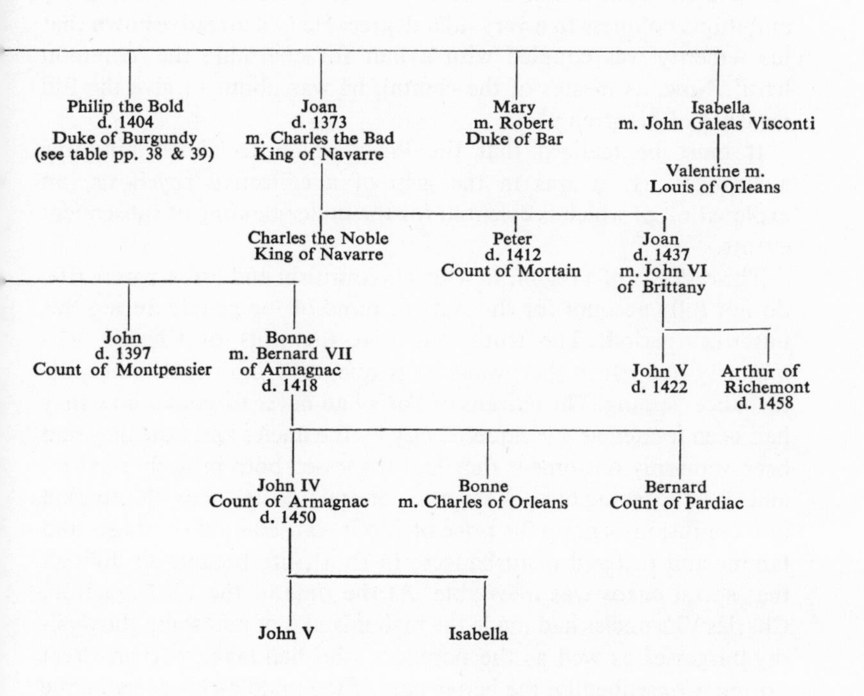
Philip the Bold
d. 1404
Duke of Burgundy
(see table pp. 38 & 39)
Joan
d. 1373
m. Charles the Bad
King of Navarre
Mary
m. Robert
Duke of Bar
Isabella
m. John Galeas Visconti
Valentine m.
Louis of Orleans
Charles the Noble
King of Navarre
Peter
d. 1412
Count of Mortain
Joan
d. 1437
m. John VI
of Brittany
John
d. 1397
Count of Montpensier
Bonne
m. Bernard VII
of Armagnac
d. 1418
John V
d. 1422
Arthur of
Richemont
d. 1458
John IV
Count of Armagnac
d. 1450
Bonne
m. Charles of Orleans
Bernard
Count of Pardiac
John V
Isabella

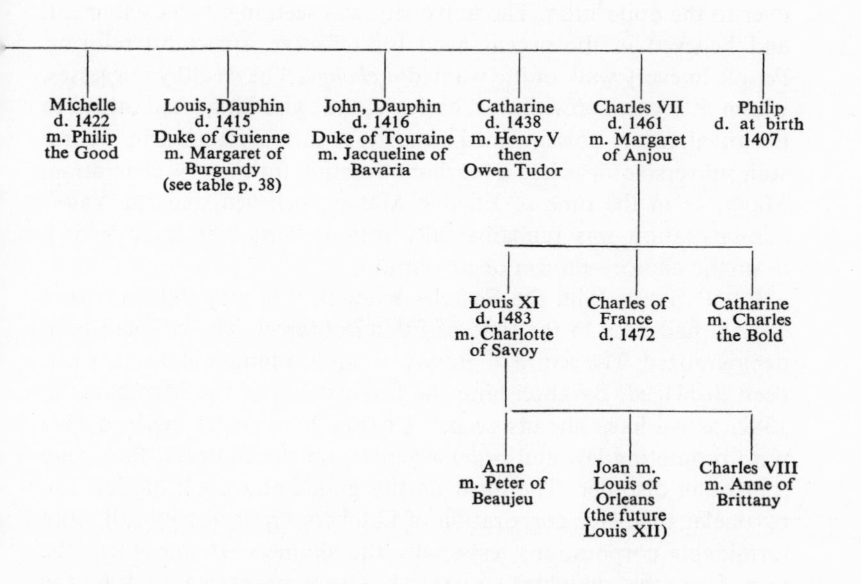
Michelle
d. 1422
m. Philip
the Good
Louis, Dauphin
d. 1415
Duke of Guienne
m. Margaret of
Burgundy
(see table p. 38)
John, Dauphin
d. 1416
Duke of Touraine
m. Jacqueline of
Bavaria
Catharine
d. 1438
m. Henry V
then
Owen Tudor
Charles VII
d. 1461
m. Margaret
of Anjou
Philip
d. at birth
1407
Louis XI
d. 1483
m. Charlotte
of Savoy
Charles of
France
d. 1472
Catharine
m. Charles
the Bold
Anne
m. Peter of
Beaujeu
Joan m.
Louis of
Orleans
(the future
Louis XII)
Charles VIII
m. Anne of
Brittany

to seize it. Duke John, as we have seen, possessed the necessary ambitious boldness to a very high degree. He had already shown that his temerity was coupled with a flair for charming the 'common herd'. Now, as master of the capital, he was about to give the full measure of his strength.

It must be realized that the Paris which acclaimed him was a strange city. It was in the grip of a collective psychosis, an explanation of which is essential for the understanding of subsequent events.

The excesses of a régime in which favouritism and bribery were rife, do not fully account for the state of mind of the people during this unsettled period. The truth was that the riots of Charles VI's minority had left in their wake consequences from which other disturbances sprang. The citizens of Paris had never forgotten how they had been treated as a conquered city by the uncles and how they had been wantonly ransomed; they had witnessed both princely rivalries and court extravagance. A severe economic crisis threw the market into confusion, sent up the price of goods, caused food shortages and famine and fostered disturbances; in short, life became so difficult that social chaos was inevitable. At the time of the 1382 reaction, Charles VI's uncles had made the rash mistake of punishing the wealthy burgesses as well as the populace who had taken part in street rioting. Consequently, the better part of the middle-classes had gone over to the opposition. The university was seething with excitement, and believed in the urgent need for effective, structural reforms. People in every walk of life wanted *a change*. The wealthy burgesses, whom fifty years previously Charles V, the 'wise king', had rallied to the royal cause, now inclined towards a sort of radicalism. Worse still, subversive ideas had a morbid attraction for the new generation. Many, as in the time of Etienne Marcel, believed that the Valois administration was fundamentally rotten. Paris was faced with a dramatic choice—reform or revolution.

But Paris, as John the Fearelss knew it, was very different from what it had been in the time of Etienne Marcel. The city had been democratized. The centre of gravity of public opinion had, as it were, been displaced. By abolishing the Provostship of the Merchants in 1382, as we have already seen,[16] Charles VI's uncles believed they were promoting law and order whereas, on the contrary, they were fomenting disorder. The most unruly guilds now took the lead, in particular the fierce corporation of butchers supported by still more formidable corporations, especially the skinners. It was, then, the men from the slaughter-houses who were preparing to lead the uncertain, restless masses; acts of violence and street battles were not likely to deter men so well-used to wielding the knife, as events were now about to show.

Such was the Paris to which John the Fearless returned. He had re-established the practice of putting up chains at night to block the streets and six hundred chains were forged by Parisian locksmiths. But as the mass of the people were a party to the disturbances, the blocking of the streets was more likely to facilitate attacks than to help in the maintenance of order. The three hundred thousand inhabitants of Paris who were living under considerable strain, with no street lighting and an inadequate police force, were now in a highly dangerous state of ferment.

For the moment, the duke took little heed of the danger. He was more concerned with making the most of his victory. He had achieved his victory by bold action, and he pressed his advantage with similarly bold moves. His desire to be considered as a dispenser of justice spurred him on. He ordered a team of politically-minded members of the university to draw up a written justification of his crime, and his obliging clerks set to work.

The men who had a share in this curious undertaking were Simon de Saulx, abbot of Moutier-St-Jean, André Colin, Nicolas de Savigny, Pierre de Marigny, Guillaume Euvrie, and lastly, Pierre aux Boeufs, who had already been associated with the controversy over the Schism. Another scholar, the author of 'The Lament of Our Lady the Church', had a hand in the affair, and played the part of chief drafter; this was John Petit, the man responsible for the famous *Justification*.

Even as early as the 17th February 1408, an extraordinary proclamation, concocted in the Chancellery of John the Fearless, claimed to prove that only the murder of Louis of Orleans could have saved France.[17] John Petit took up the same theme and developed it in the form of a diatribe in accordance with all the rules of the 'schools'. He built up his factum on a syllogism of the 'Barbara' type[18] complete with introductory statement, major premise, minor premise, and conclusion, the whole disquisition being embellished with examples, corollaries and instances, crammed with quotations, and studded with insults. It was lawful to kill a tyrant. Orleans was a tyrant, and so his death was justified. Reasons of State explained the murder and made it legitimate. Around these forceful arguments the author wove insolent and wordy variations. In the manuscripts of his work, which were widely circulated—and which even existed in de luxe copies—there were miniatures showing, with some slight variations, a wolf attacking the crown with its fangs and claws and being struck at by a lion.

Par force le leu rompt et tire
A ses dents et gris la couronne
Et le lyon, par très grant ire
De sa patte grand coup lui donne

(The wolf breaks and tugs at the crown
With fang and claw
The lion, full of wrath,
Smites him with his paw.)

The whole of the legal argument was contained in this picture-story. John, a loyal patriot, had got rid of his cousin to prevent him laying hands on the throne. '*Leu*' was a play on the name Louis; the lion was the main feature of the coat of arms of the Duke of Burgundy in his capacity as Count of Flanders. In short, tyrannicide was unreservedly commended.

This official eulogy was given an official reading at a meeting held with great formality in the main hall of the Hôtel St-Pol on the 8th March 1408, to which a large, carefully selected audience had been duly summoned. The author held the floor for four whole hours.

The king, only too genuinely incapacitated, was represented by his eldest son, the Dauphin, Louis, Duke of Guienne, in the place of honour. On either side of him sat the King of Sicily, Louis II of Anjou, the Dukes of Berry and Brittany, and the Counts of Alençon and Tancarville. A fine array of lords, dignitaries and magistrates were also present. John the Fearless, who had stage-managed the whole thing, was in his appointed place. The demonstration was meant to compel public opinion, the burgesses and the university to accept the Burgundian interpretation of the facts. Intimidation and threats were to be used to strengthen arguments based on a show of logic. The duke, clad in a wide-sleeved crimson velvet robe, spangled with gold leaves, lined with Siberian squirrel and complete with velvet amice and raised hood, took care to raise his arms and show the 'capelane' or short coat of mail, he had on underneath.

Admittedly, all those present were not taken in by the paradoxical harangue in which the dagger was presented with utter shamelessness, as a normal instrument of policy. The eulogy of the crime only convinced those who already approved of it. But no one dared to protest or even give the slightest hint of disagreement with the proceedings. Jouvenel des Ursins, who was present at the occasion, vouches for this fact: 'there was not one bold enough to raise his voice in disagreement'.

This astounding piece of stage-craft was soon officially ratified. As soon as the king had recovered from his fit, 'royal letters of pardon' were issued. The crime was 'wiped out'. The moving petition of the Orleans family thus ended in the granting of a pardon to the guilty man. Valentine, who had sought refuge in Blois, had leisure to taste to the full the bitterness of a denial of justice, achieved through a combination of effrontery and force.

The over-zealous and over-shrewd Provost, Guillaume de Tignonville, was dismissed from office, under the false pretext that he had infringed the privileges of the university in connection with some arrest or other, and he was replaced by one of John's creatures, Pierre des Essarts. Another well-known Burgundian, Charles de Châtillon, Lord of Dampierre, was given the office of Admiral of France, in place of Cliquet de Bréban, who had been appointed by the Duke of Orleans.

This was how matters stood when the scene suddenly changed, and events took another course. Incidents in the north forced the Duke of Burgundy to leave Paris and rush back to his Flemish estates. Flemish affairs now came to the fore, and it was borne upon Margaret of Flanders's son that he had other duties and tasks besides laying down the law at the Hôtel St-Pol.

Within the Burgundian Low Countries which were already beginning to take shape, the ecclesiastical principality of Liége formed a sort of enclave. An industrial town, comparable both in the trades it practised and its democratic aspirations, with the other Flemish industrial cities, Liége was unique in that it was ruled by a prince-bishop. He was especially powerful because the emperor, his overlord, was losing his power and allowed the vassal virtually complete independence.

It so happened that the craftsmen of the 'commune', inspired by the Ghent rising of 1382–1384, had seized control from the wealthy merchants. The Town Hall, which was called '*la Violette*',[19] had fallen into the hands of the artisans. Here thirty-two crafts were represented by an almost permanent and frequently stormy assembly of two hundred members. The workers of Liége had 'chambers'—or as we would say today, clubs. These were controlled by young people full of revolutionary and subversive ideas, and the most important offices were often held by men of humble social origin.

In 1407 a street-paver, Jacquemin Badut, was sent as ambassador to the pope at Avignon, Benedict XIII.

The rising fervour of the mob was bound to cause a clash with the prince-bishop. The prince, who had been ruling since 1390, was none other than John of Bavaria, the brother of Margaret, Duchess of Burgundy, the wife of John the Fearless. The chronicler, Jacques de Hemricourt, who was steeped in conservative ideas, maintained that 'a university cannot commit greater folly than to be unfaithful to and supplant its natural lord'. By 'university' he meant the whole community of Liége which was undoubtedly attempting to oust the not very devout prelate from his seignieury. John of Bavaria tried to retaliate. The conflict, which had broken out in 1394 and continued ever since, became increasingly violent after 1406. On the 26th September, the people of Liége declared that John had forfeited his rights, and demanded the appointment of a new bishop, Thierry de Perwez, whose election was engineered with complete contempt for canon law. Only two canons of St Lambert voted for Perwez. This was of scant importance, however, for in such matters, the Schism made the wildest deviations possible. John of Bavaria had sworn obedience to the Pope in Rome. In order to replace the Urbanist by a rival who had all the appearances of legitimacy, it was only necessary to make an appeal to the Pope at Avignon. Benedict XIII, delighted at this unexpected support, gave ecclesiastical sanction to the purely political move of the Liége community, and at this point the struggle reached its peak.

The Liége affair was in reality a trial of strength. The clerks, completely intimidated, took no further action. Several canons of St Lambert, who had expressed disapproval, were executed. The local knights were ineffectual and stood aside from a conflict with which they did not feel concerned. The rural population had no reason to interfere in the matter. The bishop had nobody to support him. Shut up in Maëstricht where he had taken refuge, he realized that he could at any moment fall into the hands of his enemies. It was at this juncture that he made a desperate appeal to his brother-in-law, John the Fearless. The family alliance between the Wittelsbachs and the Valois of Burgundy, arranged by Philip the Bold, was now to be put to unexpected use, in Liége.

Although he had been very keen to win the support of the common people in Paris, the duke had no intention of allowing the common people of Liége to dethrone their bishop. He realized, furthermore, that the restoration of the principality to John of Bavaria would represent an important step forward for the growing Burgundian state. And so the danger threatening the prelate forced the duke to leave Paris, notwithstanding the serious consequences which his departure might entail, and in September 1408 he headed straight for Maëstricht with his army, entering the principality by way of Hesbaye. William of Bavaria, the bishop's brother, made his entry into the principality at exactly the same moment by way of Condroz, absorbing as he went all the available troops of William, Count of Namur. These various armies met at Montenaeken. Thus reinforced, the duke joined battle with the Liége militia troops on the 23rd September 1408, on the plain of Russon, near Othée, not far from Tongres.

It was Roosebeke all over again. Repeating Artevelde's mistake, and disregarding the advice of the father of their so-called bishop, the people of Liége were rash enough to give battle. Confident in their numerical superiority they charged forward, but were caught and surrounded by a turning movement. Trapped in the same way as the people of Ghent had been trapped, they imagined that they had won the day because the enemy's centre had fallen back, and they allowed the enemy's flanks to fall on them from either side. The resistance at Othée was more heroic and the slaughter consequently greater. It was said that eight hundred militia troops remained on the field, including the new bishop and his father.

Like the people of Ghent after Roosebeke in the time of Philip the Bold, the inhabitants of Liége, incapable of further resistance, had to accept defeat and unconditional surrender.

The duke showed no pity. Two days after the military disaster, the burgesses, two by two, with bare feet and torch in hand, came and knelt before the three brothers-in-law, William and the two Johns, and begged for mercy.

John of Bavaria, a far from lenient bishop, followed only the dictates of vengeance. He had the canons and priests appointed by Perwez—and even women too—thrown into the Meuse. The municipal banners were burnt, the charters confiscated, the craftsmen's organizations disbanded, and all elective offices abolished. By sentence passed on the 24th October the town was deprived of its independence. A reign of unbridled and uncontrolled episcopal tyranny was set up throughout the principality.

Naturally, those who had made it possible for the bishop to take his revenge, saw that they were rewarded for their pains. Henceforth, John the Fearless and William of Bavaria were to have a right of way through Liége territory; their currencies were to be accepted as legal tender; the walls of Thuin, Forse, Couvin and Dinant were to be knocked down; two hundred and twenty thousand crowns, raised in the form of a tax, were to cover the cost of the successful intervention.

However, Valentine Visconti and her friends had considered the campaign, forced on the Duke by the Liége uprising, as a heaven-sent opportunity for them to emerge from their retirement. An Orleanist group was formed, and boded no good for the future. The widow recovered the initiative. Charles VI annulled the letters condoning John's crime; the queen and the Dauphin took charge under the protection of Breton soldiers sent by Duke John V, and Valentine, who had returned to the capital, renewed her plea for justice. She was supported in her cause, not only by her lawyer, Guillaume Cousinot and her chancellor, Pierre l'Orfèvre, but also by the Abbé of Cérizy, the Benedictine Thomas du Bourg. To him she entrusted the task of publicly refuting John Petit's paradoxical assertions.

The Abbé of Cérizy gave his reply on the 11th September 1408. It was read with the same solemnity as had marked the previous ceremony. Moreover, John Petit, in an attempt to out-do the Abbé, retorted with more pamphlets, the vulgar exuberance of which delighted all lovers of scandal.

At that moment, the court was all in favour of the widow. The two sisters-in-law, Isabella and Valentine, became firm allies, and the princes were in sympathy with them. There was some talk of an expedition against the Duke of Burgundy. He was known to have his hands full and people were wondering what would be the outcome of the Liége affair.

The new trend, however, ran counter to public opinion in Paris. Strangely enough, the affection which the mass of the people felt for John the Fearless, had not been in any way diminished by the Duke's hostile attitude to the Liége democrats. For Parisians, the man whose symbol was the 'levelling plane', would always be a liberal and a reformer. The average Parisian was delighted at the news of the Othée victory. It had the great advantage of saving the situation at Court, which for a time, had been highly critical.

While the widow Valentine dragged herself pathetically off to Blois, where she died of a broken heart on the 4th December 1408, Isabella and the princes deemed it prudent to retire to Tours on the 10th November, taking the king with them and leaving Paris to the Duke of Burgundy. He returned to the capital on the 28th of the same month to find his popularity unimpaired.[20]

For a time, the Orleanist faction had represented a real threat. On Valentine's death the direction of affairs passed into the hands of her eldest son, Charles, who was only fifteen and not cut out to be a man of action. All danger from that quarter now seemed to be ruled out. John the Fearless, who was not at all keen on openly assuming responsibility for starting a civil war, and could only benefit from a reputation as a peace-lover, announced that he was ready to come to terms, although he had no intention of giving way on important issues. During the negotiations, the letters of annulment were declared valid again, and the terms of the compromise agreement drawn up. It was known as the Peace of Chartres.

The cathedral setting in which the meeting and reconciliation took place, on the 9th March 1409, at Chartres, merely served to conceal the lack of sincerity on both sides under a lavish and theatrical display. The church was guarded by a contingent of soldiers from Hainault, armed to the teeth. William of Bavaria, Count of Hainault, the Duke of Burgundy's brother-in-law, had acted as intermediary and was now master of ceremonies. In the nave 'well and truly railed off', Charles VI and Isabella had taken their places, and were 'seated as if on the throne'; behind them stood the Dauphin, Louis, Duke of Guienne, the Kings of Navarre and Sicily, the Dukes of Berry and Bourbon, the Counts of Alençon, la Marche, Eu, and Vendôme, also the Constable, Charles d'Albret, and members of the *Parlement*, the *Chambre des Comptes* and the *Grand Conseil*, who had turned out in force. Two chapels in the aisles, one on the right side, the other on the left, and both enclosed by tapestry curtains—had been assigned, one to the Orleans children, the other to John the Fearless. Each party had its escort in the offing; six hundred men including a hundred gentlemen-at-arms. The ceremony was a brief one, lasting barely an hour.

Through his spokesman, John of Nielles, Governor of Arras, John the Fearless called upon the king to rid his heart of the 'grief' he felt at his brother's death, a death now 'deeply and bitterly regretted' by its instigator. The duke briefly confirmed the statement; this was, it must be admitted, a very slight concession, but his opponents made do with it. The Orleans children, somewhat ungraciously, forgave the murderer 'all the ill-will' they bore him. The Count of Vertus, the victim's youngest son, was to marry one of Burgundy's daughters. The ceremony ended with an oath of reconciliation.

Two days later, in the detailed account of the session he sent off to the Governor of Lille, John expressed himself as being particularly delighted with Charles VI's attitude:

Thanks be to God, the whole thing was done with noble ceremony and greatly to our honour and done so successfully that all parties were very satisfied and my afore-mentioned lord and his lady and other noble lords gave us a warm welcome, in particular, our son the Duke of Guienne, who most generously and without a trace of rancour, embraced and kissed us before the entire company.

In actual fact, on both sides, the pledges were false and artificial. Nicolas de Baye wrote in his *Journal* that it was a peace which was not a peace. It was called '*une paix fourrée*' (a sham peace) by the Duke of Burgundy's fool, who was in fact no fool, and whose remark has gone down in history.[21]

From the 11th March 1409, until the end of the year, except for a journey to Burgundy which lasted from the 20th April to the 13th May, and for a visit to his possessions in the North lasting from the 11th July to the 20th August, John of Burgundy remained in Paris where, under pretext of looking after the interests of the king and the dauphin, whom he overwhelmed with his protection, he reigned with undisputed authority.

As he unfalteringly pursued the plan on which he was resolved, John the Fearless showed himself to be more powerful than his father had been . . . He held court at the Hótel d'Artois, where the state in which he lived left no doubt about the extent of his authority. He showed especial kindness towards his faithful supporters among the burgesses and magistracy of Paris, whose services he recognized and whose enthusiasm he encouraged by constant demonstrations of liberality. He sent generous gifts of silver plate and casks of wine to win the allegiance of people who might be useful to him. (*In short*) he distributed gifts widely, in order to win for himself a wide circle of friends.[22]

'You can rest assured,' a merchant wrote to the Podestà of Lucca, 'that the Duke of Burgundy will remain the greatest and most powerful lord of this realm. His power rests on the armies he can draw from his estates. He can assemble so many troops that he need fear no man.'[23]

Such was, indeed, the firm belief of the duke himself. Pitiless as well as fearless, he thought he could safely satisfy his thirst for vengeance. Jean de Montagu, a financier who was loathed by the people, had been chief adviser to the princes of Orleans during the negotiation of the Peace of Chartres. John, as master of Paris, found an excuse to strike. Montagu was arrested, tortured, condemned to death and executed. He was the first victim of the terrible quarrel after Louis of Orleans.

The duke very nearly caused a reaction in Paris by this piece of cruelty. He tried to offset the brutality of his act of vengeance by making up to Isabella. Admittedly the queen did not like the duke, but she was impressed by him and confused by the force of his personality and his hypnotic gaze. Having fallen under John's spell, she placed herself, along with the Dauphin, under his protection, in accordance with the terms of the Pact of Melun, of the 11th November 1409. The authority with which the king had lately invested the queen now passed into the hands of the Duke of Burgundy.

The Dukes of Berry and Bourbon, ousted by this move, now began to lean towards the Orleans party.

It so happened that a marriage alliance had just provided the Orleanist party with the leader they needed. Charles of Orleans, formerly the husband of Isabella, daughter of Charles VI, but now a widower, took as his second wife Bonne of Armagnac. His new father-in-law, Bernard VII, Count of Armagnac, had only to raise his little finger to turn the Orleanist party into an Armagnac party. This he did not fail to do. Strongly established in southern France, the House of Armagnac was to bring the Orleanist clan the numerical support and military strength which it lacked. Berry and Bourbon added the considerable lustre of their names. Berry was, moreover, the grandfather of the new Duchess of Orleans.[24]

And so a black cloud appeared in the sky just when Duke John thought that all was at last serene. By a treaty, concluded at Gien, on the 15th April 1410, his opponents declared their unanimity of purpose. Orleans, Armagnac, Berry, Clermont, and Alençon all formally joined forces. As feudal lords, well aware of the importance of military strength, they decided to raise a common army, so that Burgundy would not be the only one able to call upon men-at-arms to support his claims. This was the first military venture on the part of the Armagnac faction, and they justified it on the grounds that it was 'for the good, the honour and the advancement of the king, the kingdom and the public weal'. Another treaty, concluded at Poitiers, strengthened the bond. The soldiers took the field, that is they set about pillaging the countryside, and civil war became imminent.

Charles VI and Isabella took fright. Their vacillating tactics had aimed at keeping the peace. The king, temporarily restored to sanity, issued an order forbidding the massing of men-at-arms. This was not so much a tranquillizing move as a counter-stroke from John, since all official power was in his hands. However, the order had no effect; the Armagnacs were already marching on Paris. But the approach of winter—hardly favourable to military operations—and the intervention of the university, led to a compromise and to yet another 'sham peace', the Peace of Bicêtre, which was drawn up on the 2nd November 1410.

This stipulated that the princes would withdraw to their estates, leaving the conduct of affairs to the Council, whose members were to be chosen by the king outside either party. In an attempt to make a fresh start, the provost of Paris was dismissed. The university was anxious for a policy of neutrality to be adopted, and as both sides wanted to placate the university, the system was given a trial. The new provost, Bruneau de Saint-Clair, was well received by the people of Paris, and it seemed that this might be the first step towards pacification.

Just at that point Charles VI had a relapse and the quarrels broke out afresh. John the Fearless realized that his rivals were becoming more and more closely united, and he complained that they were massing troops. In vain the Council repeated its prohibitions. The king, as soon as he regained his sanity, had to face bitter complaints from both sides. Each accused the other of having 'infringed the statutes'. Each declared that it was forced into action by the threatening attitude of the other.

And so the policy of neutrality, being purely theoretical, only served to bring the approaching civil war to a head. Constant pressure was brought to bear on the Council members. On the whole they favoured Burgundy. Nevertheless, they were eager to protect Paris from armed attack from all quarters. For the time being, the Armagnac faction appeared the most likely source of danger. John made the clever move of disbanding his men, and pretended to comply with the statutes whereas his opponents, unscrupulously breaking the peace, once more took the field, pillaging shamelessly as they went.

The idea that there could be no strong rule and no security except under the leadership of the Duke of Burgundy was steadily gaining ground. A well-organized propaganda campaign completed the process. Using the acts of pillage committed by the Armagnacs as an excuse, John was now ready to pit captain against captain, sword against sword.

At bottom, both sides were determined to fight. The final gesture came from the young Duke of Orleans. On the 11th July 1411, he issued, from Jargeau, letters patent, in which he sought redress for the murder of his father. He appealed to the king, the university and the Parisian *bourgeoisie*. Without waiting to see what result his petition could have, he sent off an insolent challenge to John the Fearless on the 18th July.

The gauntlet had been thrown down. John was at Douai when he received the offensive message on the 10th August. Replying as early as the 14th to his victim's heir, in such a way as to make a break inevitable, he hurled violent abuse at the duke and his two brothers. He admitted that he felt 'great joy in his heart at their challenge'.

And to Charles he added 'you and your brothers have lied, and are falsely lying now, like the traitors you are'.

The civil war had begun.

It would be useless to quibble over details; although by clever manœuvring he had succeeded in shifting the onus of responsibility on to the other side, John nevertheless considered war to be inevitable; he had prepared for it; he had provoked the outbreak, and he intended to reap all the accruing benefits. As a matter of fact, his aim was now nothing less than complete control of power in the Kingdom of France.

Anxious at the same time to keep up, for as long as possible, a pretence of wanting peace and of complying with the royal decrees, he let the Council struggle ineffectually on and waited until it implored his assistance. Finally, the inhabitants of Paris, panic-stricken at the sight of the Armagnacs plundering the Ile de France, and realizing that the queen who had fled to Melun was in sympathy with the Duke of Berry, a member of the Orleanist party, destroyed the bridges from Charenton to Melun, while inside the town pillaging and plundering were rife. On the 28th October the duke, at the express wish of the Parisian people, re-entered the city with an armed force. On the 2nd November the king, by letters patent, commissioned him to drive the enemy from the kingdom, in other words, to fight against the Armagnacs. John the Fearless managed things very well. He was now in virtual control of Paris and of the administration of the kingdom.

The victorious party was able to reorganize the distribution of power in the capital. The important posts went to faithful supporters. The Count of St Pol replaced Charles of Albret as constable; the Chevalier de Chambures replaced John of Hangest as master of the cross-bowmen. The Burgundian badge, the cross of St Andrew, was displayed everywhere. People wore it across their chests as part of their attire. It was even used to adorn the statues of the saints in the churches. The green hood with the party colours was also popular.

Since it was the king's wish that the Armagnacs should be driven out, it was right that all forms of coercion should be used against them. Why not bring spiritual pressure to bear? In the past Urban V had excommunicated the '*Grandes Compagnies*'[25] who used to lay waste the country. What were the Armagnacs but leaders of a band of outlaws? Urban V's sentence was applied to them. Priests read out a French translation of the papal bulls from the pulpit.

Operations now began. The Armagnacs ravaged and plundered.

They captured St Cloud and St Denis, but this was the limit of their success. They had, however, great ambitions. It was said that while they were ransacking the Abbey of St Denis, Bernard VII had gone so far as to place the crown on his son-in-law's head, with the promise that he would have him anointed king at Rheims. These were rash words, if he really did utter them. The opposing camp, very cleverly, made the most of them.

The Duke of Burgundy recaptured St Cloud, stormed Etampes, and routed the Armagnacs. At this juncture the approach of winter, coupled with the set-backs they had suffered, made Charles of Orleans and Bernard VII decide to postpone any further exploits until the spring.

This marked the end of the first campaign of the civil war; Burgundy had, on the whole, come off best.[26]

While the campaign was following its uneven course, the composition of the opposing parties became finally clear.

The Duke of Burgundy was supported in the first place by members of his family, his son Philip, Count of Charolais, his brothers, Anthony, Duke of Brabant, and Philip, Count of Nevers; his brothers-in-law, John of Bavaria, Prince-Bishop of Liége, William, Count of Hainault and Amadeus, Count of Savoy. Other supporters were Charles the Noble, King of Navarre, Charles, Duke of Lorraine, the Counts of Namur, La Marche, Mortain, Vaudémont, St Pol, the Prince of Orange, Marshal Boucicaut, Jean de Chalon, Lord of Arlay; John V of Brittany, an unstable and untrustworthy ally, was not to be counted on. Louis of Bavaria, the brother of Queen Isabella, was equally unreliable. Isabella herself was uncertain and fickle. The king and the dauphin were mere puppets manipulated in turn by the chief figures on either side.

The three Princes of Orleans, Duke Charles and his two brothers, Philip, Count of Vertus, and John, Count of Angoulême, had on their side Bernard VII of Armagnac, father of Duchess Bonne, John of Berry, his grandfather, Louis II of Bourbon, who had just succeeded his father, the Duke of Bar, the Counts of Eu, Alençon and Harcourt, the Lord of Albret, and also Charles de la Rivière, Count of Dammartin, the son of Charles V's minister. All these lords wore a white sash, the emblem of the faction with which they had thrown in their lot.

The nobles divided their allegiance between the two clans, the feudal lords moving from one camp to the other. Sometimes the same family supplied recruits to both sides: in the Saveuse family, two sons were 'Burgundians' and a third an 'Armagnac'; in the

Hangest family, Jean was an 'Armagnac' and Ferry a 'Burgundian'. Marshal Boucicaut followed Burgundy, but his brother supported Orleans. Any number of such instances could be quoted.

But the nobility formed only one section of the community; there were also the burgesses, the people, and the university. In order to achieve final victory, all the pieces of the intricate political chess-board had to be taken into consideration.

John the Fearless was a great schemer. What would his plan of action be? During a surprise attack carried out by the Armagnacs, the Count of La Marche, who was fighting on the Burgundian side, had been surrounded along with four hundred men and taken off to Orleans as a prisoner. One of the dead men happened to be a son of the Legoix family, who were important people in the meat trade. The duke made a special journey to Paris to attend the young man's funeral—a typical piece of flattery on his part. Moreover, he was frequently to be seen in the area of Les Halles, which was near his town house, the Hôtel d'Artois. Nobleman though he was, he was quite ready to shake hands with the working-class leaders. He cultivated the friendship of butchers, tripe-men, skinners, indeed of the whole band of 'mechanicals'—and, one might even say, of manual labourers. He distributed to the most humble the same presents which he lavished on his supporters among the nobility and the burgesses. Everywhere he was greeted with cheers; everyone had faith in him. Here, people thought, was a true liberal; he played the democrat; he even played the demagogue.

At the same time, intellectual circles had put their faith in him. The members of the university believed in the effectiveness of reform. The duke fostered this illusion. He encouraged them in the conviction that they were the enlightened leaders of the State. He strengthened them in their belief that he was the man best suited to carry their political theories into effect. All sections of the community were subjected to an intensified propaganda campaign.

Upheld by the 'mechanicals' on the one hand, and the intellectuals on the other, the duke expected to retain the support of both the burgesses and the people, and to unite all that was most vital and vigorous in the French nation. Such a combination, backed by military strength, would surely allow the prince, who by sheer audacity could work so many intricate strands into a closely-woven whole, to realize his ambition of becoming undisputed master of France.

This then was the plan, which no one had ever put into operation before. No prince of the blood had ever made such a deliberate and vigorous appeal to the emotions of the common people. John the Fearless was devoid of both prejudices and scruples. Whether he achieved his ends by fair means or foul mattered little to the clear-sighted, strong-willed statesman, who invented new political methods and put them unhesitatingly into operation, being as ready to carry out his ideas to the full as he had been to commit a crime to satisfy his hatred.

For John, as indeed for the leaders of the opposing faction, national feeling tended to be lost in the heat and ferocity of the struggle. The clear-cut patriotism of the days of Charles V and Duguesclin had by now become blurred. The son of Philip the Bold took the initiative of appealing to a foreign country for help, and what was worse, to the English. He formed an alliance with Henry IV of Lancaster; twelve hundred English, brought into Paris in spite of the butchers, who in this instance were better Frenchmen than their idol, took part in the attack on St Cloud. The Armagnacs were to turn the same poisoned weapon against Burgundy in 1412, when the Duke of Clarence swept down from Normandy to the Loire.

If one wanted to justify these appeals to France's traditional enemy, one could argue that feudal quarrels, which were in fact vendettas between families, were unrelated to patriotic sentiment, and that this sentiment, being unknown to the feudal magnates of the time, was no obstacle to intervention on the part of foreign lords, who were moreover closely linked by ties of kinship with the people they were helping, and consequently had every right to interfere in their disputes. The excuse is, however, too facile. The truth is that in the fifteenth century there were two conflicting currents: on the one hand, the international tradition of feudal loyalties, and on the other local patriotism brought about by a sudden heightening of national selfconsciousness. National awareness was sufficiently strong by now for the appeal to France's enemies who had so often attacked the kingdom, to be considered as a culpable act, which no one had any right to commit, and which brought in its train embarrassment and self-reproach. After Duguesclin's exploits, and now that Joan of Arc had been born, it was a heinous thing to form an alliance with the English and to invite them to set foot on French soil. The deed was done, nevertheless, through partisan feeling, an overpowering desire for revenge, or a thirst for power. But no valid excuse was to be found for it, as can be clearly seen in the case of John the Fearless himself.[27]

Meanwhile, John the Fearless carried out in rapid succession the various phases of his policy. On the 26th January 1412 Charles VI, at the instigation, of course, of the Duke of Burgundy, restored to the people of Paris the remaining pre-1382 franchises they had not yet recovered. The provostship of the merchants became once more an elective office; municipal magistrates were restored to their positions as assistants of the provost: the burgesses' council, in charge of municipal jurisdiction, resumed its sessions. The burgesses were triumphant, while the duke, redoubling his efforts to win the friendship of the traders, was more firmly established than ever as the idol of Les Halles.

The provostship of Paris, equivalent to the post of chief of police, was handed back to the Burgundian, Pierre des Essarts, who was at the same time a sort of minister for propaganda. To rekindle the zeal of Burgundian supporters, and to win over the waverers, he distributed vast sums both in Paris and the provinces. Intimidation was used where generosity failed. Colinet de Puisieux who had surrendered the bridge of St Cloud to the Armagnacs was hanged at Montfaucon, along with a knight from Picardy, Mansart du Bois, who was accused of treachery. Suspects were systematically rounded up, and the common people lent a helping hand to the police by attacking members of the opposing faction and half-hearted supporters, and damaging their property. In Paris, parents who did not openly support the Burgundian cause could no longer have their children baptized. No one dared bury the bodies of dead Armagnac supporters. A group of frenzied agitators, led by Legoix, ransacked the Duke of Berry's castle at Bicêtre, and destroyed works of art there. At Caen, houses inhabited by the rival party were set on fire. Needless to say, not a single Armagnac was left in Dijon. Rural areas, overrun by motley gangs of various nationalities, suffered the most appalling atrocities.

The panic created by the devastation and the fear of a close alliance between the Armagnacs and Lancaster, coupled with the fact that the Duke of Berry had put out feelers for the raising of the siege of Bourges, where he was hemmed in by John's soldiers, made the Duke of Burgundy decide to accept the mediation of the Count of Savoy.[28] On the 15th July 1412, at the Congress of Auxerre, an agreement was concluded, restoring the situation to what it had been at the time of the Peace of Chartres.

It was the deplorable state of the kingdom which had more or less forced the two parties to call off hostilities. In Paris, the king, the queen, the dauphin, the Duke of Burgundy and the Count of Vertus were cheered by the crowds. Meanwhile the Duke of Clarence and his English army went back home, the Orleanist party having had some difficulty in bringing to an end the English intervention they had so rashly solicited.

It was during the temporary lull which ensued that the memorable Estates-General of 1413 were held.

They opened at the Hôtel St-Pol on the 30th January 1413. Very few deputies came from the provinces. The Armagnac princes sent representatives but did not attend in person. The assembly consisted in fact almost entirely of Parisians and Burgundians.

Reforms in the state machinery were one of the subjects to be debated. John the Fearless had always pronounced himself in favour of such reforms. Both the town and the university gave them a prominent place in their political programmes. First, Jean de Nesle, the Dauphin's chancellor, delivered a speech, in which he asked for assistance, financial assistance, of course. This was followed by a long and involved discourse by a St Denis monk, the theologian Benoit Gentien, an empty piece of pomposity the sole purpose of which, so it seemed, was to avoid the issue. A second session was called for, and it started off with a vigorous speech from Eustache de Pavilly, a Carmelite friar and a professor at the University. Then, on the rector's instructions, a master of arts read out the 'remonstrances' of the university and the town of Paris, which lasted a whole hour and a half and were written out on a roll of parchment 'as thick as a man's arm'.[29]

It was clear that the university and the town had put their heads together; intellectuals had co-operated with merchants; brains had combined with business. The document was an indictment followed by a bill and went as far as to propose a thorough re-organization of the monarchy. Contemporary shortcomings were exposed with a ferocity which echoed and confirmed that of the *Songe Véritable*.

Dissension among the princes, failures of justice, wasteful expenditure and embezzlement, unjustified increases in the number of officials and corrupt methods of recruiting them, faulty organization of the main public bodies and public services; such were the ills plaguing France and they were violently attacked.

Public property was hopelessly mismanaged. 'Very little, or nothing at all' was devoted to public charity. The expenditure of the King, the Queen and the Dauphin had risen from 94,000 francs to 350,000. The Queen's household, which in the past had cost 36,000 francs, now cost 154,000. Where was all the money going? A good deal of it had found its way into officials' pockets. Hemonet Raguier, the

Queen's treasurer, had made such a fortune that he was able to spend 30,000 francs on his castles. Charlot Poupart, master of the mint, and Guillaume Budé, master of the garrisons, had both acquired enormous incomes, although they were known to have spent 'outrageous' sums. In fact, officials had been 'eating up' the national income for the past twenty-six years, 'without a thought for the welfare of the king or the realm, being only concerned with feathering their nests'. There was no longer any saving of money, as there had been during the previous reign. The deficit was allowed to pile up year after year and everything was 'going to rack and ruin'.

Appointments and transfers of officials were entirely haphazard. There were too many 'changes' requested by 'some people who have a say in the running of the kingdom, and God knows why they are so keen to be appointed, unless it be for the sake of the land, goods and pickings which can be obtained through the afore-mentioned appointments'. André Giffart, one of the excessive number of treasurers, was mentioned as having obtained his post through being related to the wife of the provost of Paris, and having 'stuffed his pockets' so greedily 'that he is loaded up with rubies and diamonds, not to mention silver plate'. Many posts were unnecessary. The tax officers were even worse than the treasurers and practised forgery. The savings bank was in a sorry plight: Antoine des Essarts had shared out every penny. Marise de Ruilly was supposed to hand the King six crowns a day to be spent on His Majesty's pleasures, but he squandered vast sums on his own pleasures. Yet another corrupt practice was the plurality of offices, the provost of Paris himself setting the example in this respect. Some people held four posts at one and the same time. The people of France were dismayed to see the national income 'falling into a slit purse'.

The Grand Council should consist of competent and conscientious members capable of managing the affairs of the country with speed and efficiency. But many matters dragged on indefinitely, involving negligent practices referred to as '*coulpe*'. Similarly the *Parlement* was not what it used to be. It now included young men, illiterate and unworthy members, all of them bound by family ties. The situation was still worse in the *Chambre des Comptes* where documents relating to unsettled questions were piled high, and were as good as 'buried'. There, too, it was the same story of too many officials, too well paid.

The chancellery was in no better shape, By adding various allowances to his salary the chancellor was able to increase it threefold or even fourfold. The coinage was debased and devalued.

How could this situation be remedied? By catching the tax-collectors 'red-handed' and forcing them to make restitution, by cancelling all exceptional allocations of funds, reorganizing the finances, reducing the number of agents and officials, weeding out the staff of the various public services and restoring the old rate of wages. A commission should see that these measures were carried out and make sure that all offices were elective.

In addition, all the nobles should be made to swear they would abide by the peace; in other words national unity should be established, and all parties accept a genuine truce.

The men who had drawn up the 'remonstrances' concluded their statement with an expression of confidence in the Duke of Burgundy. He had been the first to undertake the worthy task and he had promised to carry it through to its ultimate conclusion. It was only right that they should put their confidence in him.

Such a violent indictment of the abuses of the time was bound to lead to punitive measures. A commission of inquiry was set up. Officials singled out for punishment were suspended. A new provost of Paris, a Burgundian called Robert de La Heuse, known as 'one-eyed Robert', was installed in office. The drafting of an order proposing the overhaul of the State machinery was begun.

The question now was whether John the Fearless, while ostensibly supporting the reforms which he had advocated, but in actual fact using them merely as a means to power, would succeed in eliminating his rivals once and for all, in ruling in the name of Charles VI, in retaining the allegiance of his son-in-law, the Dauphin Louis, Duke of Guienne, once his apt pupil but now again breaking away and flirting with the opposite camp.

Paris then was at this parting of the ways, when the storm of the 'Cabochian revolution' suddenly burst upon the city. The butchers and their henchmen were tired of waiting for the reforms promised by the wealthy burgesses and the clerics. The Dauphin was unpopular. His equivocal relationship with the Armagnacs exasperated those who advocated immediate action. He had been rash enough to recall Pierre des Essarts, the former provost whose machinations had been exposed. At this the mob, already uneasy, could contain itself no longer and the first riots broke out. A list of traitors was drawn up and the people demanded that they be handed over. The Hôtel de Guienne was stormed. As a result the Dauphin was irresistibly driven into the Orleanist camp, while complete control of the streets passed into the hands of the butchers.

This, then, was the 'Cabochian Revolution'. It is known by the name of the most famous and fanatical of its leaders, Simon le Coutelier, known as Caboche, a skinner and the son of a tripe-dealer in the square in front of Notre Dame. He rushed forward, brandishing a standard, and thirty or forty companions followed in his wake. Gerson's house was ransacked: the famous doctor just had time to escape to the shelter of Notre Dame. Pierre des Essarts was seized and imprisoned. Fierce rioting persisted throughout the whole of the month of May. The revolutionaries did exactly as they pleased, since the police officers fraternized with the rioters. The latter had adopted as their badge the *chaperon blanc*, a reminder which could reasonably have offended a son of Philip the Bold, but by which he appeared totally unmoved. The traditional green of Burgundy was no longer enough for the more fanatical. On the 9th May, violent scenes took place in front of the Hôtel St-Pol. On the 10th, officials of the royal household, suspected of Orleanist sympathies, were arrested. The Dauphin was forced to accept the appointment of Denis de Chaumont as captain of Paris, and of Caboche himself as keeper of the bridge at Charenton. Every day brought fresh alarms.

John the Fearless had obviously lost control of the situation. He had not realized that the heterogeneous elements on whose combined support he had relied, were already at variance with each other. Both the burgesses and university authorities were alarmed at the excesses committed by the rabble. It was impossible to ensure collaboration between scholars and skinners when the latter turned even the street into a slaughter-house; on one side were wealthy, property-owning burgesses and on the other a rabble whose one ambition was to ransack what were assumed to be well-stocked mansions; on the one side, the upholders of law and order and on the other, fishers in troubled waters.

The duke had believed that he could make use of both sides, taking advantage of the prestige and commonsense of the one and the arrogant self-confidence of the other. He imagined that the 'mechanicals' would help him to gain power, and that, having won their confidence, he could at any moment halt the drive he himself had launched. This was where he miscalculated. He did not realize that he could not both foment an insurrection and check it at will; unleash chaos to serve his ends and then keep it under control.

And when the famous ordinance nicknamed by historians the *ordonnance cabochienne* was first issued during the *Parlement* session of the 25th–26th May, it was repudiated by the men who had got used to taking the law into their own hands and who had no intention of allowing themselves, at a sign from the duke, to become the willing tools of officialdom.

The scope of this famous writ must not be overestimated; it was primarily a Burgundian ordinance. The text was merely a revised version of the old *ordonnances* issued by Charles V and his ministers, the *marmousets*, with certain concessions to contemporary feeling. In drawing it up, John the Fearless's advisers had used the old edicts and the 'remonstrances' as a basis. Caboche had no hand at all in it. How could he, when the demands formulated were less extreme than Etienne Marcel's had been? The 1413 ordinance made no attempt to change the monarchical régime. It sought only to reorganize the administrative services of the country. The boldest items were those stipulating that all offices and posts were to be elective. They created a sort of trade-unionism among officials, and substituted co-option for the corrupt methods of recruitment which had been only too prevalent.

In actual fact, the ordinance was merely an attempt on the part of the Burgundians to check the Cabochian revolution, by suggesting that, since administrative reforms had been carried out, street-rioting could serve no further purpose. Such tactics were both pointless and unavailing. What did the recruitment of officials matter to slaughter-house workers? The butchers were neither concerned nor interested in the promulgation of laws. What they were after was the overthrow of existing society and the chance to use their knives. Crimes and atrocities increased in number.

In June, the dictatorship of the slaughter-house reached its height. The Cabochians indulged in unspeakable acts of barbarism. De la Rivière was assassinated in prison; his body was taken to Les Halles and then strung up at Montfaucon. Pierre des Essarts was executed on the 1st July. Torturings, hangings and massacres followed one after the other. Capeluche, the executioner, was the hero of the hour, and John the Fearless had to shake him by the hand. The duke found himself unable to change the course of events; he and his advisers were swept irresistibly along. His problem was to find a way of bringing the fanatics to heel after doing so much to encourage them. He could not fully associate himself with their extremism when the other elements supporting him shrank at the bloodshed and excesses.

There was no mistaking the fact. John had won the first round in 1408; in 1413 he lost the second.

Where could the military strength be found to halt the revolutionary frenzy? Since Burgundy was incapable of resistance, there was nothing for it but to appeal to the Armagnac faction. A third party was formed to negotiate the change of front, since a shift of opinion was now noticeable. The wealthier burgesses and the masters of the university were partly responsible for it. Jean Jouvenel des Ursins, the former provost, led the moderate party, which had the approval of the Court. The Burgundians, having lost their early ardour and realizing that they had to let events take their course and even give some help supported the new plan of action. A complete *volte-face* was thus effected. On the 25th August 1413 John the Fearless evacuated Paris, leaving the way open for Bernard VII, who now found himself master of the situation.

Unfortunately, as far as social stability was concerned, the Armagnacs had no sense of political expediency. Armagnac violet replaced Burgundian green and Cabochian white but this did not mean that order was restored; on the contrary, it merely signalled the beginning of reprisals. A new wave of terror succeeded the first which had already caused such bloodshed; it was wild and indiscriminate, attacking not only the revolutionaries, but even the more moderate Burgundians, who were in favour of a reconciliation with the Orleanist faction. Because of the blunders committed by his opponents, Duke John might soon be able to make a come-back.

In Paris, where the new masters were ruling with a heavy hand and poverty and distress were greater than ever, a Burgundian party began to form. The duke had not assumed responsibility for the excesses committed by Caboche and his followers; or if he had, he had since dissociated himself from the movement. The Dauphin, after welcoming the Orleanist intervention, was now weary of it and was again putting out feelers to his father-in-law. The annulment of the 1413 ordinance revealed how opposed the new rulers were to reform and made them highly unpopular. Public opinion, with the inevitability of a pendulum, now swung back in the duke's favour. He had been prevented from showing his true ability by an unforeseen social upheaval, but he was still the only statesman of the Valois line.

Everything seemed to indicate that John, who had been quietly meditating on his Flemish estates since the month of August, would soon be back in the saddle again. At a Council, held in Paris from the 30th November 1413 to the 23rd February 1414, the ruling faction forced through a condemnation of John Petit's *Justification*; this struck public opinion as being much more an Orleanist manœuvre than an act of reparation.

Encouraged by the signs which he deemed sufficiently propitious, John left Lille with an army on the 23rd January, and, announcing that his intention was to prevent the Armagnacs 'setting up a new king', headed for Paris. Those Cabochians who had gone into exile with him had assured him that the people would rise in rebellion, and he no doubt thought the same. But Bernard VII, although devoid of political acumen, was at least a good soldier. He held Paris, and he had no intention of handing it over. The approaches were fiercely defended. The city withstood John's counter-attack, which, it must be admitted, had been too hastily prepared.

The only result of the failure of February 1414 was a renewal of the civil war.

This set-back did considerable damage to the Burgundian cause. The Duchess was acutely distressed and the Armagnacs exultant. They besieged Compiègne, capturing it on the 7th May: on the 21st August they stormed and ransacked Soissons; Laon, St Quentin, and Péronne surrendered to them; Artois was threatened.

This was the most crucial moment in John's career. The state created by Philip the Bold, and which had expanded since his death, was shaken to its very foundations. The allies of John the Fearless, even his relatives and subjects, were wavering and almost ready to betray him. After the fall of Soissons, one of the duke's brothers, the Count of Nevers, made his submission to the king, which, at that moment, meant professing allegiance to the Armagnacs. The duke's sister, the Countess of Hainault, went to the court at St Quentin to put forward proposals for peace. She tried again in July. On this occasion she was supported by the duke's other brother, Anthony of Brabant. Charles VI, or rather the council which controlled all his actions, stiffened their resistance. Nothing less than the complete submission of Louis of Orleans' assassin would suffice. The Chancellor of France made a similar stipulation in a reply to the Flemings, who, while solemnly declaring their loyalty to the king, craved clemency for the man who was their immediate overlord.

It must be admitted that John was driven, willy-nilly, into making peace. The Dauphin, hoping apparently to safeguard the king's authority by keeping the balance between the two factions, and feeling the need to check the success of the Orleanist party, managed to arrange fairly acceptable terms for his father-in-law. He may have been influenced by the fact that the duke was known to be negotiating with the English and might, as a last resort, throw in his lot with them. Even so the Peace of Arras, negotiated on the 4th September 1414, was not very flattering to the man who had ruled France for so long. By promising not to make an alliance with the English, the duke avoided the penalty of losing one or other of his fiefs. In one of the more dishonourable clauses, John agreed to banish all those of his followers who had displeased the king, leaving the king free to decide which would be pardoned; finally the duke was not to come to Paris without the king's permission.

These clauses are such as could only be forced upon a guilty and defeated man. The slight mitigations that were agreed to do not alter the character of the Peace of Arras, in spite of what some people have asserted.

But John, who had given in at a time of grave danger, made only a pretence of complying with these terms. He was to continue to plot with the English. He was to remain obsessed with the idea of revenge, at all costs, since he was determined, like the inveterate gambler he was, to win the third round in a game in which his opponents had already taken several tricks.

Pending further developments, the Peace of Arras, a sham peace if ever there was one, created a general atmosphere of ambiguity and tension.

At this point, the situation was confused as it had never been before by various underhand manœuvres. In Paris, where no one had been consulted, the terms imposed on the duke produced varied reactions. Some people were afraid that the dangerous Cabochians would be allowed to return from exile: others, who held quite different opinions, were afraid of falling victim to a reactionary movement, the extent of which no one could foresee. The Dauphin tried to carry out a tentative policy of his own, alternately encouraging or discouraging the Armagnac extremists. Then, joining forces once more with the old Duke of Berry, his uncle, with whom for a while he had been on bad terms, the unstable prince left Paris secretly for Bourges and Mehun-sur-Yèvre. This gave the Burgundians a chance to claim that the heir to the throne had been abducted and was being worked upon by the Armagnacs.

Meanwhile, the application of the terms of the Treaty of Arras gave rise to involved negotiations which dragged on interminably. The treaty had not been ratified. The court, in order to speed up proceedings, published the letters patent of the 2nd February 1415, which were virtually letters of remission. Even so a compromise had to be arrived at on the subject of the banished Burgundians in order to persuade the recalcitrant, and not altogether sincere, duke to agree to the ratification.

Then, to crown all, Henry V of England precipitated matters by launching an offensive. He landed in Normandy, invaded France and started the Hundred Years' War again. We have now to see what course the never-ending quarrel between the Armagnacs and the Burgundians would take now that the pattern of national history had been suddenly disrupted again.

The year 1415 saw the beginning of a new phase in the Franco-English wars and therefore marked the beginning of a negative stage in the events of the century. This is a suitable moment to examine the policy of John the Fearless as head of the Burgundian State, from his accession up to this fresh crisis.

The territorial expansion directed by Philip the Bold had in fact imposed on future dukes, whatever name they bore and whatever problems they might have to face, a dual rôle: they were princes of the blood, but also the owners of vast estates existing in their own right and over which France exercised no jurisdiction. The heirs of the founder of the ducal dynasty had to conform to a growing spirit of cosmopolitanism. We have to see how the second duke took this obligation.

So far, only one episode—the Liége affair—of John's internal policy as Duke of Burgundy has been mentioned, because it was linked with his policy as a French prince.

It will soon be necessary to refer to it again, because it also marked a turning point in his policy with regard to the Low Countries, now emerging as an entity.

While working for a greater *rapprochement* with England—and, as we have seen, he had already signed important trade agreements—and at the same time adopting towards the Schism an attitude which corresponded to the feelings or the needs of his Flemish subjects, John had so far succeeded in maintaining friendly relations between the weavers and the burgesses, thus acting as a sort of peace maker between the various social classes. The peace which had prevailed in the north during the second half of the preceding reign, had persisted during his, bringing further prosperity to the manufacturing areas. It may be that when the duke aired liberal views in Paris it was partly from a desire to curry favour with the former *Chaperons Blancs*. As he spoke Flemish, a language unknown to his father, John 'was quick to win his Flemish naturalization'.[30]

At the same time he carried on the matrimonial policy which had become a tradition at the Burgundian Court. It has already been noted that, while at the French Court, he carried through the marriages planned by Philip the Bold. His daughter, Margaret, had become the wife of the Dauphin; his son Philip, Count of Charolais, married Michelle, daughter of Charles VI. Philip's sisters had been nicely married off. Mary married Adolphus of Cleves; Isabella, Olivier de Penthièvre; Agnes, Charles I of Bourbon. And Anne was to become Duchess of Bedford.

Anthony, the duke's younger brother, succeeded to the Duchy of Brabant on the 1st September 1406 on the death of his aunt Joan, whose inheritance Philip the Bold had adroitly secured for him. The two brothers, Anthony and John, had been bound by a treaty of alliance—a regular family pact—since the 21st July 1405.

When, as has already been shown, he restored his brother-in-law, John of Bavaria, Bishop of Liége, to his throne, the Duke of Burgundy became virtual suzerain of the enclave of Liége; the operation, viewed as an integral part of Burgundian history, clearly reveals with what skill John was building up his vast edifice, whose foundations had been laid and whose structure had been begun, by the first Valois.

Helped by his brother Anthony, who had strong family feelings, and by his two brothers-in-law, John of Liége and William, Count of Holland, and his cousin, William of Namur, John the Fearless controlled the whole of the hinterland stretching behind the broad sweep of coast-line between the Somme and the Zuyder Zee. The Scheldt became a 'Burgundian river', as H. Pirenne has so aptly said. And he adds:

> For centuries it had marked the boundary between France and Germany, but now there was growing up between the two countries a compact coalition of territories belonging to princes of the same family, which forced back the frontiers of the two states, as if a wedge were being driven between them.

With John the Fearless in power, the possibility of a new Lotharingia emerged, and with it the possibility of a return to the Treaty of Verdun.

On many issues prudence dictated the policy which John the Fearless, as a sovereign prince, adopted in external affairs. While supporting his son-in-law, Olivier de Penthièvre, the husband of his daughter Isabella, in his conflict with the Duke of Brittany, John was careful not to become too embroiled with Brittany but merely tried to force the Breton to revive the alliance which had existed in the days of Philip the Bold.[31]

Internally, the armed rising of the Count of Tonnerre, which was serious only in so far as the Armagnacs were able to turn it temporarily to their advantage, ended with the collapse of the rebellious vassal, and the seizure of his domain; this allowed the duke to round off his possessions in a manner that the Capetians had aimed at in the past. The annexation was perhaps as important as the purchase of the County of Charolais by Philip the Bold in 1390 had been.

Burgundy was visibly expanding while at the same time the Low Countries were beginning to fuse into a single unit. Nevertheless, the Low Countries were to be the chief zone of expansion of the ducal House.

The House of Luxemburg tried without success to recover Brabant, which had slipped out of its grasp; not daring to go beyond indignant protests, it abandoned any attempt to uphold the right of Wenceslas by armed force. He had had little prestige in Germany even before his loss of the imperial dignity, but he was in a still more crippling position afterwards. In any case, Anthony, having lost his first wife, found a means of averting a possible clash with Luxemburg, by making a second marriage. His first wife had been Joan, the daughter of Waleran III of Luxemburg, Count of St Pol. On the 27th April 1490 he married Elizabeth of Goerlitz, the daughter of the ex-emperor. This marriage was indeed an important achievement since, two years later, on the death of Wenceslas' cousin, Jöst of Moravia, Luxemburg itself was pledged to the Duke of Brabant. Thus, Anthony was expanding his state, which was a sort of twin of Burgundy, and intended to back up the Duchy. It is true that a rebellion broke out in Luxemburg, led by Seneschal Huart d'Autel. But in spite of the rebel's links with the House of Orleans and with Sigismund, now head of the House of Luxemburg in Germany, Burgundy stood firm and Anthony retained his suzerainty over Luxemburg, Limburg and Brabant. Local feeling, moreover, worked in Anthony's favour, since his subjects were satisfied with his tactful policy. And when he died prematurely in 1415, on the battlefield of Agincourt, Elizabeth of Goerlitz achieved nothing by taking refuge at Sigismund's court. The estates of Brabant stood firm. John the Fearless resolutely supported his nephew John IV, for whom he arranged a marriage with Jacqueline of Bavaria, the daughter of William IV of Bavaria, heir to Hainault, Holland, Zealand and Friesland, and who had most opportunely been left a widow by her first husband, John of Touraine, the son of Charles VI. So not only were the existing gains consolidated but new and splendid prospects began to unfold. The subsequent stages of the policy carried out by the Brabantine branch of the dynasty will be examined at the end of this chapter, in the final summary of the part played by John the Fearless in his capacity as head of the Burgundian State.

For the moment attention must be focused on Anglo-Burgundian relations, which provide the key to the highly dramatic events which occurred during the last years of John's reign, from 1415 to 1419, and their tragic culmination.

When, after the failure of the 'wooden city' episode, Philip the Bold, a faithful supporter of the fleur-de-lys as well as a good

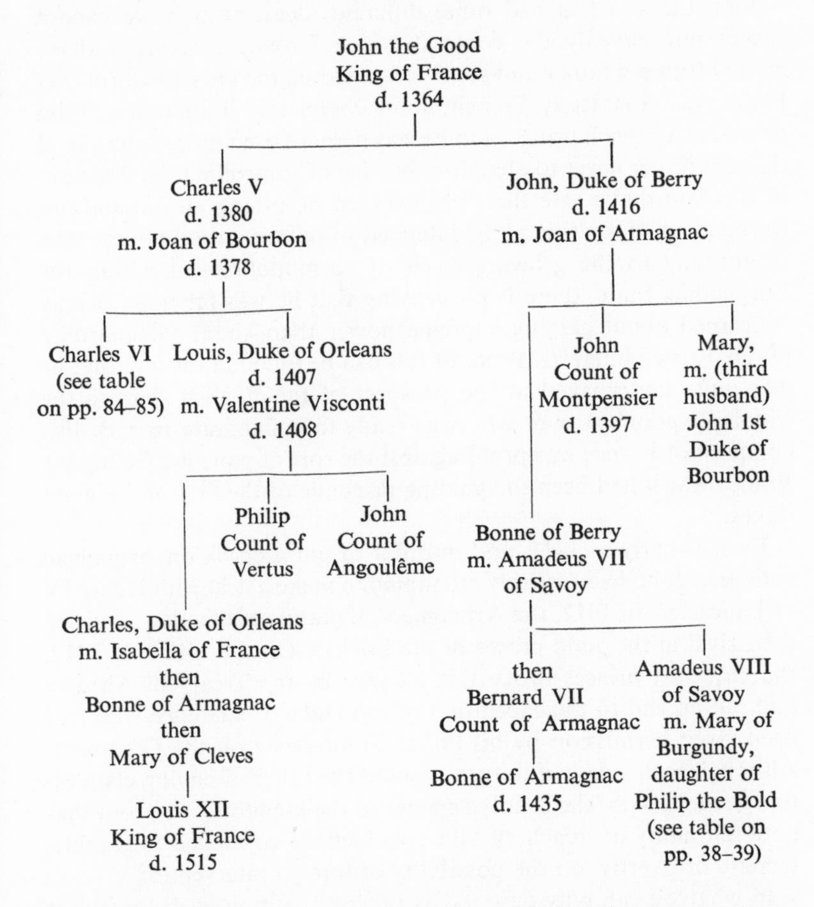

Burgundian, had directed his policy with regard to Great Britain towards peaceful relations and trade agreements, he never suspected that his attempt at a *rapprochement* would one day give rise to a pact harmful to French interests. As Pirenne has so admirably shown, Philip was 'on the whole a good Frenchman'. Even if we do not accept as gospel Monstrelet's story that Philip, on his death-bed, charged his sons to be 'good, true, faithful, and obedient to the King, Charles of France, his noble descendants, his crown and all his kingdom', it is certain that, while being self-centred enough to use the military strength of France to achieve his own ambitions in the east, he considered the interest of his seignieuries to be so bound up within those of the kingdom that, for him, expanding his estates was tantamount to helping the crown.

John the Fearless had quite different ideas, even if we cannot accept unreservedly the contrast which Pirenne declares to have existed between father and son.[32] It would be too easy to affirm that Philip was completely French, John completely Burgundian. John remained a French prince, and he was perhaps even more determined than his father never to abandon the idea of controlling the kingdom of the fleur-de-lys. He therefore avoided becoming an out-and-out Burgundian. But although he intended to pursue a dual policy, thus conforming to the growing spirit of cosmopolitanism within the Burgundian State, there is no denying that he was far more deeply concerned about gaining supreme power than about safeguarding purely French interests. Proof of this can be found in the fact that he was quite undismayed at the prospect of the English sharing the Valois kingdom. A man who was ready to collaborate in a British conquest of France was proof against the sort of patriotic feeling for France which had been the guiding principle of the first of the great dukes.

Even as early as 1411, and in order to put a check on Armagnac activities, John had furtively attempted to make a deal with Henry IV of Lancaster. In 1412, the Armagnacs, imitating his tactics, replaced their rival in the good graces of the English. On the 15th July 1412, the Orleanist princes broke this alliance by the Treaty of Auxerre and put an end to the expedition of the Duke of Clarence who had been given permission by his father to intervene on the Continent. Although each side had in turn accused the other of having clandestine dealings with 'the deadly enemies of the kingdom'—a proof that both felt guilty of treachery—the two factions continued to gamble, secretly or overtly, on the possibility of foreign intervention.

In what we can only describe as this competition in disloyalty, it must be admitted that from 1413 onwards, John the Fearless, either because he was a better tactician, or because from the English point of view he was a more desirable ally, unmistakably took the lead. It has already been shown how clandestine plots between England and Burgundy cast a shadow over the peace negotiations at Arras in 1414. When Henry V succeeded his father, Henry IV, the resumption of the Hundred Years' War became inevitable; the only question was the date. And for an English king who was out to exceed the past achievements of Edward III, the support, even the underhand and clandestine support, of the most powerful feudatory under Valois jurisdiction was bound to be of the greatest possible value.

This is a suitable point at which to sketch a portrait of Henry V, since he was to control the course of events along with John the Fearless.

Elegant, slender, athletic, Henry was slightly built and of medium height, easy and pleasant in manner. His face, with its broad forehead under a thatch of smooth brown hair, was clean-shaven and manly—a perfect oval with a straight, finely-chiselled nose, clear, sparkling hazel eyes, and a cleft chin; he gave an overall impression of coolness and rigid determination, but this outward show of iron self-control (Monstrelet calls him a 'haughty, strong-willed' man) concealed an inner fire. Georges Chastellain, the Burgundian chartist, summed him up in two lines: 'he planned and conducted his affairs himself, weighing carefully the pros and cons before embarking on any venture'.

Although a realist, he was not without ideals. Methodical, full of practical commonsense, and sure of his own strength, he was fond of conceiving vast, ambitious and far-reaching enterprises. After all, every great mediaeval prince dreamed of dominating the west and leading it in one vast crusade against the Turk. But the first problem to be solved was the union of France and England. The concept of the *double monarchy* was to be the first item in the Lancastrian programme for the reconstruction of Europe. A king of France and England, 'ruling both in Paris and London', would be the supreme champion of the Cross. The second Lancastrian bent his efforts to this end with a skill amounting almost to genius. He did not have time to give the full measure of his powers, but what he managed to do is eloquent enough indication of what he might have achieved.

Henry's intention was to make the most of the confusion in France. He claimed his Capetian inheritance, saying he had a hereditary right to the French throne. He proposed marriage with Catharine of France, the daughter of Charles VI, in order to cover up the elimination of the Valois line. On the 12th August 1415, he landed at La Hève and proceeded to overrun Normandy.

Shaken by the Treaty of Arras of 1414 and vexed by the Armagnac supremacy in Paris, John the Fearless had tried very hard to come to terms with the English during the six months preceding the invasion: he tried even harder when the landing was an established fact. He was careful to avoid committing himself, not through any qualms of conscience or national feeling, but simply because he was afraid of being caught in a mesh from which he would have difficulty in extricating himself.[33] As far as craftiness was concerned, there was little to choose between Henry and John. Each was trying to trap the other and use him for his own ends.

However, in order to come to terms with Henry, it was important not to adopt an antagonistic attitude towards him. It might seem inevitable that the resumption of Franco-English hostilities would force the French vassal to come out openly on the side of France. But John the Fearless was clever enough to evade the issue. As the Armagnacs were in control of Paris, he provoked them into declining his offer of co-operation by artfully proposing conditions which they felt they had to refuse. They feared that John the Fearless might take it upon himself to defend the kingdom, thus depriving them of their right to direct operations. John's manœuvre worked. He sulked and refused to take part in the fighting. The entire onus of facing the enemy fell on the Armagnacs, as well as the shame of the ignominious defeat at Agincourt on the 25th October.

Perhaps the two younger sons of Philip the Bold, less forgetful of their father's teachings, and more capable of patriotic feelings for France than their elder brother, tried to restore the honour of the Burgundian dynasty, thus indelibly stained by the absence of Duke John from the battlefield where the fate of Normandy was being decided. At any rate, Philip of Nevers and Anthony of Brabant were among those who gave their lives on the 25th October. Several other vassals of the Duke of Burgundy, swayed by anti-English feeling, also fought and died in the same way.[34]

Nevertheless, the Armagnacs, having chosen to fight alone—or almost alone—bore the responsibility for the appalling disaster and its consequences. Their prince, Charles of Orleans, was taken prisoner and kept in confinement in England for many long years. The Dauphin Louis of Guienne, John's son-in-law, lost heart and died on the 18th December 1415. The new Dauphin, John of Touraine, was too much of a weakling to sustain the waning hopes of the dynasty. In fact, anyone with a realistic turn of mind and a contempt for intangible factors, could very understandably conclude that the reigning house was doomed. This seems to be the only explanation of John's decision to act in 1416, after carefully refraining from committing himself up till then. Seeing English domination spread ever more widely across Normandy, and after failing to recover possession of Paris by a plot which collapsed on Easter Sunday, 17th April 1416, John resolved to come to terms with the English.

While Bernard VII of Armagnac was ruling the capital with a rod of iron, and as constable (in place of Charles of Albret who had been killed at Agincourt) was responsible for an ordinance issued on the 13th May 1416 abolishing the Great Corporation of Butchers, John the Fearless officially concluded a truce with Henry, according to which his subjects would not be involved in the war, provided they did not fight on the side of France. Then unofficially, and secretly, he made a pact by which he became a collaborator, an accomplice and an associate of the Lancastrian venture.

The truce which turned a French fief, pledged to support its overlord, into a neutral power, was in itself an act of treason.

As for the pact, it has been justly described as '*un pacte infernal*' ('a diabolical pact').[35]

The tell-tale document was drawn up in May 1417. At Calais, where they parleyed 'for a long time without letting anything be known of the matters they were discussing', John recognized Henry and his descendants as the heirs to the French throne, and solemnly undertook to pay liege homage as soon as Henry had recovered a sizeable share of the kingdom, and adding that he was prepared to offer Henry there and then 'all the help he could by secret ways and means'. The document is no more than a draft, but it is *in the duke's handwriting*. It bears no indication of date or place and is full of initials, abbreviations, and code-expressions. For instance, the enemies of the kingdom, against whom the duke is to take action, are indicated by the letters A, B, C and D. These letters signified 'all those who refuse to obey the King of England'. The unusual character of the document clearly brings out the abnormal nature of the pact, which the participants dared not formulate in the ordinary way. They thus avoided any public discussion, when they proceeded to put the plan immediately into effect. That they did so is shown by subsequent political moves; actual events provide an eloquent answer to those who plead that the duke was not guilty.

The document must have been more than a vague project. How else could it have found its way into the official English records? It explains the whole subsequent train of events; had it not reflected the intentions of the man who directed these events, it would have had no connection with them.

The best construction that can be put on the secret pact is that, being unratified in the usual diplomatic way, it left a loop-hole whereby John could effect a change of front, should a situation later arise in which there was a chance of a solution other than the disappointing Anglo-Burgundian alliance. This last hypothesis would be in keeping with the duke's constant wiliness and equivocalness.

It provides the only possible concession that can be made to those who prefer not to consider the Calais draft as a 'diabolical pact'. The fact remains that the duke, seeing the way to Paris and to control of the Valois kingdom barred by the stubborn Armagnac resistance, resorted, fearlessly and unscrupulously, to a desperate manœuvre; he was prepared to hand France over to the Lancastrians, rather than leave her to the Armagnacs, with the proviso that he would carve out his own kingdom from the remnants of the Capetian monarchy, added to the territories he already possessed, whether they were subinfeudated to France or to the Empire. His first crime had been committed with the axe in 1407; the second was committed with the pen in 1417. The axe had won him the first round, but the victory had been cancelled out by the losing of the second round in 1413. In a quite unforeseen way, the pen was to win him the third round, and indeed the whole game.

From then onwards a policy of permanent and clandestine treachery was inevitable, as subsequent events illustrate.

Henry V had achieved a master-stroke by this secret pact with John the Fearless. It was of vital importance to him to have the greatest French vassal on his side in the critical struggle which he now intended to pursue to the very end.

Badly shaken by a succession of plots, and harried by the Burgundian party, the Armagnacs became less and less capable of taking decisive action. Bernard VII, who had been in control of the administration since 1416, continued to wield his authority, recklessly and indiscriminately. He deprived the townspeople of their right to put up chains in the streets at night. He sent several members of the university into exile, and curtailed the privileges of the corporations and the burgesses. The Duke of Burgundy was obviously behind the conspiracies which involved people of every social class, for instance, a canon, a superintendent of finances, and a rich draper. According to Monstrelet there were even plots to kill the provost of Paris, Tanguy du Châtel, to murder the queen, the Queen of Sicily and the chancellor, to imprison the king, and to get rid of the King of Sicily and the Duke of Berry. From 1416 to 1417, Parisians lived in a very strange city, where bread was lacking, where, according to chronicles of the day, there was a black market in all essential foodstuffs, and where acts of criminal violence were looked upon as ordinary items of the day's news.

John the Fearless continued to threaten Armagnac-controlled Paris. In an attempt to exploit popular unrest, which physical hardship was making still more acute, John emphasized his demagogic approach. He promised to abolish all taxes with the exception of the salt-tax. From his headquarters at Chambly (now in the canton of Neuilly-en-Thelle) the duke could keep a watch on the Oise bridges, while mercenaries held the bridge at Nogent. All supply routes were threatened. By making the Lord of Toulongeon governor of Troyes, which had surrendered to him on the 30th April 1417, the duke became virtual master of Champagne, and in September, as a result of raids carried out south of Paris, Chartres fell into his hands.

Subject to pressure from both the Burgundians and the English, caught in the clutches of the two secret allies, whose complicity was unknown to them but who clearly represented an ever-increasing threat, the Armagnacs panicked. It is true that from Paris, which they controlled by terrorism, they threw out garrisons as far as Orleans, Fréteval, and Châteaudun, but they failed to prevent John the Fearless from taking the castles of Orsay and Palaiseau.

Meanwhile, the English, who found no obstacles in their way, advanced with alarming speed. On the death of the Dauphin, John, Duke of Touraine on the 4th April 1417, the title was handed on to the next heir, Charles, the future Charles VII.

The young prince who was barely fifteen years old and already overwhelmed by his lot remained listlessly for a time in Rouen, before deciding to defend Paris, which was being closely watched by eight thousand Burgundians. They occupied a succession of strategic positions around the capital—Beauvais, Beaumont-sur-Oise, Senlis, Pontoise, Meulan, Mantes, Vernon, Poissy, St Germain, Montlhéry—and so carried out a parallel campaign to that of the English, who were cutting Paris off from Normandy and manœuvring as they pleased in the northern provinces. Although the alliance was secret, both English and Burgundians exploited it to the full. It was written in letters of fire over the whole field of action.

Henry V took Caen and the Norman fortified towns;[36] he then set up a Lancastrian régime in Normandy. After the fall of Cherbourg on the 22nd August 1418, only Mont St Michel held out—an isolated pocket of resistance: it continued to hold its own, but from then onwards it was completely cut off, and surrounded by conquered territory.

John chose this moment to abduct Isabella and install her at Troyes. What was virtually a rebel government and a rival to that of the Dauphin and his Armagnac friends, was set up under Burgundian sponsorship. Isabella called herself 'Queen of France, having, on behalf of our Lord the king, government and administration of the kingdom'. The Dauphin assumed the title of 'lieutenant-general of the king', considering himself to have officially taken the place of a father who was incapable of ruling. Two separate centres of authority now appeared in France; a disastrous state of affairs at a time when the enemy was nibbling away at the divided kingdom.

To make the confusion worse, conflicting attempts at negotiation were in progress. Some people were trying to find grounds for an agreement between France and England, while others were endeavouring to persuade Armagnacs and Burgundians to unite against the common foe. Those who took the latter course were unaware of the '*pacte infernal*' and never imagined that Burgundy and Lancaster were in league with each other. Public opinion was in a state of chaos, thanks chiefly to the bitter consequences of the Pact of Calais. Faced with so many conflicting opinions, so many equivocal situations—by the Orleanist-Armagnac party, which in spite of its mistakes and its defects was the party of national defence and had assumed all the responsibilities and sacrifices such a task entailed—by the Duke of Burgundy, whose double game, or rather whose persistent deceitfulness, was so brilliantly concealed as to escape detection—by the queen, who had been installed at Troyes with John the Fearless and her rebel government—by the young Dauphin, who had been 'called upon to take over the affairs of the kingdom'—finally by the king who was almost completely senile and helpless, it is small wonder that the 'common people', that is the average Frenchman, felt lost and bewildered.

There is no denying that the acute moral crisis which was to bring fifteenth century France to the brink of disaster was already visible; nor can John the Fearless's responsibility be denied. Ambition was driving him relentlessly on towards the realization of his aims and he must have rejoiced inwardly to see the signs of confusion accumulating, since they were leading up to what he was convinced would be the crowning achievement of his career.

Perhaps it was simply the wretched conditions prevailing in Paris which suddenly opened the gates of the capital to the duke, who had been kept out since 1413. The Lord of l'Isle-Adam, John the Fearless's captain at Pontoise, succeeded in getting from young Perrinet Leclerc the keys of the gates which he had stolen from his father, a *cinquantenier*,[37] while the latter was asleep. At dawn on the 29th May 1418, Burgundian troops made a surprise entry into Paris. A rising followed, and during it Bernard VII was murdered. The provost, Tanguy du Châtel, managed to escape just in time with the Dauphin, who found refuge at Melun. The hatred of the rabble for the constable's associates could no longer be contained. So great was their fury that, according to Monstrelet, people only had to point to a man and say 'He's an Armagnac' for him to be put to death without further ado. Massacres and pillaging were once more the order of the day. Foreign banks were ruthlessly ransacked. The bloodshed mattered little to the duke, now that he had recaptured the city of Caboche.

John had just left Montbéliard, where on the 6th May, he had been settling some legal disputes with Sigismund, King of the Romans, and the Lords of the Empire, and he was heading for Dijon, by way of Villersexel and Gray, when he saw some of the king's horsemen coming towards him to announce the 'joyful entry' of his men into Paris. He stayed nearly a month in his own capital: then, on the 16th June, he joined the queen and her provisional government at Troyes. He had, however, taken the precaution of reinforcing the troops holding Paris to enable them to withstand a counter-offensive by the Dauphin. After being defeated on the 1st June, in spite of some bitter street fighting, the unfortunate Charles was finally forced to withdraw to Charenton, then to Melun, and from there he made his way to Bourges, which for many years was to be his principal place of residence; he moved between the town itself, and the castle of Mehun-sur-Yèvre, on the outskirts, which he had inherited from his uncle, the Duke of Berry, who had died in 1416.

In spite of the collapse of the Armagnacs in Paris, the Burgundian administration remained at Troyes. No doubt Duke John, who had learned his lesson in 1413, had calculated that it would be better for him if the fresh outbreak of Cabochian fury, which was once more strewing the streets with corpses, spent itself *in his absence*. Appalling acts of brigandage and terrorism were committeed. The constable's body was treated with extreme brutality; it was flayed in such a way as to show the mark of 'the Armagnac sash'. There were many victims among the clergy; four bishops were killed—Lisieux, Evreux, Senlis and Coutances—as well as the abbé of St Denis, who was held to be 'a very false, sanctimonious person'. Three hundred members of Paris university were massacred, including two clerks and ambassadors of Charles VI and the humanists, Gontier Col and Jean de Montreuil.

The Duke of Burgundy continued to ignore what was going on, remaining, as it were, behind the scenes. Unperturbed, he let events take their course. Remembering 1413, he had no intention of coming forward until the need for law and order became so acute that he would be carried along on the new current. The members of his council and his captains—Luxemburg, Fosseuse, Humbercourt and many others—begged him to enter Paris. Charles VI and Isabella also pressed him eagerly to do so. But he remained deaf to all entreaties, stuck to his original plan and bided his time.

Thirty-two days after the June massacres he finally decided to take action. He left Troyes on the 8th July and went to Nogent-sur-Seine. He stayed three days in Provins, and then, in short stages, by way of Nangis and Brie-Comte-Robert, he finally reached Paris.

He decided to turn his assumption of authority into a dazzling military display. The twelve hundred burgesses, dressed in blue, who had come to meet him half-way across the bridge at Charenton, were treated, on the afternoon of the 14th July, to a parade of five thousand soldiers. In the vanguard were fifteen hundred archers 'in close and serried rank', and one thousand men-at-arms from Picardy, in five squadrons under the command of the Vidame of Amiens, John of Luxemburg and the Lord of Fosseuse, Governor of Artois; next came the 'Burgundian battalion', the main corps of the army, fifteen hundred men all carrying lances decorated with the emblem of the plane: finally a rearguard of five hundred men under John of Chalon, Lord of Arlay and Prince of Orange.

John the Fearless, who rode close to Queen Isabella's carriage, was greeted just ouside Paris, a little beyond St Antoine, by two cardinals, the papal legates Fillastre and Fieschi, as well as by the Counts of Aumale and Tripoli, the second of whom was the King of Cyprus's brother. The procession crossed Paris and made for the Louvre, where the king awaited the queen and the duke. Charles VI kissed the queen twice and said to John: 'Fair cousin, I bid you welcome, and I thank you for all your kindness to the queen'. Then wine and spices were served. However, neither the duke nor the queen were tempted by these refreshments. If the anonymous Burgundian, who recounted this scene in detail, is to be believed, 'many people were so touched that they wept'.

John the Fearless accompanied the queen to her bedroom and then went off to his own residence, the Hôtel d'Artois.

The political situation still had to be cleared up.

Caboche was a member of the duke's household. Capeluche, the executioner, adopted a familiar tone with the prince, but his sadistic career was drawing to a close. The murder of a pregnant and entirely blameless young woman was his last glorious exploit. The duke took advantage of the popular feeling aroused by this outrage to have the executioner arrested in a tavern near Les Halles. When Capeluche reached the block, he gave his successor, who was less skilled than he was, some advice on how to tackle his job, and even displayed a sort of professional courage. Later, more terrorists were put to death.

And so Duke John ensured a return to law and order in Paris. But Parisians were depressed by the sacrifice of so many lives; their numbers had been depleted by epidemics; there was a shortage of both food and firewood, and the atmosphere of tension was made still more acute by the fact that the English were close at hand.

Almost the whole of Normandy had been conquered. Rouen, however, was still maintaining an heroic resistance. Before the siege of the town started, the inhabitants had driven out the Armagnacs in whom they had no confidence, and had placed their town under a Burgundian captain, Gruy le Bouteiller. Not realizing that the Duke of Burgundy was hand in glove with the King of England, they thought this was a way of securing effective help. The duke received the various envoys despatched to him with words of encouragement, but did not lift a finger to help the unfortunate town, which was left in the grip of famine. The terrible plight of Rouen was the clearest and most terrible illustration of the effects of the clandestine and unatonable pact of 1417. To sum up its disastrous consequences: it brought about the collapse of the French economy, debased the coinage, caused poverty and famine, created two rival governments—one in Paris, the other in Bourges—and encouraged widespread anxiety and mounting unrest.

The Lancastrian invading force was now threatening Paris. John the Fearless had gone to Provins where he had been joined by Charles VI, Isabella and their daughter Catharine. The question was: would the capital be handed over without being defended, as Rouen had been? Negotiations and counter-negotiations were in progress and the outcome of the very paradoxical situation was uncertain. There were two possibilities: either the Anglo-Burgundian alliance would have to be unmasked and ratified, or the rival parties in France would have to come to terms and combine to face the urgent danger created by the lightning advance of the invading British forces.

For a time, it seemed likely that the second possibility would be carried into effect.

At Pouilly, on the 11th July 1419, John and the Dauphin, Charles, brought together by the Lady of Giac and Alain de la Rue, Bishop of Léon, swore an oath of friendship. Fifteen lords pledged allegiance to Charles, seventeen to John. In Paris the reconciliation was celebrated with a Te Deum and the people went wild with joy. The two princes, it was said, had agreed to 'drive the English king from the kingdom',

But was the duke sincere? The terms of the Pouilly agreement remained extremely vague, and two days later, at Corbeil, where the two cousins were staying together, it was found necessary to fix another meeting for a later date.

After many delays, all brought about by John—a fact which casts grave doubts on his willingness to co-operate—it was decided that a meeting would take place on the Yonne bridge, at Montereau, on the 10th September.

The fear of assassination on either side made this famous meeting difficult from the start. However, on the appointed day the two princes met at five in the afternoon half-way across the river, on the bridge which was fortified with a machicolated tower. A small group of lords accompanied each of the participants. It was not long before tempers became frayed. Arguing that the Dauphin could not act without his father's consent, the duke refused to commit himself on any important issue. It at once became clear that the meeting was nothing but a farce. The Dauphin, disheartened, climbed down from the bridge and a confused scuffle took place. On the basis of the vague or contradictory documentation at the disposal of the historian, it is impossible to say what exactly happened. According to the highly questionable version that was quickly spread abroad, Tanguy du Châtel struck John the Fearless on the head with an axe. All that is known for certain is that Louis of Orleans' assassin was in his turn the victim of an assassination; after a long sequence of interrelated happenings the Barbette crime had its sequel and counterpart in the crime at Montereau.[38] All they that take the sword, shall perish with the sword.

Nothing is more moving in its simplicity than the day-book of accounts kept during the last journey of John the Fearless:[39]

September 16th, Sunday—Our Lord, the Duke of Burgundy, accompanied by Charles, our Lord of Bourbon, our Lord of Navailles, and several knights and squires—stopped to drink at Bray-sur-Seine—dined at Montereau on the Yonne, at which place the afore-mentioned lord was traitorously killed and murdered. And great was the confusion that day, because of the death of our afore-mentioned lord.

October 2nd, Monday—All the afore-mentioned officials and servants of the late afore-mentioned lord were dismissed from service, and the household completely disbanded.

John had not succeeded in establishing himself permanently as master of France, but by manœuvring between the Valois of France and the Lancasters of England, he had set his House well on the road towards building up the Burgundian state which was being both expanded and consolidated.

The last years of the second reign, although disappointing as far as France was concerned, were marked by positive achievements in the Low Countries, where a new power was being set up.

It has already been shown how, after the death of his brother, Anthony of Burgundy, Duke of Brabant, John the Fearless had supported his dead brother's eldest son, John IV of Brabant. But the marriage which the Duke of Burgundy arranged for John IV with Jacqueline of Bavaria, and which took place (as has already been explained) at the Hague on the 10th March 1418, was strongly disapproved of by the head of the House of Luxemburg, who, at the time, happened to be Sigismund, King of the Romans. Sigismund arranged for Elizabeth of Goerlitz, Anthony's widow, to marry the ex-Prince-Bishop of Liége, John of Bavaria, who, forgetting that the Duke of Burgundy had once rendered him a service, threw in his lot with John's enemies. He laid claim to the guardianship of his niece Jacqueline, and tried to prevent his fiefs being incorporated into the Burgundian State. At the same time Sigismund, exercising imperial rights, claimed that Brabant was subinfeudated to Germany. All John's achievements in the north were in danger of being undone.

As far as Sigismund was concerned, the Brabantine problem was more than a feudatory contest between France and Germany. His response to the people of Brabant who opposed his policy was: 'So you want to be French!'

The Brabant estates saw the matter in quite a different light. They envisaged another solution to the problem—the creation of an intermediary State which would be quite independent of both France and Germany, in short, the Lotharingian solution, and for this reason they were determined to stand up for the young duke and his protector, the Duke of Burgundy.

In this way the Low Countries became a more definite entity. The mosaic of fiefs subinfeudated to various powers were gradually being brought together by their economic interests and were becoming ever more conscious of their collective reality.

In order to break up this crystallization, Sigismund needed men and money, and he had neither. The Brabant estates coldly refused to acknowledge his imperial rights. The Count of Charolais, the future Philip the Good, was commissioned by his father to settle the Brabantine affair. He was successful in bringing about the agreement of the 13th February 1419. Jacqueline and John IV handed over to John of Bavaria and Elizabeth part of Holland, over which, however, they retained suzerainty, and kept the rest. In short, at the cost of a small sacrifice, which in any case was to prove only temporary, the domains of Joan of Brabant and Jacqueline of Hainault remained in the possession of the House of Burgundy.

The principality of Liége remained under the effective protectorate of Burgundy. In 1414, the administration set up after the battle of Othée in 1413 had been replaced by a new régime, based on a constitution freely granted by the bishop. The rights of the ordinary middle-class people vanished into thin air like those of the 'commonality'. Every year, the chapter and deputy-mayors, acting separately, drew up two lists, each consisting of twelve names. The only people eligible for inscription were eminent burgesses over twenty-four years of age, 'who either lived on their private incomes or on honest trade involving no manual work'. From the twenty-four names, the bishop chose twelve deputy-mayors for the following year, and they were solely responsible for the administration of the town. The artisan class was completely disenfranchised.

However, when this system was actually put into operation, it appeared so outrageous that emendations had to be agreed to. The bishop consented to allow the various crafts, which were gradually recovering their prosperity, a share in the administration. The population was divided up into seventeen crafts, each with the right to appoint two councillors and two people of independent means. The thirty-four councillors appointed by the crafts worked in conjunction with the mayoralty and the chapter, and together the three administrative bodies nominated two 'supreme councillors' who directed the affairs of the town. John, the Bishop of Liége, may well have made these concessions because by now he was losing interest in Liége. In September 1417 he abandoned his mitre and claimed the inheritance of his brother, William, who had died on the 31st May. The ex-prelate, who had never been distinguished by his spirituality, then threw himself into secular politics with great abandon.

Some conclusion has now to be drawn from the extremely eventful reign of the second of the great dukes.

He certainly did not fail to extend his inheritance. Whether or not he was more of a Burgundian than his father, Philip the Bold, as the great Belgian historian, Henri Pirenne, has claimed, he was certainly more Flemish.

In the conduct of the internal and external affairs of his estates he had the able support of a group of devoted administrators, first and foremost of whom were the chancellor, Jean de Saulx, Lord of

Courtivron, his successor, Jean de Thoisy, Bishop of Tournai, Thierry Gherbode, and Nicolas Rolin who also held office as chancellor. He was furthermore helped by valiant and well-equipped men-at-arms—Lannoy, Croy, Luxemburg, Villiers de l'Isle-Adam, Bauffremont, Pot, Pontailler, Vergy, Saveuse, and many others. Duke John always had a preference for the affairs of France and general political questions. He was drawn to Paris rather than to Dijon or Brussels. The English pact which was the real cause of his death, although it had remained secret, was prompted by his exasperation at being unable to find any other way of becoming the undisputed master of France. The Armagnacs had stubbornly resisted his attempt to achieve his principal aim, which was to gain control of the kingdom of the fleur-de-lys. In order to break their resistance, which found its final embodiment in the person of the Dauphin Charles, the future Charles VII, the duke considered that his only course was to seek help from Henry V, who styled himself 'King of England and France', and who was engaged in the conquest of France. The Calais pact contained all the essential elements of the future Treaty of Troyes. The policy which lay behind it can be summed up in a sentence: may France perish rather than fall into the hands of the Armagnacs. Perhaps the duke would have been satisfied with overcoming his opponents by the mere threat of help from across the Channel. Perhaps he would have repudiated the unsigned pact before it was put into full operation. But to try to carry out a pro-English policy with a man like Henry V was none the less a very dangerous undertaking.[40]

It is impossible to know to what lengths John would have carried this policy, or what would have been its outcome. But the least that can be said of him as a French prince is that he ignored both the ties of kindred and his father's teachings.

By cutting short his life on Montereau bridge, the Dauphin's henchmen removed any possibility of our knowing how things would have turned out. A wide field of conjecture thus lies open to those who like to rewrite history according to their wishes. John's reign ended on a note of puzzling and dramatic ambiguity: it was as if fate had decreed that the ambiguity which had characterized the whole of his chequered career should persist until the very end, leaving the future undecided.

CHAPTER VII

PHILIP THE GOOD

JOHN THE FEARLESS's heir was his only son Philip, Count of Charolais, who, at the time of his father's sudden death on Montereau bridge, was living at Ghent with his young wife Michelle, the daughter of Charles VI.

Who was to announce the dreadful news to Charolais? Who would approach the tall, gay, vigorous young man who was so nimble on his feet yet often incapacitated by feverish attacks? All were agreed that the delicate task should be undertaken by Jean de Thoisy . . . A group of Burgundians who had escaped from Montereau, had secretly informed Jean de Thoisy and Athis de Brimeu of the murder of John the Fearless. The two of them came to an agreement about how they would present the news. They went into Charolais's room 'their feelings firmly under control, their words carefully chosen'. The storm was about to break about the young sapling.[1]

Georges Chastellain, the Burgundian historiographer, attributes to Thoisy a lengthy speech which he certainly never made; however, his account of the effect that the news of the disaster had on the heir and his wife is, if a trifle long-winded, plausible enough. P. Champion and P. de Thoisy, from whom the preceding quotation is taken, give a brief and gripping résumé of Chastellain's account.

Philip uttered a dreadful cry. A sudden tremor passed across his face, his eyes rolled back in their sockets. His teeth were clenched, his lips parched, like those of a dead man. They had to pull his clothes off and force his mouth open. In the room full of mourners he was suffocating. Michelle, his wife, the sister of the assassin, had collapsed and lay inert beside him.[2]

As Georges Chastellain aptly says 'in that room given over to moaning, wailing and sobbing, it seemed as if there were two lifeless bodies'.

Amidst these lamentations, then, began a reign which was to be one of the longest in history, since it was to last for very nearly half a century.

The Count of Charolais, who as a result of the Montereau tragedy became Duke of Burgundy, had been born at Dijon on the 31st July 1396. Unlike his father, he was a tall, handsome prince, distinguished and prepossessing in appearance. We propose to describe, not the twenty-three-year-old prince at the time of his accession to the ducal throne, but the mature man, as depicted by his particular historian Georges Chastellain in a famous passage, which is confirmed by authentic portraits left by contemporary artists.[3]

The third duke is described by his official chronicler as being 'as straight as a die, with a strong back, broad shoulders and strong arms'. He had a thick head of hair, a broad brow, keen, proud eyes set under shaggy eyebrows 'the hairs of which bristled like horns when he was angry'. He moved with dignity and held himself proudly. He looked truly distinguished. 'His appearance alone proclaimed him emperor, and his natural graces made him worthy of a crown.'

All were unanimous on this point. It was not a question of flattery on the part of his subjects and court scribes. An Andalusian hidalgo, who was granted an audience in Brussels in 1438, recorded that 'the duke has a most noble bearing, is full of spirit, extremely pleasant, well-built, tall, elegant, lively and chivalrous'.

Philip is described as 'a supremely proud prince, touchy in his pride and subject to violent fits of anger'. He loved pomp:

> ...jewels, fine horses, splendid armour, and he knew how to make the most of them; whenever he made an official entry into a town the crowds gasped at the dazzling display. In the arranging of entertainments, jousts, tournaments, and banquets, he outshone all his predecessors. His guests were astounded by his array of jewels, tapestries, plates and dishes, and his gold-filled coffers.

His private life was free of all restraint;

> (He had) innumerable love-affairs, thirty known mistresses, seventeen officially recognized illegitimate children, from the 'great bastards' like Cornelius and Anthony—the latter became a knight of the Golden Fleece—to David and Philip who succeeded each other as Bishop of Utrecht.

But although his fits of anger were terrifying, he was fundamentally good-natured. 'One humble word,' says Chastellain,' was enough to quieten him.' And it was this 'quality of moderation', this self-control characterizing his normal behaviour, which earned for him the nick-name of 'steady' (*l'asseuré*). Posterity has chosen to refer to him as Philip the Good.[4]

Moreover, although he was 'most lickerous' by nature, he was also extremely pious. His devoutness was comparable to that of the famous paragon of chivalry, his companion Jacques de Lalaing, and his knightly virtues made him worthy to be lord of such a valiant knight. The memorialist, Olivier de la Marche, has described him fighting the men of Ghent 'not like the prince or high-ranking, important personage he was, but like a chivalrous gentleman, performing bold and valiant deeds'.[5]

Gay, lively, and a keen sportsman, he was also extremely fond of reading. He had a passion for history, which explains why he paid Chastellain for the express purpose of commemorating the events of his reign. He had a well-stocked library, and a fine collection of tapestries. The study of the history of Burgundian art shows him to have been a worthy successor of the two preceding dukes—more especially of the first duke, the famous patron of the arts, whose name he bore.

And yet, although he appears to have had such a well-defined personality, Philip leaves us with a problem, which is just as puzzling in his case as in that of one of the distant ancestors of the dynasty who bore the same Christian name as himself—the Capetian King, Philip the Fair.

Was Philip the Good really a statesman? Did he direct his policy personally, or was it the work of his ministers, and more especially his famous chancellor Nicolas Rolin? We reserve discussion of this thorny question, about which volumes have been written, for the end of the chapter. It is advisable to examine the various stages of his reign before attempting to estimate the active part played by the duke, who at least presided over events majestically and with an easy grace.

The immediate consequence of the death of John the Fearless was to throw the new duke into the arms of the King of England. As he was in duty bound to avenge his father, he considered himself fully justified in transforming the pact concluded in secret by John and Henry V into an overt, public alliance. But this decision was not just prompted, as has been too often affirmed, by an instinctive movement of anger: the matter was debated in council, family discussions were held, contact was even established with the Dauphin, and France's deplorable plight was given serious consideration. The truth was that both heart and head seemed to urge the continuation of the policy on which the duke's immediate predecessor had openly embarked. A divided France, which under Armagnac leadership seemed to be heading for disaster, was deemed incapable of holding out against the English, and so it was felt that both interest and duty compelled Burgundy to play the winning card. Philip was certainly convinced that his decision, in keeping as it was with the dictates of honour which demanded retribution for an appalling outrage, was also in keeping with his desire to safeguard both the vital interests of the Burgundian state, and those of France herself, if they were rightly understood. After due deliberation, the young duke was sure that he was fulfilling his responsibilities as a dutiful son, a good Burgundian, and a good Frenchman.[6]

The Parisian reaction to the news of the Montereau tragedy certainly influenced the discussions held at the Court of Burgundy in the direction of revenge. 'The most false and most disloyal treachery of the outrageous and hateful murder' had aroused in the capital and throughout the whole of the kingdom, a wave of violent emotion and passionate feelings of anger. The 'pitiful death' had been 'grievously' felt. The university, the burgesses and the *Parlement* had risen in protest; the cross of St Andrew had made its reappearance; the Burgundian party suddenly recovered the authority and prestige it had enjoyed during the heyday of John's reign.

Henry V, simultaneously approached both by the Dauphin and the new Duke of Burgundy, took advantage of these conflicting overtures to increase his demands. This was a natural enough move, and it seemed likely to ensure success for the clever sovereign who realized that there was no longer any man of his calibre to oppose him. Ambassadors came and went, but to no purpose.[7] The outcome was a foregone conclusion. Except for the Dauphin Charles, and the Armagnac party who were now completely discredited, everyone rallied round the conqueror, to help him in his task, and, in fact, to hand over France.

Troyes, the seat of the rebel government set up by John the Fearless (it had now become the pseudo-legitimate government) and where Charles VI and Isabella were installed, was the rallying point for all the opponents of the Dauphin, the true representative of traditional France whatever may be said against him.[8] On the 17th January 1420, Charles VI issued letters patent forbidding the inhabitants of Paris to obey the Dauphin, or to pay any attention to his messages. Thanks largely to the well-organized Burgundian propaganda-machine set up by John the Fearless, the king's instructions were widely circulated, and the feelings of the people exploited; they had been as wildly excited by the Montereau murder as they had been left unmoved by the Barbette crime. Everything—the general weariness, the intolerable impoverishment of the country, the sudden and drastic collapse of the currency, the confusion which had reached its height—combined to plunge the inhabitants of Paris and to some extent the French people as a whole, into a state of moral capitulation in which the most paradoxical and extreme solutions, diametrically opposed to national tradition, to reason and to moral principles, appeared natural and acceptable. In this nightmare atmosphere the incredible and fateful Treaty of Troyes was drawn up; it was to be the most disastrous in French history, not only because it set a seal on France's defeat and entailed immeasurable material sacrifices, but because it represented a surrender of the national conscience and the national will.

The treaty was concluded on Tuesday, the 21st May 1420. The Dauphin Charles was brazenly disinherited. His own parents referred to him as the 'so-called Dauphin of Vienne', and holding him personally responsible for the Montereau assassination they accused him 'of horrible and outrageous crimes'. Since it had been arranged during the preliminary negotiations that Catharine of France, daughter of Charles VI, would marry Henry V, the king and queen did not hesitate from now on to refer to Henry as their son. For the time being, he was to be regent of France, and on the death of Charles VI would become King of France. From that moment the two crowns of France and England were to be united under one king and Catharine's heir would reign after his father, or if need be, in his stead.

This broke with the tradition of inheritance through the male line. To suit the needs of the moment it was agreed that the crown was to be handed down through the female line. Not one of the people responsible for drawing up the astounding document ever seems to have reflected how inconceivable it was that a mad king should be allowed to break the fundamental rules of the monarchy, and the continuity of history. Passion and interest reigned supreme; the physical and moral distress was such that Paris and the main corporate bodies in the State greeted the treaty of capitulation with cheers, processions, singing and dancing.

However, one section of French soil refused to join in the general collaboration with the invader, and remained faithful to the Dauphin, who, although still lacking in personal prestige at that date, became the centre of a resistance movement.

Fine promises were made to Philip the Good at Troyes. But in actual fact, Henry V did nothing more than ratify Philip's control of 'the towns of the Somme', the castellanies of Péronne, Roye and Montdidier which John the Fearless had compelled Charles VI to hand over as security for the dowry of Michelle, now Duchess of Burgundy. The duke had no place at all in the new French administration. As soon as the English king reached Paris, he replaced the captain appointed by John the Fearless, Count Philip of St Pol, the young Duke of Burgundy's cousin, by his own brother, the Duke of Clarence. One man who had always been pro-English stood by Philip and helped to make the humiliations less intolerable; this was the old Bishop of Tournai, Jean de Thoisy. He had been one of the advisers of John the Fearless, and his former pupil Philip made him Chancellor of Burgundy in place of Jean de Saulx on the 7th December 1419.

Philip the Good[9] who had taken Crépy-en-Laonnais in March 1420, continued to execute a series of exploits alongside his brother-in-law Henry V, whose marriage with Catharine of France had been solemnized at Troyes on the 2nd June. Together they took Sens on the 11th June, and Montereau on the 23rd. John the Fearless's body having been exhumed immediately after the latter victory, the funeral of the late duke was held at Champmol on the 12th July with due pomp and ceremony, in the presence of his widow clad in deep mourning. In the meantime, Melun was laid siege to on July 7th. The Lord of Barbazon, an ardent supporter of the Dauphin, put up a brave but unavailing defence. Melun was starved into submission on the 17th November. And on the 1st December Henry V and Philip, along with Charles VI, made their entry into Paris.

Charles VI having been reinstated in his capital, the first task was to seek redress for the Montereau crime. An edifying ceremony took place on the 23rd December 1420, in a city where, now that the excitement caused by the official return of the Court had died down, the inhabitants were facing cold and famine at the start of an exceptionally icy Christmas-tide.

A 'bed of justice' was held at the *Cour de Parlement*. The circumstances were exceptional in that two kings occupied the throne; Charles VI and Henry V, the son-in-law on the right of the father-in-law. At their feet sat the Chancellor of France, Jean le Clerc, and the first President, Philippe de Morvilliers. Opposite them, the Duke of Burgundy was on a level with the Dukes of Clarence and Bedford, brothers of the King of England. Also present were the Chancellor de Thoisy, the Bishops of Amiens, Thérouanne, and Beauvais; lastly John of Luxemburg, the skilled and reckless Burgundian captain, completed the impressive assembly of noble lords. John of Luxemburg, a dashing swordsman, better endowed with ancestors than scruples, was one day to betray Joan of Arc, and the Bishop of Beauvais was none other than Pierre Cauchon, an ambitious prelate who was to acquire notoriety as the man who sentenced Joan of Arc to the stake.

At this point, we instinctively pause to reflect on the mysterious dynamics of history. The people present at this ostentatious display were blind to coming events, and unaware of the obvious and logical link between these various crimes each one of which led inevitably to the next: 1407, 1416, 1419, and finally 1431.

De Thoisy's future successor as Chancellor of Burgundy, Nicholas Rolin, was the duke's lawyer. In the duke's name he formally accused the perpetrators of 'the traitorous homicide'. He demanded that they should receive severe punishment, that they should make striking reparations, and that, as an act of expiation, they should endow various religious institutions which he enumerated at great length.

The ceremony was, fundamentally, a purely political operation.[10] The legal sanctions promised by the Chancellor of France were never to be put into operation. The making of such empty promises merely illustrated the hollowness of the spectacular ceremony, reminiscent of that organized by the Orleans children after the first crime. These pompous, theatrical displays concealed outrages of a different kind and of greater significance which were, at that very moment, jeopardizing the future of France.[11]

Now, more than ever, Henry V was in the ascendant. He was supported by Philip, who was entirely devoted to the English cause. A decree issued by the *Parlement* banished the Dauphin and declared him unfit to succeed to the throne. The Dauphin held his own, with the result that a 'free' France came into being in opposition to 'occupied' France.[12] The Anglo-Burgundian alliance gave rise to a wave of patriotic fervour, and the former Armagnac party, which had now become the Dauphin's party, tended from then on to become a frankly national party; in this way intangible factors were working against the criminal pact of 1417 and the outrageous Treaty of Troyes.

From now on there was a confused struggle, in which the English, the Burgundians or the Dauphin's party scored successes in turn. Although indecisive at first, and indeed for many long years, it was to end, thanks to Joan of Arc, and also to the enthusiastic support of the people, in a victory which became obvious long before it was actually achieved. This victory ensured the triumph of legitimacy.

As long as Henry, the great captain, was alive, the English cause continued to prosper. The Duke of Burgundy, the victor's ally, fought for him, heedless of what the ultimate outcome of the alliance would be; on the 30th May 1421 he won the victory of Mons-en-Vimeu, occupied St Riquier, and forced Jacques d'Harcourt, who was fighting against him, to retreat to Crotoy and Noyelles.

But at this juncture an advance-guard of the Dauphin's forces threatened Burgundy in the region of Charolais and Mâcon. As in previous times of crisis during her husband's reign, the dowager duchess stood firm and called for help. Philip thereupon went back to Dijon, entering the city on the 19th February 1422. He was given an enthusiastic reception; he ratified the town's privileges, and received the oaths of allegiance which had not yet been sworn. But he met with significant opposition when he tried to administer the oaths in the name of King Henry. It was important to establish to which authority allegiance was being paid and Philip was insisting that the terms of the Treaty of Troyes be adhered to. The mayor and the deputy-mayors of Dijon were loath to accept this. They tried to avoid the difficulty by an equivocation. They said they would recognize as king, without mentioning any names, the man considered as king by the Duke of Burgundy. The English—for English envoys were present—rejected this solution. 'It was finally decided to swear allegiance to the King of England at the duke's palace, and to indicate on the official record the fact that this had been done on the express instruction of Philip the Good.'[13]

There was obviously a limit to pro-English fervour, even in the duke's own capital. Philip the Good himself was less of an Anglophile than his chancellor, Jean de Thoisy. All his life he regretted not having fought for France at Agincourt, like his uncles Anthony and Philip.[14] A hint of a complete change of front, as yet quite remote, is revealed in these mental reservations, the extent and the future significance of which were never suspected by the English envoys who received the oath of allegiance from the people of Dijon in their master's name.

Moreover, the English could not fail to be reassured by the ardour with which the Duke of Burgundy resisted the Dauphin's offensive. Philip the Good, plunged once more into mourning by the death of his wife, Michelle of France, at Ghent on the 8th July 1422, nevertheless assembled his forces at Avallon and appealed for support from the Duke of Bedford, as well as from the Dukes of Savoy and Lorraine. He also summoned John of Luxemburg with his soldiers from Picardy. Reinforced by Bedford's contingents, the assembled army of which Philip took personal command at Vézelay on the 6th August, marched on Cosne which was being beseiged by the Dauphin. Seeing an army of twelve thousand men approaching, the Dauphin raised the siege, and beat a retreat. This was what Philip the Good wanted. Luxemburg's advance-guard penetrated as far as La Charité, but the main body of the Anglo-Burgundian forces turned back to Troyes. From there, Bedford hurried on to Paris, having been informed that the health of his brother, Henry V, was giving cause for alarm. Henry in fact died at Vincennes on the 31st August, at the age of thirty-four.

What was to become of the idea of the *dual monarchy* now that the man who had evolved it was dead? And what part was the Duke of Burgundy to play in the new phase now opening?

A regency had to be set up to govern for the two kings, one of whom, Henry VI, was a child, and the other, Charles VI, a madman. Philip the Good, however, refused the offer made him by Bedford, and Bedford took over the function of regent himself. He retained it when, on the death of Charles VI at the age of fifty-three on the 21st October 1422, Catharine's son, who had already been recognized as King of England, was proclaimed King of France. Monstrelet gives us a sober account of the official proclamation of the young Lancastrian in Paris over the tomb of his maternal grandfather:

> And then the king's ushers, who were present, broke their little rods and threw them into the grave, and then stood with their maces lowered and upside down; and then Berry, the king-at-arms, accompanied by several heralds and poursuivants, stood over the grave and cried: may God have pity and mercy on the soul of the most high and most excellent Prince Charles, King of France, the sixth to bear this name, our natural and sovereign lord: yet again, the aforementioned king-at-arms proclaimed: God grant long life to Henry, King of France and England, our sovereign lord.

Thus the *dual monarchy* was in operation for the first time. At this very critical junction, the royal power was represented on both sides of the Channel by one and the same prince.

At Charles VI's funeral, the procession was led by Bedford. Philip the Good remained obstinately in Arras and did not appear. He was not at all keen to see a 'regent' take precedence over him. He made so little secret of his rancour that the Cardinal-legate, the Duke of Bar, and the first Duke of Savoy, Amadeus VIII tried to bring about a reconciliation at Bourg-en-Bresse between Philip and the Dauphin Charles. Although the attempt was rather premature, the fact that contact had been established was a hopeful sign. Time and time again talks were to be resumed and then broken off, but they were never completely abandoned.

Charles proclaimed himself king at Mehun-sur-Yèvre on the 30th October and from then on, in the words of Pierre de Fénin, the chronicler, 'there were two kings in France' on the one hand 'the King in Bourges' and on the other 'the King in Paris'. Two authorities, two nations, claimed allegiance. And both were in the grip of an unprecedented physical and moral crisis.

An account of the wretchedness and moral confusion of the time does not come within the scope of the present work.[15] It is, however, important to keep the lamentable situation in mind, in order to understand how easy it was for the people living in those dark times to feel lost and bewildered.

The Duke of Burgundy, although he fully realized that he had obligations towards his allies, the English, was embarrassed by the false position in which he had placed himself. He had always felt uneasy about it and always would.

However, the onslaught launched by the Dauphin's forces on the Burgundian borders, after the talks at Bourg had broken down, roused him from the apathetic attitude he was only too ready to adopt. According to Chastellain, he was 'as honest as the day and as true as steel' and he was consequently torn between his resentment against the child-king, and his pledged word. As in the previous year, the month of July 1423 saw the Anglo-Burgundian forces once more in the field. The Marshal of Burgundy, Jean de Toulongeon, joined battle with fifteen thousand French and Milanese soldiers who were trying to reach Champagne; he beat them and relieved Cravant which Claude de Chastellux, its governor, had only managed to defend with a struggle. Then the marshal himself was captured on the 21st August at La Bussière by the Dauphin's men, commanded by Hubert de la Grolée. Antoine de Toulongeon, the marshal's brother, would have had great difficulty in holding the Mâcon frontiers, if the English, under Suffolk, had not most opportunely captured the castles of Germolles, Vinzelles and Leyre. From then on, Philip was only too glad to make the necessity of defending his own estates an excuse for not being involved, or for being involved as little as possible, in the affairs of his acknowledged lord, King Henry, whose policy was directed solely by Bedford. On Christmas Eve, one of the leaders of the mercenary bands, Perrinet Gressart, succeeded in closing the Burgundian frontier to Berry by taking La Charité-sur-Loire, an important strategic stronghold which the same captain was one day to defend against Joan of Arc.

Unable to decide what line he should take between Bedford and Charles VII, Philip inclined more and more towards the pursuit of a purely Burgundian policy. It was not surprising that henceforth he should regard such a policy not as a side-issue but as his main task.

Philip the Good's French policy may have been shifting and hesitant —first as a result of the 1417 pact and then of the still more disastrous Treaty of Troyes—but his policy in the Low Countries was clear-cut and successful. As H. Pirenne has so well said: 'the Montereau murder marked the opening of a new phase. From then on the Burgundian dynasty sought to accomplish its purpose, not in France, or by means of France, but outside France and against France'. This development was up to a point involuntary and unconscious. Philip felt himself to be French, and he was anxious to remain French; yet he pursued what was essentially a Lotharingian policy.

All that the duke gained from his intermittent relationship with Bedford, who realized full well that he needed Philip's help, was the ratification of his control over the towns of the Somme, which had been handed over as security for Michelle's dowry, and which he still retained even after her death. The duke's second marriage with his aunt Bonne of Artois[16] in no way changed the situation, nor did his third marriage, after the death of Bonne, who was his duchess for a very short time, with Isabella of Portugal.

As early as 1420, Alsace had claimed Philip's attention. His aunt Catharine, the daughter of Philip the Bold, who had married her to Leopold of Austria, had become a widow, and was thinking of getting married again to an Alsatian noble, Maximin de Ribeaupierre. The duke opposed the marriage. He not only forced Catharine to abandon her matrimonial plans, he made her agree to a donation *inter vivos* whereby her entire patrimony, with all that it would include on her death, would go to the head of the House of Burgundy. In 1421, an equally profitable transaction secured for the duke the bare ownership of the County of Namur, to which he was to succeed on the death of John III of Namur in 1429.

In the Low Countries, Philip had inherited the complex Brabantine question, but he was quite familiar with it, because, as has already been said, it had been his special care during his father's lifetime.

The marriage between John IV of Brabant and Jacqueline of Hainault had been, in Pirenne's well-founded and authoritative opinion, 'the most outstanding diplomatic success' scored by John the Fearless. Nevertheless, they were as ill-assorted a couple as one could imagine. Curiously unlike other members of the House of Burgundy, John IV was a puny, melancholy man. Such a weakling could hardly appeal, as Chastellain has said, to a woman who was 'extremely pretty, extremely gay, vigorous, and totally unsuited to a feeble husband'.[17] Passionate, sensual, and emotional, Jacqueline was highly dissatisfied with her husband, and their temperamental incompatibility was complete.

To make matters worse, they did not hold the same views. John IV, who was ready to agree to anything, provided he was left in peace, made one concession after the other to his vassal, the ex-bishop John of Bavaria, now the husband of Elizabeth of Goerlitz. In 1420 he even entrusted him with the administration of Holland. Jacqueline's indignation knew no bounds. Within Brabant the duke, who was notoriously incompetent, allowed the assemblies of the Brabantine estates a free hand. These assemblies, reacting against the favourites by whom the prince, in their view, was too easily guided, not only assumed complete administrative control but also bestowed the title of regent on Philip, the Count of St Pol, the late Duke Anthony's second son, and John IV's younger brother. Jacqueline decided in disgust to leave her despised and incompetent husband. She betook herself to her own county of Hainault, and from there she went on to England. With a remarkable disregard for propriety, she married Gloucester, Bedford's brother, who had been entrusted with the regency of England and who ruled more or less under orders from Bedford himself. This defiant marriage took place in the autumn of 1422 and 'shocked the people of the Low Countries who, still retaining vivid memories of the kingdom of Lotharingia, which Burgundy's triumphant policy seemed likely to restore, compared her behaviour with that of Lothair II'. This quotation from Pirenne, who took as his authority the Flemish chronicler, Edmond de Dynter, gives an accurate picture of the reaction which Countess Jacqueline's conduct provoked.

Gloucester prided himself on being able to renew Edward III's Flemish policy, but his real object was the purely selfish one of acquiring possessions of his own on the Continent. It looked as if the Plantagenets would trick the Valois of Burgundy out of Jacqueline's inheritance.

However, such a course was incompatible with Bedford's policy, which was based on the assumption that the Anglo-Burgundian alliance would continue. Realizing that the court of Burgundy had taken a definite stand against Gloucester, and anxious that Philip the Good should not be driven into Charles VII's camp, the 'regent of France' set to work to avoid the conflict towards which his brother was so light-heartedly heading. In 1423 he himself married Anne of Burgundy, a daughter of John the Fearless, and attempted to clear up the situation by diplomatic means.

Not only did Gloucester's ambitious dream meet with Burgundy's disapproval, it was also condemned by John of Bavaria who felt no less injured by Jacqueline's head-strong behaviour than did his colourless cousin, John IV.

Philip the Good had ceased to take any personal interest in John IV, whom he considered to be a broken reed. Gloucester had succeeded in getting the poor duke's marriage with the high-spirited Jacqueline annulled by the Church at Avignon; but Philip the Good, helped by Bedford, managed to persuade Rome to dissolve the marriage between the countess and Gloucester. He went even further; he came to an arrangement with the turbulent John of Bavaria, whereby John, who was childless, recognized him, Philip, as his heir. From then on, he could flaunt his new rights in answer to those put forward by Jacqueline and Gloucester. Gloucester, it is true, proved stubborn; he even attempted to use armed force. He landed at Calais in October 1424 with six thousand archers, occupied Hainault and got the inhabitants to swear allegiance to him as count. But Philip sent his most valiant captain, John of Luxemburg, to help John of Bavaria. Reinforced by the Hainault faction, which disapproved of Jacqueline's pro-English behaviour, he quickly forced Gloucester to beat a retreat and to re-embark for England.

Jacqueline, thrice married and without a husband, was not so easily daunted and she fought on, like the proud virago she was. However, she was besieged in Mons and captured by the Duke of Burgundy, who sent her to live in Ghent. Meanwhile, the death of John of Bavaria on the 6th January 1425 made operative, to the advantage of the Burgundian State, the terms arranged by the skilful diplomacy of Philip the Good. Burgundy had won the day.

Sigismund tried once more to put forward the rights of the Empire, but the threat was an empty one. Jacqueline, after escaping from Ghent, disguised as a page, tried without success to rekindle the fight in Holland. Sigismund, unable to leave Bohemia, failed to send her any effective help.

At the same time, Philip reacted with promptitude and vigour. Supported by the Bishop of Utrecht, Sweder of Tulenborg, and by the Duke of Guelders, Arnold of Egmont, who was backed by one of the major factions in Holland, the Kabiljaws (the other important party—the Hoeks—were fighting for the opposite side), the powerful duke had the satisfaction of seeing all the most important towns, Dordrecht, Leyden, Haarlem and Amsterdam, rally to his side and open their gates to soldiers from Picardy and Burgundy. The Dutch burgesses, who had made their money through trade, were anxious for a Burgundian victory since they considered it would be more likely to increase prosperity. The local nobility, which had rallied round Jacqueline, only succeeded in giving her party the appearance of a reactionary, feudal faction.

At this juncture we must mention a curious story, about which many sound historians have been misled. According to this tale, it was proposed to assassinate Philip the Good, and both Gloucester and Bedford were implicated in the sinister plot. Richemont and his brother, Duke John of Brittany, are said to have had wind of the affair and to have told the duke, being eager to seize the opportunity of bringing pressure to bear on him to abandon the English alliance and become reconciled with the Dauphin. The whole story is an invention, however, and should not be accepted as historical fact.[18]

What is certain, is that the victory achieved by the Burgundians in Holland was the result of a prolonged effort, carried out with remarkable tenacity by Philip the Good. Between 1426 and 1428, Philip hardly ever left Holland. Fighting at the head of his troops the chivalrous duke reaped all the glory of the arduous campaign. He comforted his allies, thwarted the indomitable Jacqueline's feverish counter-blows, while waging war unremittingly on land, and blockading the coast with his ships.

Gloucester, overriding official opposition in England, tried without success to come to the assistance of Jacqueline, whom he still considered as his wife. He himself managed to slip between the cruisers of the Flemish navy, but he was able to get only an insignificant army across the Channel, and so was powerless to act. Adolphe de Juliers, urged on by the Emperor Sigismund, launched an attack against Arnold of Guelders, an ally of the Burgundians. The effort was wasted; the Burgundians showed themselves to be proof against all attacks.

In January 1426 the Burgundian army inflicted a crushing defeat on the English at Brouwershaven, laid siege to Amersfoort, and beat Jacqueline's army at Wieringen.

By now Gloucester was gradually becoming estranged from his wife. He was less influenced by the bill of the 9th January 1424 annulling his marriage, than by the weary continuance of an inextricable situation and the natural fickleness of his nature. He became increasingly attached to his mistress, the scheming Eleanor Cobham, whom he finally married, to the shocked disapproval of many people.

This was the final blow for his forsaken and repudiated wife, who was driven into adding her signature to the Treaty of Delft. According to the terms of this treaty, dated the 3rd July 1428, she retained her title of countess, but she acknowledged Philip the Good's possession of her lands (Holland, Zealand, Friesland, Hainault) by recognizing his title of 'ruwaert' or regent. She handed over all her fortresses to him and promised not to contract a fourth marriage without the duke's consent.

This brought about the immediate collapse of the Hoek faction throughout Holland. Heedless of Sigismund's objurgations, all the towns, even the smallest, followed the example of the big cities and gave their allegiance to the duke as regent. The magnificent Flemish estates of the Wittelsbachs passed entirely into the hands of Burgundy.

The last impulsive act of the adventurous Jacqueline's chequered career in no way changed the situation. Its only effect was to hasten the transfer of her inheritance to Burgundy.

The incorrigible countess, in order to console herself for the loss of three husbands, decided to take yet a fourth. She fixed her choice on Franz van Borselen, the Burgundian governor whom she enticed from his duty and induced to rebel. They both had cause to rue the decision. Husband and wife were captured and Jacqueline was given the option of seeing her husband beheaded or surrendering her title of countess. She chose the second alternative.

And so, on the 12th April 1433, Philip the Good exchanged his title of 'ruwaert' for that of count. As for the ex-countess, now that she had been finally stripped of all her possessions, she dragged out her existence in obscurity at the Castle of Teylingen, near Leyden, where she was to die, heart-broken and consumptive, on the 9th October 1436.

Two years after the signing of the Treaty of Delft, Philip had acquired the Brabantine inheritance, and Burgundy was winning all along the line.

The pathetic John IV of Brabant had ended his days on the 17th April 1427. His brother, Philip, Count of St Pol, who was already regent, had naturally succeeded to the ducal throne. Like his father, Anthony, the younger brother was popular with the members of the estates and with the people. But unlike his father, he was determined, now that he had become duke, to pursue a policy of his own, even if this meant going against Burgundy. He tried to form an alliance with the House of Anjou. This, by drawing him closer to Charles VII, would inevitably have brought him into conflict with his cousin, Philip, who began taking steps to thwart or punish his betrayal. But no sooner had St Pol embarked on his new course, which was perhaps leading to freedom, but was certainly beset with hazards, than he died—on the 4th August 1430—most probably from natural causes in spite of what some people have said.

He left no heirs, which meant that Philip the Good, as the nephew of the late Duke Anthony, succeeded to the inheritance in due and proper form.

Heedless of Sigismund's protests, which were as violent and as ineffectual as ever, Philip had himself recognized by the Brabantine estates. Margaret of Bavaria, the late duke's aunt, who staked a rival claim, was brushed aside and on the 5th October, the head of the House of Burgundy made a joyful entry into Louvain. Here he founded a university which soon began to thrive.

To an already impressive list of titles, the son of John the Fearless could now add those of 'Duke of Lothair, of Brabant, and of Limburg, and Marquis of the Holy Empire'.

If we remember that he had bought Namur in 1421, was in complete control of the bishopric of Utrecht, was supporting Duke Arnold of Egmont in his struggle against his rival Adolphe de Juliers in Guelderland, had at his disposal the bishoprics of Cambrai and Tournai, and openly threatened Luxemburg: if we consider that, confident in the support of his new subjects in the recently annexed regions, he had no rival to fear, and had shaken off the suzerainty of both the King of France, against whom he was waging a successful war, and of the King of the Romans, whose claim to Brabant, Hainault, Holland, Zealand and Friesland forced him to behave in these counties like an independent prince, we shall have no difficulty in understanding how great an influence he wielded. In less than fifteen years, he had created a new State which included the most important towns and the wealthiest territories in the west.[19]

Thus the trend of ducal policy had veered to the north; the House of Burgundy's centre of interest had shifted. Its action in France was no longer, as had still been the case under the second duke, a major preoccupation, or even a constant obsession. With the third reign, the main energies of the Court of Burgundy were centred on the expansion and consolidation of the ducal State. This was done not so much by careful calculation as through the effect of a favourable series of events, and it provided the necessary corrective to the false position into which the ducal dynasty, founded by John the Good, had very nearly been driven by the pacts of 1417 and 1420.

The truth of this will appear very clearly when we trace, as we are now about to do, the relationship between Philip the Good and the two royal lines which were fighting for supremacy in France.

Incidentally, the prolongation of the quarrel between the Valois and the Lancastrians was the best means of ensuring the success of a Lotharingian policy, which aimed at establishing an independent state between France and Germany. Nothing could be more effective in helping such a policy to achieve a permanent result than the crippling uncertainty caused by the rivalry between the two French camps, a rivalry which was already of long standing and seemed likely to continue indefinitely.

Philip continued to support his ally Bedford, but at little cost to himself—one might almost say in a very niggardly way—and his limited participation in the Anglo-French war left him free to devote his main energies to affairs in Holland.

However restricted and spasmodic his support may have been, it nevertheless helped Bedford to maintain military superiority over Charles VII, and between 1422 and 1429 the *dual monarchy*, of which the 'regent' had assumed control, had more cause for satisfaction than disappointment. Less rapidly than under Henry V, the occupied zone under Henry VI continued to encroach steadily upon the free zone. The authority of the king at Bourges was dwindling, while the prestige of the king in Paris was increasing. The battle of Verneuil, fought on the 17th August 1427, added yet another disaster to the list of major French defeats in the Hundred Years' War, and was scarcely less serious than those of Crécy, Poitiers, and Agincourt.

Thanks to this victory, Philip the Good was able to carry out a campaign in Mâconnais which lasted until October, and which culminated in the truce of Polignac.

At the time when Gloucester's escapades were in full swing, Philip's temporary coolness brought about a slowing down of the Lancastrian advance; it was all the more marked since Richemont, the brother of John V of Brittany who had certain interests in Burgundian territory through his wife Margaret of Burgundy, became Charles VII's constable and directed a campaign which did considerable harm to the English cause in Maine. The ensuing reconciliation between Philip and Bedford—the reasons for which have already been mentioned—as well as the constable's jealousy of La Trémoille, Charles VII's favourite, prompted Richemont to withdraw to Brittany, where he confined his activities to local affairs.

The 'regent of France' having married Anne of Burgundy, Philip's sister, and curbed Gloucester's irresponsible behaviour in Hainault, found himself for a time in harmony with his brother-in-law.

He therefore exploited his advantage; his lieutenants Suffolk and Warwick harassed Charles VII's troops, who were everywhere in retreat; finally the King of Bourges suffered the crowning disaster of the siege of Orleans. He was on the point of giving in; he had serious doubts about his claim to the throne and the rumours about his illegitimacy sapped his resolve. There is no denying that he might have abandoned the struggle altogether, had not Joan of Arc appeared on the scene, and brought about an unprecedented miracle which suddenly deflected the wavering course of history in favour of the lawful sovereign.[20]

It would be inappropriate here to retrace the various phases of Joan of Arc's epic adventure—Orleans, Patay, the anointing at Rheims, the set-backs outside the walls of Paris and La-Charité-sur-Loire, where Perrinet Gressart, whose exploits have already been mentioned, broke the momentum of Joan's attack; then Compiègne and Rouen, imprisonment, trial and martyrdom. We can mention only those episodes which involved Burgundy and Duke Philip.

He was probably one of those who, at the time, did not believe in the divine mission of the maid of Domrémy, and like Bedford, he no doubt held Satan, rather than God, responsible for the irresistible upsurge of patriotic feeling she infused into the national party. The negotiations arranged by the wily La Trémoille between the court at Bourges and the duke's court were no more than a diversionary move. La Trémoille, jealous of Joan, merely wanted to thwart her military plans, and in this he succeeded only too well. The time was not yet ripe for a Franco-Burgundian reconciliation.

When, on that ill-fated evening of the 24th May 1430, the bastard of Wandonne accepted Joan's sword below the ramparts of Compiègne, after she had put her trust in his honour as a knight, he lost no time in handing her over to his chief, John of Luxemburg, who was in command of the Burgundian troops outside the besieged town. Luxemburg immediately notified Philip the Good who was then at Coudun, and he hastened to the spot. A meeting took place between the duke and the prisoner, but nothing of what transpired is known to history. Monstrelet, the chronicler, was present at the interview, but he declared that he had forgotten what was actually said—a failure of memory which has naturally given rise to a good deal of conjecture. It may be that the words exchanged in the presence of the chronicler were not very flattering to his master. Whatever the truth of the matter, the duke sent out wildly jubilant letters announcing the capture of the girl who had caused such consternation to Charles VII's opponents, and he took the opportunity of destroying, as far as possible, the belief that the deliverer of Orleans was divinely inspired.

The Duchess of Burgundy, too, was anxious to meet the amazing young woman who had been so much talked about. John of Luxemburg was too good a courtier not to allow her the opportunity of satisfying her curiosity.

The shady transactions which followed between Luxemburg and Philip the Good (but of which Bedford was the prime instigator) did no credit to any of the individuals who were a party to them. Joan was eventually handed over to the English for the vast sum of ten thousand golden crowns. From the castle of Beaurevoir, where she had been imprisoned by Luxemburg, she was conveyed to Rouen by way of Arras, Le Crotoy, Saint-Valéry, Eu and Dieppe.

The trial which preceded the death-sentence is too well known for the poignant episodes to need recalling. It is worth mentioning, however, that Pierre Cauchon, the president of the tribunal, was one of the any-purpose clerks who had formed part of John the Fearless's entourage. He had become Bishop of Beauvais through intrigue, political manœuvring and ducal favour, and it is well known that at the time of the Cabochian revolution he had kept company with the worst terrorists. A zealous advocate of collaboration with the English, and paid by them, he belonged to the class of men who put their personal interests before any other consideration.

Whatever Philip the Good's private feelings may have been while he was being kept informed of the trial, the sentence and the final agony of Joan, it is certain that the wave of patriotism stirred up by Joan during her lifetime and which continued after her death, made an impression on the court of Burgundy. Even the duke's own army felt the effects of it. Although Philip continued to be successful in Lorraine, where he sided with the Count of Vaudémont against his rival, René of Anjou (who was beaten at Bulgnéville and, in 1431, kept a prisoner for six months in Dijon where traces of his confinement in the 'tour de Bar' can still be seen) the Burgundian forces met with one set-back after another in the war against the French. They were defeated at Anthon on the 11th June, when the Prince of Orange made an unsuccessful attempt to attack Dauphiné and the siege of Compiègne was raised on the 24th October 1430. In vain Bedford tried to flatter the duke by granting him part of Mâconnais—a district which had unmistakable links with Burgundy—and by handing over Champagne and Brie, which formed a bridge between the strictly Burgundian estates and those in the north. In vain the English tried to hold Philip's allegiance by manœuvring him into a third marriage with Isabella of Portugal who belonged to a family with connections in London—the Lusitanian family of Avis, which was descended from the first Lancastrian, John of Gaunt.[21] The marriage ceremony was performed on the 7th January 1430. Yet, on the one hand, talks between Philip and Charles VII were always being resumed and never entirely broke down,[22] while on the other, Bedford's repeated set-backs as well as his growing military weakness and financial difficulties, left no doubt as to what was happening. The national feeling aroused by the Maid of Orleans was carrying all before it. On the 16th December 1431, the Duke of Burgundy deliberately refrained from attending King Henry VI's coronation, which Bedford had confidently hoped would annul the crowning of Charles at Rheims in 1429. Charles VII's claim to the throne, which had been affirmed by the Maid and confirmed by her death, was now openly supported by all men of good will. Paris was on tenterhooks, and the whole of France in a fever of excitement.

Philip the Good, who had inherited his father's popularity with the people of Paris, particularly the inhabitants of Les Halles, set great store by this popular support. However strongly he was drawn to his northern estates, he still remained a French prince of the blood. Both his natural feelings and his interests urged him not to allow Charles VII to enjoy all the prestige of victory. The Chancellor of Burgundy, Nicolas Rolin, who had in the past been very pro-English, was too subtle a statesman not to realize the need for a change of policy.

Everything, in fact, argued in favour of such a change. Charles VII was busy concluding an alliance with Sigismund, Frederick of Austria and the princes of the Empire. Anne of Burgundy had died on the 14th November 1432, and the relationship between Bedford and his brother-in-law which had so often been patched up through her agency, had now become extremely tenuous. Was Paris to be allowed to open her gates to Charles VI's heir, while the Duke of Burgundy remained the ally of a usurper who had been rejected by France and her capital? He ran the risk of finding himself, at some future date, in the position of a traitorous vassal left to face the wrath of his suzerain. There was a danger that Burgundy, caught between the German Empire and a fully-restored kingdom of France, might have to defend her future in catastrophic conditions.

The time had come to replace these dangerous possibilities by an agreement which could easily be turned to Burgundy's advantage—in short to break with the 1417 pact and the Treaty of Troyes.

Olivier de la Marche draws special attention to the personal feelings of the duke, whose French blood apparently 'was boiling in his stomach and around his heart'. Chastellain notices in his master a development of national consciousness, which ran parallel to the rise of patriotism in the country: 'as time went on, the more anxious he became to display his French heart'. Although feelings of kinship may have awakened echoes in the breast of the Valois prince who, as we have already said, regretted not having fought for the French at Agincourt, it can hardly be doubted that during the discussions in the ducal council chamber, Burgundian interests were the main consideration.

The duke had always refused to be invested with the Order of the Garter. The Order of the Golden Fleece was conceived and created as a counterpart to the English order, and we shall see later the splendour it bestowed on the court of Burgundy.

To all intents and purposes, the decision had been made. It was only a question of giving the denunciation of the existing pacts an appearance of being honourable. With this end in view, conferences were held at Nevers, then at Arras.

The man who acted as mediator between the courts of Burgundy and France was, on this occasion, René of Anjou, Duke of Bar. The former prisoner, who had received courteous treatment during his internment at Dijon, had now become an accomplice. Philip the Good arrived at Nevers on the 16th February 1435. He was joined by Charles VII's chancellor, Regnault de Chartres, Archbishop of Rheims, the constable, Arthur de Richemont, Marshal de la Fayette, and Christophe d'Harcourt who formed the French delegation. It was soon clear that everything was moving towards the settlement which had so often just eluded previous negotiators. People were heard to say that 'it seemed as if they had never been at war', and the moral of this was: 'foolish indeed the man who went to war on their behalf and got himself killed for them'.[23] Such comments revealed the general weariness and the universal desire for peace.

The most critical question which came up for discussion was that of the Burgundian demands in respect of the Montereau crime. It was soon realized that the problem was by no means insuperable.

At the same time a reconciliation took place between the Houses of Burgundy and Bourbon, which had been estranged by the quarrel.

In this less hostile atmosphere, the idea of reconciliation made such headway that, by the 6th February, preliminary negotiations had already begun. Finally, on the 7th, the negotiators parted company after agreeing to meet at Arras where, according to Monstrelet, 'a day of great parleying' was to take place with a view to the signing of the final treaty.

The preliminary discussions at Nevers had achieved the decisive step towards a reconciliation. In order to renounce the English alliance without breaking his oath, the duke had recourse to a stratagem. Banking on the general desire for peace throughout the country, which had found expression again and again through the agency of the Holy See, and the Fathers of the Council of Basle, Philip proposed that the Pope should act as mediator between the two dynasties contending for the throne of France. When the English refused to accept this form of arbitration the duke considered himself to be freed from his pledge.

Moreover, it was becoming increasingly evident that both the duke's subjects and the king's were longing for peace. When he passed through Paris on his way back from Nevers to Flanders, the duke could see that the capital and the university, both hostile to foreign domination, would not stand for a continuance of the antagonism between the senior peer of the realm and the lawful king, whose return to the capital was eagerly awaited. The Flemish people had similar feelings. Pressure from so many different quarters could only accelerate the change of front that had already begun.

Consequently, the proposals put forward at Nevers were carried into effect at Arras. In theory, the Congress of Arras was a general conference, the aim of which was to re-establish peace in the west. In nominating his plenipotentiaries for the Congress the pious Henry VI, with a certain naïve optimism, quoted the words of Christ: 'pacem meam do vobis, pacem meam relinquo vobis'. England had been invited to send representatives: the Pope sent the Cardinal of St Croix as his legate and the Council of Basle appointed Hugh of Lusignan, Archbishop of Nicosia, officially called the Cardinal of St Adrien, but known as the Cardinal of Cyprus; he was attended by two bishops, the Archdeacon of Metz and the Provost of Cracow. The Archbishop of York, and the Bishop of Winchester, Henry Beaufort, the king's uncle, both attended by extensive suites, led the British delegation. The French delegates were no less impressive: John V, Duke of Brittany,[24] Duke Louis III of Anjou, Duke

Charles of Orleans who had come back for the occasion from his English prison, the Duke of Alençon, the Archbishop of Rheims Regnault de Chartres, La Fayette, Mouy, Christophe d'Harcourt, and counsellor Jean Tudert; the Queen of Sicily was present; the university of Paris, the city authorities and several 'worthy towns' all sent representatives.

The Duke of Burgundy and the Duchess, Isabella of Portugal, arrived in person with all the pomp and ceremony that normally marked their movements. The Chancellor of Burgundy, Nicolas Rolin, was the main negotiator. With him were the Bishops of Cambrai, Arras and Auxerre, the Count of Ligny, the Lords of Charny, Commynes (father of the historian), Croy, Créquy, Halluin, and the Squire of Cleves.

The splendid and impressive congress opened on the afternoon of the 5th August in the Abbey of St Vaast, with an official session. Tournaments and jousts were held between the meetings. As was to be expected it proved impossible to find common ground for an understanding between the Valois and the Lancastrians. In spite of the cardinal's efforts, the talks between the French and English delegations were suspended on the 19th and broken off altogether on the 31st.

On the 1st September, the duke gave one of the magnificent banquets which were usual at the Burgundian court in honour of the English.[25] After the meal, the two English prelates had such a heated conversation with Philip the Good that beads of perspiration stood out on Beaufort's forehead.

A general peace being unattainable, the congress had to be content with establishing separate peace treaties between the various factions. The Cardinal of St Croix removed any remaining scruples the duke might have had. After the departure of the English, on the 6th September, discussions continued. The issue now was a Franco-Burgundian reconciliation. Bedford died at Rouen on the 14th, and when the news reached Arras on the evening of the 16th, it could only facilitate the agreement. The Treaty of Arras was signed on the 20th and made public on the 21st: the pact of 1417 and the Treaty of Troyes of 1420 were wiped out. The quarrel between Armagnacs and Burgundians had drawn to a close; in either camp, there were now only Frenchmen.

According to the terms of the Treaty of Arras, Charles VII categorically denied having any part in the 1419 crime and offered to make atonement for the murder of John the Fearless. He handed over to Philip, Auxerre, Auxerrois, Bar-sur-Seine, Luxeuil, the towns of the Somme, Ponthieu, and Boulogne-sur-Mer. However, for the sum of four hundred thousand *écus* the king was to be allowed to redeem the towns of the Somme, which formed a strategic line of fortresses protecting or threatening Paris according to whoever held them. Finally, according to article 26, during Charles VII's lifetime, Philip was exempted from the homage due for his French fiefs.

Both the honour and the interests of the Duke of Burgundy had been amply protected, but for Charles the conditions were certainly harsh. No price, however, was too great to pay for the tremendous advantage that the switch of alliances was to bring to the kingdom.

On the 21st September, Jean Tudert, on behalf of the French delegation, knelt down before the duke, and in accordance with the terms of the treaty, made the formal apology that was required in connection with the assassination of John the Fearless. The duke swore that he would harbour no resentment, and that he would keep the peace which had just been concluded. This was no empty gesture since it showed how cleverly Burgundian diplomacy had succeeded in giving to a complete change of policy, dictated by the logic of the situation, the appearance of an act of forgiveness and triumph.

Philip the Good notified Henry VI officially that the 'separate peace' which had just been concluded at Arras with Charles VII, did not entail war between Burgundy and England, but that, on the contrary, his intention was to continue his efforts to bring about a general peace. Events, however, did not justify this optimism, which was perhaps more feigned than real. In London, the Peace of Arras gave rise to a furious outburst of anger. Several Flemish or Picardian merchants were killed during mass demonstrations and even the duke's ambassadors very nearly lost their lives.[26] Henry VI retaliated by confiscating all the French fiefs belonging to the House of Burgundy. Gloucester became captain of Calais, and while ships were being fitted out in readiness to attack the principalities in the Low Countries, Flemish vessels were hunted down and seized at sea by the British. The latter gave moral support to the Bishop of Liége, the German princes, and the towns in Holland and sought agreement with anyone who might help them obtain revenge on their former ally.

The duke coped with this sudden flare-up, and used all the means at his disposal to inflict on the English the blow likely to be most damaging to their cause—the liberation of Paris. Reinforcements were sent to Constable Arthur de Richemont who was carrying out operations in the Ile de France, and a military leader who had long been associated with Burgundian policy, Jean de Villiers, Lord of Isle-Adam, also played a vital part in this decisive episode. Jean de Villiers and Michel Lallier, a counsellor of the *Chambre des Comptes*, instigated an insurrection among the Parisian people on the 31st April 1446 and enabled the constable to enter the town. Chastellain was hardly exaggerating when he said that Philip 'won back Paris and St Denis from the English and restored them to King Charles'. The Lord of Ternant, one of the bravest and most chivalrous captains in the Burgundian army, was appointed Provost of Paris.

The duke even considered the possibility of recapturing Calais and there is no doubt that he would have liked to annex the port and join it to his estates, since 'the Calais Staple' was the chief repository for English wool. The rise of the cloth industry in Britain had caused competition with the Low Countries, so much so that, at the request of his merchants, the duke had on the 19th June 1434, forbidden the importing of English wool.

The Calais venture soon proved to be hopeless. It was not long before the Ghent soldiers lost heart. The English fought back vigorously since they could ill afford to lose Calais. The siege, which began on the 9th June 1437, only lasted for about twenty days. Gloucester laid waste the whole area as far as Poperinghe and St Omer; the English fleet ravaged the banks of the Zwin; in November the siege of Crotoy ended with another set-back for Burgundy. Among the duke's own captains there was a good deal of opposition. The Count of Ligny would not agree to fight the English, and the Dutch towns entered into negotiations with them, in defiance of the duke's orders.

Even in Flanders, the duke's authority was undermined as a result of the break with the English. After the return of the militia troops to Bruges and Ghent, the towns seethed with discontent. Bruges demanded the restoration of the authority she had exercised in the past over Sluys. This dispute, which arose in August 1436, and which was only temporarily solved by means of concessions, recurred in 1437, and feelings ran so high that on the 21st May the duke was attacked when he tried to enter the town. Some members of his entourage were killed, among them Marshal Isle-Adam.

English trade, however, suffered as much as that of Holland or Belgium through the existence of this resentful hostility, which could not be allowed to last. Isabella of Portugal, charming and shrewd, if not beautiful, took it upon herself to start the necessary negotiations and bring them to a successful conclusion. It was decided that meetings would be held at Gravelines. The duke took up residence in St Omer, nearby. Henry Beaufort, Cardinal of England, led the British delegation.

Meanwhile, the situation in Flanders was improving. As in the days of Louis of Male, dissension among the Flemish towns played into the hands of the feudal power. Bruges found itself isolated and was forced to submit on the 4th March 1438.

Sigismund, who had decided to try and thwart the plans of Philip the Good now that the latter was in difficulties, fared no better than any other of the duke's opponents. He tried to make use of the Landgrave of Hesse, Louis, who, calling himself a descendant of the former dukes of Brabant, invaded Limburg with a large body of men in September 1437. At this time the *Ecorcheurs*, the worthy successors of the 'Great Companies' of Charles V's time, were laying waste Burgundian territory from Mâconnais to Picardy, and from Auxerrois to Hainault.

Fortunately for the duke, the Limburg peasants vigorously resisted the invader; they forced his army back as far as the ramparts of Aix-la-Chapelle. Then, Sigismund's death on the 9th December 1437 removed the threat from the east, which had for a time caused great anxiety at the Court of Burgundy.

The Anglo-Burgundian talks could now be pursued in a more amicable atmosphere, and with the possibility of being carried through to a successful conclusion.

Three items were on the agenda at Gravelines: the resumption of trade between the two courts, the establishment of peace between England and France, an issue which had been left undecided at Arras, and the suspension of hostilities between England and Burgundy.

Thanks to the signing of a truce which applied to Boulonnais and Artois, a partial solution to the third question was soon found. On the 29th September 1439 a treaty fixed conditions for the exchange of goods over a period of three years, and guaranteed safe trading between England on the one hand, and Flanders, Brabant and Malines on the other: it was prolonged for a further five years on the 12th January 1440 and in the following February it was extended to include the duke's French fiefs; it was in fact to be renewed at intervals, and with beneficial results, until the 1st November 1464. However, the importation of English cloth into the Low Countries continued to be forbidden and this prohibition was explicitly renewed by a writ published on the 1st December 1439.

Only on one question did the negotiators fail to reach a decision, and their failure was only to be expected. They were unable to bring about a reconciliation between the Valois and Lancastrian dynasties which were competing for the French throne. However, the negotiations went on and produced some partial results. A truce, the duration of which was not specified, was concluded on the 23rd April 1443, and covered all the possessions of the English king and of the duke: the truces arranged at Tours on the 29th May 1444 between France and England did in fact suspend hostilities in the Hundred Years' War for five years; finally a commercial treaty, signed on the 10th April 1445, settled economic relations between England and Holland.

In addition to the peace talks, Isabella of Portugal had been conducting negotiations with a view to finally securing the release of Duke Charles of Orleans. The most illustrious of the prisoners taken at Agincourt was granted his freedom on payment of a ransom. He married Mary of Cleves, Philip the Good's niece and the marriage, which was welcomed at the Burgundian court, turned the son of John the Fearless's victim into a friend of John's son. Mary of Cleves was to be the mother of Louis XII.

After the reign of Sigismund and his son-in-law Albert II of Austria, the title of emperor fell to a cousin of Albert's, Frederick of Styria, who became Emperor Frederick II of Hapsburg.

With this Frederick, a forbear of Charles V, Philip began extraordinary negotiations which very nearly led him to exchange his ducal crown for a royal diadem.

Frederick's accession to the imperial throne on the 2nd February 1440 was singularly favourable to Philip the Good's plans with regard to the imperial fiefs. Even in 1439 when the See of Cambrai had fallen vacant, he had succeeded in replacing the bishop, Jean de Gavere, who had just died, by John of Burgundy, one of his illegitimate sons, in spite of the fact that the young man was still a student at Louvain university. In 1441, the Count of Estampes, the duke's son-in-law, was made warden and counsellor of the town of Cambrai. The title of Castellan of Cambrai, which Philip had received as part of Jacqueline of Bavaria's inheritance, now became fully operative.

The duke lost no time in taking possession of Luxemburg, which he had coveted for a long time. The principality of Luxemburg, with its dependencies and the protectorate of Alsace, had been pledged to Elizabeth of Goerlitz, who had been married first to Anthony of Brabant, and then to John of Bavaria. Since Elizabeth had no children, Philip the Good could expect to inherit from her. By the act of the 14th March 1427 he had become the acknowledged heir to her Brabantine estates. However, at the insistence of his cousin, Philip of St Pol, he had considered it advisable to waive his claim in Philip's favour by the Treaty of Lierre, on the 3rd September 1427; but Philip of St Pol's death, which as we have seen occurred in 1430, had reversed the situation, and Brabant had become once more the possession of the Duke of Burgundy.

Matters were more complicated as regards Elizabeth's leasehold estates.

Being a very extravagant woman, always in debt, Elizabeth had promised to sell her rights to the duke in 1435; but having subsequently quarrelled with him, she sold them instead to the Archbishop of Trier, on the 1st May 1441. Philip cleverly succeeded in becoming reconciled with his aunt, and in getting her to acknowledge him as her general legatee by an act passed at Hesdin on the 10th January 1442.

However, the leasing of the estates, the freehold of which Elizabeth did not possess, meant that the rights still belonged to the real owner of the seigneury, who was—after Sigismund, his daughter Elizabeth and his son-in-law Albert II—Albert's daughter Anne, who was married to William of Saxony, the brother of the Elector of Saxony, Frederick II.

It took a war to disentangle this complicated situation. In August 1443, Simon de Lalaing was placed at the head of a Burgundian army whose entry into Luxemburg had been arranged in an interview at Besançon, between Philip the Good and Frederick III. Simon de Lalaing met with resistance at Diedenhofen, so the duke arrived in person to direct operations. He took several towns, including Arlon, but Luxemburg stood firm. At one moment, the chivalrous Duke of Burgundy had the idea of asking William of Saxony to settle their dispute in single combat. This offer was not accepted, and the two armies resumed their advance. Finally, during the night of the 21st–22nd November 1443, a surprise attack delivered Luxemburg into the hands of the Burgundians. The Duke and Duchess of Burgundy made their official entry into the city on the 22nd, accompanied by Elizabeth of Goerlitz. The garrison of Saxon troops who had barricaded themselves in the castle surrendered on the 11th December. Diedenhofen still held out. William of Saxony realized that the time had come for him to open negotiations. He agreed to hand everything over for the sum of one hundred and twenty thousand Hungarian florins. Admittedly, there was a stipulation that Ladislas of Hungary, Anne's brother, could buy the territories back again, but as this operation could only take place after the death of Elizabeth of Goerlitz, and as it involved refunding all monies paid by Philip the Good, either to her or to William of Saxony, there was very little fear of the magnificent estates slipping out of Burgundy's grasp.

This territorial aggrandizement, splendid though it was, did not represent the limits of Burgundian expansion in the Low Countries. The duke intervened between Utrecht and Guelders. He took part in the quarrels of his brother-in-law, the Duke of Cleves, and the Archbishop of Cologne. All the local princes came directly or indirectly into Burgundy's sphere of influence, and it was even proposed to marry the duke's heir, Charles, Count of Charolais—whose first wife, Catherine of France, had died—to Elizabeth of Austria, Ladislas of Hungary's sister.

It was during the negotiations connected with this last proposal that Frederick III's chancellor, Gaspard Schlick, made a highly significant suggestion to the third Valois duke. He offered him the glittering prospect of a royal crown. If it pleased the duke, he said, 'to have a crown, and to be king of any one of these counties, such as Friesland which in olden days had been a kingdom, or Brabant which was the oldest and finest duchy in all Christendom, and which had given birth to the most notable Christian princes, he had every hope of bringing this about'. Naturally the transaction would have involved considerable disbursements in favour of Frederick and, to some extent, of his honest broker, Schlick.

It has often been assumed that Schlick's offer was made in response to more or less open hints from the Burgundian court. The possibility can be neither confirmed nor denied. But whether he raised the matter first or not, the duke was obviously far from indifferent to it, and he gave it careful consideration. He concluded, however, that Schlick's offer was not sufficiently tempting. Burgundy's territorial expansion aimed at the restoration of Lotharingia. A kingdom of Friesland or Brabant would be far from equivalent to such an ambition. Philip wanted the kingdom to comprise all his imperial domains. He also wanted to have suzerainty over all the secular principalities of Lower Germany, from Lorraine, to Guelders and the county of La Marck. In short, if the great duke were to become king, he would insist on having part of the Reich. 'Philip's ambitions extended beyond the confines of France, in fact from the Vosges to the mouth of the Weser, from the Scheldt to beyond the Rhine, into the very heart of Westphalia.'[27] The Chancellery of

Burgundy was not afraid to hark back to Lothair. The idea obviously was to re-establish an independent monarchy between France and Germany as had been done by the Treaty of Verdun. Sooner or later, the dukedom of Burgundy along with its dependencies would have been incorporated into this newly-formed state.

The episode clearly shows what the true intentions of the great dukes were. If similar independence were ever to be granted to the French fiefs, or secured by force, the powerful State, which had so far been but a dream of the future, would become a substantial reality. In a later chapter, we shall estimate the possible existence and extent of such a State.

Frederick III, however, was quick to show his disapproval of the foundation of such a dangerous State. And had he himself been weak enough to agree to it, the whole Empire would have been against him. He refused to commit himself to more than the creation of a Kingdom of Brabant with, at the most, the addition of the imperial fiefs already held by the duke. And—a no less important restriction—he made it clear that Elizabeth of Austria's dowry would not include William of Saxony's and Ladislas of Hungary's rights in respect of Luxemburg.

Negotiations slowed down and finally ceased altogether. Philip was content to wield real power, without the addition of a crown or diadem; he was in fact as powerful as any king.

Frederick III, then, successfully avoided having to place a crown on Philip's head, but he was unable to prevent him annexing Luxemburg. Ladislas died at the age of seventeen on the 23rd November 1457. Charles VII, using as an argument the fact that he had acquired certain rights in Luxemburg and that the territory might be a source of disagreement, placed it under his protection, but Louis XI gave up all claim to it in 1462, thus allowing his uncle Philip the Good and the House of Burgundy to win the day.

We have seen that Bruges had been brought to heel as early as 1438. Twelve years later the same fate befell Ghent.

Ghent had refrained from giving Bruges support, partly through fear, partly through jealousy.

In 1451, therefore, Philip the Good decided to subject the people of Ghent to the same treatment as the people of Bruges. His plan was to institute State control. The Ghent Staple was declared 'part of the public weal', which meant that the warehouses were to be, as elsewhere, under the control of the Council of Flanders, the official organ of the whole country, and not the privileged possession of the local burgesses. Already in previous years, there had been serious brushes between the municipal authorities and the duke's administrators. In short, there was a clash between the desire for local independence and the tendency towards unification under a strong central authority. Finally, an insurrection broke out. As Pirenne has explained so well, the rebellion of the towns was no longer linked to a nation-wide movement, it was merely a last attempt to uphold outworn privileges. It was the duke who represented the interests of the country as a whole, and therein lay his strength.[28]

Flanders, as a whole, made no move, but when Ghent broke out in revolt, the duke took up the challenge.

We have already referred to the picturesque description by Olivier de la Marche, who was fond of depicting knights in battle, of the way the 'worthy duke' fought against his rebellious subjects. Victory crowned the efforts of the valiant duke. On the 23rd July 1453, the Ghent militia was cut to pieces at the battle of Gavere. The duke's horse was wounded under him. The Burgundian knights were in their element. As Olivier de la Marche has said, 'the new, young knights certainly enjoyed happy hunting'. The memorialist was right to call it a man-hunt. The light-hearted frolic ended with the pitiful spectacle of two thousand burgesses clad only in their shirts kneeling before the victor on the 30th July. They humbly asked for mercy 'in the French language'. Philip gloated over the humiliation of the proud villeins who had defied him, then made his official entry into the conquered city with a pomp and splendour that Olivier de la Marche describes: 'the duke was in full armour and mounted on the horse which had been wounded by the people of Ghent and which still had its wounds stuffed with tow in several places'. The horse was clearly intended to share its master's satisfaction at having won the day.

The independence of Ghent had been crushed. The city of the Arteveldes had fallen in the same way as Bruges. The senior members of the trade guilds were debarred from having any say in the election of the masters. The magistracy was reorganized on less liberal lines. Furthermore, the town had to pay three hundred and fifty gold *ridders* and, as a token of humility, had to block up one of its gates.

One point, however, should be made clear. Only the proud and tyrannical aristocracy of manufacturers suffered as a result of these measures. When the duke returned to Ghent in 1437, the masses proved how slender their link with the 1451–1453 ringleaders had been: they 'kissed the ground where he walked', wrote Georges Chastellain, 'and everywhere bonfires and festivities' were organized.

Liége had been reduced to obedience before Ghent and Bruges, in the days of John the Fearless, but further disturbances marked the reign of Philip the Good. John of Heinsberg, who had succeeded John of Bavaria as bishop, had tried, unlike his predecessor, to win the approval of his subjects. The 'regiment' which he granted them on the 16th July 1424 established a fairly satisfactory balance between the demands of the artisans and the claims of the wealthy burgesses. As a result, Liége prospered and there was competition with the Flemish towns, her economic rivals. This competition was anything but friendly and feelings often ran high.

For example, Bouvignes, situated in the county of Namur, and the neighbouring town of Dinant, which lay inside the principality, both highly important centres for the manufacture of copper and brass utensils, were at daggers drawn and kept each other in a constant state of alarm.

During the period of Burgundy's alliance with England, the French court took a deliberate pleasure in inciting Liége to rebel against the duke, and the unruliness of the population of the principality helped to make such tactics easy.

On the 10th June 1430, the Archbishop of Heinsberg, egged on by his subjects, openly defied the duke, and the people of Liége set fire to Bouvignes.

Philip of St Pol, on whose help they had counted, ordered the attacking force to lay down their arms. The bewildered archbishop was forced into accepting, on the 15th September 1431, a peace-treaty according to which he was to pay a huge fine of a hundred thousand 'nobles', to be supplied obviously by the burgesses, and to demolish his tower at Montorgueil.

The 1424 'regiment' had completely left out the 'mechanicals' or workers. The recent discovery and mining of coal—an economic event we shall have to return to later and the first major phase of which occurred in Philip's reign—brought the mine-workers into the limelight. They began to protest about being debarred from any part in communal affairs. They had the enthusiastic support of the locksmiths, the apprentices, and the members of the trade guilds who were likewise without electoral rights. At first, the protests made little impression and gave no cause for alarm, until certain powerful citizens realized that there was a force here waiting to be used. In 1432 some wealthy coal-owners, the Datins, tried their hand as mob-leaders, and instigated electoral riots. The workers fought in the streets, held up the normal voting procedures, and then organized their own popular elections. The revolutionary commune thus formed was crushed by the burgesses on the 16th January 1433. But the warm reception which Philip gave to the Datins who took refuge at his court, suggested that he may have had a hand in the affair or at least have been in sympathy with the rebels.

But this was just a beginning. The duke watched Liége closely and waited for a suitable opportunity; his patience was not easily exhausted, but when roused he was quick to act.

Several years went by, and other matters claimed the duke's attention. Hostility towards the burgesses of Liége persisted, and the Datins were not forgotten. The Ghent insurrection gave rise to noisy demonstrations which might have turned into a revolution if, in 1452, the Burgundian knights had lost the battle of Gavere. The messengers who brought the news of this disaster suffered by the democratic cause were very nearly hurled into the Meuse.

In the circumstances, the suppression of Ghent's independence was likely to have a logical sequel at Liége.

In 1452, the duke directed his policy to this end. He first aimed at getting his nephew, Louis of Bourbon, admitted to the Chapter of St Lambert. The officials who arrived to negotiate his admission were driven off by the crowd. Even the canons, who complained that they had to pay taxes on their property in Brabant, openly opposed his candidature.

The Duke of Burgundy could hardly accept such an open rebuff. Archbishop Heinsberg, who was not pugnacious by nature, and who felt that a difficult period lay ahead, preferred to yield to pressure and resign his see.

Philip the Good had already seized the bishoprics of Cambrai and Thérouanne: he had given them to two of his bastard sons, John (1440) and David (1451). The diocese of Tournai, formerly held by Jean de Thoisy, was now administered by Jean Chevrot, who, like his predecessor, was to complete his career by becoming leader of the ducal council. When the see of Utrecht fell vaçant on the death of Rodolphe de Diepholt, the Pope exercised his authority and translated David, Bishop of Thérouanne, to Utrecht. The duke could hardly be expected to resist the temptation of having these tactics repeated in the case of Liége. A bull announcing the appointment of Louis of Bourbon as prince-bishop was obtained in Rome.

So the man whom the canons had refused to accept as a colleague, became their superior, and started on an exceptionally stormy episcopate. It was to hold formidable complications in store for Charles the Bold, Philip the Good's successor. The main point was that, through Louis of Bourbon, the court of Burgundy succeeded nevertheless in maintaining a wary and strict control over the enclave of Liége just as it had done in the past through John of Bavaria and by the use of similar tactics.

If the Low Countries claimed Philip the Good's almost exclusive attention after the Treaty of Arras, it was because the treaty offered the duke no further opportunities for intervention in French affairs. Charles VII was most careful not to allow his too powerful vassal, before whom he had been obliged to eat humble pie, to take a leading part in the policy of the kingdom. Moreover, the king and the duke were too unlike in temperament and were separated by too many bitter memories. In 1441, Burgundian envoys noticed and remarked on the fact that the king's counsellors 'were not at all well-disposed towards the Duke of Burgundy', a curious and highly significant remark. The two cousins never met again after the Treaty of Arras, and Philip the Good did not renew his contact with the Parisian population until after Charles VII's death.

In the circumstances, the official demonstrations, which from time to time seemed to indicate friendly relations between the Valois of Burgundy and the Valois of France, cannot be taken at their face value. There was irony rather than a genuine feeling of friendship in the letter Philip sent to the king after his victory at Gavere: '. . . which things I bring to your notice', he wrote to him, 'because I know for certain that you will be overjoyed at the afore-mentioned news'.

Charles VII for his part did his best to avoid fulfilling the clauses of the Treaty of Arras. He ratified the 1435 treaty only 'because he thought that our lord of Burgundy would be satisfied with far less than had been granted to him'. The clause which stipulated that the supposed assassins of John the Fearless should be tracked down was never enforced, and the ecclesiastical institutions which Charles was supposed to set up as a gesture of atonement remained a dead letter. The levying of taxes, the exercise of seigneurage, the right to notify appeals to the Paris *Parlement*, were all perpetual sources of friction. The duke had reintroduced the custom of the former dukes of Brabant of using the formula 'by the grace of God'. In order to mollify the French court, which was offended by this practice, the duke had to laboriously explain that the formula only applied to the seignieuries which lay outside French jurisdiction.

A marriage between the Count of Charolais, Charles, the heir to the ducal throne of Burgundy, and Catherine, one of Charles VII's daughters, had been arranged in 1438: but the princess died in 1440, while still very young, and the union did not produce the results that might have been expected of it.

At the same time, with regard to the feudal coalitions which were repeatedly formed against Charles VII, Philip the Good maintained a rather ambiguous attitude, and Charles's policy in the east was hindered rather than helped. Finally, when the breaking of the Tours truces of 1444 unleashed the final campaigns of the Hundred Years' War under Charles VII—Normandy was recaptured in 1450, and Guienne during the year 1452–1453—Burgundy, using her own separate truce as an argument, maintained an official policy of neutrality, and confined herself to allowing her subjects to enlist in the king's service if they desired to do so.

The neutrality thus adopted by a French fief, as though the exemption from homage granted at Arras also relieved it of its obligation to fight in the king's service, could be seen as the first sign of a movement towards independence; of a break-away which was in contradiction with the duke's insistence that he was, and intended to remain, a French prince of the blood.

Final proof of the complete lack of cordiality in the relations between Charles VII and Philip the Good is provided, as we shall see presently, by certain aspects of the estrangement between the Dauphin Louis, the future Louis XI, and his father.

There is an oft-quoted remark that Philip is supposed to have made to envoys sent him by Charles VII. When they argued that 'although he might be lord of all his fiefs, yet he was not king', he is said to have retorted that 'he wanted all those present to hear from his own lips, that he could have been king, had he so wished'.

The great duke, who had refused one royal crown, because he considered it was not grand enough for him, was obsessed by another dream of glory; he wanted to lead the knights of Christendom in an eastern crusade against the Turk. His longing to avenge the defeat of Nicopolis was absolutely sincere, and the various attempts he made during his reign to organize a crusade must be taken quite seriously.

There is no doubt that as a child he had been greatly impressed by the glorious defeat and imprisonment of John the Fearless. Force of circumstances alone prevented him from carrying out the retaliatory campaign he longed to embark upon. Evidence of this pious endeavour marked every phase of Philip's eventful career.

For instance, he sent one of his squires, the southerner Bertrandon de la Broquère[29] on a mission to Jerusalem; he was represented by a delegation at the Council of Ferrara which discussed the possibilities of a union between the Eastern and Western Churches; he carefully worked out what his policy should be towards the Byzantine Emperor, John Paleologus; he had ships built at Nice, through the agency of the Duke of Savoy, and he hired others at Venice, some being placed under the command of Waleran de Wavrin, others under Geoffroi de Thoisy; this fleet beat off an attack launched by the Egyptians against Rhodes, and Wavrin sailed up the Danube in order to help the Hungarians with whom he joined forces at Nicopolis in 1445.

Philip had at one time the idea of securing possession of Genoa, so that he could turn it into a base from which Burgundy would launch future crusades in the east. This particular plan had no hope of success. But as the threat to Constantinople was becoming more acute, in 1451 the meeting of the Chapter of the Golden Fleece was made the occasion for a vigorous oration, delivered by the Chancellor of the Order, Jean Germain, Bishop of Chalon, in favour of the future crusade. Jean Germain was thereupon sent off to Charles VII to try and devise a plan of co-operation, which, however, the king supported only very half-heartedly.

It was while the Ghent insurrection was claiming the duke's exclusive attention that Constantinople, not having been relieved in time, fell. It is impossible to overestimate the impact made on the western world by the Turkish triumph of 1453 and the blasphemous transformation of Byzantium into Istambul. The shock of this catastrophe made the duke get in touch once more with the king. Having completed the Ghent campaign, the duke could talk of nothing but 'the holy expedition'. He formally pledged himself to the cause at a dramatic banquet known as 'The Pledge of the Pheasant', which was held at Lille on the 27th February 1454; the sumptuous details of this banquet are described in the chapter on court life.

When, in answer to the Pope's appeal, Frederick III summoned the Christian princes to Ratisbon on the 23rd April of the same year in order to organize the crusade against the Turks, Philip set out to join them. He made a triumphal march through Germany, for 'wherever he went he enjoyed every privilege as if he were the emperor in person'. Frederick III proved even more elusive than usual and sent only his secretary, Aeneas Sylvius Piccolomini, the future Pope Pius II, who, in his name, proposed the raising of an army of two hundred thousand men, to represent the Empire's contribution to the Crusade. Philip, having in the meantime fallen ill, commissioned the Bishop of Toul, Guillaume Filastre, to convey his approval. He promised to take part in person in the expedition, unless some serious obstacle came in his way. All necessary preparations were made. Flags and standards were painted in readiness. In order to prevent the Count of Charolais, then a widower, from concluding, during his impending absence, a marriage which might be detrimental to the policy of the dynasty, Philip took the precaution of arranging a union between Charles and his cousin Isabella of Bourbon. A new Pope, the Spaniard Calixtus III, sent out a proclamation stating that the crusaders would set off in March 1456. In view of his departure, the duke sent the two leading members of his Council, the Chancellor Nicolas Rolin and the Chamberlain, Antoine de Croy, to Charles VII with an earnest request for the handing over of the banner of France, the oriflamme of St Denis, so that the struggle against the Infidel could be waged under the sacred emblem. Charles VII refused on the ground that, as no peace had yet been concluded between France and England, war was still in progress. However, the Dauphin, who was estranged from his father at the time and was living in the castle of Genappe, after seeking refuge at the Court of Burgundy, justified his escapade by expressing the pious desire to accompany 'his uncle of Burgundy' who 'intended very soon to fight the Turk in the defence of the Catholic faith'.

In spite of oft-repeated proclamations, the pious intentions never materialized; the crusade did not take place. Plan after plan was made, but the duke was prevented from setting out, either by political affairs in the west or by the state of his health, which was already impaired. We shall see, however, that Charles, his son, the last of the great dukes, was also to cherish the dream of appearing before the world as the leader of western chivalry and the glorious champion of Christ.

Philip the Good had given the Dauphin Louis a cordial reception.[30] Louis had fled from Dauphiné, where the king had sent troops against him, and the heir to the throne of France, now in more or less open revolt, had taken up his abode in the castle of Genappe in Brabant. While his uncle of Burgundy maintained him in this residence along with the Dauphiness, Charlotte of Savoy, he eagerly awaited his long-hoped-for accession. When the news reached Genappe that Charles VII had died at Melun on the 22nd July 1461, Charlotte had to borrow the Countess of Charolais' palfreys in order to get to Rheims where the coronation was to take place.

The change of king immediately revived the powerful duke's ambition to play an active part in French affairs. Although Louis XI had urged him not to make the journey to Rheims an occasion for display, Philip set out with four hundred gentlemen of his household, all magnificently armed and appointed. The contrast with the very simple escort of the king, who was ill-supplied with money, was most humiliating to the sovereign. The duke looked like the guardian of his humble nephew, who happened to be king. The latter, moreover, made no bones about admitting his recent impecuniousness:

> Until recently, I held myself to be the poorest king's son that ever lived, never having experienced since childhood anything but suffering and tribulation. My wife and I, reduced to beggary, would have had no roof over our heads, and would have remained penniless, had not our uncle kept us, out of kindness and charity for a period of five years.

There could never have been a king less proud. Charles VII's son certainly did not possess his father's arrogant aloofness. The duke was exultant. Now he need no longer resent having to pay homage to a nephew who showed such humility and gratitude.

At Rheims, Philip played his customary part as doyen of the peers. As if he were anxious to show the assembled throng that the crown was his to give, the duke made the gesture of raising his arms high into the air before placing the gold circlet on Louis' head. He paid homage after high mass but he made up for any loss of dignity which this formality might involve by increased display and condescending liberality. He had taken care to bring his gold and silver plate in his vast baggage-train, and he supplied lavish quantities of his best wines for the banquet.

Louis' entry into Paris was Philip's entry too. It was the duke, an adept at organizing official celebrations, who headed the procession on the 31st August. His rich garment of black velvet was much admired; also his plumed hat, sparkling with rubies, and his white horse, the harness of which was a masterpiece of the goldsmith's art. The precious stones on both horse and rider were, it is said, words three millions! The Count of Charolais was in crimson velvet. Father and son were surrounded by pages dressed in black silk, and by nobles attired in the finest velvets.

During the days which followed, the duke monopolized the king. At the same time he tried to win popularity for himself. He allowed the townsfolk to visit the apartments of his luxurious Hôtel d'Artois, in order to see, among other marvels, the magnificent tapestries depicting the story of Gideon, the patron of the Golden Fleece. He had great pleasure in wandering through the town where he had not set foot since the Nevers meetings. He was to be seen on horseback with his niece, the Duchess of Orleans, perched behind him. He was always ostentatiously dressed, even when he visited Les Halles. It was there that, one day, he was greeted by a butcher, perhaps a descendant of one of Legoix's, or Caboche's companions, who addressed him with the words: 'O true and noble Duke of Burgundy, we bid you welcome to the city of Paris'. The new king's capital had not forgotten John the Fearless.

The king himself was entertained at the Hôtel d'Artois. He declined, it is true, to attend the most crowded receptions, in particular the fantastic banquet at which 'the cream of society was present', and where Chastellain noted his absence. Before he left for Touraine, Louis went to thank his good uncle for all his kindness, adding that he 'possibly would not have been alive, had it not been for him'. Even so, the fact that he was leaving Paris was a courteous reminder that it was time for the duke to return to his estates. Louis did not intend to turn to the court of Burgundy for advice. His methods of avoiding the tutelage of one or other of the peers were different from those of his father, but no less effective.

The fact that Philip the Good was growing old made it easier for the king to cut himself free. The duke had indulged the sensual side of his nature too well and in his declining years he sank into a state of senility.[31]

Towards the end of his reign, he allowed the Croy family to acquire an overwhelming influence over him. This resulted in the virtual retirement from office of the chancellor, Nicolas Rolin, and was highly displeasing to the Count of Charolais, the heir to the ducal throne.

The Croys formed a veritable dynasty. The head of the clan was Antoine, Count of Porcieu, a childhood friend of the duke and his chamberlain. Antoine and his brother Jean, Lord of Chimay, were both Knights of the Golden Fleece. Jean's son Philippe, who was called first of all Lord of Sempy, then Lord of Quiévrain, was, like his father, a lover of beautiful books and works of art. All were grasping by nature; they appropriated several sources of revenue and were eager to control all the affairs of state. Their kinsmen, the Lalaings and the Lannoys, supported them in their efforts.

Louis XI very cleverly took advantage of the influence exercised by the Croys. Through their agency and in spite of the Count of Charolais' protests, he succeeded in September 1463 in putting into effect the clause of the Treaty of Arras dealing with the repurchase of the towns along the Somme. He handed over the agreed sum of four hundred thousand *écus* and recovered the strategic line of fortresses.

Charolais' annoyance at this concession, in addition to his personal quarrels with the Croys, finally precipitated a break with his father. The latter, however, in spite of the fact that his faculties were declining, eventually came to realize that the Croys were in league with the king. On reflection, he regretted having given up the towns along the Somme, and he was reconciled with his son. He allowed Charles to assume leadership of the feudal league known as 'The League of the Public Weal' and to wage against Louis XI an eventful campaign, the chequered course of which will be followed in the next chapter.

On several occasions it was rumoured that the old duke had died, and just as often denied. On the 27th April 1465 he made his heir 'lieutenant-general'. He died at Bruges on the 15th June 1467. In 1473 Charles the Bold had his body and the body of the Duchess, Isabella of Portugal, who had died on the 17th December 1471, transported to the Chartreuse of Champmol. It will be explained in the chapter on Burgundian art why the duke, in spite of his splendid mode of life, could not be laid to rest, as his two predecessors had been, in a tomb that was truly worthy of him.

It only remains now to make some concluding remarks on Philip's long and eventful rule.

His contemporaries vied with each other in extolling Philip's piety,[32] his majestic demeanour, his splendid mode of life, and his powerfulness.

He was, as the old historian Pontus Heuterus said even in 1584, the founder of the Low Countries, *Conditor imperii belgici*, and this tribute is echoed by Belgium's well-known modern historian, Henri Pirenne. When we come to describe the Burgundian State, the importance of this achievement will be revealed in all its splendour.

However, although Philip left behind him this glorious and impressive achievement, he also left, as has already been mentioned, an unsolved riddle: was he himself responsible for Burgundy's fruitful policy, or was he indebted for it to his counsellors?

There is no denying that the duke had around him men of the highest ability. His first chancellor, Jean de Thoisy, who had held the office under John the Fearless, grew old and was replaced in 1422 by Nicolas Rolin; he then became a sort of honorary leader of the duke's Council, and continued to give useful advice right up to his death,[33] which occurred towards the end of May or the beginning of

June 1433. Rolin held his post for more than forty years. Jean de Thoisy's successor as Bishop of Tournai, Jean Chevrot, was also leader of the ducal Council. The Croys, the Commynes, the Pots, and many others, served the duke's cause, not to mention the many captains who helped to ensure the victories of the half-century, which was marked in turn by successful battles and advantageous treaties.

If it is now asked what part the duke played in the winning of battles, or the concluding of treaties, it can be definitely stated, as regards the first point, that he was a very brave knight. Instances and evidence of his bravery have been mentioned in passing. Whether he was fighting on the battle-field or storming towns, Philip acquitted himself as courageously as any of his captains. He adopted as his emblem the flint (that is the tinder-box which was used to spark off fire-arms), with the motto 'none other shall I have'. He excelled as a soldier. But as regards the second point, Chastellain, his historiographer, mentions his 'lackadaisical approach' to state affairs and gives such a high estimate of Rolin's authority that he seems to present the chancellor as the guiding spirit behind the policy pursued during Philip's reign.

The chancellor (says Chastellain) was in the habit of controlling everything himself; he alone handled and bore the responsibility for everything in matters of war, peace or finance; all decisions rested first and foremost with him. In all matters the duke depended on him; there was neither office nor benefice in either town or country, throughout all the duke's lands, there was neither gift given nor loan made but was done and carried through by him, or was referred to him as the supervisor of all things.

Although it is not easy to see exactly the extent of the chancellor's activities, since all official documents were drawn up in the duke's name, it is difficult not to give great weight to Chastellain's statement. It has been objected against it that during negotiations with the Council of Basle, the Holy Fathers of the Council and the Burgundian ambassadors in the city addressed themselves to the duke and not to the chancellor. It is difficult to imagine them doing otherwise if they were to show proper respect to the duke, who was extremely touchy on such matters and would have called them to order had they shown any signs of behaving discourteously. The objection is not, therefore, very significant.[34] The truth is that it is impossible to determine with any accuracy the part played by the duke. However, as in the case of Philip the Fair, it can be assumed that although Philip the Good had little natural bent for exacting administrative work and left it largely to his trusted advisers, he himself, and he alone, took the major decisions. The Treaty of Troyes may have been arranged by Jean de Thoisy, and the Treaty of Arras by Nicolas Rolin, but the number of memoranda which the preparation of this last-mentioned treaty occasioned—memoranda which have been preserved—illustrates clearly the procedure: the duke's decision was only taken after all the factors had been given due consideration. He had the professional conscience of a head of state who was resolved not to leave to others the task of settling major issues, and who was determined to assume his responsibilities in the light of history.

CHAPTER VIII

CHARLES THE BOLD: THE GLORIOUS YEARS

PHILIP THE GOOD'S only son, the fourth and last of the great dukes, the man who has become known in history as Charles the Bold, was born at Dijon on the 11th November 1433.

Philip the Good had had no children by his first wife. Michelle of France, the daughter of Charles VI, whom he had married when she was very young, had died on the 8th July 1422. The duke's second marriage with Bonne of Artois was prompted, along with other considerations, by the early expectation of an heir, for it was said that 'this lady had every hope of bearing children'. Unfortunately, this hope was doomed to early disappointment, for the new duchess died in childbirth on the 17th September 1425. Philip the Good then resigned himself to recognizing as his heir Philip of St Pol, his cousin, the son of his uncle Anthony, on condition that the agreement should be reciprocal. As it happened the Count of St Pol, who had become the Duke of Brabant, died of a mysterious illness on the 4th August 1430. Philip, who had several good reasons for being displeased with St Pol, had already remarried and his third wife, Isabella of Portugal, was pregnant. The son to which the Portuguese princess gave birth on the 30th December 1430 died at the age of twelve months, and a second son, born shortly afterwards, also died at about the same age. Philip was beginning to lose heart when at last a third son was born. From then on, the future of the dynasty depended on this child, Charles, whom his mother, in defiance of current practice, insisted on feeding herself, and on whom his father lavished as much affection as he was capable of. He lost no time in creating him Count of Charolais and Knight of the Golden Fleece. The title of Count of Charolais had already been conferred on the third duke: the fact that it was also conferred on the fourth duke underlined the House's firm resolve of establishing as the traditional appanage of the heir to the ducal throne the territorial purchase made by the first duke in 1390.[1]

Very careful attention was given to the future duke's education. One of his most prominent teachers was a scholar from Arras, Antoine Haneron, the man who founded the College of St Donat, at the University of Louvain. Of the Burgundian knights who taught the heir how to handle arms, the Lord of Auxy and Jean de Rosimboz deserve to be remembered.

Philip the Good wanted his son to be able to speak Flemish. He made him, at the age of thirteen, King of the Guild of the Voetboog in Bruges.

In addition to the influence of the duke, who was certainly fond of his son and heir but who was rather aloof by nature, Charles came under that of his mother, the serious-minded and thoughtful Isabella of Portugal. 'He never acquired', wrote Pirenne, 'even the superficial heartiness which made Philip the Good popular in the Low Countries. Passionate, but reserved, he held himself aloof from court life and had neither friends nor confidants.'[2] Only his mother had any power over him.

As for his physical appearance, he was ruddy, fairly tall, broad-shouldered but with a slight stoop; he had long arms, with which he gesticulated a great deal, black hair, a swarthy skin, clear blue eyes, and a prim mouth. His protruding jaw which was a notable feature with him and which was to remain the characteristic sign of his lineage, helped to give him 'an indefinably barbaric cast of countenance which was in perfect keeping with the passion for storms and surging seas noted by his contemporaries'.[3]

Unlike his father he was an extremely hard worker: 'more than was befitting in such a prince', observes Chastellain. But while he had his father's hasty temper, he had not inherited the good nature which enabled Philip to forgive and forget. He was an impulsive man 'strong-willed and sharp-tongued'. He was above all an ambitious man, proud, and head-strong; restraint was foreign to his nature. 'Even the half of Europe,' as Commynes said, 'would not have satisfied him.' He had a tendency to be suspicious, a tendency which he could not control; he had inherited this trait from his mother, who, as the old duke used to say with a smile, 'was the most suspicious lady he had ever known'.[4] Hard on himself as well as on others, impatient and brutal, vindictive and hot-headed, Charles was incapable of either dealing systematically with the difficulties which faced him, or of establishing any sort of proportion between his ambitions and the means at his disposal.

His youth was austere and studious; he liked reading, particularly the ancient authors. He was fascinated by history and he was especially fond of the exploits of Alexander the Great, whose father, like his own, had been called Philip. His dream was to be as great as Alexander. He had the gift of eloquence and he deliberately cultivated it. He could fire an audience with his impassioned oratory and was often carried away himself as he was rousing others. He was a keen lover of music and the arts. He was rigorously chaste—in surprising contrast to his father—yet he did not always set great store by the knightly loyalty on which the third duke had prided himself. There were occasions when he vied in dishonesty with his contemporary Louis XI, whom he had always loathed, and who returned the compliment.

Furthermore, 'the House of Burgundy, which during the succeeding reigns had become more and more estranged from France, its country of origin, finally cast off, under Charles the Bold, the last links which bound it to the kingdom'.[5] Sometimes Charles said he was English, because he was a descendant of John of Gaunt; at other times Portuguese, because his mother came from Portugal. One day he maintained that he loved France so much that he would have liked her to have six kings instead of one. No statement of political aims could have been clearer than the expression of such a wish. The last of the great dukes was quite ready to envisage the final setting up of the Burgundian Kingdom he dreamt of, on the ruins of royal France: in the memorable political speech delivered at Dijon in 1474, his plans for such a kingdom were given full and explicit expression.

Philip the Good's exceptionally long life had condemned the Count of Charolais to years of waiting no less tantalizing than those through which the Dauphin Louis, now Louis XI, had lived when Charles VII's long reign—too long for his son's liking—turned him into a conspirator. Without going quite as far, Charles the Bold was angered by the excessive influence exercised by the Croys, whose selfish intentions have already been noted, and he had contended with them for precedence on every possible occasion. Thrust aside and restored to favour in turns, the prince had only been able to make spasmodic attempts at learning how to handle state affairs. However, he had applied himself to the task with all his natural ability for hard work. He would no doubt have assumed power while his father was still alive if a deterioration in Philip's state of health had not forced the old duke to cancel his plans for a final crusade.[6]

The heir to the Burgundian State was acting as a sort of unofficial regent when the so-called War of Public Good broke out. This was the first of the crises which were to occur at intervals during Louis XI's chequered reign. Charles gave the full measure of his powers for the first time when he acted as the virtual leader of the French feudal nobility, which was at last beginning to see itself as a federation of princes arrayed against the royal authority.

In his elation at having at long last acceded to the throne after weary and anxious years of waiting, Charles VII's son tried to forge ahead too quickly. His reaction against his father's rule was too systematic. 'From the very beginning,' says Commynes, 'he thought only of revenge.' He dismissed whole bodies of officials, he made sweeping changes in the administrative machinery, he imposed new taxes on the clergy, he showed nothing but contempt for the masters of the university, he rigorously suppressed privileges and pensions, he placed restrictions on hunting rights, he provoked quarrels with Brittany on the matter of homage, and on the subject of ecclesiastical regulations; and he bought back the Somme fortresses from Burgundy. The malcontents, upset by these measures, lost no time in banding together to form a coalition. It is significant that the rebellious vassals, in order to win popular support for their cause, should have appealed to the principle of the *Public Good*.

It was a highly critical situation. Louis, who had begun by trying to crush the Duke of Bourbon, because he was the first to show his hand, was recalled to Paris by the news that the three chief conspirators, Charles the Bold, Francis II of Brittany and Charles of France, Duke of Berry—the younger son of Charles VII and nominal leader of the expedition—were converging on the capital.

Charles of Charolais had about twelve thousand men under his command. The question was whether Brittany and Berry who were steadily advancing with their contingents of some five thousand men would be able to join up with Charolais' army in time. To prevent this happening, Louis, who was usually loath to risk a battle, decided to attack the count at Montlhéry. The battle of Montlhéry was to prove to be the crucial encounter of the war.

Louis of Luxemburg, Count of St Pol, who commanded one of the Burgundian army corps, had moved his men to the foot of Montlhéry's ancient and formidable keep. As soon as he was informed of the approach of the royal troops, St Pol warned Charolais, who had taken up his position at Longjumeau. Charles sent Anthony, the 'great bastard', to give help. St Pol and Anthony set about closing the road to Paris to the king's army. But Louis XI was determined to give battle. Soon the count was informed that the king's men were advancing 'in single file' from the direction of the forest of Torfou, and that they were not very numerous. This proved too great a temptation for Charles the Bold. He would certainly have been well-advised to avoid a clash of arms and to wait for his allies Brittany and Berry, so as to hurl the full force of the combined army against his opponent. He chose to do the opposite; he charged like a bull. With a man of his impetuous nature, provocation never failed to produce the desired effect.

And so the battle began. Fiery and head-strong as ever, Charles hurled himself into the fray. But it was such a confused encounter that it is useless to try and understand what really happened; even those who, like Philippe de Commynes, were present at the battle, were only able to give a disjointed account of it.

Charles the Bold forged ahead with his page, Simon de Quingey, his standard-bearer Dubois who was holding aloft the huge banner of black and purple silk, and his bodyguard of archers, all wearing the same colours, with the cross of St Andrew emblazoned on their chests.

'The king's men had taken up position near Montlhéry castle and had in front of them a huge hedge and a moat. Beyond them stretched fields full of corn, beans and other sturdy plants, for it was good land for cultivation.' Thus, in a few masterly strokes, Commynes sets the scene.

The king's men leapt over the hedge. The impatient Burgundians pushed past their own archers and launched an attack. They charged up the hill where Louis was waiting. The Count of Maine, Admiral John of Montauban, and the Master of the Horse, Garguessale, 'shamefully' took to their heels, whether through cowardice or treachery it was difficult to tell. Suddenly the cry went up: 'The king has been captured!' Whereupon the king lifted his visor so that they could all see his face and shouted: 'Men, you can see for yourselves that I have not been captured'. And he added: 'Back to the fray and be of good cheer. If there were no more than six of us to fight these Burgundians, we would still win'.

The fight continued, very fiercely indeed. Panic ceased among the king's men as soon as he had spoken. The troops under St Pol and the Count of Ravenstein, who thought they had the upper hand, were forced back to their baggage wagons and a section of the Burgundian cavalry was scattered as far afield as St Cloud and Pont Ste Maxence.

Elsewhere, on the contrary, the royal troops took to flight. Charles saw his opponents scattered in all directions, broken by the irresistible force of his attack. Elated by his success he went on with 'the hunt'; and Commynes, who was with him, uses the word to mean that he took pleasure in the pursuit. 'An elderly nobleman from Luxemburg, called Antoine Le Breton, sought out the duke and told him that the French had reassembled on the field and that if he went on pursuing those who were fleeing he would be lost.' It was of no avail. Nor would the duke listen to the advice of the Lord of Contay. No doubt the royal army was saved by this stubborn decision to pursue the defeated flank, instead of letting it go in order to attack the centre and the other wing from the rear.

When Charolais, on his way back, passed close by the castle he saw to his great surprise that the king's archers were lined up at the foot of the keep. He thought that Louis's entire army had been routed, whereas, in fact, the main body was still intact. But now the leader of the feudal expedition had under him men who were too exhausted and too widely scattered to engage in a fresh battle. 'The ground was trampled flat where only half an hour before the corn had stood erect, and the whole field was strewn with dead men and horses.' Here we have a companion picture to the first; the two could be entitled *Before and after the battle*. Clearly Commynes had a gift for picturesque description.

On both sides part of the army had been routed, part had held its ground, so that both armies could claim victory.[7]

It was in fact an indecisive battle. But Paris stood firm and saved the monarchy. Louis went off to Normandy and came back with reinforcements. He was joined by a contingent from Milan sent by Sforza. Dissension crept into the princes' camp in spite of, or because of, the arrival of Brittany and Berry. The princes grew weary of waiting in front of the ramparts, particularly as they could rarely agree when it came to deciding what policy to adopt. They began to lose heart; perseverance had never been a feudal virtue. The king, who was well acquainted with the maxim 'divide and rule', had already begun to undermine his opponents.

Charolais, after scattering the king's archers, who were only raw recruits, at the bridge of Charenton, had pushed on to Conflans. His artillery was impressive—probably as impressive as the king's, which was under the command of 'Master Guirault'. Both sides kept up a steady bombardment. Eventually, however, they tired of this noisy exchange of missiles and 'there were several days of truce when both sides met to discuss peace'.

Commynes relates how the king 'came across the water one morning', right opposite his enemy's camp. There were only four or five captains in the boat apart from the ferryman. Charolais and St Pol were waiting on the banks of the Seine. The king asked Charolais: 'Brother, do you vouch for my safety?' and the Count replied 'My lord, yes'. The king then stepped ashore with his companions. Charles and St Pol treated him with great respect 'as was befitting', and the king, 'who was not lacking in courtesy', opened the conversation with these words: 'Brother, I know you are a nobleman, and of the House of France'. 'Why do you speak thus, my lord?' said Charolais. 'For this reason,' replied the king: 'when I sent my ambassadors to Lille and when that madman Morvilliers spoke to you in such forceful terms, you told me, through the Archbishop of Narbonne, that before the year was out I would be sorry for all that Morvilliers had said to you, and you were right.' The king spoke 'laughingly and with an open countenance'. Charles of Charolais was flattered and disarmed. Louis called him 'brother', referring to the fact that his late sister, Catherine, had been the count's first wife. He disowned Morvilliers who had recently offended him by making certain remarks. And the king, with great affability, walked up and down with Charles and St Pol on either side. People gazed at them in amazement—both the soldiers fighting in the feudal league and the guards stationed along the ramparts of the city of Paris.

Peace was certainly well on the way. It was in fact finally settled by the treaties of Conflans and St Maur, on the 5th and 29th October. Each member of the coalition got his reward, for the king was generous. Burgundy benefited considerably: the king returned the Somme towns that he had recently bought back, and added the counties of Guines and Boulogne.

On the 15th June 1467, Philip the Good's death made Charolais, already *de facto* regent, the reigning Duke of Burgundy. Having become a widower for the second time through the death of Isabella of Bourbon, Charles sought the hand of Margaret of York, the sister of Edward IV, King of England, and immediately the prospect of another Anglo-Burgundian alliance loomed large. It seemed that the Treaty of Arras might be denounced and that there might be a return to the Treaty of Troyes.

There was no denying the seriousness of the situation. If the proposed marriage took place, a fresh onslaught on the Valois royal line would be inevitable.

A series of grave events had occurred in England since the Treaty of Arras. Henry VI and his wife Margaret of Anjou, a cousin of Louis XI, had been deposed. Edward of York had replaced the Lancastrian, who was now a prisoner in the Tower of London while his wife, Margaret, had fled. Charles the Bold, as a descendant of John of Gaunt, the first Plantagenet duke of the House of Lancaster, had always shunned the House of York; the fact that he now contemplated forming ties of kinship with the Yorkists showed that reasons of State impelled him to do so. Edward and Charles together would represent a formidable threat to Louis, who tried every means in his power to prevent the marriage taking place. It was, however, celebrated at Bruges on the 3rd July 1468 with lavish flamboyance. Olivier de la Marche in his *Mémoires* gives a detailed account. When we come to deal with court life, we will refer to the hundred pages which the chronicler devoted to these wedding festivities out of the hundred and fifty he allotted to the whole of the last duke's reign. Processions, banquets, joustings, tournaments, theatrical performances—nothing was missing from the superb and costly display of Burgundian splendour. Olivier can be forgiven for having described it at such length. Being a court official, as well as an historian, he was responsible for organizing the memorable event, and his personal vanity prompted him to bequeath to future generations an exact account of every feature that was likely to enhance the fame both of the ceremonies and of the master of ceremonies.

Conscious of the danger implicit in this merry-making, Louis pondered on the course of action he should take. He sensed that a fresh storm was brewing. An idea—perhaps brilliant or perhaps disastrous—came to him, or was suggested to him: a meeting at Péronne.

Whether or not it was Cardinal Balue who suggested to Louis XI that he should arrange to see the duke at Péronne, it was undoubtedly the cardinal who arranged and planned everything, and he fell from favour because of the disastrous outcome of the episode.

The king had sensed that another feudal conspiracy was being hatched. Normandy, which had been given to Charles of France, was taken away from him again on the pretext that he had a secret understanding with Edward IV. And Charles the Bold, having become Edward IV's brother-in-law, had at all costs to be dissuaded from forming a military alliance with Yorkist England. Direct negotiation would be the best way of seeing that this did not happen. Louis had unlimited confidence in his powers of persuasion.

The king was at Noyon. He betook himself to Ham where the Count of St Pol owned a castle. On the 9th October 1468, under cover of a hunting expedition, Louis XI made straight for Péronne. Fifty or so mounted escorts rode with him, among whom figured the Duke of Bourbon, his brother the Cardinal-Bishop of Lyons and St Pol himself.

Advised of the king's approach, the Duke of Burgundy left

Péronne, 'accompanied by a powerful escort'. He invited the king to his town, which was one of the valuable fortresses recently returned to Burgundy, and installed him in the house of the local tax-collector who 'had a fine mansion near the castle', since the castle itself was 'in a poor state', and consisted only of a tower and inadequate living accommodation.

Let us keep to Commynes' straightforward and detailed narrative. He was an eyewitness and he tells of everything that happened, except that he unfortunately does not mention the part he himself played, which was considerable.

The king had hardly settled into the tax-collector's comfortable house when an army of Burgundian soldiers arrived on the scene, led by the Marshal of Burgundy and Philip of Bresse, the king's brother-in-law. The captains had the famous emblem, the St Andrew's cross.

They all pitched camp round the ramparts. The king noticed that some of the captains, for instance Antoine de Lan and Poncet de Rivière, were men who had formerly been in his service and had left him. Louis felt distinctly ill at ease. But since his plan was to inspire confidence in the duke, in order to charm him, he controlled the apprehension which he felt at being surrounded by so many men-at-arms, and asked his 'brother' to house him in the castle. As Pierre Champion, one of Louis's most painstaking historians, has said, 'the fox was about to rush into the lion's mouth'. Commynes himself might have used the expression, had he been given to literary turns of phrase.

Since he had been welcomed and treated most honourably, Louis XI could justifiably think that he would achieve his ends simply by the use of his own shrewdness. He would create a rift between the brother and the husband of Margaret of York. He had his arguments all ready, and he was sufficiently familiar with the psychological make-up of Philip the Good's son to know how to appeal to his emotions.

But suddenly the whole elaborate structure collapsed. News was brought to Péronne that the people of Liége had risen in revolt with the cry 'Long live the king!'.

It has already been explained that Philip the Good had forced the Chapter of St Lambert to accept his nephew Louis of Bourbon as their prince-bishop. Riding rough-shod over all attempts at resistance, the old duke had succeeded in installing on the episcopal throne the seventeen-year-old prelate whom Commynes himself describes as 'a man who liked good living and a gay life and who scarcely knew what was good for him and what was bad'. All efforts to resist the return to absolutism had been foiled. In vain the 'vrais Liégeois', had laid their plots, with the clandestine support of Charles VII. In vain they had chosen Raes de Heeres as leader and called themselves 'Companions of the Green Tent', a title already adopted by the citizens of Ghent who were exiled after the battle of Gavere. After the Treaty of Conflans, Louis XI, who in this matter continued his father's policy, had been forced to allow Charolais, acting on behalf of Philip the Good, to give vent to his bitter feelings. Philip, although barely conscious at the time, was carried on a litter so as to be present at the burning of Dinant in August 1466. In the following year, Charles the Bold, who had now become Duke of Burgundy, wiped out the Liége militia troops at Brusthem on the 28th October and then proceeded on the 28th November to impose on the conquered citizens a peace which deprived them of all forms of freedom, and even went as far as to abolish common law and replace it by Roman law. The Liége steps, a symbol of independence, were transported to Bruges where they were set up in the Place de la Bourse as a monument of victory. With his usual harshness, the duke who, as Chastellain says, was anxious to show the rebels 'the beard and face of a prince', ruthlessly exploited his victory. The Bishop, Louis of Bourbon, who had been driven out of the city, returned on the 30th April 1468, and entrusted administrative affairs to the Burgundian, Humbercourt. This was tantamount to the annexation of the Liége principality.

While demolition work was started on the walls of the episcopal city and tax assessments were being increased six-fold in order to meet the fine of one hundred and twenty *lions d'or* which the duke had imposed on the town, the bishop cleared the front of his palace of the stalls which blocked his view, devoted himself to music, and ordered a yacht for pleasure trips on the Meuse.

Louis XI, pursuing his clandestine manœuvres, calculated that the stronger anti-Burgundian feeling became in Liége, the more advisable it was to exploit the feeling in order to be able, at some appropriate moment, to attack the ducal authority as it were from the rear. He sent emissaries to instigate a fresh revolt which would keep Charles the Bold busy while the royal government proceeded to crush the remaining feudal leaders in such a way as to wipe out the concessions made at Conflans and St Maur.

These royal agents, who had apparently succeeded earlier than Louis anticipated, unleashed the 1468 rebellion, and this explains why cries of 'Long live the king' accompanied the fresh outbreak,

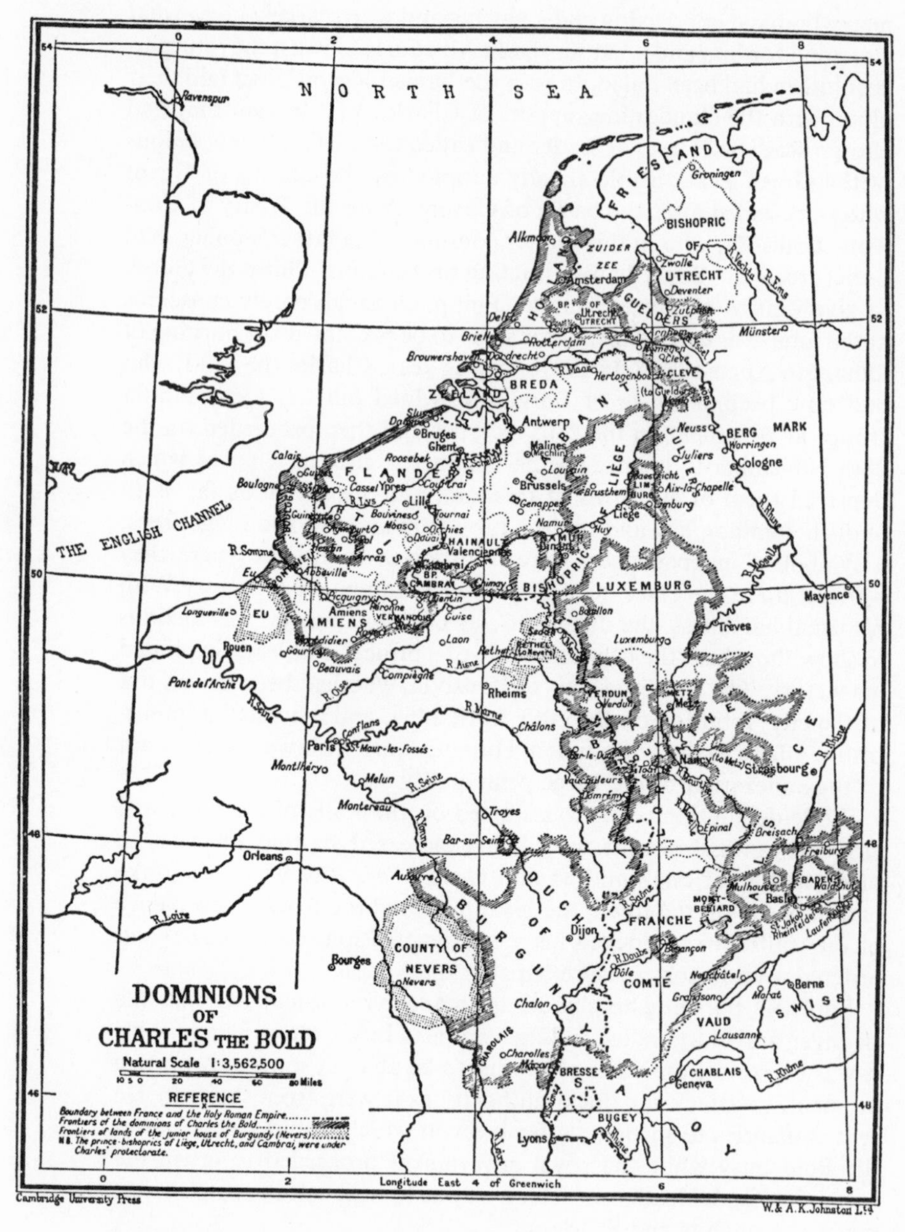

Reprinted by courtesy of the Cambridge University Press and W. & A. K. Johnston Ltd.

which, as ill-luck would have it, coincided with the king's presence at Péronne.

Philippe de Commynes explains the coincidence by a simple lapse of memory on the king's part. 'The king, when he went to Péronne, had forgotten that he had sent two ambassadors to Liége to provoke a rising against the afore-mentioned duke.' Was this the explanation that Louis himself gave Commynes, or did Commynes invent it because he could not think of any other? The true explanation was surely more complex and more subtle. It is probable that the king's plans for the timing of events had been upset and that he had arranged for the Liége insurrection to take place later. All at once Louis found himself denounced as the instigator of an armed rising in the principality of Liége when he was the guest of the immediate overlord of the principality, and which was worse, just when the latter had graciously installed him in his own castle.

This particular rising was extremely serious. The militia troops, two thousand in number, took possession of Tongres, and seized the Bishop of Liége who was in residence there. The 'enraged masses', as Commynes said, 'were overjoyed at the capture of their lord'. Messengers came streaming to Péronne with information about these events, which might be true or might be false but was certainly alarming. 'Some said that everybody had been killed, while others denied this.' But the king's responsibility for the riots was confirmed, since witnesses swore that the 'king's ambassadors' had been spotted among the rioters. 'And when the duke was told of these happenings he suddenly realized that they were true, and he was filled with fury, saying that the king had come expressly to deceive him.' The fat was in the fire. Charles the Bold, headstrong and violent, was subject to sudden attacks of rage: beside himself with anger, he was capable of anything.

According to Commynes, his first thought was to shut the gates of the town and the castle. In order to justify this action he put forward 'a pretext': he said that he had lost 'a box' containing 'valuable rings, and money'. The king suddenly realized that he was confined to his apartments. He could no longer move from the castle 'which was small'; on the duke's orders a strong force of archers 'had been stationed at the entrance'. Louis was under arrest—a prisoner in all but name. Louis was certainly not '*sans doubte*'—in other words, he was afraid. He remembered another instance in history which added to his anxiety: 'he saw that he was lodged close by the huge tower in which a Count of Vermondois had had one of his predecessors on the throne of France put to death'. There was a danger that Louis might share the fate which had befallen Charles the Simple in 929. (Charles had been a prisoner but in actual fact he had died a natural death and had not, as was commonly supposed, been murdered.)

Commynes was, at the time, Charles the Bold's chamberlain, and was on very intimate terms with him. As the son of a distinguished servant of Philip the Good, he exercised an exceptionally strong influence over the late duke's heir. The close link between the historian and his master not only explains the detailed accuracy of his account, but also enables us to appreciate the important, if unacknowledged, part he himself played in this delicate situation.

The duke, without beating about the bush, announced to his household that 'the king had come to betray him'. He informed them of the events in Liége, putting the blame on his guest. 'He was extremely angry with the king and uttered violent threats against him.' The rumour at once got about that the duke was planning vengeance, and it finally reached 'the ears of the king, who was thoroughly frightened'.

In fact, the king was very critically placed. He felt himself to be at the mercy of his most powerful vassal, the leader of the French feudal lords, just at a time when the latter had real and unquestionable grievances against him. The Liége insult, coming as it did after the violation of the treaties of Conflans and St Maur, the taking back of Normandy, and all the various deeds and actions that had occurred since 1465, revealed the king's determination to wipe out the humiliation he had suffered at the time of the 'Public Good'.

In the Duke of Burgundy's case, anger deprived him of political judgment. But all anger eventually subsides. 'On the first day fear and unrest spread through the whole town. On the second day, the afore-mentioned duke was a little calmer.' Commynes had said nothing. He just listened. He knew his master. He realized that the first flush of anger, which the slightest comment would transform into a towering rage, must be allowed to spend itself. A council meeting was called, and several solutions were envisaged. Some members proposed that the king 'should be imprisoned without further ado'; others that Charles of France should be sent for and that the treaties which had already been concluded should be revised in such a way as to establish 'a peace which would be definitely beneficial to all the French princes'. The second opinion seemed about to win the day. A horseman was ready, his mount saddled: he was to set out for Brittany where Charles had found refuge after the seizure of his duchy of Normandy. The messenger was only waiting for the

1 Philip the Bold, Duke of Burgundy, by an anonymous artist

2 3

2 Anthony of Burgundy wears the insignia of the Golden Fleece, detail from a Flemish School portrait. **3** John the Fearless, Duke of Burgundy, detail from a painting by Jan van Eyck. **4** Philip the Good, and **5** Charles the Bold, Dukes of Burgundy, from paintings by Roger van der Weyden

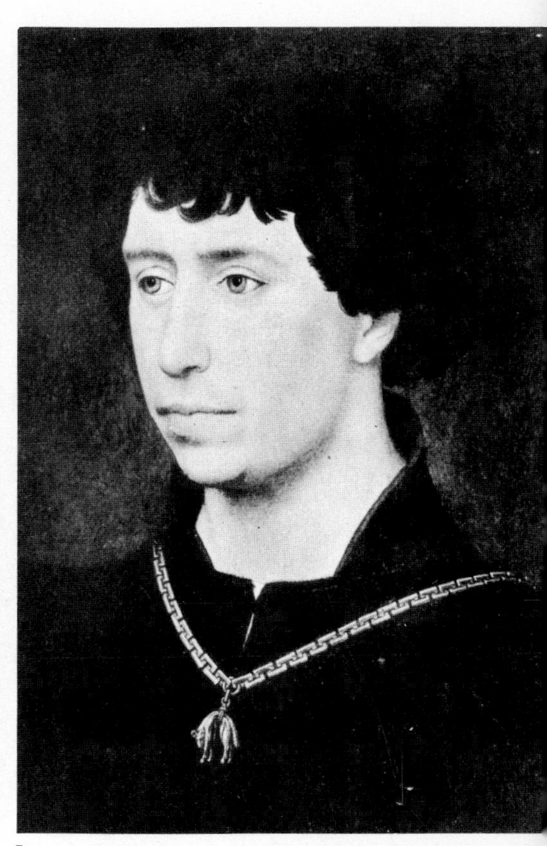

4 5

6 Detail from an anonymous artist's *Le Jardin d'Amour de Philippe le Bon* showing Philip the Good out of doors with his court

7 The Dukes of Burgundy had a magnificent town house in Dijon which was drawn in 1688 by J. H. Mansart

9

8

8 Isabella of Bourbon, wife of Charles the Bold;
9 Isabella of Portugal, wife of Philip the Good;
10 Margaret of Bavaria, wife of John the Fearless

10

11 This vivid picture of the battle of Morat comes from the *Chronicles* of Schilling of Lucerne

Duke of Burgundy's letters. The latter, however, changed his mind and cancelled the proposed journey.

The reason was, according to Commynes, that the king had 'put forward proposals', but it is more than likely that the chronicler himself acted as intermediary. He does not say so. Unfortunately, he must have considered that professional etiquette demanded discretion. Whatever the truth of the matter, the fact remains that the compromise proposals put forward by the king brought the duke's vacillations to an end. Contact had been established.

This was during the third night after the closing of the gates. The duke did not undress. Commynes describes how he paced up and down his room, from time to time throwing himself fully clothed on to his bed—but almost immediately getting up again. This jumpiness shows what an uneasy temperament he had. It is impossible to doubt the accuracy of Commynes' account. 'I lay,' he says, 'that night in his room and often I paced up and down with him.' How unfortunate that nothing of their conversation has been preserved! 'In the morning, he was in a greater rage than ever.' It took all the psychological resources and diplomatic skill of the duke's chamberlain to control the fury of his violent master, by allowing it to explode from time to time. It is difficult not to suppose that there was some connivance between the chamberlain and the king. 'The king,' says Commynes with admirable discretion, 'had some friend or other who warned him of the duke's state of mind.' Finally this 'friend' found a way of getting both Louis and Charles to accept a compromise. Burgundy was to be granted certain concessions, another appanage was to be created for Charles of France and not only were the people of Liége to be abandoned to their fate but Louis was to be forced to be present at the humiliating spectacle of their punishment.

Such were the matters to be discussed between the two parties. The obliging friend who had arranged everything acted as go-between. But the interview was very different from the discussion the king had originally dreamt of. 'When the duke entered the king's room, his voice trembled, he was so agitated and angry. Outwardly he behaved meekly enough, but his gestures and his speech were fierce.' To all the questions put to him, Louis XI 'only replied, yes'.

The Treaty of Péronne, signed on the 14th October 1468, and the complementary agreements resulting from it, ratified all the benefits Burgundy had obtained in 1465. Added to these were new sources of revenue in Picardy, the territory of Mortagne, the right to elect representatives in Amiens, homage from several new vassals in Ponthieu, Vimeu and Beauvais, the renunciation of the right of appeal exercised by the Paris *Parlement* in Mâconnais, and the right of exemption of the duke's subjects from personal service in defence of the crown. Louis could refuse nothing—there was nothing else for it but to 'reply yes' to everything.

Champagne and Brie were to be given as an appanage to Charles of France as compensation for Normandy which had been confiscated. Finally, the king agreed to accompany the Duke of Burgundy on a punitive expedition against Liége.

They set off, therefore, for the ecclesiastical principality on the Meuse. The king had with him his Scottish guards, and a few men-at-arms, the duke a section of his army; his Marshal brought up the remainder, and they all moved off in the direction of the unfortunate city which was to pay dearly for its bid for independence. 'The king and his men, although some of them grumbled, all took the cross of St Andrew.' On the 26th October the townspeople of Liége suddenly found the Franco-Burgundian forces at their gates. The king had to endure the shame of taking part in this ruthless demonstration of military might, and in the brutal extermination of men whose only crime had been to put their trust in his emissaries. People were massacred and thrown into the river. Buildings went up in flames or crashed to the ground. 'It was terrible to hear the noise made by the houses as they collapsed.' Commynes describes the looting of the churches, the flight of the panic-stricken inhabitants through the night to the safety of the Ardennes, the execution of the captured leaders, and he adds: 'Many people died of hunger, cold, and exhaustion'. So ended four days of valiant resistance and fierce street fighting. On Sunday 30th October, the duke and his troops entered the ruined city. Whereupon, throughout the whole of Burgundy, at the duke's express orders, bonfires were lit to celebrate, not only peace, but the punishment of the rebels.

The period following the Péronne incident represented the height of Charles the Bold's power. For several years he revelled in his success; but he was tormented by gnawing ambition, and had none of the noble serenity which had so greatly impressed the contemporaries of Philip the Good. The restless imagination of the fourth duke was more concerned with what he still lacked than with what he actually possessed. He was dazzled by the prospect of a vast kingdom of Lotharingia, a State of Burgundy, embracing all the Burgundies of the past. It is true that important acquisitions were still to be made, but already the disastrous effects of the duke's inability to exercise any sort of restraint were beginning to be felt.

Ever since the days of Philip the Bold, Burgundy had had her eyes on Alsace, and we have seen how Philip the Good succeeded in making himself heir presumptive to the inheritance of his aunt Catherine. In 1469 an excellent opportunity occurred for the consolidation of this advantage. Sigismund of the Austrian Tyrol, who was at war with the Swiss Cantons, sought an alliance with Charles the Bold, and in order to obtain it, signed the Treaty of St Omer with him in May. It stipulated that, in return for a money payment, Sigismund would cede Alsace, Sundgau and the county of Pfirt to the Valois of Burgundy. The traditional penury of the Austrian Hapsburgs seemed to guarantee the fact that the mortgaged territories would never be bought back.

The annexation of these territories represented an important step. It served the invaluable purpose of facilitating communications between the Burgundian domains and the Low Countries. Furthermore, the Treaty of St Omer opened up far-reaching possibilities, for by linking the Hapsburgs and the Valois of Burgundy it paved the way for the marriage of Mary of Burgundy with Maximilian, the man who was to be the grandfather of Charles V.

Mary of Burgundy, who had been born on the 13th February 1457, and was Charles the Bold's only daughter, was an even wealthier heiress than her forbear, Margaret of Flanders, had been. As Pirenne has said:

> the story of Mary of Burgundy's seven betrothals would form one of the most curious chapters in the diplomatic history of the fifteenth century. From the long procession of her suitors, Englishmen, Frenchmen and Austrians, we can see how diverse were the ventures and alliances embarked upon by her father.[8]

Preliminary negotiations for the marriage with Maximilian, the son of the Emperor Frederick III, followed closely on the signing of the Treaty of St Omer. The proposed union, which was a complement to the already existing marriage between Charles the Bold and Margaret of York, certainly gave Louis XI food for thought. Supported by Imperial Germany on the one hand, and by Yorkist England on the other, the House of Burgundy was well on the way to becoming a truly formidable power and a serious threat to the eastern flank of the Valois Kingdom.

It is true that Charles the Bold, unstable as ever, was not long in replacing the Germano-Burgundian project by an entirely different scheme. His new idea was a marriage between Mary and Charles of France, Louis XI's brother, which would be to the detriment of the king.

The duke had insisted at Péronne that Champagne and Brie should be handed over to Charles of France, because he intended to take the prince under his guardianship, so that the proposed appanage, by forming a link between the Burgundian estates, would become a disguised extension of the ducal State.

Louis had warded off this danger with great skill. Before taking leave of Charles to return to Paris, he put to the duke the following sly question which Commynes noted: 'If perchance my brother, who is in Brittany, were not satisfied with the afore-mentioned share which I am granting him for love of you, what would you like me to do?' The duke replied on the spur of the moment, *without thinking what he was saying*: 'If he does not want to take it, and if you fit in with his wishes, I shall abide by your joint decision'. Louis succeeded in forcing Charles to accept Guienne instead of Champagne and Brie. This was the lesser of two evils—but still an evil. If Charles of France, now in possession of Guienne, married Mary, the nightmare of an Anglo-Burgundian agreement was perhaps more to be feared than ever.

Louis thought he had removed this dangerous possibility at Péronne, but he had in actual fact only made it more imminent. A coalition was being formed against France. By supporting the House of Anjou, which had undertaken an expedition into Catalonia, Louis XI had incurred the hostility of an extremely clever statesman, John II of Aragon, who proceeded to join forces with England and Burgundy.[9] An ominous, triple pact was concluded between John II, Edward IV and Charles the Bold. A number of subsidiary agreements linked Brittany and several other French feudal domains to the compact group. It seemed as if a foreign war complicated by a fresh 'Public Good' conspiracy loomed ahead. The crowning blow was the marriage of John's son, Ferdinand the Catholic, to Isabella, the heiress to the throne of Castille, on the 17th October 1469, at Valladolid. This widened the anti-French circle still further. Louis tried in vain to prevent Edward IV from being dragged into war by his allies. He thought he would succeed in doing so by appealing to the Earl of Warwick, the 'King-maker' who had put the House of York on the throne. But Warwick, the head of the Neville clan, met with opposition from the Queen's relatives, the Woodvilles, led by Lord Rivers, Edward's father-in-law. Once more the spectre of the Hundred Years' War appeared on the horizon, for the great conflict was by no means over. Charles VII had not settled everything; no Anglo-French peace treaty had marked the end of the prolonged duel of the preceding reign. The final campaign of the long struggle was to be waged under Louis XI.

In order to break up the Anglo-Burgundian alliance, Louis XI decided to counter-attack. He evolved a bold plan for the dethroning of Edward and the restoration of Henry VI to the English throne.

Warwick, after a clash with Edward, took refuge in France. He was welcomed by Louis XI who effected a reconciliation between him and Margaret of Anjou, and financed an expedition against England, headed by Warwick. Edward, taken by surprise, fled to Holland and the 'King-maker', once more in control of London, released Henry VI from prison, and on the 6th October 1470, re-established him on the throne. It now looked as if there might be a Franco-English alliance against Burgundy, instead of an Anglo-Burgundian union against France.

In view of this complete transformation of the diplomatic scene, Charles the Bold, for once, felt the need to exercise prudence. He recognized Henry as king and deliberately left Edward to cool his heels at Middelburg, in Zealand, where he had taken refuge. He wrote to some English lords: 'Oh, my friends, I protest that I have always held aloof from the quarrels about the English throne: St George . . . can vouch for the fact . . . that I am a better Englishman than you are . . . .' And Edward of York's brother-in-law remembered most opportunely that 'he was of Lancastrian extraction'. After all, his mother, Isabella of Portugal, had been descended from John of Gaunt.

Louis, however, tried to exploit his advantage. He intended to use the Lancastrian restoration in England to bring about the final downfall of Burgundy with English help. French ambassadors crossed the Channel in order to work out the details of this great scheme. The war was to be pursued until the destruction of the Burgundian State had been achieved. The spoils would be shared, and Great Britain would receive the Low Countries as her reward.

Suddenly an unexpected piece of news burst on the Continent like a thunder-clap. Edward had left his place of refuge in Zealand and had set foot again on his native soil. Charles the Bold, after his initial hesitation, had come to realize that he was achieving nothing by a policy of neutrality and that he would have to support his wife's brother. He had quietly supplied him with the ships and money necessary for a counter-invasion, and Edward had resumed the struggle. Warwick was beaten and killed at Barnet on the 14th April 1471. On the 4th May, at Tewkesbury, Margaret of Anjou's son, Edward of Lancaster, was also killed and Margaret herself was taken prisoner. Henry VI was sent back to the Tower and Edward remounted the throne.

Europe was on the brink of another great war. Edward IV and Charles the Bold renewed the bonds of 1468–1469. On the 1st November 1471, the Treaty of St Omer joined Aragon, Burgundy and Naples in a triple alliance. King John II of Aragon was made a Knight of the Golden Fleece; the King of England was already a member of the Order. There was talk of an English landing in France and of the resumption of the Hundred Years' War. Everywhere people living at the time had the feeling that they were on the verge of an appalling conflagration: Bettini, the Milanese ambassador, wrote that it would be 'a fierce and terrible war'. It was feared that Edward IV might be another Henry V.

England, however, was not in the habit of entering the lists without careful preparation beforehand. Commynes himself observes that the country of parliamentary government was never in any hurry to commit herself.

Charles the Bold, on the other hand, was impatient to be up and doing. Most inadvisedly he did not wait until his allies were ready, but thought he could force Edward's hand and speed up the decision of the Parliament sitting at Westminster by launching a surprise attack. On the 28th May 1472, Charles of France, Duke of Guienne, Mary of Burgundy's betrothed, had died from natural causes. However, there was some talk of poisoning, and it was claimed that Louis XI was responsible for the deed. Sincerely believing this to be true, as can well be imagined, Charles the Bold issued a manifesto accusing Louis and took up arms. After assembling his forces below the walls of Arras and taking advantage of the fact that the existing truce had come to an end, he invaded Vermandois, and took the town of Nesle. The worst atrocities were committed; people were massacred and hanged. Roye was burnt. The most characteristic episode of this Burgundian campaign of 1472 was the siege of Beauvais. The cruelty shown by the duke, far from discouraging his opponents, fired them to even more desperate efforts. Beauvais held out and the legend of Joan Hachette —her real name was Joan Lainé—symbolizes the valiant resistance of the people of Beauvais, whose womenfolk set such a glorious example of heroism.

The defeat of Beauvais, the resolute resistance put up by the king's subjects, and the passivity of Burgundy's allies, who were not yet ready to attack, compelled the duke to accept an armistice at the beginning of 1473.

However, for Charles the Bold, this was no more than a temporary lull. In his imagination he planned a State of Burgundy even more vast and more impressive than the one over which he ruled. He was determined that the royal crown, which Philip the Good had not accepted, should not elude his grasp. At this very moment, it was offered again.

Frederick III, afraid of being caught between Burgundy on the one hand and Mathias Corvin, King of Hungary, on the other, and anxious at the same time to win the powerful duke's friendship, had recourse to the tactics that had been used with Philip the Good and once more proposed that one of the ducal fiefs should be raised to the dignity of a kingdom. This proposal was to provide the theme of a comic interlude to be enacted at Trier.

The Duke of Burgundy had rejected the proposal in the form in which it had been put to him, but like his father before him he continued to negotiate and he prided himself on being able to succeed where the third duke had failed.

In order to strengthen his hopes of success, he had hastened to press home the advantages open to him in the north. Intervening between Arnoul, the Duke of Guelders, and his son Adolphe d'Egmont, he behaved with unexampled brutality: he imprisoned the son and imposed his will on the father, and by the Treaty of Bruges of the 30th December 1472, he forced Arnoul to agree that Burgundy would inherit Guelders and Zutphen in place of Adolphe.

Frederick, disturbed by the speed and forcefulness with which his vassal had acted, deemed it advisable to make a more generous offer.[10] It was not long before a more ambitious project was afoot. The possibility of a marriage between Maximilian and Mary of Burgundy was reconsidered. Mary's father was to receive from Maximilian's father the title of King of the Romans and was guaranteed the expectancy of the imperial crown. Everything was to be settled at a meeting between the two princes at Trier.

In the meantime, the death of Duke Nicholas of Lorraine occurred on the 27th July 1473, and Charles's immediate ambitions were clarified; he intended to seize the Duchy of Lorraine and become sovereign of a state which would comprise not only Lotharingia but the Burgundia of former days and perhaps Provence too, thus conjuring up memories of both Lothair and Gondebad. Clandestine manœuvres were set in motion with a view to obtaining the inheritance of René, Duke of Anjou and Count of Provence, so as to be able to lay claim to the latter territory. It looked as if Marseilles might become once more a Burgundian port as it had been in the fifth century. The dream of kingship which had been cherished for so long was being fast realized, at least in the mind of the man who was called, for the want of any better appellation, the 'great duke of the west' or the 'great duke of the Occident'.

Frederick III arrived at Trier on the 20th September 1473. Both Frederick and Charles had given as the reason for their meeting the betrothal of Mary to Maximilian. The emperor's suite was shabby indeed compared to the dazzling and ostentatious retinue with which Charles arrived. On the following day, as if he had come to attend some triumphal ceremony of consecration, Frederick went to meet his guest, and as he drew near, Charles dismounted and greeted him on bended knee. Rising side by side, the two princes made their official entry into the ancient city cheered on all sides by a vast crowd. After the customary exchange of formal visits, a solemn conference was held in the cloister of St Maximin and the two chancellors—the Archbishop of Mainz on behalf of the Empire and Guillaume Hugouet on behalf of Burgundy—ceremoniously delivered their speeches.

The negotiations were ostensibly aimed at re-establishing peace between Burgundy and France, and organizing a crusade against the Turks. The idea of leading the knights of Europe against the Infidel appealed to the duke and indeed was never absent from his mind, but it was not part of his immediate plan of action. The true purpose of the meeting lay elsewhere—in the secret conversations on the question of the raising of the ducal State into a Kingdom.

As the discussions progressed, the more grandiose became the duke's claims.[11] For a time, there was an extremely good chance that the plan might come to something, but the duke, by his exorbitant demands, ruined the possibility. No doubt underhand manœuvres carried out by Louis XI were also a contributory cause. The discussions went on, but agreement on the details of the plan proved very difficult, and nothing could be settled. Suddenly Frederick took fright; he slipped away in a rather undignified fashion.

On the 25th November, in the middle of the night, he left Trier without informing his guest of his proposed departure, and even without settling his debts. His boatmen rowed him away as fast as they could over the misty waters of the Rhine.

Yet Charles the Bold had felt quite confident of success. He had everything ready, the thrones, the coronation garments, everything in fact that Burgundian pomp and ceremony would have demanded for such an occasion. This set-back of November 1473 was bitter indeed, but it in no way diminished Charles's tireless resolve in his pursuit of a royal crown. He turned once more, with renewed vigour, to the task of 'forging himself a kingdom'. His motto spoke for itself: 'I have set my hand to it'.

On the 23rd January 1474 Charles made his first official entry into Dijon since his accession to power. He took this opportunity of stating publicly, and more explicitly than ever before, his ambitious schemes, and dreams of grandeur. In a speech, delivered on the spot now occupied by the stone steps of the Hôtel de Ville, he reminded his hearers that 'the former kingdom of Burgundy had for a long time been usurped by the French and made a duchy of France, which fact should give all his subjects cause for sorrow'.[12]

This was a significant declaration—a virtual statement of policy—on the eve of the great war that was about to begin. In the duke's resounding proclamations, which clearly announced the intention of restoring the Kingdom of Lotharingia in its entirety, the ambitious aims of the House of Burgundy took shape and seemed within an ace of achieving spectacular success. Frederick had avoided committing himself at Trier—no doubt through a secret agreement with Louis XI—but it was not certain that he would be able to avoid the issue in the same way if Edward IV's headstrong brother-in-law renewed and put into operation the offensive alliance with England that had existed in the days of John the Fearless and Philip the Good. There was a possibility that Charles might bring the Hundred Years' War to a successful conclusion—as John the Fearless and Henry V might well have done had they lived—to the mutual advantage of York and Burgundy.

CHAPTER IX

HISTORIANS AND WRITERS

THE DUKES OF BURGUNDY were surrounded at an early date, and at their own express wish, by a group of gifted and prolific historiographers. They encouraged historical writing and had professional historians on their payrolls. The Marquis de Beaucourt, the historian of Charles VII, was even prompted to remark 'history became Burgundian history', by which he meant that chroniclers and memorialists who flourished under the patronage of the dukes occupy a dominant place among the many widely dispersed writers who left accounts of the happenings of the period.

Enguerrand de Monstrelet, a native of Picardy, was the first of the series, with his *Chroniques*.[1] They cover the period between 1400 and 1444 and include two volumes which claim to be a continuation of Froissart. But, although he followed on from the most illustrious chronicler of the fourteenth century, the Burgundian was far less gifted than his model. His narrative is dull, although full of useful information, and it reveals that he himself had a humdrum personality. 'A decent, quiet man' is the description of him given by the necrologist of Cambrai who reports his death—a short, definitive funeral oration! Enguerrand took great pains not to become involved in the quarrels which rent his own generation. He was naturally on the side of Burgundy, of that there can be no doubt, but whenever he had to deal with a difficult situation he was careful not to say too much. If necessary, rather than say too much, he preferred to say nothing at all. We have already seen that although he was present at the meeting between Philip the Good and Joan of Arc, he made a lapse of memory the excuse for not recording any of the remarks exchanged. A third volume, which is not altogether devoid of interest, although it cannot possibly be attributed to the author of the first two volumes, was added to Monstrelet's work. It has so far been impossible to discover who was responsible for this rather insipid addition.

Monstrelet's real successor was not the unknown anonymous writer but another chronicler who made no attempt to conceal his identity—Mathieu d'Escouchy. He was like Monstrelet a native of Picardy, and he carried the narration of events on from 1444 to 1461. His talent—praised by Michelet in connection with his account of the battle of St Jacques in which the Dauphin Louis defeated the Swiss on the 26th August 1444—contrasts favourably with the literary mediocrity of his predecessor. He has a lively narrative style. There is more than a hint of Froissart's inspiration in the works of Mathieu which is not to be found in the works of the intervening writer.

Mention should be made here of certain writers who provide much important information—the conscientious Pierre de Fénin, the worthy heraldist Le Fèvre de St Rémy, King-at-arms of the Golden Fleece, and the prolific Jean de Wavrin who chose *Anciennes Chroniques d'Angleterre* as the title of his work—before we go on to deal with the really great Burgundian historiographers.

The most representative of them all is undoubtedly the illustrious Georges Chastellain.[2] Olivier de la Marche, whom we shall discuss next, considered him to be the 'pearl and star of historiographers'. Robertet did not disagree since he called him a 'radiant star', proclaimed him equal to the ancients, and placed him at the head of the moderns—'but of all living authors Georges is clearly the greatest'.

The man who was known as 'le grand Georges' was born 'in the imperial county of Alost' in 1415. The date of his birth has sometimes been mistakenly given as 1405, simply on the evidence of the copy of his epitaph which presented him as being seventy on his death in 1475; in fact, as his latest biographer, M. Luc Hommel, has shown, he cannot have lived much beyond the age of sixty. He himself relates that at the age of seven he was placed in an 'infant school', where he began by learning the Lord's Prayer. In 1430 he was a young student at the University of Louvain, founded four years before by Philip the Good: but contrary to what has sometimes been supposed, it seems that he never acquired the degree of 'master of arts' since he never used the title. He supplemented his book-learning by travel, which earned for him the nick-name of 'Georges the Venturesome'—unless he acquired the name while in the service of France during the campaigns against the English between 1435 and 1446.

As early as 1434 he had been an 'esquire' in the duke's service, and he settled permanently at the Burgundian court in 1446. He then became 'esquire-pantler'; several diplomatic missions were entrusted to him, after which he received the titles of esquire-trenchant, cup-bearer, and adviser. He was a courtier, as well as a soldier and diplomat. Generous allowances were granted him and he was given various duties to perform; finally he became permanent historiographer to the House of Burgundy. Letters patent of the 25th June 1455, signed in Louvain by Duke Philip, granted him 657 *livres* and 16 *sous* a year, and commissioned him to 'put into writing the latest matters of interest, in which he was an expert; also to write up in the form of a chronicle all those deeds worthy of being remembered which had occurred to date, which were occurring now, and which might well occur again'. In addition he was granted a 'residence' in the duke's own Hôtel Salle le Comte at Valenciennes: he hardly ever left the town (except when on some private mission) for he was entirely engrossed in his literary activities, especially in the monumental chronicle which, it has been estimated, must have amounted, when finished, to no fewer than ten thousand in-folio sheets.

The prologue to this mammoth work was written shortly after the capture of Constantinople by the Turks in 1453. Book II dates probably from about 1465, but was subsequently revised.

He had already made great headway with this work when the death of Philip the Good in 1467 deprived Chastellain of his first patron. Fortunately, Charles the Bold maintained the faithful and industrious historiographer in the office which his predecessor had created for him. Charles went even further; he made Chastellain a Knight of the Golden Fleece at the Chapter held at Valenciennes on the 2nd May 1473, and appointed him as historiographer of the Order.

Thus rewarded and encouraged, Georges Chastellain continued to work until his death, which took place either on the 13th or the 20th February 1475. Fortunately he passed away before misfortune overtook the dynasty to which he had devoted the efforts of a lifetime.[3]

Chastellain's historical work is called *Chronique ou Livre de Tous les haulx faits de la Chrestienté, souverainement de ce noble royaume de France et de ses dépendances depuis l'an vingt jusqu'à maintenant*— 'Chronicle or Book of all the doughty deeds of Christendom, chiefly of the noble Kingdom of France and her dependencies from the year twenty until the present day', that is to say until 1474. Unfortunately we possess only a fraction of what he wrote and the excellent quality of the surviving fragments makes us regret still more keenly the parts that have been lost. Methodically and meticulously, he turned all his information to good account, whether it came to him from written sources or through direct contact with people. Chastellain knew the last two dukes and their households extremely well; he was informed about everything that went on and no testimony is comparable to his.

Chastellain was at once a philosopher and a man of high moral principles. He had a lofty conception of the dignity and function of the historian. He was by nature reflective and discerning. His work, official though it was, never loses the serenity which befitted his subject, and if its literary value has never been properly appreciated, this is because his archaic language, with its antiquated rhythm closely modelled on the Latin sentence, compares unfavourably for the modern reader with the lively narrative of his contemporary, Commynes. There is, however, no mistaking the fact that in the opinion of the fifteenth century, the two authors could not be compared. Only Chastellain was deemed worthy of the title of writer, and Commynes himself would have subscribed to this opinion.

Chastellain's prologue is an astonishing piece of writing. With keen shrewdness he analyses the historian's three-fold task—learned research, synthesis, and the creation of a suitable form. He estimates the true value of the various aspects of the historical discipline—textual criticism, impartiality and objectivity: and although the modesty apparent in this masterly prologue is genuine enough, it is impossible not to detect at the same time the author's conviction that he has had the ability to make what he calls 'a sifting of truth'. No other mediaeval writer was capable of expressing himself in this way, or of grasping so completely the essential function of the historian. Chastellain is not only a first-class chronicler but for whom our knowledge of the fifteenth century would have been very inadequate, he is a genuine historian, a French Thucydides who stands out among the welter of Herodotuses of varying merit who were typical of French mediaeval historiography. Even if Chastellain had stood alone, his achievement would have been enough to give exceptional eminence to historical writing in the Burgundian State.

With Olivier de la Marche[4] we return to a humbler, more ordinary level—that of the straightforward memorialist.

But although this native of Bresse lacked the intellectual power of Chastellain, his colleague and friend, he nevertheless achieved a respectable standard, and from every point of view he deserved the esteem in which his equals held him. Like Chastellain he made his career at court where he held the office of pantler. He organized many entertainments, in particular the celebrations which marked the marriage of Charles the Bold and Margaret of York, and of which he was careful to leave a long description. He was entrusted with several diplomatic missions, but it is somewhat disappointing to find that he preferred to enlarge on military exploits, parades and banquets. Chastellain died before the collapse of the Burgundian State, but Olivier de la Marche, who lived until 1502, witnessed the dismemberment of the empire built up by the great dukes. This was a source of intense sorrow to him, but his loyalty never wavered and to his great joy he acted as master of ceremonies at the marriage of Mary of Burgundy and Maximilian. The Hapsburg prince was his last master and he served him as devotedly as Philip the Good or Charles the Bold. The sincere and reliable *Mémoires* of the faithful Olivier constitute one of the most valuable and fascinating sources for the study of Burgundian history.

After these first-class writers mention should be made of several authors who dealt more specifically with the Burgundian Low Countries—men like Edmond de Dynter, Adrien de But, Jean de Haynin, and Jacques de Hemricourt.[5]

All the literary genres, whether in prose or verse, which were fashionable in the fifteenth century, were cultivated at the ducal court just as much as history was.[6]

We will deal first of all with epic poetry and romances on mediaeval themes.

At the beginning of the *Chanson des Saisnes* (*The Song of the Saxons*) we are solemnly informed that there are three main epic cycles:

> For any man of discernment
> There are only three themes,
> France, Britain and great Rome,
> And these three themes have no equal.

The French national epic, which has been called 'a primitive form of history', and which was in actual fact semi-fictitious history put into verse form for the needs of the feudal world, can hardly be considered on its own. By the fifteenth century it was rather out of favour and it often merged with the Breton epics and with those which used classical antiquity as their starting-point, if not their inspiration. As has already been seen, considerable space was allotted to this type of poem in Philip the Bold's library. They were not purely Burgundian works, but belonged to the general literature of the Middle Ages, and might even be said to be international in inspiration. Nevertheless, so assiduously were they read in Burgundy, that they gave the ducal Court a literary tone, a unique spiritual quality, which characterized the princes and the high-ranking nobles of their entourage.

It should perhaps be mentioned in passing that if both readers and collectors showed a marked predilection for *Girart de Roussillon*, a work which belonged to *Burgundia* in the widest sense,[7] their preference was surely not unconnected with the ambitions of the House of Burgundy. The prose version of *Girart* by Wauquelin deserves special mention since it enjoyed great popularity, being linked with the legend of the carrying of the body of St Mary Magdalene to Vézelay, the famous Burgundian abbey.

Alongside the epic, there existed another group of works, both in prose and poetry, which dealt with topical and political matters and relied on the contemporary scene, and to a certain extent on the world of chivalry, for inspiration. The *Geste des ducs de Bourgogne* and the *Livre des faits du bon chevalier messire Jacques de Lalaing*, belong to this group.

The *Geste des ducs de Bourgogne* is a verse chronicle. As G. Doutrepont has rightly said: 'it is one of those laboured rhapsodies which represent the final phase of the declining epic'. The author of the poem, which glorifies the first two of the great dukes, remains unknown. The work extols the chief military episodes of the two reigns—for example, the capture of Audenarde under Philip the Bold on the 23rd May 1384, the campaign waged by John the Fearless in 1408 when he helped to restore his brother-in-law John of Bavaria, Prince-Bishop of Liége, to his throne, and the glorious days of Burgundian domination in Paris. The anonymous poet never tires of expressing his admiration for the popularity enjoyed by John the Fearless:

> There was neither mason, nor roofer, nor carpenter,
> Weaver, nor fuller, nor hose-maker nor draper,
> Armorist nor goldsmith, inn-keeper, baker,
> Neither woman nor child who in order to rejoice
> Did not start shouting 'Noël' in a loud voice.

The cry 'Noël', which corresponds to the modern 'bravo', was enthusiastically taken up by the people, especially by the 'mechanicals', who were, as we know, the chief supporters of the liberal-minded duke. The author is lavish in his praise of these henchmen of his master. Pierre des Essarts, the Provost of Paris appointed by John, is also brought into the limelight alongside the prince and great importance is attributed to the office he held.

It has been commonly supposed that the anonymous author took up the pen at the express wish of Philip the Good, who was anxious to honour his father and grandfather. This is a plausible assumption, although it cannot be proved.

The *Livre des faits du bon chevalier messire Jacques de Lalaing*, which can be compared with that other '*livre des faits*' of which Boucicaut is the hero, enthusiastically commemorates the exploits of the great Lalaing—the famous paragon of chivalry, whose engaging personality and noble virtues will be described in the chapter on Court life.

The works we have just listed were inspired to some extent by what might be called Burgundian propaganda, but the tendency is most obvious in the anonymous poem called the *Pastoralet*, which aimed at bringing discredit on the Duke of Orleans and on everything connected with Burgundy's arch-enemy. The author makes little attempt to conceal where his sympathies lie, for he is writing, so he informs his readers, 'principally in honour and praise of the most noble and excellent prince, John, Count of Flanders and Artois'. In the guise of 'a piece of fiction', or '*pastourerie*' (pastoral) he depicts the state of France as he saw it, or as he wanted other people to see it. The characters who appear are given pseudonyms: Florentin is Charles VI; Belligère, Isabella; Tristifer, Louis of Orleans; Léonet, John the Fearless; Lupal, Bernard VII, and so on. Naturally Tristifer is represented as being Belligère's lover, and both are made out to be thoroughly bad and totally unscrupulous. Tristifer is trying to poison Florentin. The '*bal des Ardents*' figures as an episode in this disguised piece of propaganda and all the incidents present Léonet in a favourable light.

The work is of some literary interest in that it substitutes for the stiff and heavy verses of the epic a short brisk line with a rustic flavour which falls pleasantly on the ear and is not readily forgotten. Here, for example, is the dialogue between Tristifer and Belligère who are disporting themselves in the country:

Pretty shepherdess
Let us live happily
In this leafy wood
—My friend, let us do so
I have always been fond
Of a merry life.

In this summer weather
For joy
I want to laugh and sing
—It is my nature
And my desire
To always be as merry as possible.

In these ingenuous and thinly disguised confessions, the caricature must have been obvious to all. The author has many sly digs at the two accomplices. When Belligère imagines that she has been betrayed by her fickle lover, she complains bitterly:

> My sad heart is shaken within me
> As the wind shakes a sail.

Antoine de la Sale is on a far higher level. His treatise, *Des anciens tournois et faits d'armes* which he finished on the 4th January 1459, celebrates famous jousting contests which had taken place at the Court of Burgundy. De la Sale associated with the Luxemburg and St Pol families and it is interesting to see that the famous author of the most renowned romance of the period, *Le Petit Jehan de Saintré*, had connections with the Burgundian Court.

Surprise has been expressed,[8] understandably enough, at the fact that no writer attached to the Burgundian Court devoted his energies to a study of St Andrew, whose cross, as we know, played an important part in Burgundian politics. Olivier de la Marche tells how one of the ancient Kings of Burgundy, 'a very good Catholic', having had the apostle's cross brought to Marseilles, held it in 'such devotion and reverence' that he 'adopted it as the emblem of his troops'. Whatever the truth of the legend, the cross served as the military badge of the ducal House; it was emblazoned on the battle-flags and was used as the distinguishing mark of the Burgundian party in the quarrel with the Armagnacs.[9]

Although St Andrew was never the subject of any literary work, Burgundian hagiography produced the extremely popular *Mappemonde Spirituelle* by Jean Germain. The author of this vast compilation was a protégé of Margaret of Bavaria and Philip the Good, who paid for his upbringing and education, and he remained very attached to both mother and son throughout his whole life. He was both a priest and a man of letters. As early as 1429, he became adviser to the duke. He was Isabella of Portugal's confessor, Bishop of Nevers, Chief Chancellor of the Order of the Golden Fleece, and finally, in 1436, Bishop of Chalon-sur-Saône. He represented the head of the Burgundian State at the congresses held at Basle and Ferrara, and he was busy on the plans for the crusade when he died suddenly, on the 2nd February 1460.

His *Mappemonde Spirituelle*, dedicated to Philip the Good, was composed 'for the defence of our holy Christian faith and for the confusion of the enemies of Christianity'. The author gives a geographical description of the world, mentioning the various nations and races, then he enumerates the places made famous by the life and death of Christ, the Virgin Mary and the Apostles and 'the most renowned martyrs, confessors, virgins and widows': in short, as G. Doutrepont says, 'he put together a veritable encyclopaedia which contains details relating to several towns in Belgium; it shows evidence of extremely wide knowledge, and appears to have had great success'.

Maître Alard's translation of Chrysostom from Latin into French was a more modest undertaking; it merely offered the reader 'a short and highly moral treatise' by the famous Greek teacher, under the title of *Réparation du Pécheur*. Alard was 'Dean and Canon of the church at Leuze under the authority of the most illustrious Prince Philip, Duke of Burgundy'.

The interest in the east, quickened by the various plans for crusades which always found favour with the Burgundian Court, accounts for several works, one or two of which deserve at least to be mentioned here, for although lacking in originality, they were of considerable topical interest.

We have already mentioned the *Journey to the East* by Bertrandon de la Broquière—his name was actually Labroquère—who was sent to Jerusalem by Philip the Good.[10] Bertrandon visited Palestine, Western Syria, Asia Minor, Constantinople and Serbia. His return journey took him through Hungary, Bavaria and Switzerland. Although he had no literary pretentions, he was not without talent both as an observer and as a handler of language.

Eustace Deschamps, whose contribution to French literature includes several interesting poems and who had many links with the ducal House, produced a rather primitive translation from the Latin, a *Complainte de l'Eglise moult désolée aujourd'hui*, which, as the author himself states, was undertaken 'at the command of our Lord of Burgundy'.

Nicopolis could hardly leave Burgundian writers indifferent. The disaster and the thirst for revenge which it inspired prompted the writing of *L'Epistre lamentable*,[11] whose author, 'who does not deserve to be named on account of his great sins', was none other than the famous Philippe de Mézières, a former chancellor of the Kingdom of Cyprus and a close friend of Charles V.

Among the countless satirical writings and topical treatises to which the successive plans for a crusade gave rise, Miélot's *Terre Sainte*, which appeared in 1456, is worthy of note, as is also the magnificent parchment manuscript containing Torzelo's *Advis* along with Bertrandon's *Voyage*, and which is mentioned in an inventory made in 1467 as being one of the books belonging to Philip the Good.

We come now to what can be called profane and didactic literature.

Works on hunting, chess, and strategy, as well as encyclopaedic compilations, occupied an important place in the libraries of fifteenth-century princes. But no outstanding work of purely Burgundian inspiration can be found among the many manuscripts of this kind which formed part of the libraries of the four great dukes.

It should, however, be recalled that Christine de Pisan's *Mutacion de Fortune* was commissioned by Philip the Bold.

Perhaps, too, John Petit's *Justification*, in which he vindicated tyrannicide and commended the crime committed in 1407, should be included in this category. There is no point in repeating what has already been said on the subject of this work, the most representative of all those produced by the group of rather disreputable university clerks, ready to turn their hand to anything, who were part of John the Fearless's entourage. It should perhaps be added, however, that it was conceived and composed according to the most rigid rules of contemporary scholasticism. The mediaeval discourse had its peculiar pattern. The argument was developed pedantically according to the involutions of syllogistic composition (in the case of the *Justification*, it is a 'Barbara' syllogism). Rhetorical structures of this kind had an aesthetic appeal for the initiated, and the *Justification* must have made on the scholars of the period the same sort of impression that a fugue written for a musical contest would make today on an audience of musicians. We are now incapable of appreciating this highly specialized literary form so that a work such as John Petit's seems irritating, rather than attractive. But in order to understand why it was popular we must put ourselves in the place of the people who really derived enjoyment from it; otherwise, we cannot grasp why the mediaeval 'doctors' were held in such high esteem when today they strike us as being so second-rate. Their compositions, which to us appear heavy, obscure and diffuse, were considered by their admirers as learned, ingenious and altogether commendable productions.

The *Champion des Dames*, written by Martin Le Franc in 1442 and dedicated to Philip the Good, is more deserving of interest. It celebrates the Treaty of Arras of 1438 and presents Isabella of Portugal as the true promoter of peace.

> Through her the dreadful war comes to an end
> And peace sets to work once more
> Long live the noble duchess
> Long live the Lady of Burgundy!

The work, however, did not have the success the author had hoped for, since Le Franc, who was an ardent supporter of the rights of the man of letters, felt compelled to write a defence of it, under the title of *Complainte du Livre du Champion des dames à maistre Martin le Franc son acteur*.

The *Advertissement au duc Charles soubs fiction de son propre entendement parlant à luy-même*, by the great Chastellain himself, belongs to the same literary genre.

Charles the Bold had just acceded to the ducal throne. The '*acteur*' —in other words, the author—describes how he has 'retired to a room by himself' in order to give free reign to the grief he felt at the death of the 'august Duke Philip, the great lion, the great Duke of Burgundy, the pillar of the honour of France, and the jewel of Christian princes'. Then Chastellain has a vision. Charles appears to him surrounded by numerous allegorical figures, among whom is a youth called 'Clear Judgment', accompanied by a lady called 'Self-Knowledge'. The youth is to be the author's mouthpiece. He introduces his companion who is 'the key to all the rest' to the duke, and recalls the pomp and splendour of the dynasty. In his view, no human voice can do full justice to Philip the Good. But can Philip really be dead when human beings have virtually turned him into a god? However, the first two dukes have left behind on earth an heir to whom the speaker now addresses himself: 'Thou art the most gifted prince in the whole of Christendom, and the one with the most illustrious kinsmen' he says to him. After this exordium comes a procession of the attendants, both male and female, of 'Clear Judgment' and 'Self-Knowledge'; these represent the virtues which should be practised and the vices which should be shunned. Finally the '*acteur*' appeals to the prince, who is about to inaugurate the fourth reign: 'do not become one of those men who pervert good into evil, and who change the peace and salvation of men into anguish of heart'. The heir will eventually suffer the same fate as his predecessors: 'they have rendered their accounts; the day will come when thou hast to render thine. Therefore work at thy garland and adorn it with beautiful flowers'. After this exhortation from 'Self-Knowledge' the assembly disperses; the author awakens and feels that he must immediately commit to paper all that he has had the good fortune to hear. Obviously, Chastellain is less gifted as an apologist than as a historian.

Another similar work, the *Lyon Couronné*, by an anonymous author, also laments the third duke's death, this time half in prose and half in verse, then gives heartening advice to his successor. Philip was 'a most unconquered Caesar, the jewel of princes and

Christians, the pride of all the nobility, the true mirror, patron and example of knightly prowess'. The poet has a vision; he sees a palace from which two ladies emerge, Envy and Honest Endeavour. Between them is a young lion and each is trying to coax the lion to come to her. But help is given most opportunely to Honest Endeavour by Diligent Pursuit, Great Ability, Perseverance, and Glorious Purpose. Realizing that she can do nothing against the combined strength of her enemies, Envy, in despair, throws herself into a well.

Charles Soillot, Charles the Bold's godson and secretary, was among the men who proffered good advice to the last duke. He composed a *Débat de Félicité* in which Dame Church, Dame Nobility and Dame Labour—in short, the Three Estates—take part in a dialogue written in a mixture of prose and verse. The Court of Knowledge is consulted to determine which of these rivals holds the secret of happiness. The court settles the matter by affirming that true happiness is only to be found in Heaven.

Count Amé de Montgesoie wrote in the same vein. His *Pas de la Mort*—a title also adopted by Chastellain for one of his treatises—shows the author caught between two knights, Sudden Accident and Feeble Old-age, Death's two major agents.

The minstrels who amused and entertained the Court were often writers, and we shall see in the description of Court life, how their services were used. Being writers as well as actors, they constituted a very active and popular corporation. To be a minstrel was to be a member of an organized profession.

It was the tradition in Flanders for most of the big towns to have a '*Chambre de rhétorique*' which was a sort of society of dramatic art. Philip the Good and Charles the Bold took an interest in these groups, the productions of which did, in fact, influence public opinion. They had to be given encouragement, but at the same time they needed to be carefully watched and if necessary brought to heel. In 1455, Philip prohibited seditious verse, which proves that such verse was in circulation. Charles the Bold used even harsher measures than his father in order to curb the high-spirited maliciousness of the *chambres*, for he was often a butt for the poets' jests. On the other hand the *chambres* took part in celebrations, receptions and official entries, and were generously rewarded for their services.

In 1421 the Douai group performed an entertainment called a '*jeu de farse*' for Philip the Good. Unfortunately the title, and others of a similar nature, give no hint of the topics dealt with. But from the number of artists mentioned in official records as being players of '*farces*', '*apartises*' or '*parture*' or who are described as 'characters', and 'Morris dancers', it is clear that this type of popular theatre was greatly appreciated. Listed in these documents are such names as Phlot d'Enfer (1428), Bolequerre and Perrin Boisquement (1434), Maître Mouche (1434), Hance Crachre and many others. One man, Michaut Taillevent,[12] was a member of the ducal household, and received regular payment for his services.

At an official reception for Philip the Good, held in February 1422, the city of Dijon offered him, among other entertainments, 'several mysteries and several martyrdoms'. The 14th April 1432, the day on which Josse, the same duke's son was born, was the occasion of similar celebrations; the town of Ghent even organized a competition among the Flemish towns and contributed an entertainment of its own: Malines won first prize, Audenarde second prize.

Often in contemporary documents we find mention of similar kinds of festivities. On the 3rd January 1455, for instance, the official arrival at Lille of Isabella of Portugal, the new Countess of Charolais, was celebrated with 'historical pageants'. The birth of her daughter, Mary of Burgundy in 1457 was celebrated in the same way at Lille and Béthune. When, on the 23rd April 1458, Philip the Good returned to Ghent, after recently crushing the rebellion of the town, he was not only given a warm welcome, as we have already noted in connection with the duke's policy, but his return was also made the occasion for sensational celebrations. Along the processional route, 'platforms' had been erected and on these improvised stages, episodes with some bearing on contemporary events were enacted: Julius Caesar, surrounded by twelve senators, with Cicero facing him and praising him for having freed several prisoners after he had captured Rome; Pompey granting a free pardon to Tigranes; Mars dressed up to suggest the three Orders of the State. One group gave a flattering representation of the Altar-piece of the mystic Lamb. An elephant walked past the duke carrying a tower full of negroes, armed with arrows and shouting, 'Long live Burgundy is our cry!' The *Prince d'Amour*, a troupe from Tournai, was summoned to Quesnoy in 1461 by Isabella, Countess of Charolais, when she was organizing an entertainment in that town. In 1468, the *Judgement of Paris* was performed at Lille for Charles the Bold, but it must have been a burlesque. Although the three rival goddesses each wore a golden crown, Venus, we are told, was a colossal woman weighing about two hundredweight, while Juno was of the same height but slender as a reed, and Minerva was both hump-backed and pigeon-breasted. One can imagine with what guffaws of laughter they were greeted. In the same year, 1468, even the moving episode of the demolition of Liége was dramatized by professional actors; Georges de Brelbes, 'a jester from Béthune', received a bonus for having performed the *Destruction de Liége*.

Drama of a higher order was performed, as well as the more popular form. Although the mysteries were on the decline they still enjoyed a certain vogue. One of them was the *Mystère du Siège d'Orléans*, the author of which had no qualms about giving history some strange twists in order to work in somehow or other a part for Duke Philip.[13]

Chastellain himself composed two works, the *Mort du duc Philippe* and the *Paix de Péronne*, which were intended for performance. As G. Doutrepont says, these compositions, which were sub-titled *mystères*, could be more accurately described as historical or political morality plays.[14]

In the first, the author celebrates the splendour of the reign which has just drawn to a close and moralizes about death respecting neither fame nor greatness. Heaven, Earth, Angels, and Men, each represented by an actor, come forward to say what they think of the great prince who has just died. The character representing *Men* tells how he saw a phial 'adorned with most precious stones, descend from the celestial spheres and how everyone bowed down before it.' But the thread which holds the phial snaps—the phial falls to the ground and is smashed to pieces. This phial symbolizes destiny. The play ends with the cry of Hosanna.

It seems that the *Paix de Péronne* was performed at the castle of Aire, in 1468, in the presence of Charles the Bold and Louis XI, who happened by some miracle, and for a brief moment, to have patched up their quarrel. It was a 'mystery written to celebrate the aforementioned peace, with the best intentions and on the assumption that the terms will be observed by the contracting parties'. A note of wariness can be detected, however, in this optimistic declaration. Yet it was difficult for people not to be pleased at the touching display of unanimity between the king and the duke, even though it had been achieved at the cost of sacrificing Liége:

> Sing, dance, little children;
> You, grown-ups, join hands;
> Bend your backs and spines
> Poor ploughman in the fields,
> Be of good cheer at this time
> Of re-birth.

Sing then songs and carols,
Ye joyful guests assembled
Before the huge kitchen fire
For these two noble pelicans
Who, in order to nourish you,
Have pierced their own breasts.

Mouth and Heart, Judgement and Sense, who play here the same sort of rôle as the chorus in classical tragedy, then extol all the promises contained in the Péronne agreement. One wonders whether the enthusiastic supporters of Charles the Bold really believed in this deceptive dawn heralding a glorious day which was to have no sequel and was, in fact, to be immediately darkened by storm clouds.

Lastly, we have to mention lyric poetry. Philip the Good should head the list of poets, if he is really the author of certain verses attributed to him and which were written in reply to a request in verse made by that genuine poet—Charles of Orleans—who solicited Burgundian help to obtain his release from captivity in England. Philip's answer to Charles is couched in verse which is not devoid of charm.

S'il en était à mon vouloir
Mon maitre et amy, sans changier
Je vous asseure, pour tout voir,
Qu'en vos fais n'aurez nul dangier
Mais pardeça sans attargier
Vous verroye hors de prison
Quitte de tout, pour abregier
En ceste presente saison.

(If it were in my power
My master and friend, with no duplicity
I assure you in very truth
That there would be no uncertainty in your affairs,
And moreover without delay
I would see you out of prison,
And in short free of everything
In this present season.)

So begins the first ballad, and the second opens with the following verse:

Du cueur, de corps et de puissance
Vous mercie très humblement
De vostre bonne souvenance
Qu'avez de moi soigneusement

Or povez faire entièrement
De moy en tout bien et honneur
Comme votre cueur le propose,
Et de mon vouloir soyez seur
Quoique nul dye ne deppose.

(With heart, body and all my power,
I thank you very humbly
For the kind memory of me that you retain so zealously
And you may do with me
In all truth and honour
As your heart wishes
And be assured of my good will
Whatever anyone may say or affirm.)

There is nothing in these lines of outstanding quality, but even Chastellain's attempts at verse are hardly more successful. 'In short, if Philip is really the author, it must be admitted that he was quite as good as his hired poets, and that for once there was nothing to choose between Maecenas and Horace.'[15]

But, again according to G. Doutrepont, whose somewhat optimistic verdict we have just quoted, 'composing was only an incidental pastime for Maecenas, who was the patron and not the rival of poets'.

A 'poetaster' put into verse the burlesque 'blason'[16] by Colin Boule, who was 'chief jester' at the ducal residence. On Judgement Day, everyone is brought together, irrespective of their armorial bearings:

Pope, emperor, prelate, duke and count;

God will deal justly with everyone:

Then he will open, to the sound of trumpets,
His vast and universal chamber of accounts.

This has at least the merit of being a fresh and apposite metaphorical rendering of the 'Last Judgement'.

Several poems by Chastellain—who unfortunately, as we have already said, was less gifted as a poet than as a prose writer—should be classed under the heading of lyric verse: for instance *Le Lion bandé*. The metrical ingenuity of some of these poems delighted his contemporaries, but today they have no appeal whatever; for instance, he wrote an acrostic on Philippus, in which all the lines of each separate verse begin with the same letter of the duke's name, while each verse is supposed to be spoken by one of the great fiefs of the Burgundian State. The last one, corresponding to the letter S and to Franche-Comté, runs as follows:

Son bruyant bruit, dont luy vif abondait
Sous terre gist, ne reste mie que la fame;
Ses faits sont fés: il a fait comme on doit,
Sa mort l'amort qui toute riens affame,
Soit l'ame en bruit comme en terre on l'afame,
Sainte et sain ohiés, vive et sans vergogne
Supplie à Dieu la comté de Bourgogne.

(His noisy fame, of which he had a great deal, when alive,
Lies under the earth, only his glory remains;
His deeds are done: he did as one ought to do,
His death quietens him, as it reduces everything,
May his soul be as famous as he is on earth,
Saints, hear, in lively manner and without shame
The county of Burgundy makes a supplication to God.)

Molinet, Chastellain's successor as historiographer, also sang the praises of Philip the Good and his *Throsne d'honneur*, in lyric verse. For Molinet, Philip's throne was 'a flower among flowers' which nothing could ever destroy.

There can be no doubt that the dukes supervised this splendid literary activity personally. In spite of the fact that it produced no work which could be classed as a masterpiece, and did not achieve the brilliance of other forms of art which will be described presently, the value of some of the Burgundian literary productions should not be underestimated.

In a previous chapter we saw how well stocked the ducal library was under Philip the Bold. John the Fearless, and even more so Philip the Good and after him Charles the Bold, had an exceptionally keen love of books. They were constantly adding new volumes to their collections, and they possessed a wealth of magnificent illustrated manuscripts. Although there is no proof that the dukes had their own special school of calligraphy, as has sometimes been maintained, the orders they gave kept the various centres within their estates, or in Paris, in a state of great prosperity. Work was done for them not only in Paris but also at Dijon and in other towns inside the duchy, and more especially in the Low Countries, in Lille, in particular, in Brussels, Mons, Grammont, Ghent, Bruges, Audenarde, La Haye and in many other places. The *Bibliothèque de Bourgogne* at Brussels, where the remnants of scattered libraries or of collections which have often changed hands, have been brought together, still bears witness today to the taste of the Burgundian dukes.

Incidentally, the fact that the duke's keeper of the jewels was often entrusted with the care of these precious books, showed that they were considered as valuable possessions.[17] There were regular library officials and a checking system which made it possible to keep track of the volumes and to ascertain which had been lent, or given away. In the palace at Dijon, there was a 'library tower' and several inventories which provided information about the state of any volume at a given date.

It may be asked whether the dukes themselves were great readers or whether they merely collected books? Admittedly, their political and social obligations did not normally allow them to lead the leisurely and idle existence of the noblemen or wealthy burgesses who were free to spend as much time as they liked in their studies. But all the evidence goes to show that the manuscripts in their library were often read. Philip the Bold, like Charles V, liked to enjoy his valuable possessions. The eventful life led by John the Fearless certainly allowed him little time for recreation, but Philip the Good, especially in his old age, devoted a good deal of time 'to the study of his books',[18] and Charles the Bold, whom the memorialist Olivier de la Marche described as being particularly scholarly in his youth, is presented by the same writer as still being eager in his pursuit of culture in his later years: 'he would never retire to bed until someone had read to him for two hours, and he was often read to by the Lord of Humbercourt who was a good reader and who had a good memory'. The duchesses were equally anxious to educate themselves, especially Margaret of Bavaria and Margaret of York. Isabella of Portugal invited to her court Portuguese scholars such as Vasco de Lucena who translated Xenophon and Quintus Curtius.[19]

The account books of the period bear eloquent witness to the dukes' generosity towards writers. Scholars were warmly welcomed by the princes and were often entrusted with duties at once honourable and lucrative. Several of the authors we have mentioned were esquires, heralds, valets or counsellors. Only Chastellain, however, was made a Knight of the Golden Fleece.

CHAPTER X

ART

OF ALL THE LANDS which have been recognized as homes of the fine arts, Burgundy has, at every point in history, stood out as one of the most remarkable. It was in Burgundy that the brilliant school of Romanesque architecture was developed before Cluny made it famous throughout the whole of Christendom. Gothic art flourished in Burgundy, with the charm of its particular style, and that wonderful masterpiece, Notre Dame de Dijon, is perhaps with the Sainte Chapelle in Paris, the most accomplished, the most finished, example of French architecture. Nevertheless, when we refer to 'Burgundian art' we think, strictly speaking, of the art produced at the time of the great dukes, and in particular of the famous school of Sluter. At this period, the Burgundian State unquestionably reached one of the pinnacles of aesthetic achievement.[1]

This glorious school of art owed its inception to the patronage of the dukes. The fame it brought the Valois of Burgundy was due, then, in the first place to the initiative taken by Philip the Bold. Although the Chartreuse did not monopolize all artistic energy, it kept the Dijon School busy and so helped that school to achieve the great privilege of evolving a characteristic style.

Admittedly, the Burgundians' natural gift for sculpture played an important part in the success of the Dijon School. Nor should one fail to mention among the other favourable circumstances, the excellent quality of the stone found in the many quarries near the capital of the duchy. But the supreme factor was the sponsorship of the princes themselves. The school was an official institution; its continued existence was guaranteed and its survival ensured. The leading sculptor of the school could work at his own pace, since he was financially supported by the dukes, and had time in which to elaborate his aesthetic formulae, to perfect them and to put them into operation. The achievements of the school show how beneficial the system was.

However, an aesthetic formula alone cannot realize its full potentialities: it must be allied to the genius of a great artist, who has the ability to combine the scattered and fluctuating elements present in the artistic climate of his time, into a single, harmonious whole. The Dijon School was fortunate in having at its head Claus Sluter, the foremost sculptor of the century.

The sculptured work at the Chartreuse of Champmol had been entrusted to Jean de Marville, who was perhaps responsible for the Vierge du Portail, but Sluter, his pupil, who had succeeded him even as early as 1389, was the real leader of the new school, and it was he who ensured its fame.

Sluter was a native of Haarlem. Having been born in the Low Countries, he was a Burgundian subject: it is childish to affirm, as some critics have done, that a Dutchman cannot have created 'Burgundian art'. Surely the duke's various domains had the right to contribute to his artistic fame, just as they helped to establish his political and economic power.

It is in any case impossible to confine an artist of Sluter's stature to any one district or region. He wielded the chisel with supreme dexterity and boldness. Many of his works have unfortunately been lost, and we only know of their existence through contemporary references; but what remains, whether on the portal of the Chartreuse, or the *Puits des Prophètes*, or the tomb of Philip the Bold, is enough to put the sculptor in the same class as Michelangelo.

His work represented a synthesis of various elements: some he had received from the country of his birth, the Low Countries, at that time the centre of an all-pervading, triumphant and objective realism; others he found in his adopted country, Burgundy, which had inherited from the past a realism just as powerful as that of the Low Countries, but more human, and not without a certain intellectual content, and which had certain features peculiar to the Burgundian temperament, such as a sense of balance and a feeling for composition. Others again he borrowed from Paris and Bourges, where a French artistic revival was already under way, curbing the exuberance of inspiration by discernment and moderation, the characteristic traits of French genius. Finally, he drew from the depth of his own being the gift of assimilating what was best in the most widely divergent aesthetic systems, and the ability to reproduce the physical idiosyncrasy of his model while at the same time endowing the work with the soul of an idealized character, and to create a uniform whole with a diversity of human types.

The Jews who were used as models for the *Puits des Prophètes*—if we are to judge by the costumes, they were almost certainly acting a mystery play—might have come straight from the ghetto.[2] The figures give the impression of having been drawn ruthlessly from life. But through the concrete reality of the old Jew chosen to represent Moses and who is the most impressive of these figures, the sculptor is careful to reveal his conception of the leader of men on his way down from Mount Sinai: the eyes of the law-maker who is in a state of ecstasy after his meeting with Jehovah, still retain the reflection of the Divine presence. A comparison between Sluter's Moses and the Moses of Michelangelo produces the definite impression that these two artists are of the same calibre.

Each of the five other prophets placed round the monument is treated with equal mastery; each shows the same meticulous attention to detail, the same ability to conjure up irresistibly a human type.[3] Christ's condemnation according to the Prophecies provided the subject of the work and the scene of the crucifixion was represented on the edge of the well.[4]

Unfortunately the cross has been destroyed—an irreparable loss. But a fragment at least, and as it happens a highly significant fragment, has been preserved—the head of Christ, which is to be seen in the Archaeological Museum at Dijon.

Sluter has been hailed by critics as a realist; they have, however, been too ready to disregard the intellectual aspect of his art. His head of Christ on the cross, with its closed eyes, is essentially the work of a thinker, and shot through with the most sublime form of Christian inspiration. Far from indulging either in a harsh and facile realism which would have made the tortured face wince with pain, or falling back on the cold conventionality of the traditional style, Sluter has infused the face of his Christ with a divine grief, profound yet serene and supremely composed. We are conscious not only of Christ, but of the God in Christ. Death does not affect Christ in the same way as it would affect a man. A dead God is not a lifeless body; life in him appears quiescent, not extinct. This human frame, even when devoid of human life, must appear to have been the dwelling of a God and worthy of being so again; in short, the mystery of the Incarnation and the miracle of the Resurrection are implicit in the carving. In creating this sublime head of Christ, Sluter was surely inspired by his own faith as a sincere and practising Catholic, a faith which finally led him to end his days in a monastery.

A work as accomplished as the head of Christ bears the stamp of a mature artist. Claus Sluter did not attain such heights at the outset of his career. He had worked at Brussels before going to Dijon to collaborate with Jean de Marville, and the duke's account books make it possible to determine the exact date of some of his works. The Virgin on the portal at Champmol is not mentioned in the accounts, but the other statues decorating the portal are, and they show a development in his art which tallies with their chronological order. The patron saints—St Catherine and St John the Baptist—do not reveal the same mastery as is evident in the statues of the duke, Philip the Bold, and his wife Margaret of Flanders. The finest work of all is the statue of the Valois prince, a superb example of historical statuary and a masterpiece of its kind.

Sluter's kneeling duke is a study of the man of action at prayer. The fervour of his communion with God bestows on his reflective countenance, with its full cheeks and strongly-marked features, a religious nobility which is intensified by the extraordinary radiance in the eyes. But in appealing to Heaven, the prince is still mindful of the Earth; he is not a sinner cringing before God, but a Head of State communing with the Virgin and beseeching her to help him. And it is difficult not to believe that the closed lips are offering up a prayer which includes the request that the ducal policy may be crowned with success. Sluter's skill is such that the statue acquires all the significance of a historical document, and is at once a work of art and a representation of an actual personality. Everything, including the characteristic cloak worn by the figure, proclaims that here we have the first of the great dukes. In his treatment of the cloak, Sluter shows supreme mastery, by allowing the garment to reveal the natural lines of the body while artfully draping the material into simple, dignified folds. Sluter's school was perhaps more skilled than any other in the art of creating the illusion of drapery, and of using the folds to convey movement and even feeling. In the tomb of Philip the Bold this ability finds its most brilliant expression.

Actually, it was Jean de Marville who was commissioned to construct the mausoleum. Claus Sluter, who continued his work, did not have time to complete the monument and left it to be finished by Claus de Werve, his nephew, pupil and inheritor of his technique. It is impossible to say how far advanced the monument was at the time of Sluter's death, which took place at some unknown date between 24th September 1405 and 31st January 1406. There is no doubt, however, that it bears the indelible stamp of Sluter's workmanship. It was he who made the models of the two chief mourners and who evolved the idea—even if he were not responsible for its detailed execution—of the procession of forty-one figures arranged in strict order and each one set in a delicately sculpted alabaster niche.

It is this procession of figures, following the actual order observed at the funeral, which gives the work its startling originality. The Dijon School took a set theme, transformed it and infused new life into it. Elsewhere, such figures are impersonal and purely ornamental, but here they are given individuality, and suffused with the breath of life, so that each one has a characteristic expression, movement and stance.

In the gestures of the mourning figures, 'all the outward expressions of grief seem to have been exhausted, or rather would have been, had nature and life not provided the sculptor with an inexhaustible supply of material'. The Burgundian sculptors 'also knew how to use even costumes and folds of drapery with consummate artistry to enhance moral and dramatic expression'.[5]

The fact that it is impossible to distinguish which of the mourners were the work of Claus de Werve and which the work of Claus Sluter, reflects great credit on the nephew who assimilated his uncle's teachings so completely that he very nearly succeeded in being as great as he was. He adopted as his own, not only the style, but the artistic conceptions of the man whose enthusiastic pupil he had been. The continuity and unity of the school were thus assured.

With Claus de Werve, however, we see the first signs of a decline. John the Fearless showed less interest than his father in the Dijon School. The fact that the school's leading sculptor had his allowance reduced was a disturbing indication that interest was waning and not likely to be renewed. However, John's desire to have for himself and for Margaret of Bavaria a tomb which would be a counterpart to the tomb of Philip the Bold and Margaret of Flanders, was to keep the institution founded by the first duke active for many years to come.

Artistically, the tomb of John the Fearless, which stands next to Philip the Bold's in the Musée de Dijon, is merely a replica of Philip's in a more contemporary style, and perhaps rather more ornate architecturally. On the whole, it follows the design of the original very closely. This is all the more remarkable in that the artists who succeeded Claus de Werve and who were responsible for the second monument came from different regions: Jean de la Huerta was from Aragon; Antoine le Moiturier from Avignon. The latter, at any rate, could say that in coming to Dijon he was coming to his artistic capital, since the Dijon School had already spread its influence over a vast area, and had popularized Burgundian art throughout France, in Provence in particular.[6]

Few schools, indeed, have exercised a wider influence than that graced by Sluter. In fact, Burgundian art is found, and the Burgundian influence is evident, in all the French provinces, and in all foreign countries.

Such was the fame achieved by the tombs of the Dukes of Burgundy that they were imitated everywhere: at Souvigny in Bourbonnais, at Bourges, everywhere in fact, but more especially of course in Burgundy itself. The series was brought to a magnificent close, with some new variations, in the extraordinary tomb of the Seneschal Philippe Pot, the famous orator of the Estates General held in 1484.

This tomb certainly deserves its place in the Louvre. The unknown artist has given Sluter's fundamental conception a bold and original treatment. This time the mourners are life-size and are bearing the tomb on their shoulders. There are eight of them and each one has an individual attitude and style of movement, and his peculiar psychological make-up can be sensed in spite of the hood which is pulled down over his face. Together, they support the stone slab on which the recumbent figure—clad in full armour—reposes in an attitude of dignity and serenity.[7]

Sluter's disciples not only sculpted tombs: they often dealt with other themes, among which the Holy Sepulchre occupied an important place.

The most remarkable example of a Holy Sepulchre is the one to be seen at Tonnerre. It has been established for certain that the sculptors were Jean Michel and George de la Sonnette, and that the work was executed in 1454. The entombment of Christ is a masterly study of a nude figure which expresses with extraordinary accuracy the limpness of a dead body. The two other figures in the foreground (Joseph of Arimathea and Nicodemus, who are burying Jesus) are vigorously conceived, and the hint of meditative sadness which the artists have succeeded in giving to their movements lends nobility to faces, whose vivid characterization would otherwise reveal too clearly the commonplace features of the models used; similarly, in the five other traditional figures (the Virgin, St John, Mary Magdalene, Salome and Mary Cleophas) grief is expressed with a varied intensity which is extremely moving, without falling into rhetoric or theatricality.

Many statues of the Virgin and of different saints were produced by the various workshops of the school, whose output became more abundant as the century advanced. The artists inspired by Sluter's example must have been very prolific, because, in spite of the disappearance of many pieces of sculpture—how many exactly we do not know—museums, churches, and art collections, are full of works which can legitimately be related to 'Burgundian art'.

The towns and villages of the province are full of such statues, for instance the Virgin of St Jean de Losne and the delightful Virgin with the Rose which used to adorn a small niche in the rue Porte aux Lions in Dijon—not to mention a host of Virgins, saints and other figures, too numerous to be listed here. The task of cataloguing them, which incidentally has never yet been attempted, would be well worth undertaking.

It would be a mistake, however, to imagine that the Burgundian School produced only masterpieces. In order to survive, it was forced to increase its output, often at the expense of the quality of the work.

From these examples of inferior art, it is easier to detect the tricks of the trade and to see how what were originally qualities gradually changed into defects. Every school of art founded by men of genius eventually turns into a school of craftsmen. The inevitable price to be paid for success is that at some point mannerism creeps in. A Virgin in the Burgundian style is immediately recognizable; she is squat, dumpy and heavy-jointed; her features are so realistic as to be rather coarse; she is swathed in draperies, which are often too voluminous and, being clumsily treated by a second-rate artist, conceal the natural contours of the body, whereas formerly the contours had been so visible as to impart life to the fabric itself. A striking example of a Virgin in this uninspired fifteenth-century style is the one which survived the destruction of the Sainte Chapelle de Monseigneur, and is now on the portal of the church of Notre Dame at Dijon.

Although the craftsmen who devoted themselves to turning out copies and so changed what was originally an art into an industry have been justifiably doomed to oblivion, the best pupils of the outstanding men deserve to be known and remembered; yet so far very few of them have been resurrected. Worthy of mention are the sculptors Jacques Morel and the Sonnette brothers, roving artists who, following the example of Antoine le Moiturier, propagated the art of the Chartreuse School; and Philippe Biguerny, nicknamed

Philippe de Bourgogne, who won a great reputation for himself in Toledo and who valiantly kept the Italian influence at bay in Spain even in the middle of the sixteenth century.[8]

It was just when the fame of the school was at its height that it began to be affected, at the very centre of its activity, by new influences.

Even in Claus Sluter's day, certain new elements had crept in from the immediate neighbourhood. In 1393, the leader of the Dijon School had been sent by his master, the duke, to Mehun-sur-Yèvre and the splendours he saw there may well have helped him to give full rein to his genius.[9] At all events, by the end of the fifteenth century and even more so at the beginning of the following century, the Loire School and the Italian School had permeated Burgundian art. Of course, the Loire School itself had previously come under the widespread influence of the Chartreuse sculptors, but it had also welcomed and adapted many other elements. This was a period when the various tendencies which had competed with each other for artistic supremacy, finally intermingled: the Vierge d'Autun (known as the 'Bulliot Virgin'), for instance, represents a combination of aesthetic formulae which had previously been opposed to each other; and such monuments as the Brou tombs can be classed as masterpieces in a composite style combining all the trends.

The Dijon School, rightly understood, can be said to have persisted until the beginning of the modern era, when there emerged in France a new art which had drawn inspiration from all those various sources. Far from dying out after a period of glorious supremacy, the Dijon school survived and contributed to the development of the new, more general and more French style, so that it can be fairly said to have represented the first stage in the great French sculptural renaissance.

The sculptural genius which is the most obvious characteristic of the artistic history of Burgundy, explains no doubt why the term 'Burgundian art' refers solely to the art of statuary. Religious architecture during the period of the great dukes never seems to have achieved an individual style, and it is more than probable that the art historians would have passed the same judgement on the duke's castles, had they survived. The only historic building of the period still intact is the magnificent Hôtel-Dieu at Beaune, founded by the chancellor Nicolas Rolin; it is in a marvellous state of preservation and redolent of the atmosphere of the period. It houses the altarpiece attributed to Roger van der Weyden—a masterpiece of Franco-Flemish painting—in which the chancellor himself and his wife, Guigonne de Salins, are shown kneeling as donors.

Mention of this fine pictorial work provides a natural transition from sculpture to painting. The wonderful paintings found in Burgundy—some of which have already been referred to—were all brought in from outside. It would be wrong to conclude from this that no imitations were made inside Burgundy, but it must be admitted that as far as painting was concerned the north remained supreme. There was no reason to establish a school of painting at Dijon, alongside the school of sculpture. It was taken for granted that the dukes' commissions would be carried out in their domains in the Low Countries.

However, it should be remembered that Holland and Flanders were as much part of the Burgundian State as ducal Burgundy and Franche-Comté, and that consequently Dutch and Flemish art owed something to the dukes, in the same way as the specifically styled 'Burgundian' art did.

This, of course, does not mean that we propose to give here an overall picture of Flemish art, which occupies such an important place in general aesthetic history. The scope of the present work alone makes this impossible. It would, however, be appropriate to recall its essential outlines and to explain the presence in Burgundy proper of examples of Flemish art which reveal how far its influence had penetrated.

Flemish and Dutch art flourished in the Low Countries precisely at the time when the dukes were engaged in moulding the area into a political unit. Just as the artistic genius of Burgundy found expression in sculpture, so the artistic genius of the Low Countries was revealed essentially in painting.

If we had to name Sluter's equals in the north, first place would obviously have to be given to the Van Eyck brothers. Jan van Eyck, who was born about 1385 and died in 1441, was sent on several diplomatic missions by Philip the Good, to Portugal, Spain and the Hague. It has not been definitely established that he ever visited Italy. His treatment of religious themes was not very inspired but his gifts as a portrait painter were astounding. His eye was as keen as his brush was sensitive. It is, incidentally, impossible to establish with any accuracy which canvases were the work of Jan himself and which were by his brother Hubert, and it can be assumed that the two inseparable brothers were together responsible for a good many compositions. This is certainly the case as regards the most famous work of their joint career, the magnificent *Retable de l'Agneau.*[10]

Yet the Van Eycks owe their fame not so much to the works they left behind them as to the pupils they trained. Their main school was at the Hague. Disciples like Albert van Onwater, who painted the famous *Resurrection of Lazarus*, and Gérard van Haarlem, or Thierry Bouts, also from Haarlem, were enthusiastic exponents of the realism which formed the basis of their masters' teachings.

Roger van der Weyden—also known as Roger de la Pasture—whose school in Brussels produced a remarkable output of works between 1435 and 1464, was not perhaps a personal pupil of the Van Eycks. His fondness for pathetic effects is in striking contrast with the predilection shown by the leaders of the school for calm and philosophical serenity. But no one has succeeded in portraying powerful emotions better than Roger van der Weyden, as the amazing *Descente de la Croix*, now in the Prado in Madrid, so brilliantly reveals. It has already been mentioned that van der Weyden was apparently responsible for the altar-piece at Beaune. It immediately reminds us of Van Eyck's portrait of Rolin in the *Vierge du Chanchelier Rolin* in the Louvre, which shows such a masterly treatment of light.[11]

The second half of the fifteenth century is the richest period as regards painting in the Low Countries. Contemporaneous with Roger van der Weyden or his juniors were men like Jacques Daret, who is commonly thought to be the artist who was also known as *le maître de Flémalle*, Simon Marmion of Amiens, Hugo van der Goes, a native of Zealand, 'a neurotic whose mind finally gave way', Quentin Metys, a fine painter of bourgeois interiors, lastly the great Memling and many others who should be added to this list. The originality of the painters trained under the direction of the Van Eycks began to weaken when the Italian influence, carrying all before it, imposed its radically different style, and brought about a fusion of that style with the existing amalgam between the genius peculiar to the north and certain elements borrowed from France.

It is quite obvious that the great dukes were particularly attracted to Flemish art, which expressed so forcibly the deep-seated emotions of the most flourishing domain in their vast Empire.[12] From the time of Philip the Bold, whose broad eclecticism we have already mentioned, the dukes, as patrons of the arts, paid considerable attention to painting.

This explains why painting had a part to play in all Burgundian sculpture in the fifteenth century. The figures on the ducal tombs were painted; so too were the prophets on the well at Champmol: Moses, for example, had a red tunic and a cloak of gold lined with azure. Zachariah was given a red tunic; David was in blue, spangled with gold stars; Jeremiah was in dark blue, and Isaiah, the saddest of them all, was clad in brocade. Jeremiah's spectacles—the work of Hennequin de Hacht—were made of gilded copper. All the prophets wore gilded cloaks and stood on a green plinth. This fusion of painting and sculpture continued throughout the sixteenth century, as can be seen from the delightful figure by Antoine de Fonnette, formerly at the castle of Drée and now in the Musée de Dijon.

Painting, however, was not content to take second place; it sometimes asserted its independence, as is shown by the frescoes of Notre Dame at Dijon, which reveal unmistakable traces of Flemish inspiration.

The account-books, as well as the works which have been preserved, indicate even more clearly that several representatives of Flemish painting worked in the duchy and for the duchy.

The name of Jean de Beaumetz has already been mentioned in connection with Philip the Bold's patronage of the arts. He was a native of Artois and the duke had a high regard for him, since he was chosen to be Sluter's companion when the latter visited Mehun-sur-Yèvre in 1393. Jean Malwell from Guelders painted the statues of the prophets at Champmol, and the portrait of John the Fearless.[13] Henri Bellechose, who came from Brabant, Jacques de la Baerze and Melchior Broederlam added several works to the artistic heritage of ducal Burgundy. It was Melchior, for instance, who was responsible for the brilliant pictorial ornamentation on the two panels which form the famous altar-piece of the Musée de Dijon. Even as early as 1384 at Sluys, the same artist had painted the ship in which the duke intended to sail during the campaign against England. It was azure and gold; the poop was adorned with huge escutcheons and the sails were spangled with marguerites, the initials P.M. and the motto *Il me tarde* (I cannot wait).

Tapestry-making was closely allied to painting. It was one of the most flourishing arts in the fifteenth century and we have already mentioned, in connection with Philip the Bold's patronage of the arts, the vast number of centres which produced a succession of glorious tapestries. Arras and Flanders competed with each other. The account already given of Philip the Bold's collections[14] makes it necessary to refer again to the variety of subjects treated. Like the work of the Dijon sculptors and the Flemish painters, the achievements of the tapestry-makers won fame throughout France and Europe.

The goldsmith's craft, music,[15] as well as various minor arts and skills also contributed to the general flowering of aesthetic activity. We may be sure that if the political ambitions of the House of Valois had been realized, if greater Burgundy had taken its place on the map of the world, as a permanent and concrete reality, a rich and harmonious century of artistic production would have been its natural accompaniment in the history of culture.

CHAPTER XI

COURT LIFE

THE BRILLIANCE of the Burgundian Court shed an exceptional radiance over the fifteenth century, and the dukes obviously aimed at outshining all the other princes in this respect. In a century over which the passion for grandeur and the love of luxury seemed to exercise the tyrannical hold of a religion, the Burgundian State gives the impression of deliberately setting out to beat every record. It is almost as if it were trying, by its display of wealth, its brilliant festivities, impressive tournaments, and lavishly abundant banquets, to make good the lack of a royal crown; to imply that it deserved a crown, since it outdid in munificence those who jealously clung to the monopoly of kingship. A sort of political megalomania certainly seemed to lie behind the House of Burgundy's obsessional determination to outshine in splendour every other dynasty in Christendom, to reach the front rank of sovereign states, and to arouse universal admiration for the lavishness, munificence and discernment of the dukes of Burgundy.[1]

Banquets were a speciality of the House of Burgundy. The lavish ones given at the time of the Treaty of Arras were similar to those organized on every possible occasion as a means of winning over the guests of the great dukes. The immense kitchens with their huge fireplaces which can still be seen today in the ducal palace give a remarkable idea of the Pantagruelian menus which a gastronomical workshop of this sort was capable of devising. The lavishness and delicacy of the meals found expression in the excellent quality and extreme variety of the dishes. The length of these interminable feasts would have daunted even the most ardent epicure, if the successive series of courses had not been interspersed with '*entremets*' or entertainments, in which the ingenuity of the masters of ceremonies found full scope. The entertainments consisted of dumb-shows, '*pièces montées*' involving complicated and novel mechanical contrivances, castles manned by soldiers, acrobatic displays, and fantastic or symbolical animals. At one banquet a colossal pie was brought in holding an orchestra of twelve musicians.

The most famous banquet given at the Burgundian court was 'The Feast of the Pheasant', which took place at Lille on the 17th February 1454. The chroniclers have given enthusiastic descriptions of its splendour. The hero of the evening was a live pheasant, in the full glory of its plumage, wearing a valuable gold necklace studded with precious stones. The giant Hans represented the 'Great Turk'. Then 'Dame Church' came forward in tears, and recited a long-winded 'lament', inviting those present to come to her aid, and reminding them of the recent disaster of the capture of Constantinople by the Turks. She approached the duke first, then the guests, especially the knights of the duke's order:

> You, Oh Knights, who wear the Fleece,
> Be mindful of your most holy duties.

Then Duke Philip the Good, in full view of the assembly, swore a solemn oath that he would go on a crusade. Next the Count of Charolais made his vow, and all the lords present followed suit in order of precedence. The oath was sworn to God, the Virgin and 'the pheasant'. In this highly theatrical performance, the magnificence of the display, the profusion of precious stones and rare fabrics were in keeping with the grandeur of the great dukes, but however sincere it may have been, it did not lead to a new campaign against the Sultan. The swearers of the oath, following the example of the duke himself, were very careful to admit the possibility that they might be prevented from carrying out their pledge through force of circumstances.

For this very solemn banquet, the court was not satisfied simply with gastronomical achievements interspersed with entertainments. In addition, the attire worn by each guest was paid for from the duke's own treasury. The official documents give details of all the cloth, embroidery work, fringes, robes and ornaments supplied to the various lords, officials, and even ordinary men-at-arms called upon to appear at the banquet. The colours chosen were white, grey, and black. The duke paid for 'four hundred and fifty and a half ells of woollen cloth, half black, half grey, to make a hundred and twelve robes . . . fifty ells of white cloth, to be gathered round the sleeves of the afore-mentioned robes . . . three hundred and fifty and a half ells of a different sort of white cloth to line the forty-seven grey and black silk robes'; these latter robes were intended for the knights and gentlemen of the duke's residence who had been invited to the banquet.[2]

Ever since the thirteenth century jousting had been the chief feudal sport. The author of the poem *Guillaume le Maréchal* refers to the 'French style of fighting'—*conflictus gallicus*—in which the best jousters won so many horses and prisoners that they had to employ clerks to keep a special account of them. All through the Hundred Years' War, the tournament, which was virtually a military school for knights, won even greater popularity and was marked by increased pomp and extravagance. Mounted on richly caparisoned horses, and completely covered in armour, the knights deftly wielded their lances and swords, which were masterpieces of the armourer's and the engraver's art, and had often been brought at great expense from the east, or from Italy and Spain. The Court of Burgundy seized every possible opportunity of organizing large-scale tournaments. Competitors came from far and wide, from Scotland, Castille, Hungary, England, Portugal and Aragon. The famous jousters issued their challenges in advance and arranged to meet there; the tournaments were, in fact, international sporting events.

The somewhat uniform pattern of the contest, whether it was fought on foot or on horseback, was enlivened by a variety of novel scenic devices, some of which showed brilliant inventive touches. It was felt necessary to think up exciting new features, surpassing in splendour and originality everything that had ever been done before. And so such tournaments were devised as 'The Contest of Charlemagne's Tree', 'The Contest of the Golden Tree', 'The Contest of the Fair Pilgrim', and many others.

'The Contest of Charlemagne's Tree', for example, was held at Marsannay-la-Côte, near Dijon, during July and August 1443. Two symbolical shields were hung from a tree referred to as 'Charlemagne's Tree' and two lists were marked out—one for contests on foot, the other for contests on horseback. A superbly decorated stand was specially built for the use of distinguished spectators. An accommodation service was organized to ensure that the guests who had come from all over the world were comfortably and luxuriously installed in the nearby castles of Perrigny, Marsannay, and Couchey. In the opinion of the experts, the fighting was magnificent. On the first day, the Burgundian Charny and the Castillian Sacvedra battled on foot, using as weapons the axe and the tuck. When the contests were over, the winners, with great pomp and ceremony, bore the shields which had been hanging from the tree to the church of Notre Dame in Dijon.

'The Contest of the Fountain of Tears' was celebrated on the plain of Chalon-sur-Saône. Below a statue of the Virgin, there stood 'a lady very becomingly and richly attired, with a very simple head-dress; and she was weeping so hard that the tears ran down her cheeks and fell into a fountain which stood on her left'. In addition, there was a pavilion for the judges, tents for the knights, lists, and stands—in short, all the usual costly apparatus essential for important contests. After the fighting, there was a procession in which 'the weeping lady', who in the meantime had been somewhat neglected, came into her own again.

The excessive practice of jousting did not go uncriticized, and when the censorious Eustache Deschamps, whom we have already come across in the chapter on literature, expressed his disapproval of tournaments, he was merely voicing the view of those who had the courage to deplore the waste of human energy and material resources.

Here is a relevant quotation. The style, although by no means despicable, is less interesting than the sentiments expressed:

On se destruit pour un pou de plaisance
Où nul bien n'a fors sotie et folour,
Orgueil de cuer, vainegloire et despence
Que les chétis veulent nommer honnour,
Ou chascun pert, du bien commun l'amour
Cesse et perist, dont maint sont malostrus.
Jouste et tournois en guerre n'est qu'errour.
Que ne laissons vanité pour vertus?

(Men destroy each other for a little pleasure
In which no one gains anything except folly and madness,
Pride of heart, vainglory and expense
Which miserable wretches wish to call honour,
In which everyone loses, in which the love of the common good
Wanes and perishes, so that many become uncouth.
Jousting and war, like tournaments, are merely error.
Why do we not abandon vanity for virtue?)

The doughty knights who enjoyed great popularity, the professionals of the lists for whom the tournament was the best training ground for war, never suspected that Deschamps's sober realism was a pointer to the future.

The true knight, who rushed from one tournament to the next, also rushed, in so far as contemporary events allowed him to do so, from battle to battle.

Such was the practice of Jacques Lalaing—*le bon chevalier*, as he was called—and who was in fact the model knight of the century, the ideal representative of the last phase of chivalry. As handsome as Paris, as pious as Aeneas, as wise as Ulysses, and as fiery as Hector, but gentle when the battle was over, and always humble, and courteous, he never missed morning mass and devoted his whole life to feats of arms.

Prose writers and poets vied with each other in praising his exploits, and his epitaph, which was written by Georges Chastellain, is worthy of note:

> Here lies the man who, purer than ivory,
> Took chastity as the pillar of his fame.

It is clear that the noble race of 'parfit gentle knights' still survived from the earlier Middle Ages, and the glorious figure of Bayard was not to appear until the sixteenth century. Even in the time of Louis XIV, Condé was to capture the Franche-Comté strongholds to the sound of violins, and much later still the elegant combatants of the eighteenth century were to repeat the gestures of their ancestors, the knights-errant. Nevertheless, towards the end of the fifteenth century, guns and more modern methods of warfare were beginning to win the day against the principles of chivalry. It was already a sign of the times—a most striking sign—that Jacques Lalaing should have died, not from a well-aimed lance-thrust, but from a cannon-ball, fired by some unknown gunner without a drop of blue blood in his veins.

Alongside the knights, women played a distinctive part in courtly society. They were the queens of the banquets and tournaments. It was for them that the doughty knights took up arms and fought.

Two conflicting attitudes towards women can be traced throughout the Middle Ages. There was the hostile attitude which found rather harsh literary expression in the *Roman de la Rose*, extracts from which, if we went so far as to quote them, would soon show that Old French, like the Latin on which it was modelled, did not always observe the laws of propriety. On the other hand, there was a favourable attitude which at times even seemed to be moving towards an early variety of feminism. Christine de Pisan, who enjoyed Philip the Bold's patronage, was determined to live by her writings, and when she became a widow she proudly proclaimed her self-sufficiency:

> Seulète suis et seulète veuil estre
>
> (Alone I am, and alone I wish to be)

And when she extolled Joan of Arc, who saved France and 'did what men would never have done', Christine de Pisan was glorifying her own sex, and with good reason, since no single episode in the history of any country had ever carried a woman to the heights of fame achieved by the Maid.

Christine de Pisan's unshakeable feminism is a pointer to the distant future:

> Elle fut Tulle et Catton
> Tulle car en toute éloquence
> Elle eut la rose et le bouton
> Catton aussi en sapience.
>
> (She was both Tullius and Cato:
> Tullius because in oratory
> She had no equal.
> In wisdom she was another Cato.)

Olivier de la Marche, however, preferred the domesticated or society woman to the woman writer.

> Vous jeunes filles qui désirés honneurs
> Laissiés là lettre, tout ouvrage et escolle
> Le beau maintien qui tant a de valeur
> Aprenés-le et le faites de coeur
> Pour avoit loz qui legier court et volle
> Car je juge d'escript et de parolle
> Qu'i n'est au monde tel trésor ne chevance
> Milleur pour femme que bonne contenance.
>
> (You young girls who desire fame
> Leave writing, work, and school.
> Learn rather with enthusiasm
> Good deportment which is so valuable
> In order to have a reputation which lightly runs or flies.
> For I consider that, in writing and in words
> There is, for women, no greater treasure
> In all the world than good breeding.)

There is little point in consulting, on this precise issue, that delinquent subject of Louis XI, who was called François Villon. He would simply bring us back to the eternal feminine—the eternal feminine which has been celebrated by all poets in all ages:

> Corps féminin, qui tant es tendre,
> Poly, soeuf, si précieux . . .
>
> (Body of woman, so tender
> Smooth, soft and precious . . .)

The quarrel of the *Roman de la Rose* is linked with these widely differing opinions on the question of feminism. Marshal Boucicault considered the possiblity of an order of chivalry in honour of women, to be called 'The Order of the Green Escutcheon with the White Lady'. Philip the Bold set up a 'Court of Love' in Paris at the Hôtel d'Artois, on the 14th February 1401—'to the honour, praise, recommendation and service of all ladies and maidens'. Various issues connected with courtly love were debated, and prizes were awarded for poetic compositions which, contrary to the fiercely anti-feminist *Roman de la Rose*, sang the praises and extolled the virtues of the fair sex. This institution did not last long. Anthony of Brabant, who had helped to found it, was like many of his associates, totally unfitted for the rôle of champion of female honour.

Among the various episodes in the history of ducal Burgundy which had marked repercussions on Court life, the creation of the Order of the Golden Fleece deserves a special place.

Philip the Good's third marriage in 1429 with Isabella of Portugal was made the occasion of the institution of the Order. Although the alliance with England was still in force, the Golden Fleece was intended as an answer to the Order of the Garter. The knights of the new Order wore a gold collar to which was attached, by the middle of the back, a sheep's fleece worked in gold, as can be seen from the fine portrait of Anthony 'the Great Bastard', which is at Chantilly and is the work of an anonymous painter of the Flemish school, perhaps van Eyck.

Lavish entertainments marked the creation of the Order, whose chapter meetings were always marked by great pomp and ceremony. The privilege of creating knights was handed down the line to Charles V, and when he died, it became the prerogative of Spain and Austria.

The first patron of the Fleece was, of course, Jason, since it was the story of the Argonauts which prompted the creation of the Order in the first place. But after due reflection, it was decided that it was hardly proper to have a pagan as patron. Also, on close examination, the legend revealed crafty and somewhat dishonest behaviour on the part of the hero. Some people even seem to have seen a resemblance between Jason's unscrupulous behaviour towards Medea and Burgundy's policy with regard to France. Gideon was therefore substituted for Jason. Olivier de la Marche explains the change somewhat laboriously.[3] Jean Germain, Bishop of Chalon-sur-Saône, and the first Chancellor of the Order, was the man responsible for it. The scholarly bishop quoted from the Bible, *Judges*, Chapter VI, the passage about Gideon, a 'thresher', who laid out a sheep's fleece on the ground and prayed to God to send rain on the earth and not on the fleece. The miracle happened. Then he laid out another fleece on the ground and this time asked that the dew from the heavens should fall only on the fleece and not on the ground, and again his wish was granted. It was on this evidence that the bishop had Gideon substituted for Jason as patron of the Order, and it explains why Gideon's story, depicted on tapestry, eventually adorned the Hôtel d'Artois in Paris.[4]

The Order of the Golden Fleece was conferred on kings who were friends of Burgundy, the King of England and the King of Aragon, for instance, and also on distinguished servants of the ducal House, such as Anthony, 'the Great Bastard'.

According to custom, a college of heralds was connected with the ducal Order. The king-at-arms was called *Golden Fleece*. The heralds bore the names of counties under the duke's jurisdiction, such as Charolais and Zealand. The first poursuivant was called *Flint*—an allusion to the emblem of Philip the Good.

Court life, in all its aspects, was extremely formal. It was governed by the most rigid rules of protocol. There was a rigorous system of precedence; a complex hierarchy of court officials controlled the various services and we can judge from the promotion won by Georges Chastellain and Olivier de la Marche how, by successive stages, an able and willing man could make a career for himself. Members of the duke's household might interrupt their official public duties, to carry out confidential missions. It was from among the members of his household, whom he fed, supported and attached to his person by means of gifts, that the duke chose trustworthy agents who could be relied upon to bring the most delicate missions to a successful conclusion.

Olivier de la Marche is the typical representative of these worthy '*écuyers*' who could be counted on for devoted service of all kinds.

He did not serve the duke from a sense of duty only; he was by nature a man who loved society and Court life. No one was more convinced than he that a splendid Court and lavish entertainments were of vital importance to the prestige of the House to which he had given his allegiance. Burgundian literature as a whole tends to give rather lengthy accounts of scenes which, for our tastes, would be better summarized rather than related in minute detail. It is obvious from the way in which Olivier de la Marche enthusiastically elaborates his stories that he took a keen and significant delight in his task. His flow is inexhaustible, and he spares us no detail.

He describes the rigid formality of the ritual which governed the day-to-day existence of the dukes. The following is a typical extract describing the pantler's duties; we have cut the original as little as possible:

The duke has a chief pantler and fifty esquire assistants, who come under the authority of the chief pantler both in war and peace, and who are controlled by five gentlemen of the bed-chamber appointed by the duke and each one of whom has nine pantlers under him, who all ride as a squadron under the standard of the chief pantler . . .

When the prince is about to dine and when his table has been laid, the usher on duty goes to fetch the pantler on duty that day and escorts him to the pantry. And there the butler of the pantry hands him a napkin and kisses it as a sign of service. The pantler places the napkin on his left shoulder, one end hanging in front, the other behind. The butler then hands him the covered salt-cellar which the afore-mentioned pantler has to carry with his fingers, holding the base and centre of the dish, unlike the goblet which is held by the stem. And the pantler, bare-headed, follows the usher . . .

The pantler places the meat on the table, tastes it, then hands it to the others, one after the other. Then the pantler takes up his position at the end of the table in front of the dish and gives the duke two helpings, and each time he helps him to twelve or thirteen dishes. The meal is served in one sitting. And the pantler has to take one of the knives and put salt from the large dish into the small dish, taste it, and place it in front of the duke.[5]

The pantler takes the biscuits from the side-board and if there is an assembly of people at the banquet, he may place the biscuits before all those seated at the duke's table, but not before the others.

J. Huizinga is right when he says in his book *The Waning of the Middle Ages*, that 'the kitchen regulations are truly Pantagruelian'. The following passage is quoted from Huizinga:

Charles the Bold's meals, which had all the dignity of a liturgical ceremony, with the various services of pantlers, carvers, cup-bearers, and cooks, resembled a lavish theatrical spectacle. The Court ate in groups of ten in separate rooms and were served and treated like the master, everything being carefully arranged according to rank and status. After their meal, in order to do honour to the duke, they came to greet him while he was still at table. (In the kitchen) the cook was seated between the fireplace and the side-board on a high chair, from which he could survey the whole room. In his hand he held a huge wooden ladle which served a double purpose: with it he tasted the soups and sauces, and chased the scullions back to their work, beating them if necessary. On rare occasions, the cook himself, with a candlestick in his hand, would come to serve the food, for instance on the day when the first truffles appeared, or the first fresh herring.

The appointment of the chief cook was a major event. Olivier de la Marche, to whom we are once more indebted for details, describes the procedure.

When the position of master-cook is vacant at the prince's court, the *maîtres d'hôtel* call the kitchen squires, and all those employed in the kitchen, one by one. Each one solemnly gives his vote, attested by an oath, and in this way the chief cook is elected.

The prince, who had to support such a vast household, who was so eager to entertain on a lavish scale and who literally kept open house, not only spent fantastic sums to which the rolls in the Record Office at Dijon bear eloquent witness—even more eloquent witness than the colossal kitchen chimneys—but was also involved in a life of perpetual pageantry, which Louis XI would not have tolerated. However, all four dukes seem to have accepted it with good grace. They took a pride in their noble task, which lightened the burden for them.

Philip the Bold's patronage of the arts is in itself proof of the lavish mode of life habitual to the head of the Burgundian State. Although there is no need to refer again to features which have already been noted—in particular the ornate silver-plate and drinking cups—we should add a few details about the costumes worn by both men and women, and about certain features of private life.[6]

Documents are available which provide us with the most intimate details of how Margaret of Flanders was dressed for her son's wedding.

The duchess wore a *houppelande*, or over-cloak, of crimson silk, which revealed underneath a garment of white velvet spangled with gold stars. At these same marriage celebrations, the men wore a livery which was half green, half white, with velvet and satin trimmings to match. The duke was in green and white damask silk 'in a small check design' and 'decorated with gold spangles'.

Guests invited to the wedding were given presents such as 'ornamental clasps, lengths of silk, and jewels'.

Prince John of Rethel, the future John IV of Brabant, was born prematurely on 11th January 1403.

The preparations for his birth provide an excellent example of the arrangements that were made each time an addition to the family was expected. The two cradles normally used at a birth were sent for, the small cradle and the state cradle. The latter, used only for display, was the work of a master cabinet-maker in Paris, Jean de Liége. All the furnishings of the cradle were officially specified: sheets dyed with cochineal and embroidered with cypress gold cloth, a bright scarlet valence adorned with ten gold crosses, and a coverlet lined with ermine.

The state cradle was painted and gilded with fine burnished gold and there was a special board for the baby's head to rest on. This part of the work was done by a painter and valet to the duke, called Christopher Basan.

When Charles the Bold's heiress, Mary of Burgundy, was born, the mother lay on a couch in front of the hearth, the child in a cradle; but ceremonial beds had been set up and sumptuously appointed. Mary's room had two beds, one draped in green, the other in violet, and the two beds in the duchess's room were draped with green curtains. In the ante-room stood another large bed covered in crimson satin.

When a young Burgundian princess married, she could be counted on to take with her a fine array of dresses. Here is a list of the clothes that the future wife of Charles VI's son and heir, the Margaret who was twice to be a Dauphin's wife but never queen, packed in her baggage-train. On the day of her arrival, she appeared before her future husband in a complete outfit, an *ensemble* with an open surcoat of green silk. On the morning of her wedding, she put on a dress made of cypress gold cloth on a cochineal-tinted ground; but after the midday meal she changed into the most elaborate outfit of her whole wardrobe, a cloak made of another variety of cypress cloth with a *houppelande* to match. In this she also attended church after her wedding, for a service of thanksgiving—as Henri David remarks—for a union which was still a purely spiritual one. It was to remain so, for the first Dauphin to marry a Burgundian princess died before his tenth birthday.

The bright colours were then quickly succeeded by mourning. '*Brunette*' and '*noir de Lierre*' gradually gave way to white half-mourning, and it was not long before touches of crimson appeared on the white.

Philip the Good did not forget so easily; in his grief at his father's tragic death, he not only went into deep mourning, but retained all his life a preference for black, and although always richly dressed, usually kept to this one sober colour.

It was a tradition that every prince's Court should have a 'fool', either male or female, whose task it was to keep boredom at bay. Under Philip the Good, the fool Coquinet, according to the records, received many generous gifts,[7] and about the same time, a female fool seems to have enjoyed great popularity. She was described as being 'very graceful' and was commonly known as 'Madame d'Or'. This blonde dwarf figures in the account books on more than one occasion, and between 1421 and 1434 she took part in various entertainments.

In 1430, on the occasion of a banquet given in honour of the new duchess, Isabella of Portugal, an *entremets* was prepared; it is described by the chronicler, Le Fèvre de St Rémy.

'There was a huge *entremets* consisting of an enormous pie in which there was a live sheep painted blue, his horns gilded with fine gold.' A giant called Hans, who, as we have seen, played a part in the Banquet of the Pheasant, was on this particular day in the pie along with the sheep. He was dressed 'in the skin of a wild animal'.

When the pie was opened, the sheep and the man both jumped out. The man went 'to fight and wrestle' with Madame d'Or. A tussle between a dwarf and a giant was exactly the sort of novel exploit which the Court liked to prepare for its guests. Some new twist had to be found, so that the public did not become bored with the entertainments.

Constant inventiveness was the order of the day. The *entremets* had to be different, like the special acts with which circus masters entertain their customers. Here are a few examples of Burgundian fun: a horse richly caparisoned in scarlet silk, ridden bare-back by two trumpeters seated 'back to back', paraded backwards round the room while the riders played 'a sennet on their trumpets'; an apocalyptic monster, half-griffin, half man, was mounted on the back of a wild boar which, in turn, carried an acrobat '*en posture savante*', in other words with his feet in the air; a splendid and beautiful deer 'all white with long golden horns' was ridden by a young boy of twelve who sang a popular song: '*Je ne vis oncques la pareille*'.

It is clear, then, that intense activity prevailed at the duke's Court, where military displays were also one of the attractions. Diplomatic activity added a further excitement of its own special kind. The Court was a centre from which everything started and to which everything returned. Visiting ambassadors from foreign countries switched from business talks to entertainments, at which convention decreed they should be present. At the Court of the great dukes negotiations were conducted in quite a different manner from that customary at the French king's Court, for Louis XI had little liking for ceremony. Contemporaries of the ageing Philip the Good were fully aware of the difference in atmosphere between the two Courts. They had only praise for the vassal, and blame for the sovereign. As far as they were concerned, it was the uncle, and not the nephew, who should have worn the crown. And it was in the secret hope of wresting the crown from the hands of fate that the last two representatives of the ducal dynasty tried so strenuously to outshine the splendid achievements of the founders of Burgundy's greatness.

CHAPTER XII

THE BURGUNDIAN STATE

WHEN, AT TRIER, Charles the Bold continued to work for the realization of the dream he had inherited from his father, Philip the Good, and believed he was on the point of restoring the Lotharingian kingdom, he was really only trying to make nomenclature fit the facts. For all practical purposes, the ducal State had become the equivalent of a monarchy; indeed, as regards population and wealth, it was superior to most European monarchies of the fifteenth century, and many were far less impressive.

The fact was that, in the space of a few generations, a great power had come into being. With a combination of industry and bravery, the four dukes had pieced together a mosaic of territories which was now so extensive as to inspire respect, although no one quite knew what name to give it. In contemporary documents it is referred to either as '*le grand duché de l'Occident*' or '*le grand duché du Ponant*' (great duchy of the west) and, as it went on expanding ever further, it seemed likely to occupy, between France and Germany, a place that no state of any permanence had ever held before, pushing the former country back towards the Atlantic and hemming in the latter along the Rhine.

It constituted a formidable collection of territories, which was going to have unforeseen historical consequences. Two of the modern European kingdoms, Holland and Belgium (Holland, Zealand, Friesland, Zutphen, Flanders, Brabant, Limburg, Namur, Malines and Liége) were only a small part of it, even when combined with French Flanders, Artois, and Picardy (now three departments of France: *départements du Nord, du Pas de Calais, de la Somme*). Its coastline stretched from the Somme to the Zuyder Zee and formed a splendid maritime frontier where the estuaries of the Scheldt and the Rhine cut deeply through the sands and sheltered flourishing ports serving a hinterland which was the most active centre of mediaeval industry.

First Luxemburg and its dependencies, then Lorraine and Upper Alsace, formed a group of possessions linking the Flemish group with Burgundy proper. The latter consisted of ducal Burgundy and the county of Burgundy, also known as Franche-Comté, together with dependencies of lesser importance, such as Mâconnais, Auxerrois and the county of Charolais which, as we have seen, was the titular province of the duke's heir.

It is not surprising that the lord of such domains should have thought that only a royal crown or diadem could do justice to his majesty. Different lands and different races—from the Jura in the south, with its view of the ragged Alpine peaks beyond the Swiss plain, to the polders of Friesland in the north; from the vineyards of Mâconnais to the sand-dunes of the Helder; from the modest landing-stages along the Saône to the swelling traffic of Antwerp; from the clear Latin air on the banks of the Rhone to the pregnant mists of Zealand—contributed to the life of the unnamed state, whose complementary resources were already held together by a strong dynastic authority. The Burgundian territories contained from five to seven million inhabitants, that is the equivalent of the population of Prussia in the eighteenth century. And, by a curious coincidence, Burgundy at one point seemed about to play in France the part that Prussia was later to play in Germany. Had one of the dukes of Burgundy been like Frederick II, had the various sections of Burgundy been welded into a whole, as the sections of Prussia were, French unity would have proved as impossible at the beginning of the Renaissance as German unity was, so long as the Austro-Prussian dualism lasted. According to the German historian, Ranke, if the Burgundian monarchy had materialized, France would have been no more than 'a minor power'.

As head of a state which really counted as a great power in the fragmented Europe of the fifteenth century, the duke had a finger in every pie, sent ambassadors to every Court and, in fact, conducted a European policy.

In the east, as we have seen, he maintained close relations with Hungary, financed missions to the Holy Land, sent troops to the Danube and ships into the Black Sea. At one moment, he had designs on Genoa. At all times, he was careful to counter French diplomatic activity in Milan, Florence, Venice and Naples. He concluded an alliance with the Neapolitan monarchy and not only succeeded in thwarting French designs in southern Italy, but also worked against them in Spain by going to the help of the uncle of the King of Naples, John II of Aragon, from whom Louis XI was trying to wrest Roussillon.

It follows that Burgundian policy in Spain, which is usually neglected by historians, offers a good example of the cosmopolitanism of the dukes, of their all-pervading, international diplomacy. Its general outline is worth indicating briefly.

Even before Louis XI's accession to the throne, there was a *rapprochement* between the ducal court and the court of Aragon. About 1461, a marriage was proposed between Mary of Burgundy, the Count of Charolais' daughter, and Ferdinand, the son of John II. This was a curious anticipation of the future course of history which was already tending towards the dynastic union whose outcome would be the power of Charles V. It would almost seem that the temporarily engaged couple, Ferdinand and Mary, were destined by fate to stand opposite each other on the genealogical table of the greatest of the Hapsburgs, whichever way the wheel of fortune should turn.

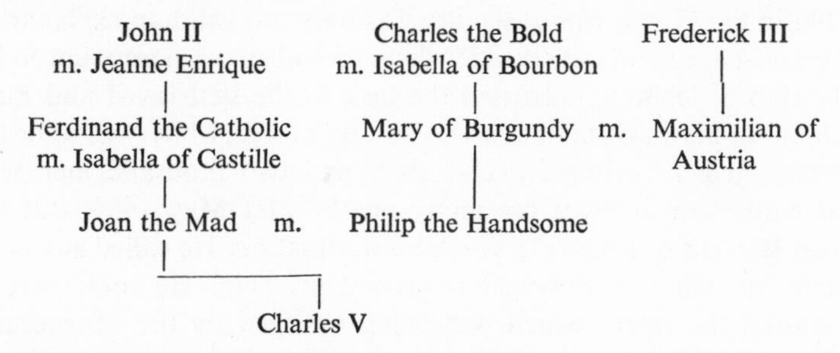

The alliance concluded between John II and Louis XI at Bayonne on the 9th May 1462, and in accordance with which French troops commanded by Count Gaston de Foix were to help to put down the Catalan Revolution,[1] interrupted the course of Arago-Burgundian friendship for a while.

Soon, however, things began to look very different on the Spanish side of the Pyrenees. The Catalan Revolution was not quelled. The Catalonians had appealed to Henry IV of Castille, against John II, but Henry had let them down when Louis XI intervened to negotiate a settlement. Louis, not satisfied with having extorted Roussillon and Cerdagne from Aragon as a reward for services which had not in fact been rendered, set about intriguing to be recognized as overlord in Barcelona. To avoid having to accept so dangerous a protector, the Catalonians then turned to the Constable of Portugal, Dom

Pedro, the heir to the ancient title of Count of Urgel, who came back from Ceuta in Morocco, where he was campaigning at the time. Assuming the title of King of Aragon in opposition to John II, Dom Pedro established himself in Barcelona.

Since Dom Pedro of Portugal, King of Catalonia, was a nephew of the Duchess of Burgundy, Isabella of Portugal, it was inevitable that close relations should develop between Barcelona and the ducal court.

They can be studied from the surviving documents. Dom Pedro made a request for help to his aunt Isabella and to Duke Philip the Good. Don Jaime of Aragon was one of the ambassadors sent to the Court of Burgundy.[2] Burgundian men-at-arms who happened to be in Barcelona agreed to fight for the duchess's nephew at the battle of Urgel.[3] Their help did not, however, save Dom Pedro from serious defeats which soon jeopardized his crown.

These Burgundian men-at-arms who found themselves by chance on Catalonian territory in 1465 were undoubtedly connected with the attempted crusade led by Anthony, 'the Great Bastard'.

Philip the Good, whose senility was only too valid an explanation of his absence from the crusade which he had so often announced his intention of leading, entrusted the task to the best-loved and most brilliant of his illegitimate sons.[4] Anthony's force, which was to be the advance-guard, included twelve ships and two thousand men who had embarked in great ceremony on the 21st May 1464. But the Great Bastard was never to reach his destination. He called at Ceuta, where the King of Portugal requested his help. He took part in liberating the town, which was being besieged by the Moroccans. On the way back, a storm drove most of his ships to take refuge in Marseilles; a few detachments provided limited support for Dom Pedro, but he was so short of men that even this help made an appreciable difference.

If the Burgundian Court did not supply great military aid to the King of Catalonia it almost succeeded in finding him a wife. Dom Pedro had made overtures for the hand of Charlotte of Savoy, a sister of the Queen of France, but Louis XI was so vexed at having been ousted from Barcelona (although Dom Pedro did not know this) that there was little hope of his agreeing to have the young King of Catalonia as his brother-in-law. He did not even reply to Dom Pedro's inquiry. Thereupon it occurred to Dom Pedro, or was suggested to him, that he should try for a union with the English royal family. It is more than probable that the suggestion was put to him, or at least encouraged, by the Duchess of Burgundy. Margaret of York, later the wife of Charles the Bold, was then in the first instance engaged to the King of Catalonia, who on the 28th March 1466 sent to his secretary a detailed description—and one which showed him to be a connoisseur of jewellery—of the ring to be presented to his fiancée.[5] According to the bill, which still survives, the diamond alone cost two hundred pounds.

But the projected marriage came to nothing, because of the death of the fiancé. Worn out by illness, disappointments, sorrow and overwork, Dom Pedro died on the 29th June.[6]

The Catalonians then offered the throne to René of Anjou, who was at once assured of the far from disinterested support of his nephew, Louis XI. This was enough to make Charles the Bold, who had in the meantime become Duke of Burgundy, revert to the initial Spanish policy based on John II. However, there could no longer be any question of a marriage-link; Ferdinand was engaged to Isabella of Castille and, as we have seen, Mary was about to be betrothed to Louis XI's brother, Charles of France, whom Burgundy was trying to win over.

A political alliance at least could be developed, and was confirmed by treaty. John II's ambassadors, Don Hugo de Urrea and Don Frances Berenguer, went first to London, then to the Burgundian Court, and a league was brought into being on the 22nd February 1469. The Arago-Anglo-Burgundian alliance thus initiated was strengthened after the restoration of Edward IV in 1471. On the 1st November of that year, a definite triple agreement bound together the Duke of Burgundy, the King of England and the King of Aragon.

This time, instead of vague assurances of friendship, the treaty contained precise and firm stipulations. Although the clauses were written in the diffuse style still favoured by the fifteenth century, they contained the terms of a defensive alliance which boded no good to France. Louis XI was mentioned at several points as the enemy of the contracting parties. It was to forestall his knavish plots that the allies gave mutual guarantees of the integrity of each others' possessions. And lest any bad feeling might still linger on between Burgundy and Aragon in connection with the breaking off of the engagement between Ferdinand and Mary, the pact was also signed by the newly-weds, Ferdinand and Isabella.

This alliance of 1471 was not one of the innocuous agreements so frequent in the fifteenth century; events were soon to show that it was an effective offensive agreement.

Its first result was to give more coherence to John II's and Charles the Bold's struggle against their common adversary, Louis XI. Encouraged by the promise of active co-operation, John II boldly launched an offensive. All over Aragon, the Duke of Burgundy was considered as working for the same ends as the sovereign of the country; proof of this ratification of the alliance by public opinion is to be found in the writings of Alfonsello, vicar of Gerona: 'The illustrious Duke of Burgundy, the comrade-in-arms of our King of Aragon, has been sent by God to fight the abominable tyrant, the King of France; the duke is pursuing the tyrant so vigorously that the latter cannot escape from his power'.[7]

Helped in this way, John II not only reconquered and pacified Barcelona, but also recovered Roussillon, which had been occupied by French troops for six years. And when the King of France sent a fresh army to besiege Perpignan, which was being defended by John II in person, Charles again responded to an appeal for help.

On the 28th March 1473, Charles the Bold sent his 'comrade-in-arms' a nobly phrased letter which is worth quoting in full:[8]

To the most excellent and puissant prince, the King of Aragon and Sicily, my lord and very dear cousin.

Illustrious and most excellent prince, my lord and very dear cousin.

First I recommend myself to you.

Having been asked on several occasions by my very dear brother and cousin the Duke of Brittany, on behalf of the King of France, our common enemy, and also by the constable of the said king, to conclude truces with him until the 1st April 1473, beginning at Easter, I agreed to do so, but on the express condition that Your Majesty's name be included, with your consent, as one of my confederates and allies. After the signing of the truces, I heard the news of the abominable and cruel murder of my cousin of happy memory, the Count of Armagnac, who was killed by the soldiers of the king, our common enemy, after the due capitulation of the castle and fortress of Lectoure, and after the king had given a solemn pledge of safe-conduct.

I learned also that the said King of France was proposing to send against you the army which had been made available through the surrender of Lectoure.

On hearing this, I immediately ordered a thousand lancers recruited in Italy and whom I intended to bring into Burgundy while the truce was in force, to set off.

It is my intention that these troops should co-operate with the Burgundian contingents against our common enemy, if he breaks the truces by attacking Your Majesty.

I shall be at the head of my forces to see that he is given no rest.

With this purpose, I am calling for the help of the very excellent and illustrious prince, my lord and brother, the King of England and of my aforesaid cousin, the Duke of Brittany. I have sent letters and messengers urging them to do as I am doing and to bring a common pressure to bear on the common enemy.

I am confident that they will do their duty; I am convinced that both the Duke of Brittany and the King of England will be vigilant and active. However, if, contrary to my expectations, they are unable to carry out this task, I for my part, am determined to go ahead without delay or reservation.

Accordingly, I have protested to the Constable of France through my ambassadors, for I wish our common enemy to know that Your Majesty's cause and mine are so closely linked and our policies so united that no one can attack either of us without the other intervening at once.

Events fortunate or unfortunate for Your Majesty are the same for me in like measure, and I have no less regard for the danger threatening your crown than for my own danger.

When the news of the concluding of the Franco-Burgundian truces arrived at the French camp at Perpignan on the 23rd May, it was an important factor in bringing about the raising of the siege and, eventually, in forcing Louis to sign the Treaty of Perpignan on the 17th September. This gave neutral status to Roussillon and opened up the possibility of a diplomatic settlement between France and Aragon.

The fact that the ducal policy could have so strong an effect at such a distance from Burgundy is a remarkable proof of the cosmopolitanism of the duchy and of the wide range of its influence.

As might be expected, the Burgundian State, being made up of bits and pieces, had no uniform pattern of institutions.

It had sprung into existence neither as a result of deliberate forethought nor through military conquest, but simply as a consequence of the accidental juxtaposition of seignieuries brought together under the same overlord through a skilful use of the principles of inheritance and purchase. It was a patchwork of territories, as can be seen from the long list of titles with which the chancellery credited the duke, and which was constantly changing according to the new accessions or secessions. Here, for instance, is the style used in an official document issued by Philip the Good:

Duke of Burgundy, Lothier (i.e. Lower Lorraine), Luxemburg, Limburg and Guelders, Count of Artois, Flanders, and Burgundy, Palatine of Hainault, Holland, Zealand and Zutphen, Marquis of the Holy Roman Empire, Lord of Friesland, Salins and Malines . . .[9]

With very few exceptions, in each of the seignieuries which came under his control the duke agreed to confirm the existing charters, to maintain traditional customs, the relative status of different functions, local organizational peculiarities and dialects,[10] merely retaining the right to establish his suzerainty and to supervise administration. As a result, the detailed study of each fief belongs to local history and would be out of place here. But it is essential to give a brief survey of the basic institutions governing the main sections of the vast patchwork: ducal Burgundy, Franche-Comté and the Low Countries.

Let us take the duchy first. We have already seen how the Capetians gave it its administrative framework, and how it consisted of five *bailliages* set up in the thirteenth century: Dijon, Autun and Montcenis, Auxois, Chalon and Montagne (Châtillon-sur-Seine). Under the Valois as under the Capetians, the bailiffs were first and foremost agents of the ducal authority. Supported by strong traditions and solid legal principles, they governed the area, protecting the interests of their master and, if necessary, voicing the needs of the population. Many of the fifteenth-century ducal bailiffs were eminent, active and creative men. During periods of peace, especially, they were responsible for some of the most definite advances in local life; at Mâcon and Autun, for instance, the bailiffs struggled inch by inch to see that the ducal authority prevailed against the pretensions and encroachments of the bishops and the ecclesiastical courts.

The dukes paid particular attention to the administration of the law. Customary law was amended by an impressive series of ordinances and, under Philip the Good, was codified in the 'General customs of the district and duchy of Burgundy', promulgated on the 26th August 1459, and which dealt with the various questions of civil law in fifteen sections subdivided into articles.

A court of appeal was set up as a check on the feudal and communal courts operating according to the ordinary practice of mediaeval law. Known as the *Jours Généraux*, it was also the court of first instance for certain privileged classes and formed a sort of *Parlement*, which met at Beaune. It included a president, about twenty counsellors and 'knights of honour'. All these officials were appointed by the duke and paid so much per session.

It should be noted, however, that the monarchy never accepted the verdicts delivered at Beaune as final; a further appeal could be made to the Paris *Parlement*. Also, the duke himself, as a peer of the realm, was and remained subject, in legal matters, to the Paris *Parlement*. On several occasions, Philip the Good and Charles the Bold were cited in the Paris *Parlement*. They never made any answer,[11] but the practice, even if it had no material consequence, enabled the monarchy to defend its right against prescription and ensured the permanence of the link between the Valois appanage and the kingdom, whatever the political circumstances might be and in spite of the exceptional power of the head of the Burgundian State, just as, in the past, the dukes of Normandy became kings of England and still remained French vassals.

Above the level of the *bailliages*, the pattern of ducal institutions was completed by the Great Council and the Estates of Burgundy both of them inherited from the Capetian period.

The Council was a governing body which met regularly from 1446 onwards and dealt with all political and administrative questions. From 1422, at least, there had been a chamber of the Council at Dijon and it had ruled the duchy to all intents and purposes. Its president was often referred to as 'the President of Burgundy'. The chancellor played an important part in the Council, and was usually its king-pin, although sometimes there was a 'leader of the Council', in addition to the chancellor. As has already been seen, Jean de Thoisy and Jean Chevrot, who were successive bishops of Tournai, were presidents of the Council.

The estates met once a year, usually at Dijon, but sometimes at Beaune or Chalon. They included representatives of the clergy, the nobility and the chief towns, the delegates of the latter acting as spokesmen for the third estate.[12] Part of their function was to vote taxes and provide for their collection, which was carried out by agents appointed by the estates.[13]

If we now move on to 'the county', the modern *Franche-Comté*, the first thing to notice is that although theoretically subinfeudated to the empire, in practice the domain had its own peculiar institutions which were unconnected with the empire.

There were many resemblances with the duchy, the chief being administration by bailiffs. The Franche-Comté *bailliages* were originally set up by Philip the Fair when he was overlord of the domain, and were definitely confirmed by the Valois dukes. At the beginning of the fourteenth century, there were two Capetian *bailliages* at Vesoul and Poligny, called respectively 'upstream' and 'downstream' (*bailliage d'Amont*, *bailliage d'Aval*). In 1442, Philip the Good added the bailliage of Dôle, a subdivision of the *bailliage d'Aval*.

The Franche-Comté *Parlement* had been permanently established at Dôle by a ducal ordinance of the 30th May 1396. It asserted its authority by summoning the principal barons to appear as occasion arose. It displayed its power still more clearly in 1460 by publishing 'The General Customs of the County'. Thanks to this codification of the customary law, all the Franche-Comté courts were able to operate in accordance with a fixed, written text.

Moreover, to ensure a better training for his lawyers and councillors both in the county and the duchy, Philip the Good founded a university at Dôle, also in 1460; it developed rapidly and was particularly noted for its law school.

It was in the fifteenth century, too, and also at the instigation of the dukes, that the Franche-Comté estates first emerged. Their origins are obscure but it is clear that they were an off-shoot of the communal movement and first came into being in 1384. This, at least, was the year in which, for the first time, the duke-count, instead of sending his commissioners from town to town to ask for tribute and collect it, called a meeting of the delegates of the communities of the '*bailliage d'Amont*'. A little later, the same method was applied in the '*bailliage d'Aval*', and eventually the two assemblies were made into one and became the estates.

They included representatives of the two tax-paying classes, the clergy and the burgesses; the nobility, except in special cases, made payment in the form of personal service. In the course of the century, the three classes came together at Salins. In Charles the Bold's time, when the Salins estates were called upon ever more frequently for contributions, they took the precaution of stipulating that funds raised in the county should be used exclusively in the county. The tradition was gradually established of granting no contribution for external use.

It is obvious that, under the Valois, the power of the duke-count was well organized in Franche-Comté. But it was very conscious of being limited by the presence in the very heart of the county of an 'imperial city', Besançon, which formed a self-administering enclave.[14] It was a kind of republic, with elected magistrates. Its independence was somewhat curtailed through the strenuous efforts of the dukes, from Philip the Bold to Charles the Bold, who exploited the internal struggles between the bourgeois oligarchy and the common people. They used, in fact, more or less the same tactics as at Liége, but they did not produce the same violent upheavals at Besançon, for understandable reasons. In the end, they came to exercise a sort of protectorate over the town (the term used in the contemporary texts is *gardienneté*). A captain and a judge, permanently installed in the town, represented the duke-count's interests and kept a watchful eye on the republic, whose privileges were left intact, at least in theory.

The two Burgundies were linked by one institution common to both, the *Chambre des Comptes* in Dijon.[15] However, the single financial control it exercised did not prevent the two Burgundies from being very different from each other. Yet although they remained separate, even jealous of each other at times, and with conflicting atmospheres and aspirations, they managed to collaborate and each contributed, in its own way, to the glory of the dynasty.

The administrative achievement in the Low Countries was no less remarkable than in the duchy and the county.

In Flanders, Philip the Bold established a *Chambre des Comptes* based on the previously existing feudal institutions. The area served by this chamber showed that it had been set up as an instrument of unification. However, the first duke's heirs did not bring their successive annexations within its scope, and so its radius of action remained what it had been in the time of the first duke.

Another noteworthy innovation on Philip's part was to fix the chamber permanently at Lille, which was contrary to previous usage, and to institute two sessions per day, one in the morning and another in the afternoon. The chamber was also provided with permanent premises and a salaried staff. Its function was to keep a check on the financial operations of the bailiffs and other functionaries and its jurisdiction extended to the towns along the Somme.

Justice was put into the hands of a Council of Flanders, which corresponded more or less to the *Jours Généraux* of the Duchy of Burgundy, except that it did not always meet in the same place. It was held in Audenarde from 1405 to 1407, Ghent from 1407 to 1439, Courtrai in 1439, Ghent from 1440 to 1447, Termonde from 1447 to 1451, Ypres from 1451 to 1463 and lastly in Ghent, from 1463 onwards.

The Council included the 'President of Flanders', eight counsellors, a public prosecutor, a lawyer concerned with fiscal matters, a clerk of the court, a receiver of writs, ushers and a '*garde des Chartes*', or keeper of the records.

It was a bilingual institution, both Flemish and French being used as working languages, whereas the *Chambre des Comptes* used only French.

The estates of Flanders were organized in the same way as those of the other great domains subinfeudated to France, such as *Langue d'Oil* (the northern district), *Langue d'Oc* (the southern district), Champagne and Normandy. Their meetings took place in Brussels, Ghent, Bruges and certain other towns, according to the decision of the duke. The three biggest towns in Flanders—Ghent, Bruges and Ypres—were generally referred to as 'the three members of Flanders'.

Like Burgundy, Flanders was divided into *bailliages*, but the local bailiffs were under the general authority of a chief bailiff, known as 'the sovereign bailiff of Flanders', who was directly responsible to the duke. A typical administrative career was that of Colart de Commynes, Lord of Renescure and the father of the historian, Phillipe de Commynes. He was appointed governor of Cassel in 1429, bailiff of Ghent in 1432 and sovereign bailiff of Flanders in 1435. Later he was made a Knight of the Golden Fleece, and he died in 1453.

Anthony, Duke of Brabant, following the example set by his father, Philip the Bold, endeavoured to give a systematic and coherent organization to the duchy he had inherited from his great-aunt.

In 1406, he set up a *Chambre des Comptes* and a Council of Justice at Vilvorde. Later, the chamber was to extend its jurisdiction to Holland, Zealand, Friesland and Luxemburg. But the Council was short-lived and was superseded by the estates, through the lack of authority shown by John IV, Anthony's eldest son. In 1422, the Council was officially replaced by a body representing the nobility and the larger communes.

When Philip the Good took over Brabant, he had to handle the province carefully because it was in a touchy state, John IV's weakness having allowed the estates to behave independently and given a sense of emancipation to all classes. Fortunately, the third duke was tactful enough to smooth over the difficulties. He tightened up the administration of justice by means of reforms which were applied in successive stages. Finally, he set up a high court, known as 'the Court of Brabant', which was presided over by the Chancellor of the Duchy and included a public prosecutor as well as six judges, four appointed locally and two by the duke. It was the supreme legal authority in Brabant.

In Holland, Friesland and Zealand, this function was fulfilled by the 'Court of Holland', which at first consisted of nine officials. Like the Council of Flanders in Philip the Bold's time, this court originally had financial as well as legal responsibilities, but in this case, too, there was eventually a separation of functions. The Court continued to be the legal body, while a *Chambre des Comptes* was set up at the Hague and, in 1463, combined with the one in Brussels.

In Hainault, the administration was under the centralized control of a 'great bailiff'; Luxemburg was administered by a lieutenant-governor.

As a rule, local administration was in the hands of natives of the provinces concerned, Flemings in Flanders, Dutch in Holland, and so on. But the University of Louvain, founded by Philip the Good, attracted students from all parts of the Burgundian State.

A remarkable attempt at unification was made with the publication of the *Thionville Ordinances*, in 1473. A *Parlement* was set up at Malines to take over some of the functions formerly exercised by the Great Council and to act as a Court of Appeal for the whole of the Low Countries. The financial system was reorganized by the abolition of the *Chambres des Comptes* at Lille and Brussels and the setting up of a single authority, called a court, for the whole territory. It was established at Malines, which was also made the seat of a *Chambre du Trésor* and a *Chambre des Généraux*. Charles the Bold had a special liking for Malines and since he had a still keener sense than his father of the existence of the Low Countries as an entity, his aim was to make the town into the administrative capital of the area.

Although, as we have just seen, the institutions of the Burgundian State were not unified, there had to be some central authority through which the duke could keep a check on all the provinces.

This rôle was fulfilled by the Great Council, which moved about with the duke, and by the chancellor, whose duties remain to be defined.

The most representative of all the Burgundian Chancellors was Nicolas Rolin. He was born at Autun about 1380, and was first a lawyer in Paris and then at the *Parlement* of Dôle. As the assistant of Jean de Thoisy, John the Fearless's chancellor, he displayed such efficiency in carrying out the various tasks and missions entrusted to him that when the time came for his master to resign his office, Rolin became chancellor, while Thoisy retained the position of leader of the council.

The chancellor was not only the Lord Privy Seal, and the head of the various departments of the chancellery; in Rolin's case, he acted virtually as a prime minister.

Rolin was entrusted with the seals on the 3rd December 1422 and he retained them until his death on the 18th January 1462, although at the very end of his career there was a definite decline in his power through the influence acquired by the Croy family over the elderly Philip the Good. Nevertheless, for the space of some forty years, Rolin, a shrewd and subtle burgess, had a large share in the making of internal and external policy. We have seen that this was so in connection with certain concrete details and we have noted Georges Chastellain's evidence as to the range of the chancellor's activities. Rolin was concerned with every issue. He seems to have played the part of an unapproachable power behind the scenes who kept everything under his control and, if necessary, accepted responsibility for the taking of unpopular measures. He had an outstanding capacity for work and was an expert in many different fields. His successor as chancellor was Pierre de Goux; then, under Charles the Bold, the post was filled by Guillaume Hugonet, who also served the Duchess Mary, and with a fidelity which eventually cost him his life, since he was sacrificed, along with Humbercourt, to the resentment of the Flemish.

Like many other ministers known to history, Nicolas Rolin, while tirelessly serving the interests of his master, also took care of his own fortune. There is no reason, however, for posterity to pass harsh judgement on so able a man. His patronage of the arts is an additional point in his favour. It was he who founded the famous *hospices* at Beaune, and as has already been noted, he is to be seen, along with his wife Guigonne de Salins, in the traditional attitude of the donor in the famous triptych attributed to Van der Weyden, which is one of the permanent glories of Beaune.[16]

Alongside the chancellor, there were other officials whose functions, in many cases, covered the whole range of the duke's possessions; the Marshal of Burgundy, who was head of the army, the Admiral of Flanders, in charge of the naval forces, the chamberlain, the master of the horse, and all the various court dignitaries who were, as we have seen, both numerous and splendid.

As regards the finances of the state, there were administrative offices in charge of the interests of the duke's possessions as a whole. In addition to the tax-collector of the Duchy of Burgundy and the tax-collector of the Low Countries, there was a *receveur de toutes les finances*, or general tax-collector. On a lower level, there were, of course, many local tax-collectors. An official called the *trésorier-gouverneur* acted as inspector and checked the accuracy of the revenues. The seal-tax was collected by the *audiencier*, payments were made by the *argentier*, and the master of the *chambre aux deniers* kept a careful account of the expenses incurred by the duke and his costly household. Revenue from taxes was about a hundred thousand pounds. In 1455, the duke's total income was estimated to be nine hundred thousand ducats, which was the equivalent of the total revenue of the Republic of Venice; the Republic of Florence had only a quarter of that sum and the Pope half.[17]

As a result, the head of the Burgundian State was in a position to support not only his expensive household and the complicated administrative services but also an army in keeping with the size of his domain and his political ambitions.

Charles the Bold, imitating Charles VII, created 'ordnance companies', of which there were thirty-two. With the addition of the feudal contingents of the ban and the arrière-ban, the duke could mobilize some fifteen thousand men under the flag with the St Andrew's Cross, supported by three hundred cannon, not counting the heavy artillery in the fortresses and walled towns. He also had Swiss and Italian mercenaries. Charles the Bold had a military mind.[18] He built up the Burgundian army carefully and competently, and if his diplomacy had been sound, his military machine would have proved extraordinarily powerful. He almost succeeded, incidentally, in obtaining the services, as captain of his Italian mercenaries, of the famous Colleone, whose equestrian statue still stands in the shadow of St Mark's, but the Venetian Republic in the last resort refused its authorization, although the medal-maker, Candida, had put his diplomatic skill at the duke's service. Occasionally, the recruitment of mercenaries came up against an obstacle of this kind, but usually the only problem was to find sufficient money.

Whatever the ducal revenues and the taxability of the Burgundian subjects, the financial resources of the state were exceeded every year, which meant that the deficit was permanent and that, in the manner of modern states which are in the habit of anticipating the future by means of borrowing, the Duchy of Burgundy, like its neighbours, had to have recourse to various expedients.

Advances were made by money-lenders whose speciality it was to come to the help of princes, and who usually accepted securities. We have seen that on one occasion Philip the Bold pawned his jewels. Precious stones, gold plate and even crowns were used as securities. But the modern reader should not feel too sorry for the great feudal lords who had to part temporarily with their possessions. The pawning operations were not essentially different from the manipulation of the gold reserves which is current practice in modern banks.

Among the great international financiers that the State could appeal to in time of need was Dino Rapondi, who has already been mentioned in connection with the ransoms paid after Nicopolis. He was a skilled technician, and his resourcefulness was such that, according to Froissart's admiring comment, 'all financial operations can be made through him'. He did not lack honour during his lifetime, nor, indeed, after his death, since he was buried in the Sainte Chapelle at Dijon and a statue was placed there in his memory (it survived until the eighteenth century) showing him with a large alms-bag hanging from his belt.[19] Other natives of Lucca rendered similar services—Thomas Portinari, for instance. Bruges was the centre of their activities. Italian bankers, Florentines in particular, put their considerable international credit at the disposal of the economic development of the Low Countries, an outstandingly hard-working and prosperous region.

And so we are naturally led to give a rapid sketch of the social and economic situation, which is the final aspect of the Burgundian State that has to be dealt with in this summing-up.

The wealth and prosperity of the state presided over by the great dukes impressed their contemporaries. 'A land of promise' was the expression applied to Burgundy by Philippe de Commynes, who was in a position to have an opinion. And he added: '. . . the subjects of the House of Burgundy were very prosperous because of the lasting peace and because of the goodness of their prince, who did not tax his subjects heavily'.

Only towards the end, when danger laid a burden on the country, were the financial resources of the population strained. The ducal policy, which aimed at keeping the Franco-British fighting outside the frontiers of Burgundy, spared the duke's subjects the terrible hardships suffered by the population in other territories sub-infeudated to France. Apart from a few scattered pillagings by mercenaries or occasional unrest after a bad harvest, as in 1438, the Burgundian fiefs were peaceful and agreeable to live in.

Everything tended to favour economic development. In the duchy, agriculture and trade enriched the peasants and town-dwellers. There was a busy port at Auxerre. Châtillon produced cloth like a Flemish town. The ports along the Saône were important stages on the inland waterways, and exported the famous and choice wines of the Côte d'Or. From Chenôve, where the dukes had their celebrated wine-presses, to Rully and Mercurey, the vines were tended more carefully and produced ever more sought after vintages, which were transported at great cost to Flanders and England. There was considerable building of dwelling-houses at Beaune; the *hospices* were erected and decorated with works of art. Dijon had between six and seven thousand inhabitants about 1436 but by 1460 the total was between twelve and thirteen thousand. Although the modest 'house with the monkeys' decorated by Claus de Werve continued to serve as the town hall, the seven parish churches, the Sainte Chapelle, the abbey-churches, the convents and twenty well-built chapels made an impressive line of spires against the sky. The town became livelier and, as it stood at a cross-roads, it had to increase the number of its inns. Its streets were loud not only with quarrelsome swarms of pack-asses but also with hundreds of travellers of all kinds—Italian ambassadors going to Paris, mendicant friars putting up for a few days at the new Franciscan monastery, and wealthy companies of southern merchants on their way to, or from, the markets of Troyes. It is understandable that Burgundy should always have been thought of as a much travelled-through area.

In the Low Countries, international trade and large-scale industry worked hand in hand. Although rivals, to some extent, on the political level, the two forms of economic activity were at the same time partners, whether they wished to be or not. The upper middle-class and the workers were interdependent.

Chastellain celebrates the wonders of the exceptional towns of the north: 'their inhabitants, who are numberless, their riches, their power, their familiarity with merchandise, their abundance of goods of every kind'. Commynes, for his part, speaks admiringly of the delights of life there: 'receptions and banquets greater and more lavish than anywhere else, bathing-parties and other entertainments'. The standard of living, to use the modern phrase, was exceptionally high.

It was this prosperity which ensured the soundness of the ducal currency; at the same time, the latter helped the former. As a result, a very careful watch was kept on the coinage and minting was strictly supervised.

It is true, however, that an occasional cloud appeared in the economic sky of the Low Countries. The political situation sometimes had unfortunate repercussions.[20] Also, technical developments produced unforeseen consequences. The cloth-making industry declined, because the production of textiles began in England. The English suddenly realized that since they supplied the raw material they could just as well work it up themselves instead of sending it to Belgian weavers, and so the beginnings of a protectionist policy hampered the export of English wool. At the time, the experts thought that this would be only a short-lived crisis, but they were wrong; it was a permanent shifting of the centre of gravity of the industry.

But, while the big weaving-mills lost their trade, the smaller ones remained very active. Cassel, Bailleul, Poperinghe and Tourcoing continued to develop. The production of linen increased; tapestry-making was established. An important grain-market was set up in

Ghent. Luxury industries flourished in Brussels. Coal-mines were started at Liége and metal-working became a separate industry.

Ghent was the chief town of Flanders, '*caput Flandriae*', as a traveller from Nuremberg, the doctor Jerome Munzer, noted in 1495. He was an observant tourist and he tells how he climbed to the top of a tower and saw the town spread out below 'like a star', and surrounded by fields studded with wind-mills. Another traveller, Tafur, a Spaniard, was also struck by the windmill as being a characteristic feature of the landscape; he noted that peat was the normal fuel and beer the ordinary drink. At the same time, he declares that no army would be strong enough to break through the defences of Ghent, which can be manned in a moment by sixty thousand foot-soldiers, since every citizen has his armour and his lance. According to Munzer, Ghent covered about the same area as Paris, but he adds that, because of the decline of the Low Countries, so many inhabitants had left that about half the houses were unoccupied, which, of course, had not been the case in the time of the dukes. Munzer also mentions that the houses were large and well built, and that the town could be turned into a fortified island in the space of three hours by the flooding of the moats. The nobles, weavers and 'mechanicals' shared the government. There was close co-operation between the town and the surrounding countryside. The inhabitants lived on trade and, at the fair, there was so much linen thread and wool, so many bales of cloth of all kinds, that it seemed, says Munzer, that the whole of Germany had disgorged its possessions. There was a grain-market and a general market, both of them near St Jacques.

Bruges had as much the air of a capital as Ghent. In spite of the falling off in the weaving industry, the town was still at the height of its prosperity, which found splendid expression in artistic achievements. To the rich heritage of monuments left by the reign of Louis of Male, further additions were made in later years: between 1393 and 1396 an upper storey was added to the magnificent belfry; the church of the Holy Sepulchre was completed in 1427, the Damme market in 1464 and the Gruthuse palace in 1465. On feast-days, the decorations on the houses, the illuminations and processions were of such fairy-like splendour that they dazzled the inhabitants themselves, as well as strangers. Visitors, like Munzer, who saw the normal life of the town, were struck by the setting, the architecture and the great economic activity in progress. Set on a rich plain thick with windmills, the town was surrounded by a circular wall, comparable to the one at Milan, a town of about the same size. The canals and little bridges were reminiscent of Venice; the streets were carefully paved; there were fine squares, pleasant gardens, well-dressed inhabitants, and plump, ruddy-cheeked women in bright-coloured dresses, whose amorous ardour was as great as their religious fervour. These were the things which struck the visitor as much as the lively activity at the exchange or the well-stocked markets. Each 'nation' or nationality had it semi-basement shops under the arches of the Exchange. The merchants of the Hanseatic League brought beer, skins, wax, Russian furs, wood for cabinet-making and building and pitch for ships. Spain sent wool, iron, silk, fruit (chiefly figs, grapes and oranges), oils, rice, wines, grain, and the small ewe-skins that were in such demand by skin-dressers. Tafur remarks that the oranges and limes were as fresh on arrival as if they had just been picked. England despatched wool, lead, tin and London cloth. Venice supplied spices and gold and silver cloth. The French contribution was mainly wine, especially but not entirely from Burgundy, and the excise duty on it was the principal source of fiscal revenue for Bruges. In return, the markets sold the products of Flemish industry: woollen cloth dyed in various colours, fine linen and carpets. Munzer also mentions the *Palais de Justice*, with its gilded statues of the counts and countesses, and the *Hôpital.* He admires the sheltered port of Sluys and compares it to Lisbon, which is bigger and deeper. In painting, the Flemish Venice can rival Florence; like Florence, too, it is a great financial centre, the greatest banking town in the north. The Italian banking houses have branches there, and along the Lys as along the Arno, before embarking on any elaborate undertaking, it is normal to obtain credit.

Philip the Good was not exaggerating when, in 1450, the period of Bruges's greatest prosperity, he proudly declared that the town was: 'the most renowned in the world through the merchandise that can be found there and the merchants who come there'.

Brussels,[21] although less active, had a ducal palace, which Tafur visited in 1438, under the guidance of John of Luxemburg, Lord of Hautbourdin, an illegitimate son of St Pol. He admired the duchess's court, which included no less than two hundred ladies-in-waiting, living at her expense. In the streets, he admired 'many attractive houses', as well as the *Hôtel de Ville*, and outside the town, the ducal residence of Tervueren, which had vast gardens, about a league in circumference, filled with wild deer. The attractions of life in the future Belgian capital were also celebrated by Eustache Deschamps, who praised the good capons and Rhine wines that could be obtained there.

Antwerp was in Brabant and its importance did not make itself felt until the fourteenth century, when it began to supplant the port of Sluys, linked with Bruges, and to get the better of its nearest rival, Malines.[22] It owed its lasting predominance to the rise of the Burgundian State. As the port of Limburg, it benefited from the coal-mining which developed in the latter province.[23] At the same time, it took over the Malines 'staple'. Its relations with the dukes were more harmonious than those of any other town of the Low Countries, and so it was more favoured than the others. Its two annual fairs, one at Whitsuntide and the other on the feast of St Baven (1st October), were as remarkable as the ancient fairs of Champagne; Tafur writes, 'they are the finest in the world'. He adds that the main part of the fair was held in a big square but that business was also carried on elsewhere: pictures were sold in a Franciscan monastery, tapestries in a church dedicated to St John, jewellery and gold plate in a Dominican monastery, and merchandise of various kinds in other churches and religious houses. The fairs were extremely well attended because 'the finest merchandise in the world was on sale', and it was all 'laid out in orderly fashion'. Outside the town, just beyond the gates, was a long street with great stables on one side and inns on the other. The duke did not disdain to visit the Antwerp fair, and Tafur, who had seen those of Geneva and Frankfurt, maintains that 'none is comparable to this one'. The fact was that Antwerp's trade was booming. The Scheldt and its tributaries carried both agricultural and industrial produce to the port. Its commercial Exchange, the earliest, was opened in 1460 and proved most valuable. And the activity at Antwerp encouraged and accelerated the development of the hinterland around Liége, so that eastern Flanders forged ahead, while Bruges and maritime Flanders were slowly declining.

Liége recovered its prosperity. It had suffered under Philip the Good and was still further harmed by Charles the Bold's determination to wreak vengeance for the disaster of 1468, but it gradually revived towards the end of the century, thanks to the great development of its coal-mines and to the incomparable richness of its agricultural land. Munzer claims that in summer the wheat there was as tall as a horseman and he comments: 'it is a great gift of Nature'. Liége was, in fact, exceptionally rich both agriculturally and industrially.

As for the Dutch towns, before the fifteenth century only Dordrecht, which was visited by ships from the Hanseatic towns and from the Baltic, had any international trade, but now Amsterdam began to show signs of activity. Nevertheless, Holland and Zealand, like

Artois, Hainault and Brabant, remained predominantly agricultural and cattle-breeding areas. Along the coast, fishing was a major activity, particularly in Friesland and around the Zuyder Zee. The practice of curing and barrelling herrings was introduced at the beginning of the fifteenth century and was soon to give rise to a flourishing trade.

The very variety of the territories ruled over by the ducal dynasty was a source of wealth and a factor making for economic prosperity. The multifarious products and activities of the mosaic of provinces which, for want of a better name, is referred to as the Burgundian State,[24] were complementary to each other and made up for the absence of a collective spirit. However, other historical combinations —such as the composite Hapsburg monarchy, which survived until the shock of the First World War proved too much for it—are proof of the fact that, in certain conditions, the dynastic link can provide dissimilar but complementary countries with a lasting mode of political existence.

CHAPTER XIII

CHARLES THE BOLD'S MISTAKES

THE ANGLO-BURGUNDIAN ALLIANCE which marked the peak of Charles the Bold's career admittedly contained great possibilities. Edward IV and Charles had renewed the bond which united John the Fearless and Henry V. The formidable alliance whose combined forces had very nearly paralysed the France of Charles VII, now threatened to strangle the France of Louis XI. It seemed likely that the new phase of the Hundred Years' War which was now beginning would end in a decisive victory for the allies.

It was a crucial moment. It looked as if Louis XI, whose ambition had been to dismember the State of Burgundy in conjunction with the Lancastrian King, Henry VI, would be forced, after that unfortunate monarch's second fall from power, to accept the dismemberment of France through a coalition between York and Burgundy.

This is, of course, what the two brothers-in-law hoped for. With this end in view, they signed, on the 25th July 1474, the Treaty of London, which gave a hint of the grim prospects ahead. To the clauses taken from the secret pact of 1417 and the fateful Treaty of Troyes of 1420, were added further clauses promising substantial rewards to the Burgundian State. The Duke of Burgundy was to recognize Edward as King of France. Edward was to land on the Continent with more than ten thousand men before the 1st June 1475, and Burgundy was to supply another ten thousand men to help him. The duke's domains at present under French jurisdiction were to be exempted from all forms of homage. They would be increased by the addition of a vast area—also exempted from French overlordship—comprising the county of Eu, Picquigny, the Somme fortresses, certain territories belonging to the Count of St Pol (those which were not dependencies either of the crown or of the Duchies of Normandy and Guienne), the diocese of Tournai, the counties of

Guines and Rethel, the French part of Barrois, the county of Champagne, the diocese of Langres, the county of Nevers and the barony of Donzy.

In this way, in addition to his extensive possessions under imperial jurisdiction, the duke had the prospect of gaining absolute control of a vast and continuous empire, which would be wrested from the dismembered Capetian monarchy and would include even Rheims with its impressive cathedral, where the King of England and France —admittedly a much diminished France and one hardly worthy of the name—would merely have the right of admittance on coronation day, according to the stipulations of a special article of the pact.

The fact that these plans were intended to be put into execution shows to what extent Burgundy's dreams of aggrandizement presupposed the destruction of the greatness of France.

To dream, however, was not enough, nor was it enough to sign pacts; it was also essential to have the means of carrying plans into effect, of translating diplomatic agreements into concrete, tangible results.

With a document as favourable to Burgundy as the Treaty of London in his possession, Charles the Bold ought to have remained on the defensive in the east, cultivating the friendship of the many neighbouring states and directing all his energies towards his preparations for the English invasion in the west.

He did exactly the opposite and, the Yorkist attack having been put off until July 1475, he not only kept Germany in a greater state of suspense than ever concerning his covetous designs, he also intervened actively within the empire's sphere of influence. His final and greatest blunder was to allow himself to be drawn into a German quarrel concerning the Archbishopric of Cologne. To support his young kinsman, that discredited prelate, Robert of Bavaria, he did not hesitate to lead his army off to the Rhine where he proceeded to besiege Neuss—to while away the time as it were. Several captains in the Burgundian army had so few illusions about the shortness of the siege that, according to Molinet, they 'took pleasure' in arranging their tents like so many little castles with galleries and gardens.

The most vigorous condemnation of this aberration on the part of Charles the Bold at an important turning-point in his career was made by Commynes.

> And God had allowed his mind and judgement to become disordered, for all his life he had striven to open a way into France for the English, and at this moment when the English were ready, he remained stubbornly determined to embark on an impossible undertaking.

Commynes, now in the service of Louis XI, saw very clearly how mistaken his former master was.[1]

Still further mistakes were committed during the year 1474, which marked the turning-point in the fortunes of Burgundy.

The duke had handed over the administration of his domains in Alsace to the bailiff Pierre de Hagenbach, a greedy and brutal official who, by his repeated blunders and acts of violence, drove the towns and rural areas to rebel against him and his master.

At the same time, certain incidents caused alarm among the Swiss, and the cantons, apprehensive lest an attack should be made on their sturdy independence, were forced into the surprising and paradoxical move of forming an alliance with the House of Austria, hitherto their sworn enemy.

It is hardly necessary to say that Louis XI's handiwork can be detected in the various agreements entered into and the various moves made with a view to encircling the unruly duke, whose restless ambition had spread fear and alarm among all his neighbours, since he had announced in his speech at Dijon that he intended to restore the Kingdom of Lotharingia.

Frederick III, and Sigismund of Austria, dismayed at the excessive authority wielded by the great duke and by his now openly warlike policy, were willing to lend a sympathetic ear to France's proposals. Louis, the 'universal spider', now allied to the Swiss, who were to supply him with mercenaries, provided he paid them well enough, spun his web. He hemmed in Edward's brother-in-law, and could now reasonably hope to make enough trouble for the duke in other quarters for the latter to be unable to send really adequate help to the English king when he landed.

In 1474, Alsace rose in revolt against Hagenbach. The situation was complicated by the fact that Sigismund was able to buy back the Alsatian territories, by means of a loan from France.[2] This spelt immediate disaster for Charles the Bold's plans on the Upper Rhine; on the Middle Rhine, Neuss still held out against his assaults thus frustrating his secret aim, which was to become Protector of the Electorate of Cologne, as he was already of the ecclesiastical domains of Utrecht and Liége.

Pierre de Hagenbach helped in no small measure to bring discredit on his master. By his tyrannical rule he aroused the most violent protests from the freedom-loving populations under his control. Through sheer obstinacy, the duke refused to pay any heed to the protests; he even went out of his way to defend his 'landvogt' or bailiff. Suddenly riots broke out. The unpopular governor was arrested at Brisach by the rebels, who received reinforcements from Strasburg. Within a few days the territory was cleared of Burgundian troops. A wave of rejoicing swept over the country: mingling their joy at their deliverance with the Easter ceremonies which were being celebrated at the same time, all the inhabitants, even the little children, sang:

> Christ is risen, the governor has been captured
> Let us rejoice!
> Sigismund will console us, Kyrie Eleison![3]

Since Sigismund immediately reoccupied the formerly mortgaged territories, the duke found himself legally deprived of lands he had shown himself incompetent to govern. All things considered, this was a staggering reversal of fortune.

Having hastened to Brisach on the 30th April 1474, Sigismund ordered Hagenbach to be tried by judges appointed at his, Sigismund's, request, by the municipal magistrates. An impressive list of charges was levelled against the 'landvogt'.

In order to comply with legal formalities, the accused was granted a lawyer who said:

> My Lord Pierre de Hagenbach recognizes no judge or Lord other than the Duke of Burgundy by whom he was commissioned and from whom he received his orders. He had no right to query the orders he was given; his duty was to obey. It is surely well-known that soldiers owe allegiance to their lord and master.

The judges deliberated for a long time. Finally at seven o'clock in the evening, by torchlight, after declaring that they alone had the right to pronounce sentence in connection with the crimes of which the 'landvogt' was accused, they had him brought in and condemned him to death. He showed no sign of emotion and the only favour he asked was that he should be beheaded. Eight executioners from different towns offered their services. The one from Colmar, reputed to be the most skilful, was chosen.

Before going to his execution 'Hagenbach was deprived of the rank of knight and of all his honours'.

The tragic fate of his bailiff threw Charles the Bold into one of his most violent fits of rage; but the event failed to teach him any lesson of moderation or wisdom. The Swiss in alliance with the towns of Alsace and in the pay of France, beat the Burgundian forces at Héricourt on the Luzine on the 13th November 1474. The emperor signed the Treaty of Andernach (on the 31st December 1474 and the 17th April 1475) with the King of France.

While stubbornly continuing to besiege Neuss which still held out against him, the duke was informed that the English landing would take place, as planned, in the summer of 1475, and at the same time found himself faced with a new opponent, whom Louis XI had roused against him, René II of Lorraine.

Heavy pressure had been brought to bear on the Duke of Lorraine, not only by the King of France, but also by the Emperor Frederick III and by all those who were alarmed at Burgundy's ambitions. On entering the coalition formed against Burgundy, René decided to issue a formal challenge on the 10th May 1475.

The herald arrived at the camp below the walls of Neuss. Having read the challenge to the duke, he threw down at his feet the blood-stained gauntlet, symbolising the war to the death he had just announced. Then, fearing a terrible outburst of anger from the prince, he fled in a panic. The duke had him brought back, coolly and graciously made his reply and, according to custom, ordered him to be given a fine robe and a sum of money.[4]

Charles apparently thought that this was an excellent opportunity to gain control of the Duchy of Lorraine, which would be a magnificent and final addition to the Burgundian State.

However, by hurling the Duke of Lorraine against Charles on the very eve of Edward IV's intervention, Louis XI had played a decisive stroke. The masterly skill of the 'universal spider'[5] helped by the repeated blunders committed by his rival, was about to precipitate, to the advantage of the French royal line and to the detriment of the House of Burgundy, the dramatic events of the year 1475; Charles's mistakes of the previous year had heavily mortgaged the future.

The Lorraine challenge was exceptionally serious because the king had anticipated the date fixed for the invasion by the signatories of the Treaty of London. Taking advantage of the fact that the existing truces expired on the 1st May, which meant an automatic return to a state of war, Louis, contrary to his usual practice, launched an offensive. This was proof that he had the sort of flexible intelligence which could adapt itself to circumstances.

By sending troops into Burgundy and Franche-Comté[6] Louis intended to exploit the fact that Charles was immobilized on the Rhine. He also hoped not only to divert part of the duke's army but also to frighten the French vassals who were obviously wondering whether they should form yet another Public Good coalition to join up with the Anglo-Burgundian faction. The king may even have hoped to discourage Edward IV at the last minute, because he also ordered his ships to patrol the Channel at the same time, in order to impress the English king.

From a military point of view, the fiercest attack was directed against Picardy, where Louis XI commanded his army in person. From the 1st until the 18th May, he took a whole series of fortified towns, including Bray-sur-Somme, Ancre (later known as Albert), Montdidier, Roye, Moreuil, Corbie, and Doullens. Then on receiving a false report that the English were attacking in Normandy, the king retreated. However, it was at Calais that Edward made his landing on the 4th July.

There can be no doubt that of the two signatories of the Treaty of London, Edward IV was the one who respected the agreement more faithfully. The invading army which he had assembled and which he commanded in person, comprised at least thirteen thousand fighting men. Never, according to Commynes, had a finer army crossed the Channel.[7] These forces were appreciably greater than the minimum stipulated in the treaty. Nearly all the barons and lords of England took part in the expedition, notably the Dukes of Clarence and Gloucester, the king's brothers; the Dukes of Norfolk and Suffolk, the Earls of Ormond, Northumberland and Arundel; Anthony Woodville, Earl of Rivers, brother of the Queen; Lord Boyd, Lord Scrops, Lord Ferrers, Lord Stanley, Lord Hastings, Lord Howard, Lord Grey of Ruthyn, and one hundred and fifty knights. The men-at-arms were superbly equipped and the archers were mounted. It was not an English habit to take to the field unless all the equipment was in perfect order.

The artillery, under the command of John Sturgeon, was impressive. The English had with them an entirely new device for making trenches, a sort of giant plough, pulled by fifty horses. Greatly improved camping gear had been provided and the king, who liked his creature comforts, had ordered for his own personal use a leather-covered, collapsible wooden house.

This, then, was the splendid invading army which Charles the Bold ought to have been ready to welcome and which it would have been only elementary commonsense to support, once the landing had taken place, with as great a force as Burgundy could muster.

Before setting sail from Dover, Edward, following the usual procedure, sent a challenge to Louis by a herald-at-arms, calling upon Philip VI's descendant to hand back the Capetian Kingdom to the lawful heir. Louis, of course, refused to agree to this; but he was careful to explain to Garter King-of-arms, who had brought the message, the reasons which, according to him, ought to predispose England and France to conclude a satisfactory agreement. He handed the bearer of the challenge three hundred crowns and thirty ells of crimson cloth, and promised him a further three hundred crowns if an agreement were reached. Garter King-of-arms, surprised by the welcome he had received, responded to Louis's courteous behaviour by suggesting that if a herald were sent to the English camp, he might—through the mediation of Lord Stanley and Lord Howard—obtain assurance of safe conduct for French envoys.

Charles the Bold had at last decided to raise the siege of Neuss. Before making off, he held a magnificent banquet for the German princes, his allies, then he went straight to Calais with a small escort. Seeing no sign of the promised ten thousand men, some of the English accused him of treachery. The duke thereupon explained that only the problem of supplies had prevented him from bringing up his army. He proposed to follow a plan which he had worked out during the siege of Neuss. The English, who were strong enough, he said, 'to conquer France and Italy even as far as Rome', would make their entry into France through Vermandois, eventually reaching Rheims by way of St Quentin and Laon. In the meantime, the Burgundians would wipe out the forces of the Duke of Lorraine, who had thrown in his lot with the King of France, and by way of Barrois, join up with their allies in Champagne.

Charles the Bold stressed several important considerations in favour of this plan: the French army only protected Normandy; the key to Champagne was in the hands of a friend, a kinsman, the Count of St Pol, Louis of Luxemburg, who, in spite of being constable of France, had not been given any military command by his king, and for very good reasons; finally, once crowned at Rheims, Edward would have no difficulty in being recognized as lawful King of France, and most of the fleur-de-lys vassals would rally to his cause.

Edward agreed to this splendid plan. On the 16th or the 18th he took the field with Charles. The English made their way through Ardres and Guines and on the 19th set up camp near St Omer. Then from St Omer, by way of Thérouanne, they reached Fauquembergue on the 23rd, then Ruisseauville and Agincourt where they spent two nights. By way of Blangy and St Pol they went on to Doullens, where they were rejoined by Clarence and Charles the Bold who had left Edward at Fauquembergue in order to visit Arras, one of his possessions about whose fate he was still somewhat anxious. At Doullens, the king and the duke spent three days inspecting the troops.

From then on, Louis XI saw quite clearly what the enemy faction was up to, and he acted accordingly. The fine army which Charles VII had organized and which his son had reinforced, constituted, if firmly controlled, a powerful defensive weapon. The King of France left a few troops in Normandy under the command of the bailiff of Rouen and the marshal of Gamaches, while he himself made for Beauvais which he reached on the 31st July, undeterred by the fact that the plague was raging there at the time. He gave instructions for the defence of Beauvais, and gave thought to the problem of Rheims. He ordered the defence-works to be put in good condition, and on the 28th he commissioned Raulin Cochinart to speed up the work, which had now become urgent.

While Louis of Bourbon, the Admiral of France, set fire to two villages on the outskirts of Arras, beat the town's garrison and captured John of Luxemburg on the 27th July, the king, on the 28th, commissioned Torcy, St Just and L'Isle to burn down Doullens as soon as the enemy vacated it.

After the inspection of the troops, Edward had resumed his advance. On the 1st August, the English reached Acheux, on the 2nd Ancre, and Curlu on the 3rd. Crossing the Somme, they set up camp at Eclusier Vaux, near Péronne, on the 5th, with the river behind them.

Louis XI then left Beauvais, passed through Creil, where the royal artillery was assembled, on the 4th August and on the 5th arrived at Compiègne. He continued the while to speed up the efforts of the townspeople of Rheims who were working night and day to strengthen their fortifications. The Grand Master, Antoine de Chabannes, Count of Daumartin, was at Noyon with a brilliant team of military captains. The king, for his part, had an equally brilliant staff around him. It was felt that operations essential to the outcome of the war were imminent.

In the circumstances, it was of vital importance to get possession of St Quentin. This stronghold was still in the hands of St Pol, whose intentions were more than doubtful. He was pursuing a policy of his own and steering a devious course between the rival princes. He was in an extremely embarrassing situation, because in the present state of affairs he was reluctant to commit himself. Both sides pressed for his support and he could not make up his mind which to follow. Time was running short; the English had arrived at Eclusier, and on the 6th August the Duke of Burgundy reached

Péronne. St Pol sent a messenger to Péronne with a sealed letter in which he promised to obey the duke. On the strength of this promise, Charles informed Edward that the stronghold would be handed over. Edward, satisfied that this would be the case, sent part of his army off to St Quentin. The English expected to be received with enthusiasm, but to their stupefaction, St Pol opened fire and brought out his skirmishers. After a clash of arms, during which both sides sustained losses, the English advance-guard returned to camp in driving rain.

This was a bitter disappointment. From St Christ, lying to the south of Péronne, the English were able to overrun the area as far as Falvy, but the French army could retaliate by doing the same. On the other hand, Edward had counted on a rising of the French vassals. But the uncertain course of events made the feudal lords hesitate to commit themselves. Had the Duke of Burgundy taken his full share of responsibility alongside his royal brother-in-law at the head of the coalition, they would perhaps have been won over. The fact that the best part of the Burgundian forces were immobilized in the east, could only encourage a wait-and-see attitude. Even the Duke of Brittany, whom the English had expected to declare himself immediately, did not stir. Yet Edward had fulfilled his engagements towards Francis II: Andley and Duras, who had been commissioned to take the two thousand archers promised to the duke into Brittany, had been officially appointed on the 12th June. Francis still preferred to wait, since he was negotiating in secret with Louis XI. The English, because they had got wind of this or because they were uncertain, decided against marching into Brittany.

So many disappointments made the 'white rose' king somewhat sceptical, even with regard to Burgundy, his ally. After all, there was no actual proof that the Burgundian army was capable of inflicting a speedy and crushing defeat on the Duke of Lorraine. The plan put forward by Burgundy could, of course, be a trap and there was in any case a danger that it might throw the onus of the campaign on the English. Even Charles the Bold's behaviour aroused suspicion. In order to protect his subjects in Picardy, he had denied the English access to the towns in the area, and would not even allow them into Péronne. Such measures certainly protected the people, but they put Burgundy's allies in a very awkward position. Between Amiens and St Quentin they had no stronghold on which to fall back. Bad weather would soon set in, and they could see no prospect of finding winter quarters. Forced to set up camp in a region which had been stripped bare by the French attack of the previous spring, Edward began to hanker after the life of pleasure he had been accustomed to lead in London. This was a far cry from the light-hearted and successful campaign envisaged by the handsome Yorkist monarch.

Commynes points out somewhere that it was a typically Italian procedure to negotiate even while hostilities were in progress. It was a method with which Louis XI was not unacquainted, and he intended to apply it on this occasion. This was the meaning of the welcome he gave to Garter King-of-arms.

Before reaching the Somme, Edward IV had sent the Ulster King-of-arms and two poursuivants to Louis. The King of France commissioned the Admiral, Louis of Bourbon the bastard, to receive these emissaries, after which the Ulster King-of-arms had a secret conversation lasting two hours with the King; when he left he was given the sum of two hundred golden crowns. A clandestine transaction was now afoot and Louis XI was in his element. Edward, unable to shake off the impression that his alliance with Burgundy would bring him nothing but disappointment, was increasingly inclined to accept the idea of an immediate and no doubt advantageous peace treaty, which would allow him to spend on pleasure the money he would save on the campaign.

Charles the Bold had set out once more for Lorraine, and was entirely engrossed in the war with René II. Edward consequently felt that he was free to act. As it happened, the English had just taken a prisoner, the first one of the campaign—a valet in the service of Jacques de Grassay, a gentleman of Louis's household. Edward had the valet set free. He was questioned on his return to the French camp and the account he gave made the King of France decide to send an emissary to the English. Mérindot was chosen, dressed up as a herald, and sent off to try his luck.[8]

The plan was a complete success. Mérindot was brought before Edward IV as soon as he reached the English lines. He announced that the King of France desired to live at peace with the King of England; he explained to the latter the risks he ran in continuing the campaign and assured him that it would be an easy matter to conclude an honourable and permanent agreement; finally he suggested that safe-conduct should be granted to ambassadors, and that the English sovereign should choose the place and time for parleying. Louis XI was prepared to grant safe conduct to the negotiators appointed by Edward.

As a matter of fact, the success of the mission was a foregone conclusion. Edward granted the safe-conduct which had been asked for and decided that the talks should take place between the French and English lines. A herald was sent off from St Christ to deliver the safe-conduct for the British ambassadors. Contact had now been firmly established and negotiations could begin.

Four Frenchmen and four Englishmen met at Dives on the 14th August. The Admiral of France, Louis of Bourbon, Jean Daillon, a nobleman from Lude, Jean Héberge, Bishop of Evreux, and Jean Blosset, a nobleman from St Pierre, were chosen by Louis XI; and William Dudley, Dean of the Chapel Royal, Lord Howard, John Morton and Thomas St Léger, a knight and one of the king's bodyguard, by Edward IV. Continuing a well-established tradition, the English started by claiming the French crown, or at least, Normandy and Guienne. This, however, was a pure formality; more concrete proposals were to follow. Edward said he would be satisfied if Louis were to pay him seventy-five thousand crowns within two weeks, which sum would cover the expenses incurred during the war. A treaty was to be concluded, stipulating friendship between the two kings. Louis was to grant Edward an annual pension of fifty thousand crowns for life, and he was to bear the cost of the Dauphin's marriage to one of the English princesses, who was to receive a guaranteed annual dowry of sixty thousand pounds.

Louis XI showed how shrewd he was by accepting these conditions straightaway. Never had negotiations been carried out with such speed. On the very next day, the French plenipotentiaries transmitted to their colleagues their master's decision to accept the terms. The English king had been taken at his word, and the Hundred Years' War was virtually at an end.[9]

Charles the Bold was on his way to Lorraine where he intended to pursue his private quarrel, and it was on the 12th August, on arriving at Valenciennes to hold a session of the Hainault estates, that he learnt the astounding news of negotiations between the two kings.

He turned back at once, and made for Péronne. He raced to the camp at St Christ, but what had been done in the meantime could not be undone.

On the 19th the duke approached his brother-in-law. He asked him if it were true that he had been negotiating with France. On being told this was the case he flew into a rage. He upbraided Edward in English.[10] He made bitter comparisons between his behaviour and the behaviour of previous English kings. Edward replied in the same vein. He reproached his accuser with not having abided by the stipulations of the Treaty of London. The next day, the duke had another interview with Edward, who refused either to repudiate his action or to assure Charles of his support. Finally Charles left the camp proudly affirming that he could do without the English, and that he would prove it by refusing to conclude a truce with the French until the English army had been back on their native soil for three months.

This brought to an end the Anglo-Burgundian alliance which had caused Charles VII's heir such uneasiness.

By now the English and French armies were fraternizing. Tables laden with food had been set up at the gates of Amiens, and the English ate and drank as guests of the King of France. One morning as many as nine thousand of them were said to have been seen helping themselves to the lavish spread. At the Picquigny meeting which took place on the 29th August, treaties were drawn up which, once they had been put into operation, set the official seal on the reconciliation between the two royal dynasties which were from then on to live at peace.[11]

With his army already assembled Louis XI might have been expected to fight it out with Burgundy immediately after the Picquigny settlement, especially as the duke scornfully refused to be included in the Anglo-French truce.

But Louis intended to revert to his favourite tactics; he preferred to manœuvre in secret and hem in his opponent by the use of diplomacy, rather than run the risk of a pitched battle.

Burgundy was still in a very strong position in spite of the mistakes that had been committed by Duke Charles. The treaties of friendship concluded by Charles the Bold with John II of Aragon were still in force. In addition to the Arago-Burgundian alliance, and we have already seen how close an alliance it was, a Burgundo-Neapolitan agreement had been concluded, and just at this time the possibility of a marriage between Mary of Burgundy and Prince Frederick of Taranto—the son of Ferrando, King of Naples—was being discussed. Frederick was with his prospective father-in-law and ready to take part in the onslaught on Lorraine.

Thanks to pressure brought to bear by the House of Aragon, Charles acquired another ally, Sforza of Milan who, although he had up till then been heavily committed to the French alliance, now changed sides. Savoy, too, was secretly involved in these manœuvres. Yolanda of Savoy, although Louis XI's sister, had no hesitation in encouraging the Milano-Burgundian rapprochement. She did so by stealth. While ostensibly negotiating with Berne and belonging to the anti-Burgundian coalition, she had in actual fact been working for the other side, and on the 30th January 1475 had arranged the Treaty of Moncalieri, between Sforza and Charles the Bold.

If therefore, after the English withdrawal, Charles had executed a complete *volte-face*; if he had freed himself from his commitments in the east, and, together with his allies, had boldly faced Louis XI —he might have succeeded in frightening the king into concluding a tolerable agreement, such as Edward had obtained. But he was obsessed by the Lorraine question and his ambitious projects in the east. His policy was, in consequence, to postpone operations in the west, and to settle, by force of arms, not only the Lorraine question but the Swiss question too, for he was eager to wipe out the bitter defeat inflicted by the surprise attack at Héricourt.

With his customary guile, Louis XI encouraged his opponent in this policy, because it served his own secret purpose. He therefore agreed to sign the nine-year truce of Soleuvre with the duke on the 13th September 1475.[12] Both parties somewhat unscrupulously abandoned alliances to which they were already committed. Charles renounced the Aragon alliance, and Louis the alliance with Lorraine. It was definitely the king who got most out of the shady transaction. By isolating John II, he deprived Charles of help which could have had far-reaching implications; but above all, he felt sure that René would be roughly handled by Burgundy and would stubbornly resist the duke; furthermore, in spite of the truce, he intended to give clandestine support to Lorraine. As a crowning piece of duplicity on the part of both contracting parties, an agreement concluded by 'private letter', handed St-Pol over to the king's justice.

It was while Charles the Bold was carrying out a lightning campaign in Lorraine and had taken possession of the strongholds and capital of the duchy[13] that Louis XI, in connivance with the duke, took his revenge on the constable.

For years, St-Pol had been playing a triple game, giving his allegiance to Louis, Edward and Charles in turn. Edward, with whom the St Quentin affair still rankled, had before returning to England handed over to Louis a letter in which St-Pol criticized the Treaty of Picquigny and implored the King of England not to count on it, since the clauses would not be respected by his co-signatory.

Having been thus exposed, the count, dreading retaliation on the part of Louis XI, turned to the Duke of Burgundy. Once within the safety of the duke's estates, he had promised Charles that he would hand over St Quentin, and he had obtained from the duke's chancellery letters bearing the Great Seal and guaranteeing his safe-conduct. The king then seized St Quentin. Whereupon the duke, who claimed not to understand what was happening, and probably acting on the false presumption that St-Pol had been guilty of a fresh breach of faith, himself committed an open and glaring act of disloyalty by breaking his promise and handing his guest over to the king's 'justice'.

In this affair, there was very little to choose as far as duplicity was concerned between the Valois of Burgundy and the Valois of France.

Jean Blosset, Lord of St Pierre, came to take St-Pol into custody.[14] The constable was brought before the *Parlement*, condemned to death, and beheaded in front of the Town Hall on the 28th December 1475.

Charles the Bold was now subjugating Lorraine with a heavy hand. The capital was in his hands. Elated by the success of his punitive expedition Charles was determined not to stop there. René II's act of defiance had been given the punishment it deserved. But the Swiss, too, ought to be taught a lesson for having dared to launch the surprise assault on the duke at Héricourt. At this point, the entire policy of Charles the Bold, now flushed with his triumphs, was dictated by a desire for revenge.

Louis XI had foreseen that this was exactly how the duke would react, and he had, consequently, negotiated for a truce at Soleuvre. He fully expected that his formidable opponent would eventually bring about his own destruction by continuing his blind and headlong course, like a trapped bull charging from one end of the arena to the other. The king made only a show of neutrality. He had helped René in the past and would continue to help him in the future. He concluded, with the Swiss, the '*Union Perpétuelle de Constance*' which had been arranged on his behalf by his ambassador Jost de Sileneu, Bishop of Grenoble, and which was to make the 29th March 1474 so memorable a date. Roussillon had been occupied, thanks to Burgundy's ill-timed betrayal of John II of Aragon, and thanks to the fact that the whole of Spain was engrossed at this moment by the problem of the Castille succession.[15] The French feudal lords were quiescent.[16] There was nothing to prevent Louis XI from keeping a close watch on the events which were about to be enacted in the east. Although he had signed the Soleuvre truce, the king knew full well that long before the nine fateful years had elapsed, the fate of Burgundy would have to be settled once and for all.[17] Three great Burgundian disasters were now about to be enacted, like a trilogy, on the vast stage of history, and were to mark the culmination of the Machiavellian schemes laid by the 'universal spider'.

CHAPTER XIV

THE END OF A REIGN AND THE END OF A DYNASTY

THE STRUGGLE BETWEEN the Duke of Burgundy and the Swiss had now entered an acute phase. The help which the cantons had given to the Alsatian towns, the agreements they had concluded with France, the designs which the people of Berne had on the Vaud region, the surprise attack launched at Héricourt on the 13th September, the connivance which existed between the Swiss and René II of Lorraine—all these factors made war between Burgundy and Switzerland inevitable. Swiss pride had been wounded to the quick, and French money helped to provide arms for the indomitable mountain race. The Count of Romont, Jacques of Savoy, the Duke of Savoy's uncle and Governor of Franche-Comté had aroused the hostility of the people of Berne, his neighbours, and had provoked them into issuing a challenge which they followed up by a full-scale attack. In order to inflame Charles the Bold still further Louis repeatedly advised him to exercise prudence and offered to act as mediator in the quarrel, while hoping all the time in his heart of hearts that it would bring about the duke's downfall. To preach moderation was the surest way of encouraging Charles to plunge whole-heartedly into the war.[1] The inevitable happened. Charles made no attempt to use diplomacy in order to straighten out the confused situation brought about by his own mistakes; his one aim now was to impose his rule everywhere by force of arms.

He wished, to begin with, to settle the Swiss question once and for all. The first campaign against the Cantons was launched in January 1476, with some fifteen thousand men. Charles attacked the stronghold of Grandson, and after a fierce bombardment, it capitulated. Charles immediately proved himself to be both cruel and ruthless. Believing that the Swiss peasants could be terrorized into subjection, he ordered four hundred of the town's defenders to be hanged by three executioners, while other victims were flung into the lake.

Emboldened by the success of these exploits,[2] Charles decided to march on Neuchâtel and close the Val de Travers, that is the highway to and from Franche-Comté, to the Swiss troops. With this objective in view, he sent his men to occupy the half-ruined castle at Vaumarcus.

On the 1st March, the Swiss confederate forces, roused to indignation by the atrocities committed at Grandson, decided to make for Vaumarcus. Their plan was to lure the enemy troops in this direction and then to attack them in the rear with a force specially reserved for this operation.

The duke completely failed to realize that this was a planned manœuvre and fell straight into the trap which had been set for him. As he moved towards Neuchâtel, he was rash enough to send his advance guard into a narrow pass on the slopes of Mt Aubert on the morning of the 2nd. Here the Swiss halted his advance and hurled his men back in confusion.

The morning mist was just clearing. In order to give his advance guard time to reform, the duke placed his artillery on the right hand slopes of the Corcelles plateau so that it could cover the point at which the Swiss would emerge. The infantry took up their position behind the cannons. The cavalry, under the command of Louis of Chalon, Lord of Châteauguyon, climbed the slopes of Mt Aubert with the object of falling back, to the right, on to the enemy's flank. But as it happened, the aim of the artillery fire was poor and totally ineffective, and Charles was in too great a hurry to hurl his foot-soldiers against the enemy formations which Louis of Chalon had failed to break up.

In the meantime the Swiss force moving towards Vaumarcus and which had been informed that the battle had begun, came up by way of a ravine and rushed into the attack. Caught unawares by their unexpected and noisy arrival, which was announced by the din of the horns of Uri and Unterwalden re-echoing through the mountains, Charles rashly ordered his men to give ground. His intention was to allow himself space for greater freedom of manœuvre or to take cover behind the river Arnon, which protected his camp. His orders were misunderstood and finally caused a general panic. A crushing attack launched by the Swiss flung the Burgundian soldiers back—some to the Arnon, some to a nearby swamp. The duke did his best to stop the rout until he himself was swept along in the general stampede.[3]

Having been attacked in a pass where they had no freedom of

movement, the Burgundians had no other course but to take to flight. What was more serious they had to abandon a vast amount of precious booty to the enemy, who were themselves astonished at having won such a complete victory.

The duke's personal treasures were saved, but he left behind five hundred pieces of artillery, four hundred tents, six hundred flags, four hundred pounds of silver plate, tapestries, pieces of embroidered cloth (some of which are now in the Musée de Berne), the 'Sancy', the duke's diamond, his hat, sword, the die-stamp of his secret seal (now in the Archives d'Etat at Lucerne) and many other trophies. On the Burgundian side, the victims included Châteauguyon, Quentin de la Beaume, Louis Rolin and Jean de Lalaing.

The unexpected defeat at Grandson could admittedly have been made good; nevertheless, it left a deep impression throughout the western world. The proud and mighty duke who aspired to kingship and who had struck fear into all the neighbouring states, was not invincible after all.

Fearing that Louis XI might attack him in the rear after his defeat on the 2nd March, Charles hurriedly sent the Lord of Contay, Louis the Young, to the king. The latter, who had been informed of the outcome of the battle some time between the 8th and 10th March at Notre Dame du Puy, where he had gone on a pilgrimage with Commynes, had made his way to Lyons, where he could follow the course of events more closely. He received Louis the Young most courteously and set his mind at rest. There was no question of abandoning the existing truces. Nevertheless from the snatches of topical ditties he heard during his stay, the duke's emissary could measure the effect the incident had had on public opinion.

The duke's authority had in fact been seriously impaired. All those who had been intimidated by him, now took fresh heart. Flanders was debating whether to send help or not. Guelders was in a state of feverish uncertainty. The Duke of Milan had already opened negotiations for a return to the French alliance. René of Anjou, who at one point had effected a rapprochement with Charles the Bold and who had even considered making him heir to Provence, now took fright and sought only to reingratiate himself with his nephew, the King of France. Finally, Savoy, still playing a double game, was careful to keep open a line of retreat. Only John of Aragon showed no reaction. He made no effort to maintain relations with the duke who had most unscrupulously thrown him over at Soleuvre, and resigned himself to the loss of Roussillon, because he considered it would be only temporary. While fulfilling his life's ambition—the establishment of

Spanish unity—he looked forward to the day when either he or his son would eventually restore the old frontier, once the mighty power of Spain had been consolidated.

The King of Naples, who normally followed in Aragon's wake, did in fact remain faithful to the loser of the battle of Grandson; it was difficult for him to abandon his pre-war policy because Frederick, Prince of Taranto, as Mary of Burgundy's suitor, was still with his prospective father-in-law. Frederick had fought at Grandson and intended to take part in the preparations for revenge. The Neapolitan prince had in his entourage a doctor called Angelo Cato, the future Archbishop of Vienna, who was attending the duke. In the meantime, Louis was distributing gifts to the Swiss more generously than ever.[4]

Commynes has painted an unforgettable picture of Charles the Bold after Grandson, and there seems no doubt that it was his friend, the man in fact to whom the *Mémoires* were dedicated, who supplied him with material.

The duke's health was gradually deteriorating and his morale had suffered a grievous blow. He had become in fact a neurasthenic. His disposition underwent a profound change; normally of a sanguine temperament he had so far avoided wine, preferring more cooling drinks such as tisanes and rose-hip syrup; he now however felt the need of tonics and stimulants. He let his beard grow, vowing that he would not cut it off until he had recovered his military prestige. Angelo Cato, however, made him shave. But, now more irascible than ever, the duke, in Commynes' unequivocal phrase 'was losing his faculties'.[5] On all sides, the duke could see his enemies, who 'had previously been lying low', coming boldly forward and 'sticking out their horns'. These vivid expressions which recall Commynes's style, come actually from Molinet.

Although his subjects did not go so far as to betray the duke, on the whole they showed very little willingness to make sacrifices for his sake; it is certain that not even his most loyal subjects were fired by the sort of national feeling which can alter the course of history and has a stabilizing effect in time of crisis.[6]

In an attempt to hurry on the marriage between Mary and Maximilian which was once more under consideration and now seemed likely to replace the Burgundo-Neapolitan marriage plan, Frederick III agreed to sign a pact at Lausanne on the 14th April 1476. Although this meant that the emperor and the House of Austria abandoned the Swiss alliance, it was a diplomatic victory of slight importance. The defection, genuine or feigned, of the unstable emperor which was paid for by the surrender of Alsace and the consequent collapse of the improbable Austro-Helvetic *entente*, were not events likely to affect the balance of power one way or the other.

Only a decisive victory of the Burgundian forces over the cantons could extricate the duke from the perilous position in which he now found himself, and he fully realized the fact. In spite of his impaired health, he feverishly assembled an army at Lausanne with the intention of achieving his revenge. It is difficult to assess the total strength of his army—he probably had less than ten thousand men.[7] Furthermore, his preparations were a glaring instance of improvisation which boded ill for the future.

The Duke of Milan tried in vain to dissuade the Duke of Burgundy from taking up arms again so soon. The voice of prudence went unheeded. According to the wise Commynes, 'his ears were blocked, and his mind disordered'—shrewd comment and a clear pointer to what was going to happen. It was impossible for Charles, in his distraught mental state, to follow a sober course; he could only think of recovering his lost prestige. He could not 'face the world', he asserted, 'until he had wiped out the shame of having been defeated by a race of savages'.[8] The more obstacles he encountered, the fiercer his ambition became. The duke had no intention of calling a halt after settling his account with the Swiss. He would, he said, pursue the King of France even to Paris, and, in addition, he would occupy Savoy. These were rash prophecies, and they cast a revealing light on the man who could utter such vain boasts so soon after losing a major battle.

However, the Burgundians succeeded in forming the army which was to carry out the retaliatory campaign. The Count of Romont and the Prince of Taranto were to be the main leaders, under the supreme command of the Duke of Burgundy in person. The Swiss were conscious of a great danger hanging over them. They urged the King of France to take his share of responsibility in the struggle which could not now be avoided. Jost de Silenen, Bishop of Grenoble and chief intermediary between the Cantons and France, was sent off to Louis who was still at Lyons. The bishop begged Louis XI not to leave his secret allies to 'bear the whole brunt'. But Louis, imperturbable as ever, continued to pursue his usual tactics of giving advice and money. Obviously, he was firmly convinced that the Swiss, backed by reinforcements from Lorraine which René II came to command in person on 2nd June, were capable of getting the better of the enemy formations since the two armies were more or less of equal strength and since the deluded Charles was about to hurl his hastily assembled forces into battle, without any adequate training.

On the 27th May 1476, the Duke of Burgundy left Lausanne. He encamped for a week about six miles from the town, on the Morreus plateau. On the 4th June, he set off for the Broye Valley by way of Echallens and arrived beneath the walls of Morat in the Canton of Freiburg on the 9th. The evening before, Butenberg, a distinguished citizen of Berne, and a former pensioner of the duke's but now hostile to him, had made his way into the small fortified town overlooking the south bank of the lake of Morat with a force of between fifteen hundred and two thousand men. Morat, which the Bernese had taken from the Count of Romont, represented a sort of front line of defence for Berne. A thousand or so men occupied Freiburg in the same way. If the Morat-Freiburg line collapsed, the valleys of the Sarine and the Sense, with the bridges at Gummeneu and Laupen, would form a second line of defence.

After Romont had reconnoitred as far as the outskirts of Harberg, he came back and hoisted his colours to the north-east of Morat, while Charles the Bold took up his position to the south of the same fortress on the hill slopes at Courgevaux. It was the 10th June. The next day the siege of Morat began.

The town was in touch with Berne by way of the lake. The duke kept his men hard at it digging trenches while his heavy artillery maintained a steady bombardment. The defenders, far from being alarmed, even made several energetic sorties. A violent assault launched on the 10th June was unsuccessful and inflicted heavy casualties on the attacking force. On the 22nd events took a sensational turn. Frederick, the Prince of Taranto, on the express orders of his father, King Ferrando of Naples, left the camp. The Burgundian court's renewed proposal for a marriage between Mary and Maximilian had angered Ferrando, who felt he had been tricked, while at the same time Louis XI had undermined the friendship between Burgundy and Naples by offering Frederick the hand of his youngest daughter, Joan the Lame, the future Duchess of Orleans.[9] The King of France, after winning back the friendship of Sforza of Milan and of the Emperor, and after reoccupying Roussillon, and legalizing his position with regard to Aragon by a series of truces, had succeeded in robbing the Duke of Burgundy of his one remaining ally, the King of Naples.

By a remarkable coincidence, on the very day that Frederick of

Taranto abandoned his one-time prospective father-in-law, René II of Lorraine arrived in person to offer his services to the cantons.

This then was the military and diplomatic situation when the final operations were launched near Morat.

With the lake behind them, and with no possible line of retreat open to them in the event of a defeat, the Burgundians were attacked by the Swiss army on the 22nd. The sturdy mountain race knew every inch of the ground. Furthermore they had the slope in their favour and could make full use of the converging valleys, and take cover when necessary in the woods.

While Butenberg kept Romont's men busy, the duke allowed himself to be caught unawares by the enemy offensive, and was unable to capture the initiative.

In the morning a group of enemy soldiers crept through the forest of Morat, but on seeing the Burgundian troops solidly lined up between Cressier and Coussiberlé, they withdrew. The rain was pouring down. At eleven o'clock the duke, thinking that all was quiet for the time being, and that the enemy had gone, ordered his men to return to their quarters. At noon, however, the enemy forces, having advanced under cover, emerged in a body right opposite the Cressier line, and succeeded in reaching the plateau, in spite of the heavy barrage from both the English archers and the Burgundian cannons. The Duke of Lorraine and Hans de Hallwyll, who were leading the Swiss advance guard, were moving along a narrow path. Charles, in order to hurl his cavalry at the enemy ordered his artillery to move back, and as at Grandson, the order produced panic and confusion. The infantry began to give ground, while the cavalry tried to restore the battle. With the arrival of the Swiss rear-guard under the command of Gaspard de Hertenstein, the disaster was complete.

An appalling massacre ensued. Many of those who fled were drowned in the lake. It was obvious that the mercenaries, who had been assembled in far too hasty a fashion at Lausanne, who were poorly led and inadequately trained, were no match for the sturdy Alpine troops, filled with patriotic enthusiasm.

Louis XI's expectations were thus fulfilled. Even the picked troops fighting alongside the duke were unable to control the confusion and were caught up in the general rout. The casualties at Morat were far heavier than they had been at Grandson. About eight thousand men —mostly infantrymen—lost their lives. Their bones were laid in two huge charnel-houses on either side of a chapel of remembrance.[10]

The Burgundians left behind less booty than at Grandson; even so, rich fabrics, priceless furs, weapons of exquisite workmanship, a portrait of the duke and an ornate and costly chapel fell into the hands of the victors.

The duke had galloped without stopping to Morges on Lake Geneva and attended mass there on the morning of the 23rd. About six o'clock in the evening he arrived at the residence of the Duchess of Savoy at Gex, where he stayed until the 27th. Finally, by way of St Claude, Poligny and Arbois he went to settle at La Rivière in Doubs. It was from this small stronghold that he issued orders for a new army to be reassembled, whatever the cost. Neither the energy he displayed, nor the cheerfulness which, the Milanese ambassador says, he showed, can possibly deceive the student of history as to the defeated duke's true frame of mind. Commynes bears witness to the fact that he was 'most despondent' about 'the mishap'. It was indeed difficult for him to be otherwise.

Charles did not possess Louis XI's ability to pause for reflection after a disappointment, nor his genius for planning in secret the sort of well-timed and shrewdly calculated recovery which could rectify the most disastrous mistakes.

On the contrary the duke was given to impulsive action. In Charles's view, the attempt to retrieve his fortunes should be made without delay. Now more than ever before he was at the mercy of his headstrong nature; as Commynes says: 'the more involved he became, the more confused he grew'.

The most eloquent proof of this is to be seen in the ill-timed act of violence which was carried out at that very moment at the ducal court, against the Savoy family. The Duchess of Savoy, Yolanda, Louis XI's sister, had been favourably disposed towards Burgundy, although she had been careful not to commit herself completely to the point of entering into an alliance with her brother's enemy.

Pretending to believe that the king was about to seize Savoy, the duke suddenly made a dramatic move in complete defiance of international law, but which was supposed to forestall the king's attempt. Yolanda, who was now a widow, had been acting as regent since the 3rd July 1475. The duke resolved to arrest her and her eldest son, the eleven-year-old Duke Philibert. Public opinion everywhere was shocked by his action.

From Gex, where the Duke of Burgundy had been her guest after his defeat at Morat, Yolanda had set off for Geneva. She was overtaken about two miles from the town at Grand-Sassonex by Olivier de la Marche who had been commissioned to carry out the daring exploit. The memorialist has given his own account of the incident and, conscious of the odiousness of the task assigned to him, he made his apologies to posterity in the following terms: 'I did it in order to save my life, because the duke, my master, was such that everyone had to do as he ordered on pain of losing their heads'.[11] The attempt was only partially successful. Philibert and his little brother, Charles, were 'hidden away' by one of the men accompanying Olivier, Ludovic Taglianti from Ivrea: the young princes were first of all concealed in the cornfields bordering the highway, then they were taken to Chambéry by the major-domo, Geoffroy de Rivarol. The duchess, perched behind Olivier de la Marche, was taken through the Jura mountains to St Claude. From here she was transferred first of all to Rochefort-sur-Nenon, near Dôle, then to Rouvre castle, not far from Dijon.

The ill-used Yolanda appealed to her brother for help. Louis was only too glad of the opportunity to free Savoy from Burgundian domination.

Geoffroy de Rivarol, the emissary acting on behalf of the captive duchess, addressed himself first to Commynes, who referred the matter to the king. Rivarol was at once given an assurance that action would be taken without delay. Charles of Amboise, Lord of Chaumont, was commissioned to carry out the operation in his capacity as Governor of Champagne, and it was a complete success. The Lord of Chaumont, with the help of two hundred men-at-arms carried off Yolanda from Rouvre and took her to Langres. Since leaving Lyons, the king had gone by boat from Roanne to Tours, and he sent for his sister to join him at Plessis manor. 'He went to meet her at the gates of Plessis du Parc and greeted her amiably with the words: "I bid you most welcome, Madame Burgundy." She realized from his expression that he was only teasing and demurely replied that she was a loyal Frenchwoman.' This was just what Louis wanted. Savoy had never been an ally of the Burgundian State, but it had been favourably disposed towards the duke, and its return to the French fold completed the switch of alliances started by Anjou, Naples and Milan.

The Duke of Burgundy was now completely isolated. The second disaster in Switzerland had dealt a crucial blow to his prestige. The estates which he summoned in Flanders, Burgundy and Franche-Comté were far from amenable. A policy based on war and imperialism always proves disastrous to powers which consist of a conglomeration of races held together by a purely dynastic authority and without any common aspiration.

Of the territories annexed at the point of the sword since Charles's accession, only Lorraine remained in the hands of the over-impetuous duke, who was still bent on imposing his will without delay on all the neighbouring states.

It was inevitable that Lorraine should be prompted to seek her freedom after the two victories won by the cantons. René, Duke of Lorraine, had been one of the heroes of Morat. He had fought for the Swiss, and was determined to get his own country back as a sequel to the Burgundian defeat.

In August 1476, René made an attempt to take Nancy, but it was premature and failed. The duke had to be satisfied with the capture of Lunéville and Epinal which he achieved by a daring advance. He then withdrew to Strasburg, where, with reinforcements from the towns of Alsace and the Rhineland, he assembled a fresh army. Finally he returned to Nancy which was inadequately protected and recovered his capital by a surprise attack on the 6th October.

Whether the Duke of Burgundy had been unable to act quickly enough in Lorraine to ward off the surprise attack, or whether he did not have the means of doing so, the fact remains that the fall of Nancy was yet another shock for him, and a terrible one. Perhaps his defence plans had been held up because the troops from Luxemburg, on which he had counted, failed to arrive in time. Perhaps, too, he had reckoned that the garrison entrusted with the defence of Nancy and which had given in almost without striking a blow, would hold out for longer than it did.

The fall of Nancy, coming as it did after Grandson and Morat, now sounded the death-knell of Burgundian supremacy.

Leaving his camp at La Rivière on the 25th September, Charles the Bold set off with the object of defending the capital of Lorraine, which he had won by force of arms. He made for Toul, by way of Besançon, Vesoul, Joinville, Bulgnéville and Neufchâteau. Having reached Toul on the 11th October, six days after the fall of Nancy, he had the choice of withdrawing or attempting to recapture the stronghold he had lost. Ignoring the fact that his forces were inadequate, the duke chose the latter course. He decided to 'run after the ball' as Commynes so picturesquely said, borrowing his expression, on this occasion, from the game of *longue paume*. The duke was indeed running after an elusive—and an illusory—ball.

It was certainly a gamble to attempt to recapture Nancy at this point, for René II's armed strength was far superior to that of his opponent. Thanks to the financial and diplomatic help that Louis XI had gladly given him, he had at his disposal twelve thousand Swiss, in addition to his own troops. Even French men-at-arms, with the king's clandestine encouragement, embraced his cause.[12]

Thus reinforced, René II took up his position at St Nicolas de Port with about fifteen thousand men. Charles the Bold, who, in spite of previous set-backs, was still confident in his star, coolly and calmly laid siege to Nancy. The sudden desertion of the Count of Campobasso, whatever one may think of his motives,[13] made the situation of the besieging forces, which were already too few in number, even more critical. According to the definite figures given by Olivier de la Marche, out of a total of about ten thousand men, whose names figured on his active list, Charles had not, in fact, more than two thousand men fighting for him.

This being the case, the forces were unevenly matched. The fourth duke, in making this stubborn attempt to defy fate, undeterred by the hopeless discrepancy between the two armies, lived up to his nick-name as never before. The only answer he could give the Count of Chamay who put forward the objection that the enemy had overwhelmingly superior forces, was the boast that he would give battle even if he had to fight alone.[14] The duke, in the blind pursuit of his lost prestige, would heed no advice and, according to the reliable Commynes, 'spoke like a mad man'.

Fought on the 5th January 1477 in these hopeless conditions, the battle of Nancy was bound to be an appalling disaster.

Charles arranged his army on a plateau to the south-east of Nancy between the river Madeleine and the river Jarville, both tributaries of the Meurthe. Jacques Galéot, the *condottiere* who had remained faithful to him, took up his position on the hill-slope opposite Tomblaine with the advance-guard which spread out to form the left flank; the rear-guard, which formed the right flank, was lined up near Saurupt woods, from which René II was expected to emerge. The Burgundian artillery, therefore, conscientiously blocked this exit.

The Swiss commanders decided to repeat the tactics used at Morat, by circumventing the enemy formations concealed behind the woods at Jarville. The attacking forces crossed the river Heillecourt and reached the plain of La Malgrange; then falling back to the right, through Saurupt woods, they emerged directly behind the Burgundian rear-guard. Jean de Bauder, who belonged to the company of young Jean de Lorraine, the son of Count Antoine de Vaudémont, was carrying the huge banner of the Annunciation.

The unexpectedness of the attack caused almost immediate panic and confusion. Once more the horns of Uri and Unterwalden spread terror, as they re-echoed noisily through the hills. Many Burgundians took to flight, others were massacred on the spot. Campobasso and his Italians, having gone over to the enemy, cut off all the escape routes across the Meurthe. Galéot and his companions, who were able to get away in time, rushed off to entrench themselves in Metz.

A vast amount of booty was left behind. The Burgundian camp was pillaged by soldiers from Lorraine and Alsace and by the Swiss. What could not be taken away was burnt. The duke's helmet was sent to Louis XI; his ring, which had been picked up by a Swiss soldier, was given in 1478 by the Schacht brothers to the Duke of Milan; the duke's tunic, which some Alsatian soldiers had torn from his body, was hung up in Strasburg cathedral as a war trophy, but unfortunately it afterwards disappeared; the flags are in the arsenal at Soleure, militia troops from the town having taken part in the battle. The duke's drinking cup, which was taken away by Henri Strübin, master of the artillery, is at Liestall, which had sent men to reinforce the Basle contingents. Lastly, the insignia of the Order of the Golden Fleece were, according to Commynes, sold in Milan for two ducats.

The body of the last of the great dukes, which was identified by Charles's broken teeth and by certain scars left by a wound he had received at Montlhéry, was discovered, two days after the battle, naked and mutilated, in the muddy pond of St Jean, on the frozen surface of which the battle had been fought. The fortunes of the State founded by Philip the Bold, and which his successors, including the last of the line, had never ceased to promote and expand, collapsed with the death of the fourth Valois.

Commynes has described in vivid terms the delirious joy with which Louis XI received the news of the Nancy disaster. The outcome was even better than he had expected. Not only had Burgundy's military might collapsed, but the formidable duke himself had been killed. It is not surprising that the messengers who brought the news received a lavish welcome.

The king was at first so surprised and overjoyed on hearing this news that he hardly knew what expression to adopt. After he had spoken for a moment with the afore-mentioned messengers, he heard mass and then ordered the table to be laid and invited them all to dine with him. He had with him his chancellor and several members of his council and as they dined they continued to talk of these matters . . . On rising from table, the king withdrew and decided on the distribution of some of the lands which had been in the possession of the afore-mentioned duke, assuming that he really was dead.

While joy reigned at Plessis, where the king was already planning his next moves, dismay overwhelmed Duchess Mary at Ghent; she was completely distraught 'at the time of this terrible disaster', to quote Commynes once more.

Surrounded by the unfriendly Flemish, by advisers whose loyalty was questionable, Mary, an orphan and less than twenty years of age, found herself at the most tragic turning point of her existence. The Burgundian State had been crippled and was tottering on its foundations. It had no duke, no money, no army. The spirit had gone out of it and fear and uncertainty filled the void. The young princess, conscious of the heavy burden she had inherited, was afraid of making a false move. She did not even dare to grant an audience to Spanish ambassadors who had just landed in Flanders.[15] She felt that, at such a time, she could not risk incurring the wrath of her formidable suzerain, the king, by some move which might arouse suspicion. Yet, as her god-father, the king might also become her protector.

At first sight, it might appear that the death of the fourth duke raised a straightforward legal problem, similar to the one which had been settled with so little trouble, rather more than a hundred years previously, on the death of Philip of Rouvre. The only question which might have caused difficulty was the revertibility of the ducal appanage in the absence of a male heir. In actual fact, events did not follow a juridical course. It soon became clear that considerations of a much higher nature would have to be taken into account. The France of 1477 was more powerful than the France of 1381 and had much better control of her actions. Louis XI was a statesman of an entirely different calibre from John the Good. Furthermore, Europe was beginning to take shape; new powers were coming to the fore; everywhere feudal principles were giving way to the growing consciousness of the existence of the State.[16]

Louis could adopt either of two possible attitudes towards the deeply-distressed duchess who was for the moment completely lacking in resources—he could be either her friend, or her enemy. Louis, however, avoided making the choice; he was anxious to combine the advantages of both possibilities. Manœuvring, shamming, insinuating and lying—these were the involved and fluctuating tactics he chose to adopt. Commynes did not approve of his policy. In his opinion, his master, whom he had admired on so many occasions, had 'gone astray' in this matter, which was admittedly a particularly difficult one. 'Being free of all fear, he was not granted by God the ability to set about this affair in the right way.' No severer or fairer judgement could be made. This criticism by Louis XI's companion is a basis for, and a justification of, the serious reservations that impartial historians have made about Louis XI.

While acting with great brutality in the north, where he seized Arras and Cambrai, and at the same time marched on Péronne, Louis sent into Burgundy proper a well-equipped army of six thousand men led by a triumvirate consisting of Jean de Chalon, Prince of Orange, Georges de la Trémoille, Lord of Craon, and Charles d'Amboise, Governor of Champagne. At the same time, he sent the people of Dijon a famous letter, dated 9th January, in which he condoled with the subjects of the late duke and expressed his feelings towards the young duchess, his 'god-child'. The letter ended with the highly significant words: 'We hereby inform you that you should submit to no other authority but ours, and that we will defend the right of our afore-mentioned god-daughter, as we have already said.'

Nobody could have indicated with greater clarity than Louis did himself in these few lines the double game he was determined to pursue. While insisting that Burgundy should surrender to him, he was at once claiming to protect the duchess and robbing her of all she possessed. He felt confident that he could also seize Ghent, and gain control of the Low Countries. Commynes was certainly right. Louis's behaviour was an excellent illustration of the proverb about not biting off more than one can chew.

In order to cover up his manœuvres, the king put forward the idea of a marriage between Mary and the Dauphin Charles. The Dauphin was only seven, whereas Mary was nineteen. Nevertheless, Commynes was in favour of an immediate betrothal which, in his opinion, would provide an amicable solution to the problem of Burgundy's future and the one most advantageous to the French crown. As a matter of fact, in addition to the disparity in the ages of the couple, there was another obstacle, which was the reluctance of the Low Countries and Franche-Comté to be annexed to the Valois Kingdom.

However, the proposed marriage served as a pretext for sending the royal army into Burgundy. It reached Dijon on the 1st February. Within a very few days the whole of the duchy was occupied without any serious opposition. The estates of Burgundy gave an official reception to Jean de Chalon, a native of Franche-Comté, who had gone over to Louis XI, and who was acting as Louis's representative. Provided Burgundy was allowed to retain her privileges, the assembly was prepared to accept Louis's pretence of being the duchess's guardian and future father-in-law.

Official circles in Burgundy appeared, then, to have accepted the *fait accompli*. Mâconnais,[17] where memories of previous French domination still persisted, followed the same course, at the instance of Jean de Damas. The towns were cleverly taken over, and controlled by La Trémoille. Promises and bribes did the rest. In short, the people of Burgundy, bewildered by events, were unable to express their local patriotism.

Everything would have gone off perfectly if the intrigues of Jean de Chalon and the brutality of La Trémoille, both of them natural trouble-makers, had not suddenly provoked a revolt in Dijon, from the 26th to the 29th June.

It was a popular rising. With cheers and shouts of 'Mary of Burgundy!' the populace seized St Nicholas's tower and tore down the royal banner. The president, Jean Jouard,[18] who tried to restore order, was butchered.

The rebellion spread from the capital to the whole of the region. At one moment the entire duchy appeared to be in a state of ferment. Beaune, Semur, Châtillon, Seurre, Verdun and many other less important centres, which were either in open revolt or seething with excitement, threatened the local governors or the captains, by setting up a sort of league of independence—inefficiently however, and somewhat late in the day.

The outburst was no more than a flash in the pan. The subtlety and vigour with which Charles d'Amboise handled the situation, put the confusion to rights. He had been appointed Governor of Burgundy on the 12th October, and, like the skilful statesman he was, he allowed the revolt, which for a time had given cause for alarm, to subside.

The towns were brought into subjection, sometimes not without the use of force as, for example, at Seurre, and in the small towns of the Saône area, because Franche-Comté, which was violently opposed to French rule, continued the resistance. An impressive military machine and strategically placed garrisons soon restored law and order.

Louis XI himself travelled to Dijon on the 31st July 1479. At St Bénigne, he received the oath of the new vassals now under the immediate jurisdiction of the crown. However, on the 3rd August he withdrew to the fortified castle of Talant, with a promptness which gave the impression that he had little faith in Burgundy's conversion.

At bottom, he felt that he had forced Burgundy into allegiance. The possibility of another flare-up of local patriotism could not be ruled out. This explains why soon afterwards the king had an impressive castle built, not so much to protect the conquered territories as to keep them under firmer control. At the same time he was careful to appoint men whom he could trust to executive posts in the *Parlement*, *la Chambre des Comptes* and in all the administrative departments which the newly constituted 'province' had inherited from the dukes.

But the Duchy of Burgundy did not represent the entire Burgundian State. The whole vast extent of Charles the Bold's inheritance was soon to be fought over throughout the entire field of European politics. Spain remembered the former Arago-Burgundian alliances and was sympathetically disposed towards the heiress of the man who had held up the French offensive in Roussillon. The Flemish estates were on the defensive and determined to have a say in settling the future of the Low Countries. England, also concerned about the future of the Low Countries, was watching and waiting. Margaret of York, Edward IV's sister and widow of the late Duke Charles, was staying with Mary, her step-daughter. Mary had regained her self-control: she now spoke and behaved like a duchess. Although the communication she addressed to the estates of Burgundy on the 23rd January 1477, exposing the duplicity of her so-called protector who was robbing her of her inheritance, had very little effect in the duchy, she at least answered the ill-advised proposal of marriage with the Dauphin by becoming betrothed to Maximilian. From among her many suitors, the famous heiress chose the man whom she considered to be most fitted to defend her inheritance—the emperor's son.

Just as he had been unable to put a stop to the marriage between Ferdinand and Isabella, which, by unifying Spain, made her a constant menace to France, Louis could not prevent the marriage between Mary and Maximilian, which was to turn Austria into France's future enemy. Commynes's criticism was only too true. As a crowning misfortune for France, the son of Maximilian and Mary, Philip the Handsome, was to marry Joan the Mad, the daughter of their Catholic Majesties, and the grandson to issue from these various unions was no other than Charles V. By throwing Burgundy's heiress into the arms of an Austrian archduke and future emperor, Louis XI was laying in store for the kingdom which he had just delivered from the English wars yet another Hundred Years' War, the long, historic duel with the Austro-Spanish Empire.

Louis himself experienced the first effects of the coming struggle. Although he succeeded in holding Burgundy, Picardy and Artois, he had to let Maximilian take Franche-Comté, Flanders and the Low Countries, and for a time there was confused warfare. The imperial victory at Guinegatte, on the 29th July 1479, led to the compromise of the Treaty of Arras, of 23rd December 1483, whereby Louis XI, already sick and near the end of his career, settled the difficult question of the Burgundian inheritance under cover of yet another marriage proposal. Mary of Burgundy had died at Bruges on the 27th March 1482, as the result of a fall from her horse. It was arranged that her daughter, Margaret of Austria, should marry the Dauphin, who would renounce his English fiancée in her favour. Ducal Burgundy and Picardy were to be recognized as French possessions and certain of Maximilian's estates—Artois, Franche-Comté, Mâconnais and Auxerrois, Salins, Bar-sur-Seine and Noyers—were to form Margaret's dowry.

It seemed that everything was about to be settled in friendly fashion, with the whole magnificent domain of the Low Countries remaining in the hands of the future emperor. Very soon, however, all the arrangements broke down. During the regency of the Beaujeu, Charles VIII's betrothal to Margaret of Austria was broken off and, as everyone knows, Charles VIII married Anne of Brittany, whereupon the Franco-Austrian dispute flared up again.[19] The treaty of 1483 had to be modified by another treaty—the Treaty of Senlis, May 1493. France restored Artois and Franche-Comté to Philip the Handsome, Maximilian's son, but retained possession of the other domains. The Austro-Spanish Empire, then, kept the Low Countries which had already been acquired, along with the two provinces handed back at Senlis. Burgundy, to which Charles V laid claim, only just escaped being incorporated into the German Empire. It was handed over by François I when he was a prisoner in Madrid after his defeat at Pavia; it owed its survival as part of France to the declaration made by the estates that they would not accept transference to a foreign power—a declaration which was confirmed by the military recovery of the valiant Renaissance king.[20]

The political achievements of the great dukes were, then, not entirely lost. Although the state which they had built up had been dismembered, the fragments that remained bore eloquent witness, throughout succeeding ages, to the keenness of their endeavour, and the effectiveness of their exploits. Burgundy remained part of France; Franche-Comté eventually returned to France; Flanders, Artois and Picardy followed the same course, while the kingdoms of Belgium and Holland, moulded by the fifteenth-century princes who did not succeed in winning a royal crown for themselves, proclaim to the modern world that the men who first founded them were of truly royal stature.

CONCLUSION

IT IS ABUNDANTLY CLEAR—the succession of princely reigns which spanned the century of the great dukes is sufficient evidence of the fact—that it was the ambition of the Valois of Burgundy to restore the Kingdom of Lotharingia, or to create a new State of Burgundy embracing not only the Lotharingian lands but all the various domains which had belonged to Burgundy at various times, from the early Middle Ages onwards. It is clear too, that at the height of the last of the four ducal reigns, this ambition was very nearly achieved.

The prize that Philip the Good failed to obtain from Frederick III in 1477 and that Charles the Bold allowed to slip through his fingers during the farcical negotiations at Trier, in which the same emperor played so undignified a rôle, would hardly have eluded the grasp of a victorious duke, once he had brought the last phase of the Hundred Years' War to a glorious conclusion. The carrying out of the Treaty of London, following on the 'infernal pact' of 1417 and the Treaty of Troyes of 1420, would have allowed the Anglo-Burgundian alliance to culminate, round about 1475, in a peace treaty imposed by sheer military superiority, a new Treaty of Brétigny which would have paved the way for the formation of a new Europe in which the ducal state, transformed into a vast monarchy and freed from all feudal ties, would have been at liberty to extend its numerous and firmly linked domains in all directions.

It may be argued that the lack of any racial or linguistic unity, and the absence of any community of interest, prevented these domains from ever being united by bonds of fellowship, and that consequently the failure of the venture was a foregone conclusion. But to make a pronouncement of this kind implies gratuitous acceptance of the dangerous dogma of historical determinism.[1] It would also be to overlook the fact that similar historical groupings, the Austro-Hungarian Empire, for instance, have found adequate reason for coming into existence and for continuing to exist, by linking up their interdependent economic systems, and grouping themselves around a single dynasty.

It would be more accurate to conclude that the fate of the growing state was determined by the interplay of those major considerations which usually provide the true explanation of the dynamics of history. Perhaps the dukes failed to behave in such a way as to ensure success. Perhaps, in order to build up their state whose existence or non-existence was not dictated by the natural order of things, they should have been less preoccupied with the interests and susceptibilities of a French feudal dynasty, and should have developed a whole-heartedly cosmopolitan spirit, instead of constantly trying to reconcile cosmopolitanism with the temptations and changing perspectives of the French kingdom's internal politics.[2] Perhaps they should have followed the course adopted by John the Fearless and repudiated their ties of kinship with the French royal line, resolutely and without any qualms of conscience, whereas, as we have seen, Philip the Good eventually reverted to French patriotism. To win a decisive victory over Louis XI with Edward IV's support, they should have avoided the mistakes, which Commynes pointed out at the crucial moment. In short, they should have had the ability to deal with their problems one by one and to solve each as it presented itself, promptly, yet unhurriedly.

The last of the great dukes, because of his impatient and impetuous nature, brought the whole structure crashing to the ground. The collapse was, however, only an incidental fact, which might have been very different. The successive mistakes committed by Charles the Bold were not historically inevitable. Imagine for a moment that by some accident of heredity in the double line of the Valois, Louis XI had been Duke of Burgundy and Charles, Dauphin and then King of France. Had things fallen out this way, it is not at all certain that French unity would have been assured or that the might of Burgundy would have been doomed to disaster.

However, the final outcome was clear; it was a decisive defeat. The powerful State of Burgundy, which had appeared like a blinding flash across the horizon of history, suddenly, and for ever, vanished, on the fatal day of the Nancy disaster.

But nothing can destroy the splendour of her achievements: the impetus she gave to the Low Countries, which were to keep their place in the future; the prestige of a magnificent court; the memory of a school of writers and historiographers, which thrived under the great dukes' active patronage; and lastly the splendour of an art which takes its place among the most glorious achievements of peoples and princes, and shows Burgundy's awareness of an ideal of beauty and her efforts to achieve it.

NOTES

Chapter I: From Kingdom to Duchy

1 The term is used by Sidonius Apollinaris, a contemporary and eye-witness of the invasions. For an account of Burgundy in the early Middle Ages, readers are referred to the *Histoire de Bourgogne* by Henri Drouot and Joseph Calmette (Paris, Boivin, 6th Edition).

2 Marseilles was occupied by Gundobad's Burgundians at the time of the war waged by Clovis, in alliance with Gundobad, against Alaric II, King of the Visigoths. While Clovis was able to extend his frontiers from the Loire to the Pyrenees as a result of the famous Frankish victory of Vouillé during the campaign of 507, Gundobad gained control of Provence. He lost it again a short while later through the intervention of Theodoric the Great, King of the Ostrogoths. But the fall of the Ostrogoth monarchy after Theodoric's death resulted in the region between the Alps, the Rhone and the sea becoming a sort of autonomous principality ruled by a duke who was a native of that region, Mauronte. Martel, helped by Childebrand, brought Mauronte into subjection and for the second time incorporated Provence with Burgundy. It will be seen in Chapter VIII that, seven hundred years later, in the fifteenth century, a strange quirk of history came very near to reproducing this pattern of events for the third time.

3 For further information on these trends, readers are referred to the first chapters of my book *Charlemagne, sa vie et son œuvre* (Paris, Albin Michel, 1945).

4 The meaning of the words *comitatus* and *pagus* at the time of the Carolingian dynasty is defined in the work quoted in the previous note, p. 221, n. 12.

5 An analysis of this dynamic development and its effects can be

found in my book, *L'effondrement d'un Empire et la naissance d'une Europe* (Paris, Aubier).

6 At the time of the Carolingian decline, a lay abbot was a lord who had acquired, in the temporal affairs of a monastery, the administrative rights which normally belonged to the abbot. A cleric carried out all ecclesiastical duties, the lay abbot being without the right to perform them. But the lay abbot claimed the major share of the profits. This was one of the abuses abolished by the religious reforms of the eleventh century.

7 c.f. J. Calmette, *La Société féodale* (Paris, Colin, 6th edition, 1947).

Chapter II: The Achievements of the Capetians in Burgundy

1 'To enjoy the freehold thereof and to pass it on to his heirs': such were the terms of the grant made by Henry I to Robert. In spite of this wording, it should be understood that the younger brother was the vassal of the elder and owed him homage. The dukes never disputed the right of the crown to subinfeudate. In short, the terms used by Henry meant that, apart from the exercise of his feudal duties towards the crown, the duke was henceforth master of the duchy. Within the limits of ducal subinfeudation, he was the king's true representative. The whole of the future destiny of mediaeval Burgundy was contained potentially in the assignment of 1031. J. Dhondt, *Note sur les deux premiers ducs de Bourgogne*, in *Annales de Bourgogne*, 1941, p. 30 onwards, upholds the thesis that Robert the Pious had himself given Burgundy to Robert, having previously intended it for Henry before the death of his elder brother Hugo. Thus there is some justification for attributing to the second Capetian king the deliberate policy of leaving the royal throne to his eldest son and Burgundy to his second son, with the object of strengthening the position of the holder of the royal crown. This attempt at systematic policy is perhaps worth mentioning in passing.

2 The nickname Landless (Sans Terre) often attributed to Robert —and in any case a gross exaggeration—is historically doubtful. See Jean Richard's note in the *Annales de Bourgogne*, 1946, p. 111.

3 It is curious to notice that the only truly outstanding member of the Capetian dynasty, St Louis, owes his place in history to his moral qualities, rather than to his ability as a statesman. His political achievements were undeniably both effective and beneficial, but he is chiefly memorable for his virtues. c.f. my account of St Louis in *Les Grandes Figures*, a work published

under the editorship of S. Charléty, Paris, Larousse, and in my *Etudes Médiévales* (Toulouse, Privat, 1946).

4 This happened after the disappearance of Hugh, son of Aimon, of whom no trace at all can be found later than the 2nd February 1053, when he signed after Robert I.

5 c.f. J. Calmette, *La Société féodale* (Paris, Colin, 6th edition, 1947).

6 For example, a crusader, about to leave for the east and needing money to pay for his equipment and the long and costly journey, would be overjoyed to receive such a sum of money. He might get the money by agreeing to a compromise; the duke would bear the initial cost but his heirs would derive permanent benefit from the transaction. In the departmental record offices of the Côte d'Or, there are innumerable documents showing how allods —that is to say estates held in fee-simple—became fiefs. We can quote, as an example, the declaration made by Guy de Semur at the end of the thirteenth century: 'I have surrendered my allod to our seignieur, Robert, Duke of Burgundy; and received it back as a fief, the agreement to take effect from the drawing up of the present deeds'. Guy did not mention money. Other sources give more detailed information: for example, in April 1260 Hughes de Saint-Privat, in exchange for a similar investiture, received from the duke twenty-five pounds in '*monnaie viennoise*'.

7 From the last quarter of the twelfth century onwards the practice of dividing the country into *communes* was becoming widespread in Burgundy. The duke granted each *commune* a charter and in exchange exacted from the towns a contribution which represented the price of their freedom. Dijon paid out five hundred silver marks. Argilly paid fifteen *sous*. By increasing his revenue in this way, the duke was able to acquire both land and vassalages.

8 The researches of Ch. Petit-Dutaillis have shown that the re-establishment of such functionaries as bailiffs and seneschals was initiated by the Plantagenets when they were organizing their domain on the Continent, and that Philip Augustus had in this respect copied his rival, Henry Plantagenet II. The great vassals of Capetian subinfeudation, in their turn, imitated the King of France.

Chapter III: Philip of Rouvre and the Problem of Succession

1 The royal dynasty of the Capetians ruled over France for three hundred and forty-seven years, from 987–1328; the ducal dynasty of the Burgundian Capetians lasted for three hundred and thirty

years, from 1031 until 1361. It is obvious that the junior branch was every bit as vigorous as the senior. Furthermore, it would seem that, in both cases, the line became extinct more or less by accident. Philip of Rouvre inherited the dukedom at the age of two and a half, on the death of his grandfather Eudes IV, on the 3rd April 1349. He had as regent, first Eudes's sister, Joan of Burgundy, then his aunt, Joan of Boulogne, who was also Queen of France. She was second wife of John the Good, who, as it happened, was Philip's guardian.

2 A typical example of a seventeenth century problem of succession was that of Charles IV of Spain which kept chancelleries busy for a long time in advance. One complicated scheme after another was devised. The Burgundian succession of the fourteenth century gave rise to no such preparation.

3 The reader should refer to the tables on pages 20 and 12. The table on page 12 also shows how well-placed Charles the Bad was to lay claim to certain parts of the estate. For further information on the possibly justified rights of this prince, and for legal details concerning the Burgundian estate, see the interesting studies published by several jurists in the *Mémoires de la Société pour l'histoire du droit et des institutions des anciens pays bourguignons* (1935–1936), also the concise study written by Pocquet du Haut-Jussé on the same problem, in the *Annales de Bourgogne*, 1937. It appears certain, however, as the aforementioned writer points out, that there never was at any time a 'Navarrese party' in Burgundy although Ernest Champeaux, one of the jurists of whom mention has just been made, believed there was; the few isolated supporters of Charles the Bad never went beyond individual acts of rebellion. On the other hand, Pocquet du Haut-Jussé is quite right to contrast the Burgundian estate with the Breton estate. In Burgundy there was no clash, as there was in Brittany, between two conflicting interpretations, and two powerful parties.

4 Readers anxious for more information on events in French history which are referred to here and which will be referred to later, will find all the relevant details in my work on Charles V, *Les Grandes Etudes Historiques* (Paris, A. Fayard, 1945). The same work explains why the French and Burgundians of that time rejected the King of Navarre's 'rights'.

5 Letters published by Dom Plancher, *Histoire de Bourgogne*, Vol. II, *Preuves* Nº CCCVI p. CCLXVII–CCLXVIII, bear the date: 'given at Cistiaus, on the 16th day of February, in the year of grace CCCLXII'.

6 For example, one document reads: 'Our lords of the Council of the aforementioned seignieur, being at that time at Rouvre, instruct the aforementioned governor to take great care within his area not to reveal the death of the duke'.

7 According to the conventions which prevailed in the royal chancellery, these official letters, published by Dom Plancher, *Histoire de Bourgogne*, Vol. II, *Preuves* N° cccxII, merely give the month of publication, without any mention of the day; but as the month in question was November, it is clear that the death of Philip of Rouvre having occurred on the 21st, there was just enough time to receive the news, and draw up and publish the letters, on the 30th November at the latest.

8 It is perhaps worth quoting the essential part of these letters patent, the reference for which has already been given in the preceding note: 'Joannes Dei gratia Francorum rex. Notum facimus per presentes tam presentibus quam futuris, quod, cum nuper, per mortem charissimi filii nostri Philippi ducis Burgundiae, ducatus Burgundie com juribus et pertinentiis universis nobis in solidum *jure proximitatis non ratione corone nostre debitus* ad nos fuerit devolutus, et in nos jure successorio translatus, ac a nobis tanquam noster acceptatus, ipsum eumdem ducatum Burgundie . . . nostre felici corone Francorum de nostra certa scientia et auctoritate regia donamus, unimus, conjungimus et inseparabiliter solidamus . . .'

9 c.f. Tourneur-Aumont, *La Bataille de Poitiers* (Paris, 1940); my *Charles V* where the rehabilitation thesis is refuted; and F. Lot, *L'art militaire et les armées au Moyen Age* (1946), I, p. 370.

10 This promise of investiture was obviously linked with another project. In December 1362, a rather curious marriage was under consideration between Philip and Joan I of Naples, Countess of Provence. Had this marriage taken place, the whole of the former kingdom of Burgundy might have been reconstituted, Gundobad's kingdom, in fact, which had extended as far as Marseilles. But this proposed union, even supposing that it had ever been contemplated at all, was very soon abandoned. The Queen of Naples' third husband was not Philip, but James III of Majorca (c.f. for this plan which never materialized Maurice Prou, *Etudes sur les relations politiques du Pape Urbain V avec Jean II et Charles V*, pp. 11 and 14 and documents 2 and 3; Paul Fournier, *Le royaume d'Arles et de Vienne*, p. 497).

11 Dom Plancher, *Histoire de Bourgogne*, V. III, *Preuves* N° III.

12 The constitution of the appanaged duchy of Burgundy has been

studied by Pierre Petot in *L'avènement de Philippe le Hardi en Bourgogne*, one of the series of juridical works quoted in n. 3 above. Petot points out that Charles reserved the right to impose taxes on the duchy and discusses the subsequent application of this right. We shall come back to this point in Chapter XII, p. 248 n. 0. See also J. Faussemagne, *L'apanage ducal de Bourgogne dans ses rapports avec la monarchie française* (law thesis, Lyons, 1937).

Chapter IV: Philip the Bold: the Statesman

1 c.f. Etienne Picard, *La dévotion de Philippe le Hardi et de Marguerite de Flandre* in *Mémoires de l'Académie de Dijon*, v. XI, 1914. The choice of Anthony as the name of Philip the Bold's second son showed the latter's predilection for this saint. The Duke of Berry, Philip's brother, born on the 30th November 1340, celebrated his birthday saint, St Andrew, in similar fashion.

2 The appanage was a gift *ad panem*, that is the prince of the blood was expected to maintain himself from it. John the Good had been most generous in the creation of appanages for his sons. Charles, the eldest, the future Charles V, held, in addition to Dauphiné—he was the first descendant of the royal line to possess this province—the duchy of Normandy and during his regency was commonly referred to as the Duke of Normandy; Louis had received Anjou and John, Berry. For information on the Burgundian appanage, see Jean Faussemagne's thesis: *L'apanage ducal de Bourgogne dans ses rapports avec la monarchie française* (1363–1477) (Lyons, 1937).

3 See page 213. Paul Colin in *Les ducs de Bourgogne* (Brussels, 1941), a very superficial work of poor critical value, refers however, appropriately enough, to the 'magnetism' of Philip the Bold.

4 E. Petit (de Vausse), *Ducs de Bourgogne de la maison de Valois, Philippe le Hardi* (Paris, 1904). Only the first volume of this history has been published, and only the first volume, too, of Otto Cartellieri's *Geschichte der Herzöge von Burgund, Philipp der Kühne* (Leipzig, 1910). Readers are referred to the first of these two works, which deals with an aspect of Philip's reign which will not be touched on in the present work, his campaigns against the mercenaries. They took place between 1363 and 1369 and brought him into conflict, first as John the Good's lieutenant, and subsequently as duke, with the leaders of *Compagnies* which, helped by men from Franche-Comté, were pouring into Burgundy, and sacking the countryside. The struggle was bitter and chaotic

and was pursued with great tenacity first by the duke in co-operation with his bailiffs then by Marshal Boucicaut and the Count of Sancerre (Petit, I, 47–253). Philip succeeded in ridding the duchy of these troublemakers and his popularity was due, to a very large extent, to this valuable achievement.

5 *Histoire des ducs de Bourgogne de la Maison de Valois*, I, p. 81. The references for this and the following quotations are to the ordinary edition in eight volumes of M. de Barante's work, the *nouvelle edition, Librairie académique* (Paris, Didier et Cie, 1860). As regards the merits and demerits of this work, there is nothing to be added to what has already been said in the Introduction.

6 For the political aspect of the marriage, see Pirenne, *Histoire de Belgique*, v. II, bk. II, ch. 1. At the time of his marriage, the duke is described as being most meticulous in matters of personal hygiene. He had a *maître des déduits*, or 'master of the duke's pleasures'; he bathed in essence of damask roses and used violet-scented powder. Contrary to the usual assumption it was not at all unusual to take baths in the Middle Ages. Michelet's famous and graphic definition: 'five hundred years without a bath', is an over-simplification resulting from a total misunderstanding. See my book *La Société Féodale*, p. 182.

7 The denunciation of the Treaty of Brétigny was a masterly stroke of diplomacy on the part of Charles V. For details of this curious episode and the ensuing wars, readers are referred to my book on Charles V, Chapter XVII *et seq*.

8 It was in 1371, during one of these stays, that Philip settled the dispute which for a while had caused a very serious rift among the Burgundian nobles, and which arose from a quarrel between the Rougemont and the Blaisy families. Humbert de Rougemont had been a member of the retinue which accompanied Philip to Ghent. On his return he had been captured and robbed of his possessions by Jean de Blaisy. Blaisy claimed that his crime settled an old family score, since he was avenging the death of his cousin, Garnier de Blaisy. Some of the lords of the duchy had taken sides for Blaisy, others for Rougemont. The duke arranged for Rougemont to be held prisoner in the house of one of his friends, Leray, and for the two adversaries, after reaching a settlement, to drink together in the presence of their mutual overlord, a most appropriate way to set a seal on their reconciliation.

9 In 1371, and in 1372, Philip fought in Périgord and Saintonge (Petit, I, 271–290). In the middle of February 1371, he left Chalon-sur-Saône, joined John of Berry at Clermont-Ferrand

and, in accordance with orders received from Charles V, they marched together towards Montpont, a fortress in Périgord, which was being beseiged by the English; but on hearing that Montpont had fallen, the two dukes turned back. In the middle of August 1372, Philip joined Olivier de Clisson and Duguesclin in Poitou. He helped in the capture of several towns and, after a journey through Brittany, was present at the fall of Thouars, the crowning achievement of the campaign. Consequently, he took part, along with his brother and brother-in-law, Berry and Bourbon, in the triumphal entry into Paris, bringing back many prisoners, including Jean de Grailly, Lord of Buch. These campaigns were waged with only a small force and interspersed with feasting and banquets; although Philip acquitted himself honourably he was fond of gambling, particularly with Duguesclin and Clisson, and so lost vast sums of money.

10 Louis of Bourbon was the brother of Joan of Bourbon, Charles V's wife, who had died on the 6th February 1378 of puerperal fever. The word *marmouset*, which means 'grotesque figure', was applied in the everyday language of the fourteenth century to the grimacing figures used as door-knockers and fire-dogs. A more detailed account, including bibliography and references, of the 'uncles' régime' at the time of the minority of Charles VI, can be found in the work by J. Calmette and E. Déprez, *L' Europe occidentale de la fin du XIV siècle aux guerres d'Italie*, part I, which is volume VII of *L'Histoire du Moyen Age*, in *L'Histoire Générale*, published by G. Glotz (Paris, Presses Universitaires, 1937).

11 Louis of Male owes his surname to the castle where he was born and which was situated about a mile and a half from Bruges. A similar instance of this practice has already been mentioned in the case of Philip of Rouvre. It should be noted that the custom of calling princes by the name of their birthplace was common in the fourteenth century. All the sons of Edward III of England, except the eldest, were given their names in accordance with this custom. The most famous of them, after the Prince of Wales, known as the Black Prince, was John of Gaunt (Ghent); Edmund of Langley, Earl of Cambridge, has already been mentioned. The Black Prince's son, who succeeded his grandfather Edward III in 1377 as Richard II, was called Richard of Bordeaux.

12 Historians usually refer to this insurrection as the insurrection of the *maillotins*, but the word was not used at the time. The *maillets* (mallets) in question were policemen's bludgeons. The

insurgents seized these leaden mallets and struck down their opponents. For details of these brutal incidents, see my book *Chute et Relèvement de la France sous Charles VI et Charles VII* (Paris, Hachette).

13 *Tuch* meant 'woods', just as *maquisards* comes from *maquis*, Corsican 'scrub'.

14 This is how, according to De Barante, *Histoire des Ducs*, I, 138–139, the second van Artevelde came to be chosen as leader. The account, incidentally, is taken almost entirely from Froissart. One of the chief commanders of the *Chaperons Blancs*, Pierre Dubois, was the man responsible for van Artevelde's emergence. 'One evening, Pierre Dubois went to see Philip van Artevelde and said to him: "If you follow my advice, I will make you the greatest man in Flanders". "How could that be?" replied Philip van Artevelde. "We have urgent need at the moment of a supreme commander of great repute. You would be given the direction and administration of the town of Ghent: you would become the living embodiment of your father, Jacob van Artevelde, who in his day was so beloved and feared in Flanders. I could easily put you in his place. But until you are fully acquainted with the situation—which you will be very soon—you must act in accordance to my advice." "Pierre," replied Philip, "you are asking me to undertake a very important task. I believe you, and I promise you that if you give me this position, I will do nothing without consulting you."' On Dubois's recommendation, the crowd acclaimed Artevelde. It should be noted that the entire account of the Flemish crisis is, in Barante's work, presented in a light which is consistently unfavourable to Artevelde and his supporters; the fact is that Barante adopted the views of the chroniclers who provided him with his material, and who, like Froissart, the typical historian of the age of chivalry, were steeped in the spirit of feudalism. Artevelde's *cruelty* is frequently criticized. The cruelty of the 'young lord of Enghien' who, after capturing Grammont, 'held by the inhabitants of Ghent', ordered the town to be burnt, and 'five hundred people, men, women and children' to be put to death, is presented as a perfectly natural manifestation. The author simply adds: 'The Count of Flanders praised him highly for this successful exploit'.

15 M. de Barante, *Histoire des Ducs*, I, p. 149.

16 Ibid. p. 151. 'The count finally succeeded in escaping from the town, alone, and on foot. He wandered aimlessly about, since he did not know the roads, which was only to be expected of a

prince unused to walking. He saw a man-at-arms coming towards him and hid in the bushes, but recognizing the voice as that of one of his own knights, who had in fact married one of his illegitimate daughters, he called out to him. "Ah, my lord, I've been looking for you everywhere in the town and in the surrounding country," exclaimed the knight. "Quickly, get me a horse", said the count, "for I can walk no farther, and let us set off for Lille, if you know the way." Nearly a whole day elapsed before they found a horse. Finally the count was provided with a peasant's mare and made his entry into his faithful town of Lille, riding bareback and still clad in his valet's shabby smock.'

17 In the fourteenth and fifteenth centuries, *mécaniques* (mechanicals) meant skilled workers using tools. Some historians misunderstanding the term have been led into curious misinterpretations. It is important to give the word, which is used constantly in the documents of the time, its true meaning. It refers to the *avant-garde* of the working class.

18 Ypres had welcomed the king and contributed forty thousand francs. Cassel, Bergues, Bourbourg, Gravelines, Poperinghe, Tourhout and other towns surrendered, thus deserting the *Chaperons Blancs*. For further details concerning the surrender of these towns, readers should consult M. de Barante's detailed account in *Histoire des Ducs*, I, 165. For events in Flanders as a whole the best work is still *L'Histoire de Belgique* by Pirenne, which could be quoted at every step. In addition to H. Pirenne's work, see the excellent study by H. Laurent and F. Quicke, *Les Origines de l'Etat bourguignon, l'accession de la Maison de Bourgogne aux duchés de Brabant et de Limbourg*, vol. I (Brussels, Royal Academy of Belgium, 1939).

19 In the papal bull, *Nupercum vinea*, Urban VI had called upon the English to fight on his behalf; in the bull *Dudum cum vinea* he had stated his intentions clearly, and in the bull *Dudum cum filii Belial* he had solemnly called upon clerics to take part in the campaign. Those who set out and died on the way would become martyrs. For this curious episode, see the thesis by Edouard Perroy, *L'Angleterre et le grand schisme* (Paris 1933), ch. v, *L'intervention anglaise en Flandre*.

20 c.f. Edouard Perroy, *op. cit.*, pp. 197–198. Some extremely shady bargaining went on amongst the French, the English and the Flemings. In England, the Bishop of Norwich was accused of 'corruption'. It is a fact that Charles VI had offered the prelate 15,000 francs, and it is certain that, although he himself may not

have accepted a bribe, several of his commanders did. After an examination of his accounts, Despenser was declared 'not guilty' before Parliament, but he was convicted of 'presumptuousness'. His revenues were seized for two years, and this put an end once and for all to his vainglorious ambitions. British pride had suffered a severe blow. Several of Despenser's confederates were fined (for instance, commanders Elmham, Trivet, Faringdon, Ferrans and Fitz-Ralph) for having sold the King of France their garrisons, their provisions or their prisoners.

21 See the interesting article by Léon Mirot, *L'Emploi du flamand dans la chancellerie de Charles VI* in the *Bibliothèque de l'Ecole des Chartres* 1896, p. 55. Louis of Male had already allowed the use of Flemish in his chancellery (H. Pirenne, *Histoire de Belgique* II, 188).

22 Cabaret d'Orville, *Chronique du bon duc Loys de Bourbon*, edited by Chazaud (*Société de l'Histoire de France*), p. 181. Eustache Deschamps, edited by Queux de Saint-Hilaire, VI, N° 1145.

23 When Charles V released the three castellanies from royal suzerainty in order to induce Louis of Male to give his daughter in marriage, Philip had promised to restore the towns to the French kingdom as soon as they came into his possession. His failure to keep his promise represented the first set-back for French influence. He justified it on the ground mentioned above, but also by arguing that Margaret had promised her father she would not allow the Walloon castellanies to be released (H. Pirenne. *Histoire de Belgique*, II, 176).

24 See the genealogical table, pp. 38–9. Catherine had been affianced first of all to William of Bavaria, but William married her elder sister, Margaret, as has already been explained.

25 *L'apparicion maistre Jehan de Meun et le Somnium super materia schismatis d'Honoré Bonet*, edited by Ivor Arnold, p. 100. 'Vidi cum eram juvenis, te, o princeps dominabilis, vocari et nominari Philippum sine terra. Nunc fecit tibi Deus largissimum nomen grande juxta nomen magnorum qui sunt in terra.' It should be remembered that Philip did in fact 'lack' land before receiving the appanage of Touraine, whereas his brothers, being older than he was, were already provided for.

26 Details of the manœuvres and counter-manœuvres of the two dukes can be found in the work by Jacques d'Avout, *La querelle des Armagnacs et des Bourguignons* (Paris, 1943), p. 27 onwards. It is perhaps conceivable that in its early stages the quarrel was to some extent caused by Margaret of Flanders' hatred of

Valentine Visconti, and that it can be explained by the powerful duchess's jealousy of another woman who was rather too pretty. But there is not enough justification for blaming the Court of Burgundy for the malicious rumours that were current about Valentine. Her unpopularity sprang from various causes. The fact remains, however, that the dukes were everywhere at daggers drawn. Their interests clashed even in the west, where Philip, in order to thwart Louis, had himself appointed not only guardian to the young duke of Brittany, who was a minor, but regent of the duchy as well (Pocquet du Haut-Jussé, *Philippe le Hardi, régent de Bretagne; Discours de réception à l'Académie de Dijon*, 20th December 1933, and by the same author, *Les séjours de Philippe le Hardi en Bretagne* in *Mémoires de la Société d'Histoire et d'Archéologie de Bretagne*, v. XVI, 1935. In the east, Orleans relied on the support of Luxemburg, Philip on the support of Bavaria. Philip made Isabella assume control while in actual fact he used her as a cloak for his own activities, as has been clearly pointed out by Jacques d'Avout, *op. cit.* p. 71. For the Genoa affair, see the same author, p. 40. He draws attention to a letter from the Doge of Genoa, Adorno (*Archives départementales du nord*, B.1252, No. 13276) in which the Doge thanks the Duke of Burgundy for his action in the royal Council of State; this document leaves no doubt about the game the prince was playing. The causes of the dissension between the two dukes was the subject of a paper read at the 1935 *Congrès de l'Association bourguignonne des Sociétés savantes* at Dijon by Léon Mirot, and entitled, *Les raisons de la rupture entre Philippe le Hardi et Louis d'Orléans*. The complications of Italian politics in their relationship to France are the subject of a thesis by Michel de Boüard, *La France et l'Italie au temps du Grand Schisme* (Paris, 1936).

27 At one moment in December 1401, an open break between the two almost occurred, and with both sides massing men-at-arms, the spectre of civil war suddenly loomed large. The danger was averted just in time thanks to the intervention of Bourbon and Berry who both wanted peace, and thanks also to the mediation of Isabella of Bavaria (J. d'Avout, *op. cit.*, p. 68).

28 c.f. Pocquet du Haut-Jussé, *Le retour de Nicopolis* in the *Annales de Bourgogne*, 1937, p. 296. F. Lot, II, pp. 217 *et seq.* Some Moslems called John of Nevers 'The Son of the King of Flanders'.

29 M. de Barante, *Histoire des ducs*, II, 55 (adapted from the *Religieux de Saint-Denis*, ed. by Bellaguet, III, 149). The author

wrongly gives the duke's age as *seventy-three. Soixante-treize* instead of *soixante-trois* may be a printer's error. The mistake reappears in the biography of *Jean de Thoisy, evêque de Tournai* by Pierre Champion and Paul de Thoisy, *Bourgogne France–Angleterre au traité de Troyes* (Paris, 1943), p. 24. Here it is furthermore stated: 'The liquidation of the duke's debts, which amounted to 119,455 francs, proved no easy task'. According to documents quoted by P. Champion and P. de Thoisy, p. 25, John of Thoisy, who was in charge of the transaction and who, as attaché to the chancellor of Burgundy, Jean Canart, Bishop of Arras, had to pay himself his salary and travelling expenses, was obliged to take several tapestries in lieu of payment.

Chapter V: Philip the Bold: Patron of the Arts

1 Most of the information used in this chapter comes from the excellent studies written by my former pupil Henri David: *Philippe le Hardi, duc de Bourgogne protecteur des arts* (Dijon, 1937), *Philippe le Hardi au début du XVe siècle*, and sumptuary extracts, Dijon 1945, taken from the *Annales de Bourgogne*, September and December 1944 (I. *Patriarcat d'un prince du sang.* II. *Les ors du couchant*). The author of these studies, a research-worker at the *Centre National de la Recherche Scientifique*, is an expert on the history of Burgundian art.

2 *Inventaire du mobilier de Charles V*, edited by Labarthe (Paris, 1871), *Documents inédits*.

3 Moranvillé, *L'inventaire de l'orfèvrerie et des joyaux de Louis I duc d'Anjou*, in the *Bibliothèque de l'Ecole des Chartres*, 1901. As 'King of Jerusalem', Louis had his portrait inscribed on his seal between two eagles (René Gandilhon, *Inventaire des Sceaux de Berry* (Bourges, 1933), pl. X, after a plaster cast in the Archives Nationales, Depaulis collection).

4 Paul Gauchery, *Influence de Jean de France, duc de Berry, sur le développement de l'architecture et des arts à la fin du XIVe et au début du XVe siècle*, Congrès archéologique, Bourges, 1898 (Société française d'archéologie); Hiver de Beauvoir, *La Librairie de Jean de Berry au château de Mehun-sur-Yèvre* (Paris, 1860); P. Durrieu, *Les très riches heures du duc de Berry*, in the *Gazette des Beaux-Arts*, 1904; Henri Malo, *Les très riches heures du duc de Berry* (reproductions) published in the review *Verve*, 1943. The highly epicurean motto of John of Berry, which recurs over and over again throughout his collections was *le temps venra* (the time will come).

5 F. D. S. Darwin, *Louis of Orleans*, p. 91 onwards. A letter from John of Berry to Philip the Bold, dating from the end of 1399, throws a curious light on the artistic rivalry among the princes: 'Order a Saint James the Greater for me, because Orleans, my nephew by marriage, is having a Saint James the Lesser made for me' (Otto Cartellieri, *Philipp der Kühne*, p. 146). These presents were worth fabulous sums. A Saint John the Baptist given by Philip to John on the 24th June 1388 cost 2,500–2,800 golden francs: in 1389 a Saint Nicholas cost 6,400 (H. David, *Philippe le Hardi, duc de Bourgogne, protecteur des arts*, p. 12). It is impossible to list here the mutual gifts and New Year's presents which passed between the Valois princes. Some instances will be found in the article by H. David already quoted, *Annales de Bourgogne*, 1944. See too B. Pocquet du Haut-Jussé, *Les dons du roi aux ducs de Bourgogne* in the *Mémoires de la Société pour l'histoire du droit et des institutions des anciens pays bourguignons*, 1939 and 1940–1941.

6 An account of Bartholomew the Englishman was given by Ch. V. Langlois in the 1911 edition of *La connaissance de la Nature et du Monde au Moyen Age*; the account was omitted in the 1927 edition. Corbechon's translation was made in 1372. For further information on the translation and the various copies, see Claude Herfray-Rey, *Jean Corbechon, traducteur de Barthélemy Langlais*, Ecole des Chartres (Thesis), 1944, p. 59 onwards, and in particular p. 66.

7 It should be recalled that before his accession to the ducal throne, Philip had been on the point of marrying Joan of Naples (see Chapter III, n. 10). On the subject of Philip's liberality, see p. 33. It should furthermore be noted, in connection with St Louis, that in 1375 the duke bought, for one hundred golden francs, a girdle traditionally supposed to have belonged to the saint-king.

8 Henri David, *Philippe le Hardi duc de Bourgogne, protecteur des arts*, p. 15. On p. 16 the author gives a list of the Arras weavers who had the honour of supplying the duke: Jean Cosset, Vincent Boursette, Gilles de Marquais, Pierre de Bapaume, Jacquemart Davion, Pierre le Comte, Philippot de la Vigne, André de Mouchy, Gilles Eglantier, Colart d'Aussy, Huart Valois etc. We must not leave out Michel Bernard, mentioned on p. 69. The tapestry representing Duguesclin was linked with the duke's stay in Brittany according to Pocquet du Haut-Jussé, *Les séjours de Philippe le Hardi, duc de Bourgogne, en Bretagne*, quoted above, Chapter IV, n. 26.

9 c.f. Henri David, *op. cit.* in the previous note, page 11, and *Patriarcat* by the same author, p. 10. Drinking cups were a special feature of table services at that time. They were found, as H. David points out, in a variety of forms: 'sometimes they were plain, sometimes scored (ornamented at the base with *hachures*): some were *poinçonnés*, that is, decorated with various designs, or with scenes engraved in sunk carving; others on the contrary were fashioned in relief in the solid metal, embossed and "glassed", that is a fusible substance was melted in with the precious metal.' Philip possessed an extremely varied collection of drinking cups: 'tankards, bowls, goblets, mugs and *creusequins*, quart and pint pots, together with ewers, bottles, flagons and flasks among which is worth noting as typical of current taste, a drinking cup of antique silver adorned with "images" and called, at the Burgundian court, "Julius Caesar's tankard": the duke used it as an "alms pot" and people put in it whatever was left over from banquets for distribution to the poor.'

10 The following passage describing the duke's headgear is taken from *Les ors du couchant* by Henri David, p. 39. 'Towards the end of his life the duke wore, in winter, thick felt hats half way between a toque and a bonnet, of which there is a splendid example in the well-known portrait at the *Musée de Versailles*: this was his official or ornamental headgear which he wore on state occasions. Two of his other hats which he wore in the country or when travelling were somewhat startling: he favoured black "Lombardy style" straw hats, to protect him from the sun, with knitted cords, buttons, fringes and tassles all made of silk: he had other hats too, also made of straw, to "protect him from the rain". One of the prince's favourites was a hat of deep-pile velvet, black for mourning; to the above should be added a few high hats "in the German style", suitably lined with sable or Prussian beaver.' Philip's brother, John of Berry, had no rival as far as hats were concerned. He was known to possess one trimmed with gold and decorated with sapphires, emeralds, rubies and pearls (E. Teilhard de Chardin, *Registre de Barthélemy de Noces, officier du duc de Berry* in the *Bibliothèque de l'Ecole des Chartes*, 1891, p. 251). For Philip, elegant boots, ankle boots and gloves were just as important as hats, H. David notes for example, that in half a year, the duke and his son Anthony went through 217 pairs of gloves.

11 c.f. Henri David, *op. cit.*, in note 10, p. 6. The author rightly observes that the prince often stayed in the castles

belonging to the royal family as well as in the houses he owned himself, and it could be added that he was frequently entertained by his brothers, especially by John of Berry, whose castle at Mehun-sur-Yèvre was well known to, and much admired by, the duke. Many details about the architectural works commissioned by the duke are given in financial documents quoted by David, *loc. cit.*, pp. 20–25.

12 The Chartreuse is the subject of a thorough study by Cyprien Monget in three volumes (Dijon, 1898–1905). For more recent works, readers should refer to David, *op. cit.* in the previous note, p. 28. L. Armand-Calliat gives precise details of some of the ornamentation which has survived at the castle of Germolles since the time of Philip the Bold in a note in the *Annales de Bourgogne*, 1942 (pp. 311–313). Mention should also be made of the work on the craftsman of the Chartreuse, by Henri David, *Claus Sluter, étude historique et artistique*, in the Collection des grands sculpteurs français, Paris, Pierre Tisné.

Chapter VI: John the Fearless

1 Henri Pirenne, *Hist. de Belgique*, II, 209; Pierre Champion and Paul de Thoisy, *op. cit.* (see Chapter IV, n. 29, of the present volume), p. 28. Colville, *Les Cabochiens et l'Ordonnance de 1413* (Paris, 1888), p. 29.

2 The two authors quoted in the preceding note take the battle of Nicopolis as the epitome of John's career. 'He had broken through the first ranks of the Turkish army. He had won one battle and he now intended to win a second, but this brought about his defeat and capture. Such behaviour was typical of him during the whole course of his life. He would plunge into the fray, gain the upper hand, and then be carried recklessly on by the very force of his own momentum, like a wild boar' (*op. cit.*, pages 27–28). This last comparison is only partly true, because it underestimates his cunning. Incidentally, the Nicopolis ransom was Philip the Bold's responsibility, for John, although 'Count of Nevers', was not in charge of the county and drew no revenue from it (B. Pocquet du Haut-Jussé, *Jean sans Peur, son but et sa méthode* in *Annales de Bourgogne*, 1942, p. 181).

3 Monstrelet maintains that Duke John won his surname at the Battle of Othée. This victory over the town of Liége is referred to on page 90.

4 It was usual for a feudal lord to ratify privileges without delay and to receive homage at the same time as he rendered homage to his

overlord. John's official staff as Count of Nevers, which had formed his household under John of Véléri's direction, replaced the staff of Philip the Bold (Léon Mirot, in the *Annales de Bourgogne*, 1939, p. 132). John acted both as overlord and vassal, rendering immediate homage to the king for fiefs held under French jurisdiction. This act of homage was performed with great alacrity, even before the official entry into Dijon: John the Fearless left the procession to make its leisurely way under the command of his younger brother and Count Arthur of Richemont while he set off for Paris, dashing back later to catch up with them at the gates of Dijon. The 1404 act of homage was solely concerned with the fiefs inherited from Philip the Bold. Those which he inherited from Margaret of Flanders were liable to homage only in 1405 after the death of the duchess. The additional act of homage is mentioned here because it involved an interesting show of force on John's part. One cannot fail to be struck by the rapidity of John the Fearless's movements. See, on this point, Léon Mirot's work, *Jean sans Peur de* 1398 *à* 1405 in the *Annuaire-Bulletin de la Société de l'Histoire de France*, 1938.

5 In spite of the existing truces referred to in the previous chapter, constantly recurring incidents threatened to cause a fresh outbreak of hostilities. Louis of Orleans' challenge to Henry IV took the form of accusing him of having dethroned Richard II. Henry haughtily replied that he considered it beneath his regal dignity to pit his strength against a nobleman of inferior rank.

6 Marcel Thibault, *Isabeau de Bavière, reine de France, sa jeunesse*, Paris, 1903, p. 426. As the author died before completing his work, there is no complete life of the queen—a regrettable gap in historical biography.

7 The most dramatic reconciliation was one which took place in 1406, at the double wedding solemnized at court—the marriage of Charles of Orleans to his cousin Isabella of France, and the marriage of the Duke of Touraine, the king's son, to Jacqueline of Bavaria. Isabella, the widow of Richard II of England, was marrying the eldest son of the Duke of Orleans, Charles, Count of Angoulême. 'She was older than he was, and she was only a child: she was losing her title of queen so she cried a good deal. The marriage celebrations were held at Compiègne: at the same time the marriage of John, Duke of Touraine, the king's second son, to Jacqueline of Bavaria, the daughter of the Count of Ostrevent, took place. All the princes vied with one another in lavish display. The Duke of Burgundy appeared as ostentatiously

arrayed as ever his father had been; the gifts he offered were no less impressive. The mottoes, *I will vex him* and *I hold him fast*, the emblems of the knobbly stick and the plane featured prominently in the embroidery-work, on the banners, and in all sorts of adornments. The two dukes had collars made of them and these they handed out to their followers and favourites; they each exchanged collars and swore henceforth to be brothers in arms and fellow knights; and then each appeared wearing the motto which was directed against himself, so completely did they seem at that moment to have forgotten their differences.' (M. de Barante, edition already quoted, vol. II, p. 99).

8 Colville, *Les Cabochiens et l'Ordonnance de 1413* (Paris, 1888), p. 20. Isabella was in a difficult situation: she was carrying on a flirtation with Louis, who supported Wenceslas of Luxemburg in Germany against Robert of Bavaria, and the queen, who had remained very German and Bavarian, needed John's help to uphold her family's claims in the Empire.

9 Guillaume de Tignonville, bailiff of Chartres in 1399, had been appointed to the Provostship of Paris, the chief police post at that time, on the 6th June 1401. His investigation into the affair was published by P. Raymond, *Enquête du Prévot de Paris sur l'Assassinat de Louis, duc d'Orléans* in the *Bibliothèque de l'Ecole des Chartes*, 1865. At the funeral service, John the Fearless had held the cloth which covered the coffin along with his uncles Bourbon and Berry and his cousin Anjou, 'King of Sicily'. It was rumoured among the people that blood had been seen trickling through the boards of the coffin, and it was recalled that the body of a murdered man bleeds if the killer approaches.

10 The investigators very nearly went off on the wrong track. They first suspected some betrayed husband, since Louis was a notorious rake whose conjugal infidelities were too numerous to count. The famous 'Orleans bastard', John of Dunois, was the result of Louis' affair with the Lady of Chauny, Mariette d'Enghien.

11 According to P. Cauchon, *Chronique de la Pucelle*, edited by Vallet de Viriville, p. 381, Parisians made the comment: 'Blessed be the man who struck the blow, for had Louis lived, he would have brought destruction on the whole kingdom'. Monstrelet, a Burgundian it is true, writes: 'The common people were overjoyed at his death, for the aforementioned Duke of Orleans caused them grievous suffering by extorting from them, in the name of the king, heavy tolls and aids'. The fact that Louis, in his hostility towards the English and his eastern policy, was consciously

following in the steps of Charles V, did not enhance his prestige in any way, since he carried on the policy with no sense of tact, timing or discrimination; and too obviously to serve his own interests, as was evident in his Avignon policy.

12 M. de Barante, in the edition quoted, pp. 115–116, writes: 'It was said that the Duke of Orleans, never discreet on the subject of his love-affairs, boasted one day at table that he had a room full of portraits of women who had granted him their favours, and that the Duke of Burgundy, happening one day to enter this room, saw there the portrait of his wife. Margaret of Bavaria, the wife of Duke John, was indeed a handsome woman, but she had always had the reputation of being chaste. Some people believed that the Duke of Orleans was not telling the truth but merely boasting. It was even claimed that the Duchess had been obliged to complain to her husband about the brazen and insolent behaviour of the Duke of Orleans.'

13 Thomas Basin, edit. Ch. Samaran, I, 11, c.f. J. d'Avout, *op. cit.* p. 89.

14 M. de Barante, edition quoted, II, 117.

15 P. Cauchon, *Chronique Normande*, edit. by Ch. de Rodillard de Beaurepaire (Rouen, 1876, Société des Antiquaires de Normandie, p. 382.) While staying at Amiens, the duke, according to the chronicler Pierre de Fénin, had 'two spear-heads painted above his door, one sharp, the other blunt, intimating that he was prepared either for war or for peace' (M. de Barante, II, 119).

16 See page 48. A *garde de la Prévôté* had replaced the *Prévôt des Marchands*, but he was only commissioned to deal with finance and municipal administration. The restlessness of the Parisian people was due to a very large extent to their nostalgic memories of the time when they had enjoyed independence as a commune.

17 This document is to be found in the 'Archives du Nord' and it has been analyzed by Cartellieri, *Beiträge zur Geschichte der Herzöge von Burgund.* For details of Jean Petit's pamphlet, see Colville, *John Petit*, *La question du tyrannicide au commencement du XVe siècle* (Paris, 1932), and my review of the book in the *Journal des Savants*, April, 1933.

18 A word invented by mediaeval scholars to help them to remember a certain form of syllogism. (Translator's note.)

19 This word, which is used in Le Mans to indicate the prison, was at first linked by Henri Pirenne with '*violon*', a slang French word for jail. But later, the same scholar (third edition, p. 274) ruled

out the possibility and admitted (with T. Gobert, *Les rues de Liége*, 1901, IV, 166) that the name originated from a sign—a violet—which marked the premises used by magistrates in the 13th century.

20 P. Champion and P. de Thoisy, *op. cit.*, maintain that John the Fearless was planning to bring off a *coup d'état*, similar to the Duke of Lancaster's against Richard II, and to become King of France as Henry IV had become King of England. But Richard II had no heir. Charles VI always had a son ready to succeed him. There is no lack of evidence to show how risky such a plan would have been on John's part. Pocquet du Haut-Jussé, *Jean sans Peur, son but et sa méthode* (*Annales de Bourgogne*, 1942, p. 195) is right to deny the existence of any such plan. In any case, even if John cherished the dream, he never revealed the fact by any overt act. The help which he later gave Henry V would seem to be totally inconsistent with such an interpretation. c.f. J. Avout, *op. cit.*, p. 198. The policy of John the Fearless seems to have been partly prompted by his financial requirements. He needed the share of the tax-money that Charles V had granted to Philip the Bold, and he was afraid that he would be deprived of this contribution if he allowed the reins of government to fall into the hands of his opponents.

21 Nicolas de Baye, *Journal*, edit. Tuetey (Société de l'Histoire de France) I, 360. Jouvenel des Ursins gives an account of the remark made by the duke's fool: 'And the Duke of Burgundy had in his entourage a very clever fool, who was said to be a wise fool, and who went to buy an ecclesiastical medal (*une paix d'église*) and had it plated with gold (*fourrée*) and said that it was *une paix fourrée*. And this was the sort of peace it turned out to be.' For further details on the Peace of Chartres and Arras see Léon Mirot, *Autour de la Paix de Chartres*, in the *Annales de Bourgogne*, 1931, and J. d'Avout, *op. cit.*, p. 107 onwards.

22 J. d'Avout, ibid., p. 120; Colville, *Les Cabochiens*, p. 94.

23 Brun, *Lettres avignonnaises*, XIII, 1936. Letter dated the 24th December 1407.

24 Bonne of Berry, daughter of the Duke of Berry and widow of Amadeus VII of Savoy, had married Bernard VII of Armagnac, brother and successor of John III of Armagnac.

25 Bands of mercenaries who ravaged the countryside at the beginning of Charles V's reign. (Translator's note)

26 At one moment a quarrel between lord and vassal which arose between the duke and the Count of Tonnerre, Louis de Chalon,

encouraged the Armagnacs to attempt an attack on Burgundy. The Duchess, Margaret of Bavaria, coped vigorously with the situation, which for a time was quite serious. Duke Charles of Lorraine, the ally of John the Fearless and John's brother, the Count of Nevers, intervened. The Armagnacs seized Rougemont, but after a siege lasting ten days, the Count of Lorraine recaptured it and finally Louis de Chalon was driven out of his own castle at Tonnerre by Jean de Vergy, Marshal of Burgundy.

27 J. d'Avout, *op. cit.*, p. 145 onwards, emphatically defends the opposite point of view, which we cannot accept. It is worth remembering that Burgundians and Armagnacs alike accused each other of coming to terms with the English, 'the deadly enemies of the kingdom'. This proves that both sides were fully aware of having misbehaved: c.f. P. Champion and P. de Thoisy, *op. cit.*, pp. 90 and 92. Furthermore B. Pocquet du Haut-Jussé is right to point out that the pact concluded between John and an English king openly at war with France, was a much more serious matter than the appeal for intervention made by the Armagnacs during a period of international peace—or at least of international truce. On the nature of the 1417 pact, the same author has views very similar to ours, as can be seen from his article *Jean sans Peur, son but et sa méthode*, in the *Annales de Bourgogne*, 1942.

28 Amadeus VIII of Savoy was the brother-in-law of John the Fearless through his marriage with Mary of Burgundy, daughter of Philip the Bold, and, through his mother, Bonne, the grandson of the Duke of Berry.

29 Published by H. Moranvillé under the title *Remontrances de l'Université de Paris et de la ville de Paris à Charles VI sur le gouvernement du royaume* in the *Bibliothèque de l'Ecole des Chartes*, 1890.

30 J. d'Avout, *op. cit.*, p. 111.

31 Relations between Burgundy and Brittany are the subject of a special study by B. A. Pocquet du Haut-Jussé, *Deux féodaux, Bourgogne et Bretagne* (Paris, 1935) (in the *Revue des Cours et Conférences*).

32 Pirenne, *Hist. de Belgique*, II, 209. 'In him, the Burgundian had completely superseded the Valois. The power he had inherited from his father and his general interests extended too far beyond the frontiers of the kingdom for him to be able to behave like a vassal of the crown. Having a Bavarian wife, a daughter married to Adolphus of Cleves, a sister married to an Austrian and a brother married to Elizabeth of Goerlitz, this little man . . . had

ceased to embody either the character, the habits or the inclinations of a fleur-de-lys prince.' Yet in fact he still wished to remain a French prince, and his career acquires its distinctive character from the fact that he shared his time, his activities and his energies between the two aspects of his dual vocation as a prince of the blood and a head of State.

33 J. d'Avout, *op. cit.*, p. 22, gives a detailed account of his manœuvrings.

34 *Op. cit.*, p. 238, 'The Duke of Burgundy, who was moping at Dijon, had kept his Burgundian nobles with him. But it was more difficult for him to impose his orders on the knights of Artois and Picardy on whose land the battle was being waged, and their names figured prominently among the dead. Jean de Croy, Lord of Renty and his son Jean . . . the Lords of Brimeu, Poix, Roncq, Liedekerque, Lichtervelde, Moy, Jeumont, Wavrin, Louis de Chistelles, Colart de Fiennes . . .' On the subject of Agincourt, see Lot, *op. cit.*, II, p. 9 onwards.

35 J. Calmette and E. Déprez, *op. cit.*, p. 336. J. d'Avout, *op. cit.*, p. 244 gives a different and unacceptable interpretation. For reasons already given (correlation between subsequent events and the terms of the pact) it is not possible to agree with Newhall, *The English Conquest of Normandy* (Newhaven, 1924, p. 54), that the pact was a plan which never matured. The relevant document can be found in Rymer's well-known selection, *Foedera*, IX, 394. As we point out, the draft which preserved the 'diabolical pact' for posterity, bears no date, but it was almost certainly drawn up on May 6th 1417 when Henry V and Duke John conferred at Calais. Paul Colin's account of the affair in *Les Ducs de Bourgogne*, p. 135, is full of inaccuracies and unfounded suppositions.

36 Here, in chronological order, are the towns captured by the British in their ever more rapid campaign: Caen, 4th September 1417; St Pierre-sur-Dives, 20th October; Alençon, 23rd October; Falaise, 2nd January 1418; Bec Hellouin, 4th May; St Lô, 12th May; Coutances, 16th May; Evreux, 20th May; St-Sauveur-le Vicomte, 25th May; Pont de l'Arche, 5th July; Domfront, 10th July; Cherbourg, 22nd August. In 1417, the Normans were given formal notice either to swear an oath of allegiance, or leave their homes and possessions.

37 A city official who read out public notices to the burgesses. (Translator's note)

38 Jouvenel des Ursins, who had the advantage of being a contemporary, admitted even at the time that it was impossible to know

what exactly had happened at Montereau. The murder remained shrouded in mystery all through the reign of Charles VII, which explains why the king, even after the Treaty of Arras, was able to avoid taking any action against those of his advisers who were suspected, but whose alleged culpability could not be proved (see Albert Mirot, *Charles VII et ses conseillers assassins présumés de Jean sans Peur*, in the *Annales de Bourgogne*, 1942, p. 187 onwards). Readers anxious for further, if unimportant, details, should refer to the extremely thorough, if somewhat embroidered, account of events given by J. d'Avout, *op. cit.*, pp. 293–300. If the axe-blow was a pure invention, it was obviously prompted by the moralizing desire to make Louis of Orleans' murderer suffer the same fate as his victim. For information concerning the disinterment of the supposed remains of John, and a report of questionable authenticity on the state of his skull, see the *Mémoires de la Commission des Antiquités de la Côte d'Or*, XIV, 1901–1903. A. Kleinclausz, *Histoire de Bourgogne*, pp. 146–7, disagrees with the version according to which the duke was killed with an axe. An oft-quoted but inaccurate remark is attributed to one of the monks of Champmol. As he showed the famous skull to Francis I who happened to be visiting the monastery in 1521, he said: 'Sire, this is the hole through which the English got into France'.

39 Published in J. Calmette, *Textes et Documents d'histoire* (Paris), p. 127.

40 The opinion given here on John the Fearless differs only slightly from the one expressed by B. Pocquet du Haut-Jussé, *Jean sans Peur, son but et sa méthode*, in the *Annales de Bourgogne*, 1942, p. 182 onwards. I believe, however, that Pocquet du Haut-Jussé puts too systematic an interpretation on the duke's policy, which owed far more than he thinks to empirical considerations. For John the Fearless's 'diabolical' side, see Paul Durieu, *Jean sans Peur, duc de Bourgogne, lieutenant et procureur général du diable ès parties d'Occident*, in *Annuaire-Bulletin de la Société de l'Histoire de France*, XXIV, 1887. The following judgement by P. Champion and P. de Thoisy, *op. cit.*, pp. 174–5 is worth remembering:

'John the Fearless had inspired fear: and he died a victim of that fear.

'For a long time he was caught in the vicious circle of his own ruses and in the confusion of his clandestine pacts with the English.

'He could not speak his mind openly for fear of incurring the disapproval of his own supporters.

'So he deliberately curried favour with the people, shaking all and sundry by the hand, even the executioner. But he was always having to act out of character, to use hired assassins, and to hold his own by aggressiveness.

'Twice he had to start all over again, reconstructing his whole career, from the beginning. He had been hailed as the master of Paris. But he was conscious in the background of the reproachful glances of those who accused him of having "driven the English into France".

'John the Fearless had decided to brazen it out. He swore he had never signed anything. After all there was no proof. Yet Duke John could not forget the words addressed by the Dauphin to his herald: "If our Lord of Burgundy desires the king and us to consider him as a kinsman, let him go and drive out the King of England".' (Quotation taken from Le Fèvre de Saint-Rémy, edited by Morand, p. 79).

Chapter VII: Philip the Good

1 P. Champion and P. de Thoisy, *Bourgogne France-Angleterre*, pp. 167–74. Chastellain, edited by Kervyn de Lettenhove, I, 43–9. There is an excellent little book on Philip the Good, entitled *Philippe le Bon*, by Paul Bonenfant (Brussels, 1943) in the collection *Notre Passé* (with bibliography). c.f. too J. Huizinga, *La physionomie morale de Philippe le Bon*, in the *Annales de Bourgogne*, 1922.

2 *Op. cit.* Chastellain refers to Thoisy and Brimeu as the 'two elderly lords'. Thoisy had been entrusted with the political education of the future duke.

3 Georges Chastellain, edited by Kervyn, VII, 220. The quotation which follows is taken from *Andanças é viages de Pera Tafur por diversas partes del mundo avidos* (1435–1439) (Madrid, 1874). Collección de libros españoles raros é curiosos, VIII, 248.

4 See P. Bonenfant, *op. cit.*, pp. 18–19: and for an explanation of the nick-name, see the bibliographical details given by the same author, p. 122. The fact that he was quick to forgive most probably accounts for the laudatory epithet. For further details of the first documents in which the third duke is referred to as Philip the Good, see Bonenfant's article on this subject, *L'origine du surnom de Philippe le Bon*, in the *Annales de Bourgogne*, 1944, pp. 100–3.

5 See Chapter XI, p. 226. In the fifteenth century, piety and chivalry were inseparably linked.

6 Bonenfant, *op. cit.*, pp. 27–34 takes more or less the same view; but he remarks quite rightly that the English alliance was highly dangerous, and adds: 'Could the career of "the great duke of the west" have followed the course it did, if Henry V had not died on the 31st August at the age of thirty-four?' A family council was held at Malines, and a meeting at Arras (18th October 1419). Margaret of Bavaria, the widow of John the Fearless, was thirsting for revenge. Presumably she influenced her sister Isabella. For further details concerning the spirit of revenge which prevailed at the Burgundian court, see Huizinga, *Le déclin du Moyen Age*, p. 25.

7 Philip himself received Thomas Beauchamp, the then Count of Warwick, at Ghent, and sent Marshal Claude de Chastellux and Antoine de Toulongeon to Mantes, the English headquarters where Henry V was in residence.

8 E. Déprez, in *Un essai d'union nationale à la veille du Traité de Troyes* in the *Bibliothèque de l'Ecole des Chartes* (1938), has disclosed that, according to documents intercepted by the English military intelligence and kept in the Record Office in London, a last-minute attempt was made by some of the Dauphin's followers, in particular by the Archbishop of Paris, Gérard de Montagu, to reconcile the Dauphin with his mother and father and with Burgundy, his brother-in-law. The Dauphin's legitimacy, and his exclusive right to rule in place of the mad king, were advanced as eloquent arguments. But the die had been cast. The bishop's patriotic feelings did not evoke a sufficiently strong response. c.f. my book *Chute et relèvement de la France sous Charles VI et Charles VII* (Paris, Hachette, 1945).

9 It was at Mons-en-Vimeu that Philip was made a knight.

10 This has been clearly shown by P. Champion and P. de Thoisy, *op. cit.*, pp. 232–6.

11 The only actual punishment for the Montereau crime was the execution of 'Big Henry'. He was a minor figure, whose part in the affair remains obscure. He was captured, accused of having been involved in the assassination of the 10th September, handed over to the Dowager Duchess Margaret and condemned by the Dijon magistrates. He was dragged alive on a hurdle through the streets of the ducal capital, beheaded in the *Place du Morimond*, and his limbs were displayed on four of the town's gates, while the rest of his body was burnt in front of the duke's palace. It

may seem surprising that the identity of the person really responsible for the 1419 crime was never revealed. It is safe to assume that the French court, in spite of, or because of, the Treaty of Arras, chose to let the mystery remain unsolved, since the revelation of the truth would have entailed sanctions which were better avoided. History has thus suffered as a result of this calculated deception.

12 Concerning the various aspects of this situation, see the book already referred to, *Chute et relèvement de la France sous Charles VI et Charles VII* (Paris, Hachette, 1945). There is nothing far-fetched or artificial in comparisons with the modern situation; they merely help to illustrate more clearly the fundamental truth about human psychology and the causes of events.

13 P. Champion and P. de Thoisy, *op. cit.*, p. 253.

14 Le Fèvre de Saint-Rémy, I, 239, heard Philip the Good say when he was an old man that 'it was sad that he had not had the good fortune to take part in the afore-mentioned battle, either to perish in it or to survive'.

15 For a description see the work quoted in note 12.

16 She was the widow of Philip of Nevers, John the Fearless' brother who was killed at Agincourt. She died in childbirth on the 17th September 1425.

17 Georges Chastellain, edited by Kervyn de Lettenhove, I, 210.

18 C. Rutherford, in *The Forgeries of Guillaume Benoit*, the *English Historical Review*, 1915, has shown that the whole story was based on the word of a forger. There may, however, have been some Machiavellian plot to bring discredit on the Bretons.

19 Pirenne, *Hist. de Belgique*, II, 227.

20 J. Calmette, *Jeanne d'Arc* (Paris, Presses Universitaires, 1946), in the *Que Sais-je?* series. The introduction to this small volume contains a statement of the attitude the historian must adopt towards the problem of the supernatural.

21 The marriage with Isabella of Portugal received the blessing of the Bishop of Tournai, Jean de Thoisy, on the 7th January 1430 at Sluys, and the celebrations were held at Bruges. Four days later, during the course of the festivities, Philip founded the 'Order of the Golden Fleece', in honour of the new duchess, about which more will be said in Chapter XI. An account of Isabella has been given by C. Latten, *Isabelle de Portugal, duchesse de Bourgogne et Comtesse de Flandre* in the *Revue de Littérature comparée*, v. XVIII, 1938. The author outlines the princess's political activities, but says nothing that was not already known. Paul Colin, in

Les ducs de Bourgogne, p. 163 onwards, has given a summary, based on chroniclers' tales, of the 1430 celebrations and rejoicings.

22 The relationship went through the following stages: before opting for the English alliance, Philip had agreed to hear his brother-in-law, the Dauphin, plead innocence in respect of the murder of John the Fearless. But having chosen the path of vengeance, and having taken part in the negotiations leading up to the Treaty of Troyes, Philip waged war alongside Bedford against Charles VII; we have already seen however how the Cardinal, Duke of Bar, the legate of Martin V, and Duke Amadeus VIII of Savoy, tried to bring about a reconciliation between the two Valois, the king and the duke. The negotiations, conducted at Bourg by Chancellor Rolin for the Burgundians and Chancellor Martin Gouge, Bishop of Clermont, for the Dauphin's party, ended in failure on the 22nd January 1423. They were resumed after Verneuil, following the marriage between Richemont and Margaret of Burgundy, the former Dauphiness, and were helped by the efforts of the Houses of Anjou and Brittany, since Charles VII had married Mary of Anjou in 1422, and Margaret of Bavaria, Philip the Good's mother and a sworn enemy of the 'Armagnacs', had died on the 23rd January 1424. Arthur de Richemont, having become Constable of France with the consent of Burgundy, his brother-in-law, acted as a link with Charles VII's mother-in-law, Yolanda of Sicily; Gloucester's campaign on the Continent was an additional cause which almost brought about a reconciliation. Philip the Good's marriage to Bonne of Artois, at Moulin-Engilbert on the 30th November 1424, also helped, since the new duchess was an ardent advocate of the Valois coalition. A lull in the fighting left the duke free to launch attacks against Gloucester and Jacqueline. At the same time, two of the Dauphin's henchmen, who were universally considered to have been implicated in the Montereau affair, Tanguy du Châtel and president Louvet, were sent away from the Valois court—one to Beaucaire as captain, the other on a mission to Provence. Bedford, however, put an end to Gloucester's indiscretions, made important concessions to Burgundy, married Anne, Philip's sister and gave fresh impetus to Burgundo-Lancastrian friendship. Also, the favours bestowed by Charles VII on Georges de la Trémoille put an end to the prestige which Richemont and Yolanda of Sicily had enjoyed at the court of Bourges. This was virtually a return to the Treaty of Troyes. But is is clear that fresh

efforts to effect a rapprochement with the Valois were constantly being made, and Anne of Burgundy often had to intercede in person to prevent her brother slipping over to the side of her husband's enemies. When Joan of Arc's victory brought the dual monarchy to the verge of collapse in 1429, Bedford appointed Philip governor of Paris, a post which he refrained from taking up, but the step helped to save the capital since it coincided with the signing of a truce with Charles VII which halted Joan's offensive (see J. Calmette, *Jeanne d'Arc*, p. 84). What was happening in fact was that the duke was offering his services to the highest bidder—Lancastrian or Valois. The time was not yet ripe for a major 'switch of alliances', but repeated fluctuations of policy were preparing the way for it. Philip was drawn towards Bedford for a time when the capture and death of Joan seemed to justify Henry VI's claims. Later, after Anne of Burgundy's death, he engaged in negotiations with the other side, and soon the removal of La Trémoille which had been engineered by Richemont's friends (see J. Calmette, *Chute et relèvement de la France*, p. 184), made it possible for the long, drawn-out, wavering negotiations, which have not yet received the detailed historical study they deserve, to move towards the long-awaited and on the whole inevitable settlement.

23 Du Fresne de Beaucourt, *Histoire de Charles VII*, II, 519. Reports had been drawn up at the court of Burgundy on the problem of whether or not to negotiate with the Dauphin. Chancellor Rolin put forward a remarkable diplomatic statement showing why Burgundy should abandon England and support France (c.f. Frederick Schneider, *Der europaïsche Friedenskongress von Arras 1435, und die Friedenpolitik Papst Eugeñius IV und des Baslerkonzils*, Graz, 1919).

24 John remained as enigmatic as he had been all his life. It was impossible to say whether he was pro-English or pro-French; he was waiting to see which would be the winning side. Actually, at the court of Brittany, John followed one policy, Richemont another (B. A. Pocquet du Haut-Jussé, *Deux féodaux*, previously quoted, p. 153, n. 1, and by the same author *Le connétable de Richemont, seigneur bourguignon* in the *Annales de Bourgogne*, 1936).

25 Several banquets were held at Arras. 'And Heaven knows what splendid feasts and banquets took place there,' says Guillaume Gruel in *Chronique d'Arthur de Richemont* (Paris, Levavasseur, 1890, Société de l'Histoire de France), p. 377.

26 'An unfortunate jingo movement' Ramsay calls it, in *Lancaster and York* (Oxford, 1892), I, 475.

27 P. Bonenfant, *Philippe le Bon*, pp. 73–4. See also by the same author, *Le Projet d'érection des Etats bourguignons en royaume en* 1447, in *Le Moyen Age*, XLV, 1935. The author accepts the truth of the official denial by the Chancellery of Burgundy to the effect that 'the idea had not been put forward by his Lordship'. Denials of this sort were usually just a matter of form. In any case, it is hardly conceivable that Frederick III could have proposed the scheme, had he not known that he was flattering his partner's secret wish. In the previously quoted article in *Le Moyen Age*, there are interesting details about the secret negotiations. J. Huizinga, in *L'Etat bourguignon, ses rapports avec la France et les origines d'une nationalité néerlandaise*, in *Le Moyen Age*, 1930–1931, has also given some useful information on the subject.

28 Pirenne, *Cambridge Mediaeval History*, VIII, 358, chapter X, in connection with Philip the Good: 'The insurrections of Bruges (1436) and Ghent (1450–1453) against him had none of the character of national risings; they were the last attempts of the two great towns to defend privileges which no longer corresponded to their real interests. It is sufficient to remark that the rest of Flanders left them to fight alone; this shows that they were only fighting for an out-of-date parochialism'. The truth could not be more clearly expressed.

29 Labroquère, near St Bertrand de Comminges (Haute Garonne, in the canton of Barbazan). His interesting account of the journey has been published; it is edited by Scheffer, *Le Voyage d'Outre-Mer* (Paris, 1892), *Recueil de voyages et documents pour servir à l'histoire de la géographie*, XII.

30 See my book, *Autour de Louis XI* (Editions de Fontenelle). The reader will find here full details of the Dauphin's stay in Burgundian territory.

31 The first sign of this diseased state of mind was seen in a sudden fit of anger against his son. After a violent scene, the duke galloped off one evening, alone, and got lost in the depths of a forest. The episode is related by Chastellain. The whole story is told in my book quoted in n. 30, in Chapter IV, p. 71 onwards.

32 The following passage, dealing with the capture of Luxemburg in 1443, is taken from M. de Barante, *Histoire des ducs*, IV, p. 264. 'Messages were sent at regular intervals to the duke. At two o'clock in the morning, he got up and put on his full armour,

called for his horse and got all his men ready, but he was anxious not to miss hearing mass and saying his prayers, which he always did on rising. His pages and his servants, who were already mounted, were becoming impatient. New messages were constantly arriving to say that all was going well. Everyone was eager to be off. "His lordship," they complained, "could well put off his paternosters to another time." So eager were they, indeed, that his chief squire, Jean de Chaumergis, could not refrain from urging him to make haste. The duke was always cool and collected and never lost his self-control unless there was a good reason for doing so. "God has granted me victory," he said quietly, "he will be able to hold it for me, and he can do as much through my prayers as he can through a whole army of knights. Besides my nephews and my bastard son are there with a large number of my subjects and servants; with God's help they will hold out until I arrive." And the good duke unconcernedly finished saying his prayers.'

33 There exists a letter written by Thoisy on the 25th May and the news of his death was received at Tournai on the 9th June (P. Champion and P. de Thoisy, *op. cit.*, p. 360).

34 P. Bonenfant, *Philippe le Bon*, p. 27. Bonenfant could have quoted from Cartellieri, *Am Hofe*, p. 185, the statement made by a Bishop of the Golden Fleece, Guillaume Fillastre, on the subject of Philip: 'I have seen him to go bed at two in the morning and get up at six and yet never have an idle moment, always being busy either reading books or drawing the bow or taking part in some healthy sport, or attending the Council of State, when the occasion demanded it'. We do not consider that this statement weakens Chastellain's affirmation—on the contrary, it would seem to corroborate it, since according to Fillastre, the duke only gave up his time to political affairs when he was compelled to do so; he was by no means lethargic or inactive but preferred to read or indulge in some sport or other.

Chapter VIII: Charles the Bold: the Glorious Years

1 It was a very common practice at the time to bestow on heirs presumptive a title which marked their special relationship to the throne: there was the Dauphin in France, the Prince of Wales in England, the Prince of Asturias in Castille, the Prince of Gerona, the first-born of the House of Catalonia in Aragon, the Prince of Viane in Navarre, the Duke of Calabria in Naples, the Viscount of Castelbon of the House of Foix, the Viscount of Lomagne of

the House of Armagnac, etc. Charles's godfathers were Charles de Nevers and Jean de Croy: Agnes of Burgundy, Countess of Clermont, was his godmother. His second Christian name, Martin, was given him because he was christened on St Martin's Day.

2 H. Pirenne, *Histoire de Belgique*, II, 290.

3 Ibid., p. 291, probably taken from Olivier de la Marche, II, 207. Georges Chastellain describes him as follows: 'his face was a little fuller than his father's and he had a fairly dark skin; he had bright, laughing and angelically limpid eyes, which, in reflective mood, made him look the very image of his father'. See, too, John Bartier, *Charles le Téméraire* (Brussels, 1944), which is particularly interesting as regards Charles's early years and his immediate entourage. According to Bartier (p. 13) Haneron had a calming influence on the duke.

4 P. Bonenfant, *Philippe le Bon*, p. 85.

5 H. Pirenne, *Histoire de Belgique*, pp. 293–4.

6 P. Bonenfant, *Philippe le Bon*, pp. 91–2. The departure was to have taken place in May 1464 from Aigues-Mortes; then it was postponed until 1465, and, in the meantime, Anthony, 'the Great Bastard', Philip's illegitimate son, left Sluys on the 21st May 1464. On p. 238 further mention is made of this advance party, which was in fact the only force to set out.

7 The text of the two conflicting *communiqués* can be found in my book *Le grand règne de Louis XI*, p. 110. For details of the total strength of both armies, see F. Lot, *op. cit.*, II, p. 86 onwards.

8 Pirenne, *Hist. de Belgique*, II, 299. A Spanish candidate could be added to the list, for one of the first, if not the first, suitors was Ferdinand the Catholic, son of John II of Aragon. See J. Calmette, *L'origine bourguignonne de l'alliance austro-espagnole*, in the *Bulletin de la Société des Amis de l'Université de Dijon*, May 1905. For Burgundy's policy in Alsace see Louis Stouff, *Les possessions bourguignonnes dans la vallée du Rhin* (Paris, 1904): *Catherine de Bourgogne et la féodalité de l'Alsace autrichienne, ou essai des ducs de Bourgogne pour constituer une seigneurie bourguignonne en Alsace* (Paris, 1913).

9 For further details of the energetic policy pursued by the House of Aragon, which cannot be given the space it deserves here, readers can be referred to three previous works of mine—*Le grand règne de Louis XI*, which has already been quoted, *L'unité espagnole* (Paris, Flammarion), and *La Question des Pyrénées et la Marche d'Espagne au Moyen Age* (Paris, J. B. Janin).

10 J. Huizinga, *L'Etat bourguignon, ses rapports avec la France et les*

origines d'une nationalité néerlandaise, in *Le Moyen Age*, 1930–1931.

11 Although it is difficult to give exact details it would seem that the proposed solution was to make a double kingdom—Burgundy and Friesland. This is at any rate the opinion of J. Huizinga, in the work mentioned in the previous note.

12 Henri Chabeuf, *Charles le Téméraire à Dijon*, in the *Mémoires de la Société Bourguignonne de géographie et d'histoire*, 1903. The periods of hostility between France and Burgundy between 1470 and 1475 were marked by diversionary attacks on the part of the royal troops against Mâconnais and even against the actual duke-dom of Burgundy. A painstaking and well-documented account of these details of military history which are beyond the scope of the present work, has been given by J. Robert de Chevanne, *Les Guerres en Bourgogne de 1470 à 1475* (Paris, A. Picard, 1934). This study was completed by *Episodes des dernières luttes au duché de Bourgogne* (1470–1475), the author's contribution to the Twelfth Congress of the *Association bourguignonne des Sociétés Savantes*, held at Dijon on the 26th, 27th and 28th May 1935, Dijon, 1937, p. 45. Mention should also be made of André Leguai, *Dijon et Louis XI*, in the *Annales de Bourgogne*, 1945, and F. Lot, *op. cit.*, II, pp. 106 onwards.

Chapter IX: Historians and Writers

1 The reader is referred to the following editions of each one of the Burgundian historians whose works are worthy of note before Chastellain: Monstrelet, ed. Drouët d'Arcq, 6 vols. (Paris, 1857–1862); Mathieu d'Escouchy, ed. Fresne de Beaucourt, 3 vols. (Paris, 1863–1864); Pierre de Fénin, ed. Mlle Dupont (Paris, 1837); Jean de Wavrin, same editor, 8 vols. (Paris, 1859–1863). All these editions form part of the collection of the *Société de l'Histoire de France*. There is a slightly more recent edition of Jean de Wavrin, the William Hardy edition, 5 vols. (London, 1864–1891), in the Roolls series. Jean Strenger, *Notes sur les rapports entre la continuation anonyme de Monstrelet, les Mémoires de Jacques de Clercq et les Chroniques d'Angleterre de Jean de Wavrin*, in the *Annales de Bourgogne*, 1946, has drawn attention to certain repetitions in these authors which are explained by the fact that they all used the same authority, Jean Chartier.

2 Georges Chastellain, *Oeuvres*, ed. Kervyn de Lettenhove, 8 vols. (Brussels, 1863–1866). The study by Kennet Urwyn, *Georges Chastellain* (Paris, 1937), should be checked by reference to

Dupire's account, in *Humanisme et Renaissance*, v. I, 1938. See too Luc Hommel, *Chastellain*, and on Commynes, Gustave Charlier, *Commynes*, in the Belgian series *Notre Passé* (Brussels 1945), *La Renaissance du Livre*. According to Luc Hommel, Chastellain was born in 1415. To these should be added, Molinet, *Chronique*, ed. Georges Doutrepont and Omer Jodogne, 3 vols. (Brussels, 1935–1937), in the Old Belgian Chroniclers series; N. Dupire, *Jean Molinet, la vie, les oeuvres*, thesis, Paris, 1932.

3 Although he had always been a good Burgundian, Chastellain was determined at the same time to remain a good Frenchman and the following sentence, which does him credit, is worth remembering (ed. Kervyn de Lettenhove, IV, 21): 'For I am not English, but French, neither Spanish, nor Italian, but French, and I have written of the exploits of two Frenchmen, one a king, the other a duke.' A noble declaration which reveals, moreover, how mistaken historians have been in imagining that patriotism did not exist in the fifteenth century.

4 Olivier de la Marche, *Mémoires*, ed. Beaune and Arbaumont, 4 vols. (Paris, Société de l'Histoire de France, 1883–1888); H. Stein, *Olivier de la Marche, poète et diplomate bourguignon* (Brussels, 1888), *Mémoires de l'Académie de Belgique*, XLIX; *Nouveaux documents sur Olivier de la Marche* in the same collection, 1932; *La date de naissance d'Olivier de la Marche* in *Mélanges Pirenne*, 1926.

5 Edmond de Dynter, *Chronicon ducum Brabantiae*, ed. P. de Ram, 3 vols. (Brussels, Commission royale d'histoire de Belgique, 1854–1860); Adrien de But, *Chronique*, ed. Kervyn de Lettenhove (Brussels, Coll. des Chroniqueurs belges, 1870); Jean de Haynin, *Mémoires*, ed. R. Chalon, 2 vols. in 1 (Mons, Société des Bibliophiles de Mons, 1842); *Chroniques relatives à l'histoire de Belgique sous la domination des ducs de Bourgogne*, ed. Kervyn de Lettenhove, 3 vols. (Brussels, 1870–1876); Jacques de Hemricourt, *Oeuvres*, ed. Bormans, Bagot and Poncelet, 3 vols. (Brussels, 1910–1931), same series.

6 Georges Doutrepont, *La Littérature à la Cour de Bourgogne*, (Paris, Bibliothèque du XVe siècle, 1909), and by the same author, *Les mises en prose des épopées et des romans de la chevalerie du XIVe siècle et du XVe siècle* (Brussels, Académie de Belgique, 1939), classe des Lettres, vol. X. For the brief account given in this chapter we propose to follow the basic plan used in the first of these works. Readers are referred to it for bibliographical details which would take up too much space in the

present work. Nor is there room to mention here contemporary or subsequent works by such scholars as Desonay, Dupire or Jodogne. As regards editions of works, for brevity's sake we shall mention only Kervyn de Lettenhove (Brussels), Coll. des Chroniqueurs Belges; Chastellain, *Oeuvres*, ed. Kervyn de Lettenhove, already quoted; Antoine de la Sale, *Oeuvres complètes*, ed. Desonay, 2 vols. (Liége and Paris, 1941).

7 Edward Billingsham, *Gérart de Roussillon, poète bourguignon du XIVe siècle* (New-Haven, Yale University Press, 1939; Paris, E. Droz, 1940); c.f. an account of this work in the *Annales de Bourgogne*, 1930, p. 36 onwards.

8 Georges Doutrepont, p. 226. Olivier de la Marche, I, 49–50. Part of the supposed cross of St Andrew which had been kept in the Abbey of St Victor at Marseilles, was taken by Philip the Bold to Brussels.

9 For the origin of the emblem, see the *Annales de Bourgogne*, 1939, pp. 150–1.

10 See chapter VII, n. 29. For information on other accounts of travels and pilgrimages which can more or less be compared with Labroquère's work, see G. Doutrepont, p. 246. Bertrandon was an esquire trenchant. He died at Lille in 1459. On the subject of Deschamps, who is mentioned a little further on, readers should refer back to pages 51 and 65.

11 The full title was: 'Lamentable and consolatory epistle on the subject of the deplorable defeat of the valiant King of Hungary by the Turks before the walls of Nicopolis in the Empire of Bulgaria, addressed to the most powerful, valiant and wise royal prince, Philip of France, Duke of Burgundy, and also addressed, in subject-matter and not in form, to the most excellent princes and kings of France, England, Bohemia and more especially of Hungary and consequently of all the kings, princes, knights and commons of Catholic Christendom, by an old hermit of the Celestine Order in Paris, who, on account of his great sins, does not deserve to be named'.

12 Michaut le Caron, known as Taillevent, was a valet. An actor of farces and a *rhétoriqueur* in the service of Philip the Good, he was the author of several poems mentioned by Doutrepont, *op. cit.*, p. 152 onwards; but Emil Roy, in his review of Doutrepont's work (*Revue bourguignonne publiée par l'Université de Dijon*, 1910) draws attention to the fact that Doutrepont confused Taillevent and Pierre Michaut (c.f. Piaget, in *Romania* XVIII, 1889, pp. 439–52) who had also acquired a certain degree of fame.

The *Psautier des Vilains* is among the works attributed to Taillevent. The *Pas de la Mort* was apparently not the work of either Taillevent or Pierre Michaut, as some historians have believed.

13 The author imagines that the town of Orleans is being threatened and that messengers have been despatched to Philip the Good. The latter sends his herald to tell the English attacking force that he will withdraw his troops if the siege is not raised. The English give an insolent reply. Philip declares that he will take his revenge when the time comes. Obviously, this is not a true representation of the facts, although the man who sold the Maid to Bedford did actually, *in his own good time*, break with the House of Lancaster —but not until many years later and for reasons which were totally unconnected with the Orleans affair. c.f. on this point, F. Lot, *op. cit.*, II, p. 37, n. 6, which we have no room to reproduce here.

14 G. Doutrepont p. 363. He gives details, which we have no room to reproduce here, of this type of play.

15 G. Doutrepont, *op. cit.*, p. 379.

16 A type of poem popular at this time which described the qualities of an object in minute detail. (Translator's note)

17 Usually, however, books and jewels were entrusted to two different officials. Normally the barber was the librarian, while the keeper of the jewels was chosen from among the prince's 'cup-bearers'. Under Philip the Bold, Maître Richard le Comte was put in charge of the books. He was simultaneously chief barber, librarian and valet to Philip. He was succeeded, it seems, by Franchequin de Blandeke, then by Antoine Forest. Under John the Fearless, Philippe Jossequin held the post; under Philip the Good, Jean de la Chesnel and Jacques de Brézilles; under Charles the Bold, Charles de Visen.

18 On the subject of Philip the Good's fondness for reading, c.f. the statement made by Bishop Guillaume Fillastre, already quoted in Chapter VII, n. 34.

19 Ch. Samaran, *Vasco de Lucena à la cour de Bourgogne*, in the *Bulletin des Etudes portuguaises et de l'Institute français au Portugal* (Coïmbra, 1938); Robert Bossuat, *Vasque de Lucena traducteur de Quinte-Curce* (1468) in the *Bibliothèque d'Humanisme et Renaissance*, v. VIII (1946); the last mentioned study has revived attention in the Portuguese writer who was so highly thought of by the Burgundians of the day and who was one of the ornaments of the court of the Duchess Isabella. On the subject

of Mary of Burgundy's literary tastes c.f. ch. XI in Georges H. Dumont's book, *Marie de Bourgogne* (Brussels, 1945).

Chapter X: Art

1 Louis Courajod, in his lectures at the Ecole du Louvre (L. Courajod, *Leçons professées à l'Ecole du Louvre*, 3 vols. (Paris, 1887–1890) was the first critic to do full justice to fifteenth-century Burgundian art and to recognize Claus Sluter's school at Dijon as representing an essentially original form of Franco-Flemish art, which combined purely Dutch and Flemish elements with all that was most fertile in the revival of French art. Since then, Burgundian art has been the object of several studies. Raymond Rey's very fine book, *L'Art Gothique* (Paris, H. Laurens) sums up the present state of knowledge on the subject and includes up-to-date bibliographies. On Claus Sluter see: A. Kleinclausz, *Claus Sluter et la sculpture bourguignonne du XVe siècle* (Paris, undated): Ænne Liebreich, *Claus Sluter* (Brussels, 1936), *Recherches sur Claus Sluter* (Brussels, 1938), and H. David, who has already been mentioned in n. 12, chapter V.

2 From the ghetto at Dijon, it has been said. It is true that Jews had been banished on the duke's orders before Sluter came to Dijon. But it is by no means certain that they had all left Burgundy. It may also be supposed that Sluter used sketches which he had made while in the Low Countries. After a visit to Holland, my pupil Henri David has suggested that this is a likely assumption. He adds that it is difficult not to compare Sluter's work with some of Rembrandt's portraits of old men, for Rembrandt and Sluter had a great deal in common. David concludes: 'The remarkable and striking skill with which the sculptor carves the Jewish figures would seem to confirm his Dutch ancestry, and the fact that his youth and years of professional training had been spent in the urban centres of what was later to become Holland'.

3 It is worth quoting a singularly appropriate comment on Sluter's Moses, made by Raymond Rey in the work already mentioned in n. 1. 'His face is lined, his beard flowing, his eyes deep-set, the expression of his mouth bitter, and he has two horns rising from his forehead (*cornuta facie*, according to the Rouen Passion play) representing the rays of light which were visible to the Hebrews after he came down from Mount Sinai and which were the supernatural sign of the man who had seen God face to face'. Rey says of the other prophets: 'David is the typical oriental monarch, sumptuous and solemn; Jeremiah, clean-shaven and

bowed by age, is pondering over his book; Zachariah seems prostrate with grief, while Daniel and Isaiah are deep in discussion, one with sharp, expressive, aquiline features, the other a bald, broken and discouraged old man. Each prophet is shown in the act of unfolding a scroll on which is inscribed the Prophecy concerning Christ's passion'.

4 The cross was in its place on the 30th June 1399, but the six statues of the prophets, which were to be placed round the hexagonal base of the monument, *were not added until* 1406. They therefore represent the last phase of Sluter's style, when his art was at its peak.

5 Apart from André Michel, *Histoire de l'Art*, III, 596, the main works to be consulted are: Henri Drouot, *La mort de Sluter et la fin de sa carrière*, in *Bulletin monumental*, 1911: *Le nombre des pleurants aux tombeaux des ducs de Bourgogne*, in *Revue de l'Art chrétien*, 1911; Henri David, *L'Art de Sluter d'après les Prophètes de Champmol*, in the *Revue belge d'archéologie et d'histoire de l'art*, 1934; *Claus Sluter, tombier ducal*, in *Bulletin monumental*, 1934. Of the works of Sluter which have been lost, mention should be made of the 'pastoral' scene at Germolles. This has already been referred to on page 67 in connection with Margaret of Flanders' liking for pastoral settings. In a lead niche, and sheltered from the 'wind and rain' by 'eight panels', was a group consisting of the duke and duchess seated under an elm and surrounded by a flock of sheep. This idyll in stone may, or may not, be connected with Sluter's visit to Mehun (Henri David, *Mehun-sur-Yèvre et Germolles*, in the *Annales de Bourgogne*, 1936) but it certainly links up with the literature of the time and more especially with the duchess's predilection for pastoral themes. See too Henri Drouot, *Autour de la Pastorale de Claus Sluter*, in the *Annales de Bourgogne*, 1942, pp. 7–24.

6 For information on the general influence exercised by the school, readers are referred to R. Rey's book, already quoted, and to the bibliographical details which it contains. Readers may also care to consult Henri David, *Quelques artistes méridionaux en Bourgagne*, in the *Annales du Midi*, 1936.

7 Henri David, *Autour du tombeau de Philippe Pot*, in the *Annales du Midi*, 1942. See also David, *Annales de Bourgogne*, 1947, p. 206 onwards for a discussion of Schaeffer's attempt at cataloguing the works.

8 See my *Histoire de l'Espagne* (Paris, Flammarion). A certain Jean de Bourgogne is mentioned as being in the service of the Arch-

bishop of Toledo even as early as 1495 (De Laborde, *Les ducs de Bourgogne*, I, CXXXIII, note.)

9 There has been a good deal of speculation about the real object of the mission with which the duke entrusted Sluter in 1393. It may be that he was asked to give an expert opinion on work commissioned from André Beauneveu by John of Berry and to see that the orders were being properly carried out. Or perhaps the Duke of Burgundy wanted his master sculptor to have the opportunity of learning from the works of art which had delighted him at his brother's castle. Even if we accept the first explanation, which is the least likely (see Henri Drouot, *La visite de Claus Sluter à André Beauneveu*, in the *Revue du Nord*, August 1936) it is difficult to avoid the impression that Sluter was strongly attracted by Beauneveu's art. It was thanks to Beauneveu and perhaps to other influences too, that the French style, as practised at Paris and Bourges, made its impact on Sluter. It would be possible to give a more accurate account of the famous visit, if Beauneveu's works had not been lost. But since they have, we have no means of estimating his personal influence. That it was considerable cannot be doubted, because he was a great artist. He was, like Froissart, a native of Valenciennes and was much admired by the chronicler, who did a little discreet advertising for him in his writings, with the result that Beauneveu received valuable orders from the noble lords who were also Froissart's patrons.

10 The 'Van Eyck' question and the question of how oil-painting began, are dealt with by R. Rey in the work already mentioned. It can also be recommended for its bibliography of books on Flemish painting, such a bibliography being impossible to reproduce here.

11 On the subject of this work, we would like to quote the following remarks by Raymond Rey: 'The oratory in which the solemn communion is taking place is reminiscent of a wealthy Bruges interior with windows opening on to a delightful urban landscape. And the vista which occupies the centre of the picture and stretches beyond the gardens and the terrace of the palace as far as the eye can see, reveals a profusion of minute details, all observed with striking realism. This is yet one more portrayal of nature in which men and inanimate objects are fused together in mystical harmony'.

12 Henri David, *Au pays de Claus Sluter*, in the *Annales de Bourgogne* (1939), p. 194 onwards, attributes great importance to the

part played by Malwell and argues that Philip the Bold thought more highly of him than of Sluter himself, since Malwell was paid twelve 'gros' per day, whereas the famous sculptor was only paid eight.

13 Henri David, *Au pays de Claus Sluter*, in the *Annales de Bourgogne*, 1939, p. 192 onwards, has some very shrewd comments on the way the dukes drew upon the artistic wealth of their '*pays*'.

14 For details about the Dutch and Flemish painters and the web of influences around them, the reader is referred again to Raymond Rey's book in which the chief representatives of each school are appraised with sober accuracy and shrewd judgement. Malwell's portrait of John the Fearless was painted in 1413 and intended for the King of Portugal. During his visit to Portugal, Jan van Eyck painted a portrait of the Infanta Isabella, who was to become the Duchess of Burgundy. It is regrettable that practically nothing is left of Malwell's work; for this reason it is impossible to estimate his influence which was certainly important. It also means that Malwell does not occupy the place he deserves in the history of art. As Henri David has said: 'Only a few panels from the duke's oratories dealing with religious themes, and which are preserved at the Louvre, give us some inkling, if they are by him, of what his real gifts were'.

15 We have already had occasion, and shall have again later, to mention certain goldsmiths by name as well as characteristic specimens of the goldsmith's craft, in connection with Philip the Bold, page 68, and the Court of Burgundy, p. 228. As regards music the dukes had choristers, harpists and minstrels attached to their households. Singers of both sexes came to the Court even from foreign countries. The young singers of the duke's chapel at Dijon formed a choir which was extremely highly thought of. A veritable school of Burgundian music which played an important part in the formation of Renaissance choral art, was set up. Jossequin Despres was the school's chief representative in the time of Mary and Maximilian. Among the musicians belonging to the period of the dukes, we should mention Gilles Binchois, Pierre Fontaine, Jacques Vide, Nicolas Grenan, and Gilles Joye, whose most characteristic works, along with those of a few other composers, have been very well edited (Jeanne Marix, *Les Musiciens à la cour de Bourgogne au XVe siècle*, 1420–1467 Paris, Editions de l'Oiseau-Lyre, 1937)). Interesting details are given by Maurice Emmanuel in his study, *L'art choral bourguignon*, in the *Mémoires de l'Académie de Dijon*, 1925. See also the information given by

Norbert Duffourcq in his two theses: *Esquisse d'une histoire de l'orgue en France*, Paris, 1935, and *Documents inédits relatifs à l'orgue en France*, Paris, 1934, in which Dijon organs are mentioned (p. 47) in connection with the years 1440, 1447, 1470. One organ-maker referred to (p. 50) was of Flemish origin. In the second thesis, p. 73, there are highly interesting passages on the same subject.

Chapter XI: Court Life

1 Otto Cartellieri, *Am Hofe der Herzöge von Burgund* (Basle, 1926). The author of this 329-page volume, which includes 25 plates and a genealogical table, has no new documents to offer, but he makes good use of the existing ones by a judicious choice of quotations. The same author has also written two studies on the marriage of Charles the Bold and Margaret of York: *Theaterspiele am Hofe Karls des Kühnen von Burgund*, in *Germanisch-Romanische Monatschrift* IX, 1921, and *Ritterspiele am Hofe Karls von Kühnen*, in *Tijdschrift voor Geschiedenis*, XXXVI, 1921. A French edition (O. Cartellieri, *La Cour des ducs de Bourgogne*, translated by F. Caussy) of the first work was published in 1946 (Paris, Payot, *Bibliothèque historique*). The long-winded descriptions of Burgundian celebrations are sometimes wearisome. Yet J. Huizinga, *Le Déclin du Moyen Age*, p. 312, is right when he says: 'However, to be fair, we should understand the function that these celebrations fulfilled in society. They still retained something of the significance that celebrations have for primitive peoples—they were a supreme expression of culture, a collective outburst of joy, and a manifestation of solidarity. During periods of great change, such as that of the French Revolution, celebrations of this kind were again to fulfil a social and aesthetic function'.

2 For details of 'The Feast of the Pheasant', see Cartellieri's special study, *Das Fasanenfest*, in *Historisch-politische Blätter*, CLXVII, 1922. See also by the same author *Die Sitterliche Gesellschaft am burgundischen Hof*, in *Historische Zeitschrift*, 1915.

3 Olivier de la Marche, *Mémoires*, ed. Beaune and Arbaumont, *Société de l'Histoire de France*, IV, 164–6. Yet Jason was not forgotten. Speaking of the collars which had just been distributed, Monstrelet says: 'each one had, hanging from it in front a golden fleece like the one, and in remembrance of the one, that Jason conquered on the island of Colchos'. Chastellain however says: 'in memory of Gideon as well as Jason', thus reconciling both

parties. According to J. Doutremont, *La littérature française à la cour des ducs de Bourgogne*, p. 152, Gideon replaced Jason as early as 1431.

4 Jason's exploits had often been depicted on tapestry, since his adventures had a strong appeal for artists. The idea of tapestries honouring Gideon's exploits dates only from 1448, when they were ordered from Tournai for the Chapter House of the Order. Chastellain mentions that they were in evidence at the chapter meeting held at The Hague in 1456. He refers to them in enthusiastic terms: 'hanging in that room, there was the most glorious tapestry ever seen at a king's court' (ed. Kervyn de Lettenhove, II, 190).

5 Olivier de la Marche, *Mémoires sur l'Etat de la Maison du duc;* this extract is taken from J. Calmette and H. Drouot, *La Bourgogne* (Paris, H. Laurens, *Anthologies illustrées des provinces françaises*). The passage quoted refers to the 'tasting' of the dishes. The '*officiers de bouche*' had to taste them before serving them to see if they were ready and to make sure they contained no poison. The meat was subjected to tests of another kind by the use of certain substances, which, it was believed, had the property of revealing the presence of harmful ingredients. 'Unicorn's horn' was considered to be a testing agent. On this subject, see Edmond Faral, *La vie quotidienne au temps de Saint Louis* (Paris, Hachette), p. 165.

The details which follow are taken from Henri David, *Philippe le Hardi au début du XVe siècle, extraits somptuaires,* in the *Annales de Bourgogne*, 1944.

At the same period, the Count of Charolais had a fool called Andrieu de la Plume.

Chapter XII: The Burgundian State

1 Spanish history of the period is expounded in greater detail in my two books: *L'Unité espagnole* (Paris, Flammarion), and *La question des Pyrénées et la Marche d'Espagne au Moyen Age* (Paris, J.-B. Janin). A proper study of Burgundian policy in Italy and the east will only be possible when the relevant documents, widely scattered in various archives, have been brought to light and collated.

2 Archives of the Crown of Aragon (at Barcelona). *Intrusos, passim,* Madrid, Biblioteca de la Academia de la Historia, Salazar, A 7, folio 52.

3 Archives of the Crown of Aragon, *Intrusos*, No. 43, folio 34.

Alonso de Palencia, VII, 7 (ed. of the *Biblioteca de autores españoles*). For further details, see my article *Dom Pedro, roi des Catalans, et la Cour de Bourgogne*, in *Annales de Bourgogne*, 1946.

4 See p. 164, for the links between the projected crusade and the general policy which had led up to it.

5 Archives of the Crown of Aragon, *Intrusos*, No. 27, folio 65: 'El Rey Secretario muy amado nuestro. Vista vuestra lettra, vos respondemos que, acomodandose el precio del diamente, luego fagays aquel engastar en oro fino: el engaste no sea sobergo, porque mas sea favorecida la piedra; e sera ab anillo tal que venga bien al dedo en que se ha de levar. E festo esto, queremos se de en mano de nuestro secretario Pellicer, el qual la tenga, fasta que sea tiempo de las sposalles, si a Dios sera plaziente.' In another document written not in Castillian but in Catalan dialect, Pedro commissions his agents to try to buy 'un diamant o robi o esmeralde' worth a hundred *nobles* (English gold crowns). The ring was to be presented in the king's name to 'doña Margarita' who is referred to as 'germana del illustrissimo rey d'Anglaterra y de França' (Madrid, Biblioteca de la Academia de la Historia, Salazar, A 7, folio 54, Letter to Barthomeu Gari). The reader will have noticed that Dom Pedro counters Louis XI's hostility by giving Edward of York the title of 'King of France and England'. In connection with the embassies entrusted with the marriage negotiations, see my book *Louis XI, Jean II et la Révolution catalane* (Toulouse, 1903), p. 261, and J. Ernest Martinez-Ferrando, *Pere de Portugal, 'rei dels Catalans'* (Barcelona, 1936), p. 104 onwards.

6 He had appointed as his heir his nephew, the Portuguese infante, but the Catalonians disregarded his will, despite the arguments put forward by the Duchess of Burgundy in a letter in Portuguese, which she sent to Barcelona (J. Calmette, *Louis XI, Jean II et la Révolution catalane*, p. 531). The Burgundian chancellery obviously included a Portuguese department; several letters from the Duchess are to be found in the Catalonian archives. As regards this letter, the only one in Portuguese, see my article *Deux lettres du XVe siècle en portugais aux archives municipales de Barcelone*, in *Etudes médiévales* (Toulouse, Privat, 1946).

7 Fidel Fita, *Los reys d'Arago y la Seu de Girone* (Barcelona, 1873) Part II, p. 28.

8 The Latin original is given in J. Calmette (*Louis XI, Jean II et la Révolution catalane* (Toulouse, 1903), p. 367.

9 J. Calmette, *L'origine bourguignonne de l'alliance austro-espagnole*,

in the *Bulletin de la Société des Amis de l'Université de Dijon*, 1905 and *Etudes médiévales* (Toulouse, 1946).

10 As has already been seen, the Flemish dialect was a recognized language. It was the official medium in Flanders, just as Walloon was used in the provinces of Liége, Luxemburg, Namur and parts of Hainault and Brabant; at Mons and Tournai, legal documents were drawn up in the Picardy dialect, which was the prevailing medium to the south and south-west of the present-day Franco-Belgian frontier.

11 They always looked upon the proceeding as a deliberate insult on the part of the king. It must be admitted that the monarchy always made it as spectacular as possible. For instance, in 1466, an usher of the Paris *Parlement* came to Ghent 'on St Andrew's Day, at the very moment when the duke and all the glorious company of the Golden Fleece, together with Charles of Orleans, were about to sit down at table, and delivered a summons calling upon Philip the Good to appear in person before the Court, in connection with some matter concerning a former leader of the skinners' guild'. The quotation is from J. Huizinga, *Le Moyen Age* (1931), p. 24 onwards. Huizinga gives other instances too. See also John Bartier, *Charles le Téméraire*, quoted in n. 3, Chapter VIII.

12 The following were considered as the chief towns: Dijon, Arnay, Autun, Avallon, Beaune, Chalon, Châtillon, Flavigny, Montbard, Semur and—from the fifteenth century onwards—Nuits and St Jean de Losne. Others, that figured intermittently on the list were Noyers, Montréal, Talant and Montcenis. In connection with Dijon in the time of the last two dukes, interesting remarks are to be found in André Leguai, *Dijon et Louis XI* in the *Annales de Bourgogne*, 1945–1947.

13 There exists no specialized study on the council. Billioud has dealt with the estates in *Les Etats de Bourgogne aux XIVe et XVe siècles* (Académie des Sciences, Arts et Belles Lettres de Dijon, 1922); a cognate study is Edouard Andt's, *La Chambre des Comptes de Dijon à l'époque des ducs valois* (a thesis, Paris, 1924).

14 Georges Gazier, *Du mode d'élection des magistrats municipaux à Besancon du XIIIe siècle à la conquête française* (1674), in the *Bulletin du Comité des Travaux historiques, philosophiques et historiques*, 1932–1933.

15 Under John the Fearless, it was proposed in 1408 to establish another *Chambre des Comptes* in Besançon, but nothing came of the plan.

16 There is no full-scale, single study on Rolin, as there is on Jean

de Thoisy (c.f. Chapter IV, n. 29). Paul Bonenfant, in *Philippe le Bon*, p. 122, gives a list of the fragmentary discussions of his rôle. I myself have dealt with the main works devoted to the chief officials of the dukes, in *L'Elaboration du Monde moderne*, p. 110.

17 H. Pirenne, *Histoire de Belgique*, II, p. 403. In connection with the individual officials and the handling of funds, extremely interesting information was found in contemporary documents by B. A. Pocquet du Haut-Jussé, *Les Chefs des finances ducales de Bourgogne*, Dijon, 1937, in the *Mémoires de la Société pour l'histoire du Droit*, *fascicule* 4, 1937. Unfortunately, no general study of taxation has been made; there is nothing, in particular, on the royal tax in Burgundy. Pierre Petot, in *L'avènement de Philippe le Hardi en Bourgogne* (*Mémoires de la Société pour l'histoire du droit et des institutions des anciens pays bourguignons*, 1936) shows that Charles V, after reserving his right to raise a tax in the duchy, took the personal decision of allowing his brother to raise *even their father's ransom* for his own benefit, and that Philip so arranged things that the royal right fell into abeyance. As we have seen, John the Fearless took it upon himself to authorize or forbid the collection of the *taille* stipulated by the Royal Council. A thorough study of the question would throw light on many obscure points.

18 c.f. the details given in F. Lot, *L'art militaire*, II, p. 114 onwards.

19 Jean Perron made a drawing of it in 1726, and a copy of this drawing is in Paris: MS 3901 at the Arsenal (L. Mirot and E. Lazzareschi, *Lettere di mercanti Lucchesi da Bruges e da Parigi* Lucca, 1929, in *Bolletino Storico luchese*, p. 180).

20 Louis XI tried to wage economic warfare and to organize a sort of blockade of Charles the Bold's territories. For this aspect of their conflict, which had so far escaped notice, see the curious revelations of René Gandilhon in his Toulouse university thesis, *Politique économique de Louis XI*, Rennes, 1940.

21 G. Desmarets, P. Bonenfant and Fr. Quicke, *Le développement territorial de Bruxelles au Moyen Age* (Brussels, 1935).

22 Tafur visited Malines, which he describes as a 'charming' town although small. He adds that the duke liked to rest there 'as in a garden'. He points out that the duke had no residence there but stayed at an hostelry so well appointed that it would have been comfortable enough for the greatest princes of the earth.

23 Maurice Jans, *Histoire économique du duché de Limbourg sous la Maison de Bourgogne* (Brussels, 1938). The second part, *Les*

Mines, is particularly interesting. It shows how important Philip the Good's reign was in connection with the exploitation of mineral resources. The author studies the history of each mine with the most praiseworthy mastery of detail. As regards Lille, there is much interesting information in R. Marquant's *La vie économique à Lille sous Philippe le Bon* (Paris, 1941), *Bibliothèque de l'Ecole des Hautes Etudes, fascicule 277*.

24 Chastellain, Kervyn de Lettenhove edition, II, 150, expresses the idea of the Burgundian State when he says that Philip the Good was referred to as the '*grand duc du Ponant*'; Molinet calls him '*le très grand et renommé duc d'Occident*' (Doutrepont and Jodogne edition, II, 591).

Chapter XIII: Charles the Bold's mistakes

1 Nothing is known of the relationship between Commynes and the king between 1468 and 1472. But during the night of the 8th August 1472, Charles the Bold's companion left him in order to join Louis XI at Ponts-de-Cé. There can be no doubt whatever about the date of his desertion, because on the 8th August at six o'clock in the morning the duke signed a document announcing the confiscation of all the deserter's possessions since, said the duke, he 'has, on this day, withdrawn his allegiance from us and joined the opposite camp' (Mlle Dupont's edition of Commynes, *Société de l'Histoire de France*, III, 11). Commynes himself (*Mémoires*, III, XI) informs us that he went over to Louis at Ponts-de-Cé, where the latter happened to be at this time. Charles the Bold never forgave his former servant. He was not included in the amnesty granted during the truce of Soleuvre in 1475 (Olivier de la Marche, edit. Beaune and d'Arbaumont, *Mémoires*, bk. II, ch. VII, vol. III, p. 211).

2 On the subject of the last duke's relations with Switzerland and Germany, which cannot be studied in detail in the present volume, Toutey's thesis, *Charles le Téméraire et la ligue de Constance*, Paris, 1902, is still worth consulting. Basle and Strasburg supplied Sigismund with the money he needed, but the King of France acted as surety. The following remarks by M. de Barante (*Hist. des ducs*, VI, 371) on the paradoxical Austro-Swiss alliance are worthy of note: 'A hundred and fifty years of the most bitter fighting in which so many lords and knights had lost their lives; the deadly hatred and mistrust which existed between the exiled princes and their rebel subjects; all the possible sources of discord which still remained—all was for-

gotten in the fear inspired on the one hand by Duke Charles's ambitions, and on the other by the despotic rule of Lord Hagenbach. The tyranny exercised by the cruel governor and his constant threats aroused a fierce determination to break free, not only among the people of Alsace, but among the Swiss too. It seemed as if he were a reincarnation of Gessler, the Austrian *landvogt* of former days whose death had been the first sign of approaching freedom.' By his despotic rule, Hagenbach did indeed recall the tyrant whose name has remained in the legend of William Tell.

3 M. de Barante, *Hist. des ducs*, VI, 377. The following quotations relating to Hagenbach have also been taken from the same author, pp. 379–81. The title of '*landvogt*' corresponds exactly to that of *baillif.*

4 M. de Barante, *Hist. des ducs*, VII, 23. Charles the Bold, on this particular occasion, behaved in a more chivalrous manner than the Black Prince did in circumstances which, if not similar, were at least comparable. See my book, *Charles V*, pp. 283–4.

5 The expression 'universal spider' to describe Louis XI was first put into circulation by the Burgundian chroniclers, Chastellain and Molinet. They did not in fact realize how near they were to the truth. Unfortunately for him, the duke was indeed the buzzing and imprudent fly caught in the royal spider's web. No attention should be paid to the innuendoes of Paul Colin who in *Les ducs de Bourgogne* calls Charles 'the so-called Bold' and 'Bold against his will' (p. 247).

6 Further details of these events and the history of the war and ensuing peace of 1475, which must perforce be omitted here, can be found in *Louis XI et l'Angleterre*, by J. Calmette and G. Périnelle (Paris, Picard, 1930). (*Mémoires et Documents*, published by *La Société de l'Ecole des Chartes*, XI.)

7 'Never had a King of England, since King Arthur, brought so many men at once across the sea' (Commynes, edit. Calmette, II, 77). F. Lot, *op. cit.*, II, p. 89 onwards, after a thorough discussion of the question, amends the figures which were previously thought to be correct.

8 Mérindot was a valet in the service of Olivier Mérichon. He was a little man, very glib of tongue. Commynes, who tells the story, was commissioned to explain to Mérindot exactly what was expected of him. At first the poor fellow was alarmed at the thought of carrying out such a dangerous mission, but the king's clever companion succeeded in persuading him, by promising

him money and a post as tax-collector in the Ile de Ré, his place of birth. The reason for his being selected was that, not being one of the regular heralds, he could if necessary be disowned. A tunic was cut out for him from a trumpeter's banner, and he was given the tincture of one of the admiral's heralds and sent on his way. Only Commynes and the master of the horse, Alain Goyon, Lord of Villiers, knew of his mission (Commynes, edit. by Calmette, I, p. 295 onwards).

9 The motives justifying Louis' decision are easy to understand. The danger was that Charles the Bold would have a breathing-space in which to finish off his Lorraine campaign, St Pol time to hatch fresh plots and the hesitant French vassals a chance of taking action, should some unforeseen military development give them a hope of being in at the kill. Louis XI realized that this was a unique opportunity to bring hostilities to a close. By settling the Anglo-French quarrel, he put an end once and for all to the Anglo-Burgundian alliance and nipped the threatened 'Public Good' conspiracy in the bud. The king had never given more striking evidence of his shrewdness and clearsightedness than by his quickness of resolve on the 14th August 1475.

10 Commynes describes the scene and remarks that Charles the Bold spoke in English: 'The Duke of Burgundy, on hearing the news, came in great haste from Luxemburg where he happened to be, to see the King of England and arrived accompanied by only sixteen horsemen. The King of England was most surprised at the duke's sudden arrival and asked him what brought him there. He realized full well that the duke was angry. The afore-mentioned duke replied that he had come to speak with him either alone or in public. Then the afore-mentioned duke asked him if he had negotiated for peace. The King of England replied that he had signed a nine-year truce which applied to himself and to the Duke of Brittany; he begged Charles to give his consent to this truce. The duke thereupon flew into a rage and spoke English, for he knew the language, and he listed all the splendid deeds performed in France by English kings and all the trouble they had taken to win honour in France . . . he wanted them to know that he did not need their help, and that he would conclude no truce with the King of France, until the King of England had been back on his native soil for three months.'

11 The treaties, known as the Treaties of Picquigny, were in actual fact signed at Amiens and in the English camp. They comprised several clauses: (1) a seven-year truce (and not a nine-year truce

as Commynes mistakenly stated in the passage quoted in the previous note); (2) A war indemnity of seventy-five thousand crowns to be paid by the King of France to the King of England; (3) an arrangement concerning the forthcoming marriage of the Dauphin, Charles, son of Louis XI with Elizabeth, Edward IV's eldest daughter, and the assignment of a dowry of sixty thousand crowns as income to the future Dauphiness when she came of age (the marriage never took place); (4) a pension for life of fifty thousand crowns a year to be paid to Edward IV by Louis XI twice yearly—half at Easter and half at Michaelmas. Briefly, this meant that the problem of the disputed Capetian claim to the French crown was finally settled, for the Valois retained the inheritance and in return made a cash payment to the Plantagenets.

12 Soleuvre is in Luxemburg; the truce was not signed at Soleure in Switzerland, as so many historians have supposed.

13 Pfister, *Histoire de Nancy*, I, 403. The siege of Nancy was begun on the 24th October and the town fell on the 30th November 1475.

14 People said jokingly that there was war in Paradise and that St Peter had taken St Paul prisoner. The dramatic details of his trial and execution can be found in my book *Le grand règne de Louis XI*, pp. 182–6. Commynes gives an account of an amusing scene which occurred when Louis was trying to precipitate a quarrel between Charles the Bold and St Pol. The Lord of Contay, a gentleman in the Duke of Burgundy's service, happened to be with the king at the same time as one of St Pol's men, the Lord of Sainville, whom Commynes refers to as Ceville. Louis XI made Contay hide behind a screen, called an 'ostevent' by Commynes, and gave orders for the count's emissary to be admitted. 'The king came and sat down on a stool *very close* to the afore-mentioned "ostevent" so that we could hear all that Louis of Ceville said. The only person with the afore-mentioned lord was a certain Monsieur du Bouchaige. The afore-mentioned Ceville and his companion began by saying that their master had sent them to talk with the Duke of Burgundy and had remonstrated with him on several occasions in order to dissuade him from being friendly with the English, and as he said these words, thinking thereby to curry favour with the King of France, the afore-mentioned Louis of Ceville began to imitate the Duke of Burgundy, stamping on the ground and swearing by St George. The king laughed loudly and asked him to speak up because he was becoming rather deaf. Ceville, without any hesitation, willingly started all over again.

Monsieur de Contay, who was with me behind the screen, was completely dumbfounded and would never have believed it, if he had not heard it for himself.'

15 Later, on pp. 272-3 we will indicate the reasons for this change in the Spanish situation: the reader, however, will find a thorough investigation of this question in the books quoted in Chapter XII, n. 1.

16 The 'Lectoure' incident, which had cost Count John of Armagnac his life on the 4th March 1473, had brought the French vassals once more into submission (Ch. Samaran, *La Maison d'Armagnac au XVe siècle et les dernières luttes de la féodalité dans le Midi de la France* (Paris, 1908) (*Mémoires et documents*, published by the *Société de l'Ecole des Chartes*, VII), pp. 185–94.

17 An analysis, incomplete however, of the duke's mistakes, can be found in the biography by Marcel Brion, *Charles le Téméraire, grand duc d'Occident* (Paris, Hachette, 1947). The author is right in stressing Charles's arrogant tendency to underestimate his opponent's resources. He even asserts—with some exaggeration, for there were other reasons for Charles's downfall—'all the mistakes he committed came from the fact that his contemptuous attitude blinded him to the realities of the situation'.

Chapter XIV: The End of a Reign and the End of a Dynasty

1 Alluding to an incident which occurred between Savoy and Switzerland, Olivier de la Marche, III, 209, and Commynes, II, 105, asserted that the war waged by Charles the Bold against the Cantons was caused by 'a wagonload of sheepskins', and Montaigne, *Essais*, III, X, noted this fact as an illustration of the philosophical idea that 'our most violent states of agitation spring from paltry causes'. The same idea is expressed in Pascal's famous remark about Cleopatra's nose. In actual fact, however, the load of sheepskins was not the cause of the war. An account of the true causes is given by Hoch and de Mandrot, *Morat et Charles le Téméraire* (Neuchâtel, 1876), Hans Wattelet, *Die Schlacht bei Murten* (Berne, Polygraphische Geschichte, 1926), and Toutey, *Charles le Téméraire et la ligue de Constance*, a thesis, Paris, 1902. This is how the origin of the war is explained by M. M. Reymond, Chief Paleographer of the Canton of Vaud, at Lausanne, in his contribution, *Les objectifs des Suisses dans la guerre de Bourgogne*, to the Twelfth Congress of the *Association bourguignonne des Sociétés savantes*, held at Dijon on the 26th, 27th and 28th May 1935, Dijon 1937, pp. 49–50. 'When at St Omer in 1469, the Duk

of Austria transferred his Alsatian domains to Charles the Bold, the King of France cleverly spread abroad the rumour that the two princes were preparing to attack Switzerland. Although there was no truth in this, the accusation gained credence, thanks to the efforts of the people of Berne who had for a long time wanted to gain possession of Vaud which would give them control of the highway between France and Italy and of the road to Lyons. The Baron of Vaud was a Prince of Savoy, Jacques, Count of Romont, a prominent figure at the court of Burgundy'. At the beginning of the war, the Bernese did indeed send an army into Vaud. However, as M. Reymond explains, Louis XI, in spite of his alliance with the Swiss, had no intention of allowing Vaud to be annexed to the canton of Berne. His idea was rather to unite Vaud and Savoy, but he died before he could put this plan into execution.

2 Several historians have quoted moving passages from the *Chronique de Neuchâtel*, which was supposed to have survived in fragmentary form and which aroused the enthusiasm of Michelet (*Louis XI et Charles le Téméraire* in the 1837 edition, p. 382); but it is only a pastiche written by the supposed discoverer of the fragment, de Pury, as has been shown by A. Piaget and Th. de Liebenau (see B. de Mandrot, Vol. I of his edition of Commynes, *Société de l'Histoire de France*, p. 346, n. 2). For details of the total strength of the armies c.f. Lot, *op. cit.*, II, pp. 118–19.

3 It would appear that the Italian mercenaries were the first to take flight. 'The duke shouted to them to come back, hurling abuse at them, and striking wildly at them with his sword. Overcome with fatigue, exhausted by grief and rage, he was almost the last man left, when he too, being without camp or army, was forced to flee. He went blindly off, attended only by five of his followers. He rode without stopping for six miles until he reached Jougne on the road through the Jura mountains. "Ah, my lord," his fool said to him during this dismal retreat, "we're well and truly Hannibalized!" ' (M. de Barante, *Hist. des ducs*, VII, 144). To appreciate the piquancy of this remark, it must be remembered that ever since he had embarked on the punitive expedition against the Swiss, the duke had been obsessed by the story of Hannibal and his crossing of the Alps.

4 Garsias du Faur was entrusted with the distribution of these gifts (Degert, *Les Toulousains et les origines de la diplomatie française*, in the *Revue historique de Toulouse*, VIII, 1921. For information, about Angelo Cato reference can be made to Benedetto Croce.

Il personagio italiano che essorto il Commynes a scrivere i 'mémoires', Angelo Catone, in *Atti della Academia di Scienze Morali e Politiche*, v. LV, Naples, 1932).

5 The Neapolitan ambassador, Palomar, corroborates Commynes's testimony (Gingins-la-Sarra, *Dépêches des ambassadeurs milanais sur les campagnes de Charles le Hardi, duc de Bourgogne de 1474 à 1477*, 2 vols. (Geneva, 1858), I, 363. On the subject of the marriage between the Prince of Taranto and Mary of Burgundy which did not take place, see my survey *Le projet de mariage bourguignon-napolitain en 1474 d'après une acquisition récente de la Bibliothèque nationale*, in the *Bibliothèque de l'Ecole des Chartes*, LXII, 1911).

6 Mâconnais and Charolais were invaded. For details of the defence preparations and the operations as a whole, see Robert de Chevanne, *La guerre en Bourgogne de 1470 à 1475. Etude sur les interventions armées des Français au duché de Charles le Téméraire* (Paris, A. Picard, 1934). In another context, the author states that the 'famous battle' fought on the 20th June 1475 took place at Montreuillon (Nièvre) (Robert de Chevanne, *Episodes des dernières luttes au duché de Bourgogne*, 1470–1475, a paper read to the Twelfth Congress held at Dijon on the 26th, 27th and 28th May 1935, *Association bourguignonne des Sociétés savantes*, Dijon, 1937, p. 45). On the subject of the loyalty of the people of Franche-Comté to Charles the Bold readers are strongly recommended to refer to G. Gazier, *Les rapports de Charles le Téméraire avec la ville de Besançon*, quoted in the *Annales de Bourgogne*, 1938, p. 148. For details of the attitude prevalent among the mass of his subjects c.f. John Bartier, *Charles le Téméraire*, p. 196.

7 F. Lot, II, 121, corrects Commynes, II, 121 and note. The duke had spent nearly eleven weeks at Lausanne and had devoted all his time to getting an army ready. M. de Barante, *Hist. des ducs*, VII, 161, says: 'Soon his army grew to nearly the size it had been before. In addition to his own men who had rejoined him, five thousand men-at-arms arrived from Ghent and Flanders, six thousand from Liége and Luxemburg, and four thousand from Bologna and the papal estates, for the Pope was well-disposed towards him. He also called upon the band of English soldiers who had been in his service for a long time; there were three thousand of them and they were the best fighting men in his army.' These English soldiers, to whom Commynes refers (Calmette edition II, pp. 131 and 133) were under the command of a certain Jehannin Collepin, whom Olivier de la Marche also mentions in the Beaune and

Arbaumont edition, III, 288. There had been few casualties at Grandson—perhaps a thousand or so—so that a large number of survivors were available for active service again; some however had deserted. c.f. Lot and my account in the *Annales du Midi*. The figures given by M. de Barante are certainly excessive. For instance, the English numbered only a hundred and twenty.

8 Gingins-la-Sarra, II, 210: 'Vivere al mundo con questa infamia de essere stato rotto da questi populi bestiali.' The duke's state of mind accounted for the rather lukewarm support given by his immediate entourage. Baseless legends have, however, been circulated about the attitude adopted by Burgundian subjects, and in particular by the subjects of the duchy itself. On this point see J. Billioud, *Les Etats de Bourgogne au XIVe et XVe siècle*, pp. 141–53, and my review of this work, *Bibliothèque de l'Ecole des Chartes*, LXXXIV, 1923, p. 127.

9 There exists a biography of Joan—largely if not entirely based on historical fact—by the Duc de Lévis-Mirepoix, *Jeanne de France, fille de Louis XI* (Paris, 1943). The author, however, does not appear to have known about the marriage proposal mentioned here.

10 M. de Barante, *Hist. des ducs*, VII, 181–2: 'The Swiss, in accordance with ancient custom, spent three days on the battlefield, in order to prove to all comers that victory was indeed theirs, and then proceeded to bury the dead. A huge ditch was dug near Morat and the bodies were thrown into it and covered with quicklime. Four years later when the bodies had rotted, a chapel was built and the bones were taken from the ditch; the chapel was commonly called 'The Burgundian charnel-house' and bore the following inscription:

Deo Optimo Maximo
Inclyti et fortissimi Burgundiae ducis exercitus
Moratum obsidens ab Helvetiae caesus
Hoc sui monumentum reliquit

(To God who is very good and very great—the army of the famous and valiant Duke of Burgundy which laid siege to Morat and was defeated by the Swiss—here left this monument.)

'For more than three hundred years this charnel-house was carefully preserved. Then in 1798, French soldiers passing through Morat on their way to subdue the Swiss, felt that the Burgundian charnel-house was an insult to the glory of France, so they destroyed the chapel and scattered the bones.' Jérôme Münzer who travelled through Switzerland in 1494 estimated the losses at 24,000 men, according to information he obtained from the local people. He noted the Latin inscription on the chapel (E. Déprez, *Jérôme Münzer et son voyage dans le Midi de la France en 1494–1495*, in the *Annales du Midi*, 1937, p. 54).

11 Antonio d'Appiano, writing from Geneva to the Duke of Milan on the 29th June, expresses his indignation at the outrage committed at Grand-Sassonex in the following terms: 'Questa arrestatione de la illustrissima Madama cusi villanamente fata, de laquale tutto il mondo dice que gia mia non se oldito dire la piu iniqua ne la piu villana cosa dopo chel mondo e creato'.

12 It should be mentioned in passing that Alfonso V of Portugal tried to act as mediator. In the hope of winning French support in his struggle against Ferdinand the Catholic and Isabella, with whom he was at that moment contending for the possession of Castille, he fancied he would be able to settle everybody's quarrels. See my book *L'unité espagnole*, p. 127 onwards, for further details of this extraordinary episode.

13 The question has been dealt with by Benedetto Croce, *Un condottiere italiano del quattrocento, Cola di Monforte, conte di Campobasso, e la fede storica del Commynes* (Bari, 1934), and in my study *Campobasso et Commynes*, in the *Annales de Bourgogne*, 1935. B. Croce proved that, a few days before, Charles the Bold had struck Campobasso with his iron gauntlet during an argument and that consequently the *condottiere's* defection was an act of revenge. I think however, that I have cleared Commynes of the accusation of dishonesty levelled at him by the Italian historian in this connection. It is, moreover, impossible to white-wash Campobasso completely. We cannot, as B. Croce would have us do, compare the behaviour of a military captain who went over to the enemy in the thick of the battle and changed sides at the crucial moment, with the behaviour of Commynes, who left Charles the Bold in order to enter Louis XI's service. As regards the blow with the gauntlet which had been endured in silence, Campobasso's behaviour may be excused on the grounds that it was a reflex action; but even so, it is difficult not to look upon it as a *betrayal*. The circumstances may be termed extenuating or even justificatory but the brutal fact of the desertion remains. Had Campobasso remained faithful, it is unlikely that he would have prevented the battle of Nancy from ending in a Burgundian disaster. Nevertheless, his *volte-face* contributed in no small

measure to the duke's collapse, and the blow with the gauntlet, whether deserved or not, was, as it happened, grimly atoned for.

14 Molinet, in the edition already mentioned, I, 229: 'Even if I had to fight alone, I would still fight'. In actual fact, mediation on the part of the Pope could have saved his honour and avoided the disaster (Toutey, *op. cit.*, p. 374). Pfister, *Hist. de Nancy*, I, 476, has written a very thorough study of the battle of Nancy. There is a good deal of uncertainty about where the body of the last duke—and also that of his third wife, Margaret of York—were buried. They may be at Bruges, near the tomb of Philip the Good. Henri Drouot, in *Les restes de Marguerite de York et de Charles le Téméraire, Annales de Bourgogne*, 1937, p. 259, gives the essential facts connected with this curious problem.

15 J. Calmette, *Une ambassade espagnole à la cour de Bourgogne*, in the *Bulletin hispanique*, January, 1905. For details of events relating to Burgundy under Louis XI, see André Leguai's interesting study, *Dijon et Louis XI*, in the *Annales de Bourgogne*, 1945–1947.

16 The arguments for and against the revertibility of the ducal appanage have been set out by Jean Faussemagne, *L'apanage ducal de Bourgogne, ses rapports avec la monarchie française* (1363–1477) (a Law thesis, Lyons, 1937): the conclusion is that, being a controversial issue, the matter could be approached in a variety of ways according to the political interests of the parties involved, and could only finally be settled by diplomacy or by war. The same was true, but to an even greater extent, of the various dependencies which made up the Burgundian State as a whole. Actually the Burgundian succession was the first of the major *European* questions which had to be faced by the first modern powers. It was one of the causes—perhaps the chief cause—of the rivalry between France and the House of Austria. For details of this aspect of the problem, see my book *L'Europe et le péril allemand* (Paris, Aubier, 1947), *Les grandes crises de l'histoire*.

17 Useful information on the subject of Mâconnais and its links with, and differences from, the duchy, can be found in Jean Roussot's article *Le Mâconnais et la Bourgogne*, in the *Annales de Bourgogne*, 1946.

18 Jouard was 'president of Burgundy' in the sense in which the expression has already been defined on p. 243 of the present work.

19 A curious document, discovered and published in part by A. Voisin—*Français ou Bourguignons*, in the *Annales de Bourgogne*,

1941, pages 38–9, throws some light on the intrigues carried out from the Low Countries to Burgundy. For details of the crisis in the Low Countries at this period, c.f. Georges H. Dumont, *Marie de Bourgogne* (Brussels, 1945).

20 c.f. Henri Hauser, *Le Traité de Madrid et la cession de Bourgogne à Charles Quint*, in the *Revue bourguignonne*, v. XXII, Dijon, 1912. The same author has given a summary of the episode in *Les Débuts de l'Age moderne*, v. VIII, of *Peuples et Civilisations*, Paris, Alcan, p. 387. 'François, when a prisoner in Madrid, signed everything he was asked to sign (13th January, 1426); "in accordance with the wishes and pleasure of the emperor", he promised to hand over Burgundy . . . Before he had even reached Bayonne (17th March) it was clear that the exorbitant treaty was already a dead letter . . . At Cognac, on the 22nd May the princes formed a confederation with the support of the Pope and the people of Venice; their pretext, a general peace campaign; their instrument, François freed from the obligations to which he had agreed in the sombre castle, where his children had now taken his place as hostages. The diplomatic campaign, was backed by what would be called today a parliamentary campaign. Although there was still a "Burgundian party" in Burgundy, the duchy, since Louis XI took it over (covered moreover as it was by the treaty of neutrality which applied to all Burgundian territory) had had no cause to complain of French rule. When everything had been settled it was not difficult to get the estates of Burgundy to issue, on the 4th June—and the estates of the Count of Auxonne on the 8th June—a declaration forbidding the king from surrendering those subjects who wished "to remain under the jurisdiction of the French crown, and who did not wish to be handed over to the afore-mentioned emperor". Here surely in this declaration, which may not have been entirely spontaneous but would have served no purpose had it not corresponded to local feeling, is one of the first expressions of "the rights of peoples to self-determination".'

Conclusion

1 J. Huizinga, *Le Moyen Age*, 1930–1931, p. 170 onwards, makes some penetrating observations on this subject. The Burgundian, Gaston Roupnel, in *Histoire et Destin* (Paris, 1943), puts forward a brilliant and plausible thesis, with his customary skill. His book makes extremely interesting reading, and abounds in astute observations, but the main argument—that everything which

happened had to happen—is based on a piece of *a priori* reasoning which is very far removed, in our opinion, from the *a posteriori* approach of historical analysis.

2 J. Huizinga, in the work already mentioned, note 1, *Le Moyen Age*, 1930–1931, p. 5, has given a shrewd analysis of their dual policy.

INDEX

Figures in italics refer to the illustrations

B

L

N

O

P

R

Y

THE ENGLISH ROYAL HOUSE

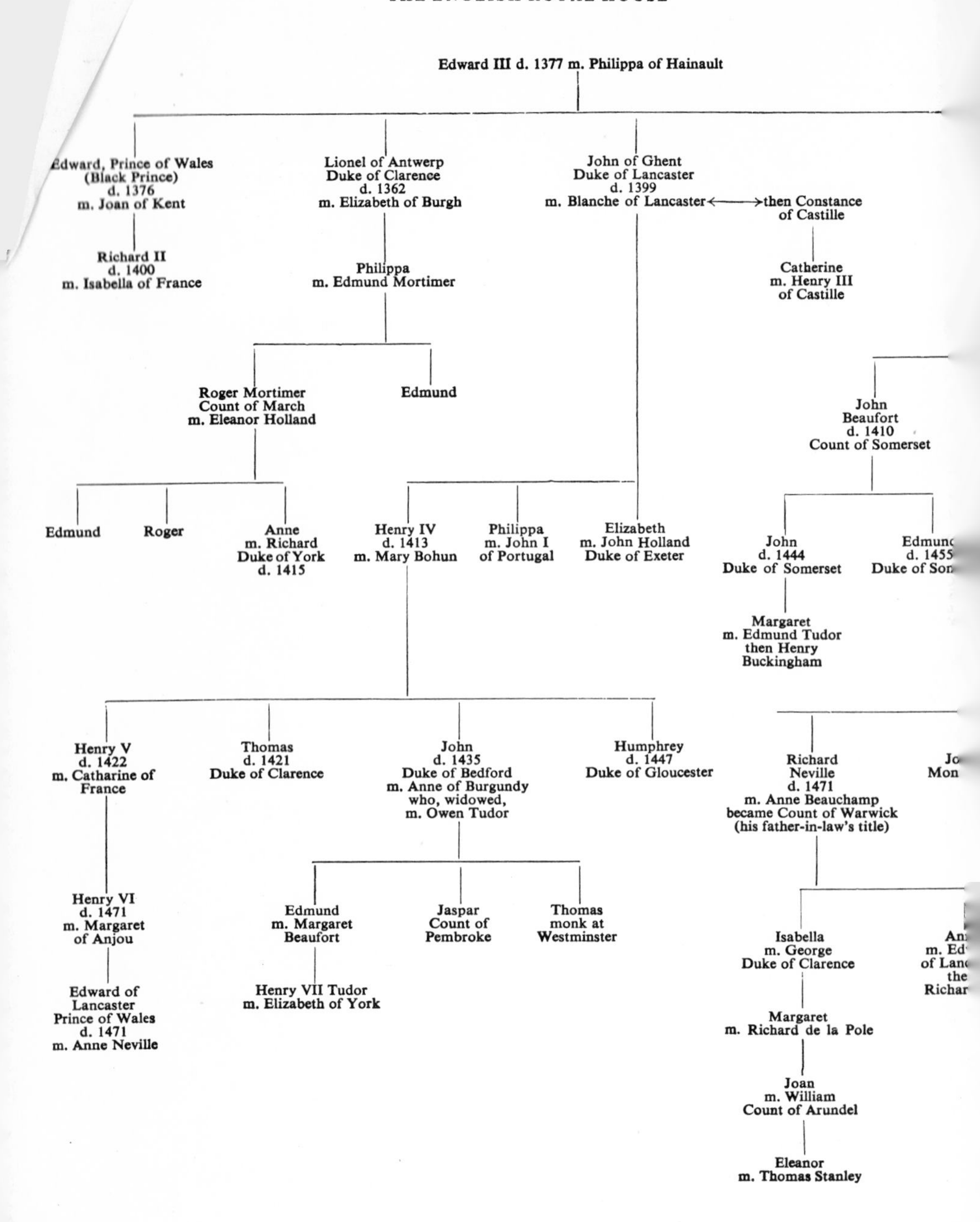

THE ENGLISH ROYAL HOUSE

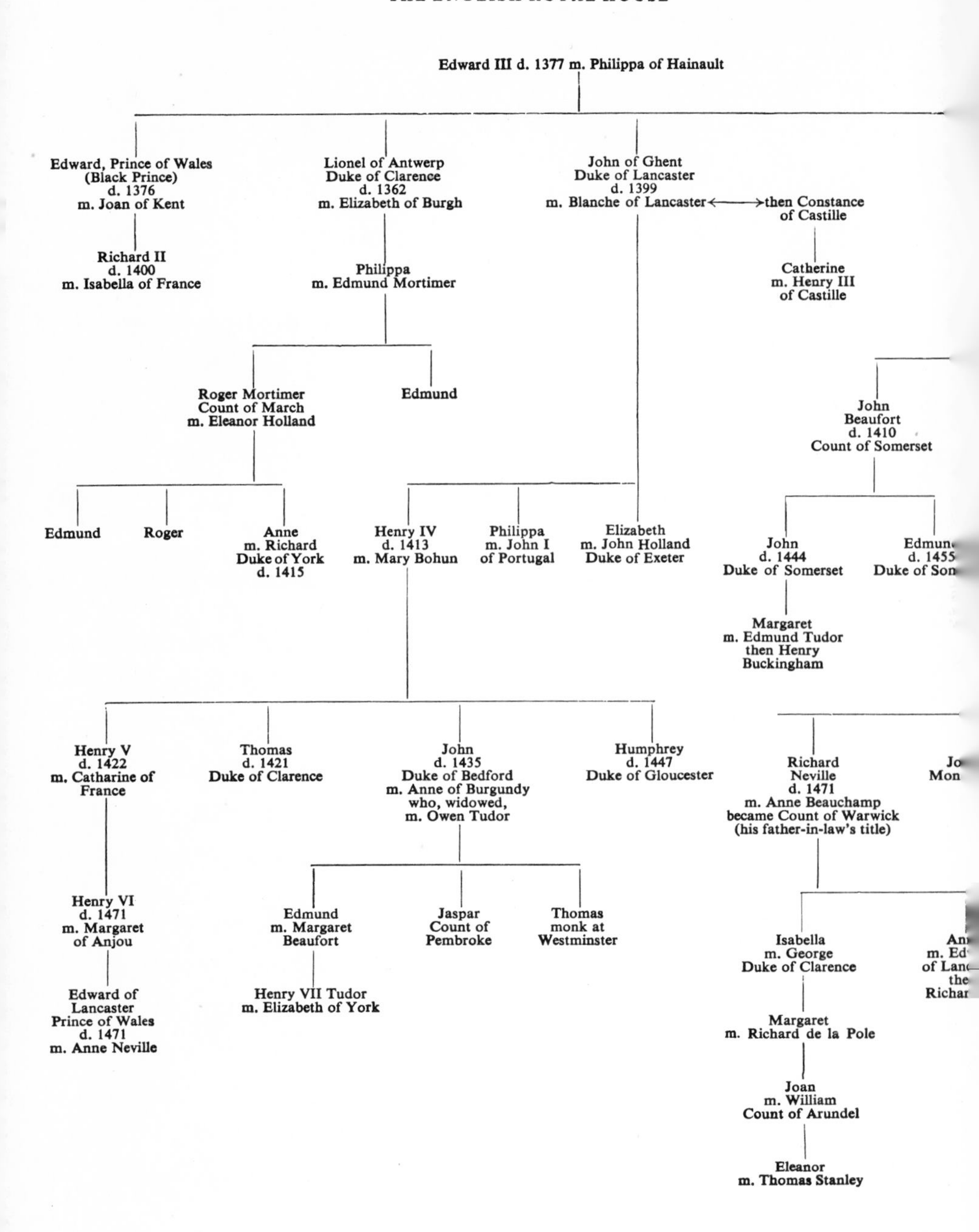